GRACE

Robert Lacey's bestselling books include *Majesty*, his definitive study of the British royal family. *The Kingdom*, the standard history of modern Saudi Arabia, and *Ford: The Men and The Machine*, the story of Henry Ford and the Ford Motor Company that was made into the successful TV mini-series, starring Cliff Robertson.

Educated at Bristol Grammar School and Selwyn College, Cambridge, Robert Lacey now lives in Florida with his wife, Sandi, and younger son, Bruno.

GRACE

ROBERT LACEY

PAN BOOKS

First published in Great Britain 1994 by Sidgwick & Jackson

This edition published 1995 by Pan Books
an imprint of Macmillan General Books
Cavaye Place London SW10 9PG
and Basingstoke

Associated companies throughout the world

ISBN 0 330 33894 3

1 3 5 7 9 8 6 4 2

A CIP catalogue record for this book is available from
the British Library

Phototypeset by Intype, London
Printed and bound in Great Britain by
Cox & Wyman Ltd, Reading, Berks

To Sandi, my wife

CONTENTS

PART FOUR
PRINCESS

The Road from La Turbie

SHORTLY BEFORE ten o'clock on the morning of Monday, 13 September 1982, Gendarme Frederic Mouniama was emerging from a baker's shop in the French hillside village of La Turbie. The young policeman was fond of a croissant with his coffee, and he was heading for the police station with the pastry in his hand.

A brown Rover car was coming through the village, travelling from the direction of Roc Agel, the weekend home of Prince Rainier and Princess Grace of Monaco – and as it drew to a halt to let the young gendarme cross the road, Frederic Mouniama realized that the Rover was being driven by Her Serene Highness Princess Grace herself.

She smiled at him from behind the wheel. Her seventeen-year-old daughter, Stephanie, was sitting beside her in the passenger seat. Princess Grace was by no means the face on the movie screen, the lithe and impish Grace Kelly who had come to Monaco nearly thirty years ago. That film star Grace had filled out significantly since then in face and body. But she still had her presence, that elegant and particular Grace Kelly glow, and as Frederic Mouniama stepped out across the road in front of this living legend, he instinctively tipped the hard brim of his képi to her, nodding his head.

1

Arriving at the police station, Gendarme Mouniama was just putting his croissant down on his desk when the emergency phone rang. A car had gone off a hairpin bend on the CD 37, the road from La Turbie down toward Monaco and the sea. Mouniama must get there straight away.

It was not ten minutes since he had left the baker's shop, and now the young gendarme was speeding down the twisting road with a colleague, the siren on their car sounding and the blue light flashing. It took the police car four or five minutes to get to the bend, and as Mouniama looked over the edge, he could see the grey and dusty belly of a car lying upside down beside a house in what seemed to be a flower garden. There were four or five people milling round the car – they must have come out of the house – and when the policeman got to the spot, he found they were comforting a dazed girl who was convulsed with sobs. 'Sauvez Maman!' she was weeping. 'Sauvez Maman!'

Staring at the mangled wreckage, Mouniama realized it was Princess Grace's brown Rover that he had seen no more than fifteen minutes earlier, and peering inside through the one still viable door, the gendarme took a hard look at the princess herself. She was lying flat inside, on her back, as if the upturned roof were a bed, one leg bent sharply sideways, her eyes closed, totally unconscious. There was no sign of blood. She was not dead, but there was no obvious sign of life.

For the next twenty-nine hours Frederic Mouniama, his fellow gendarmes and the forensic experts and detectives of his gendarmerie company were to work nonstop, without breaks for food or sleep, measuring the road, interviewing witnesses and retracing the path that the Rover took, trying to solve the mystery. How had it happened? Which princess had been driving? Had there been some sort of sabotage? And through it all Frederic Mouniama kept seeing the lady smiling, slowing her car and stopping, so that a young gendarme could cross the road with a pastry in his hand.

She had first driven in these hills when she was twenty-four, making a film for Alfred Hitchcock called *To Catch a Thief*. She had come back the following year for a film festival, and the year after that she was back again, this time to marry a prince. That was in April 1956, when Grace Kelly, movie star, was at the summit of her loveliness. She had a bounce to her walk, a sort of smile in her posture. With her blond hair and firm jawline, she had that strong, almost sterile collection of north European features that add up to what is called the classic American beauty. In the early years of the twentieth century, the noble families of Europe competed to recruit the handsome and wealthy 'dollar princesses' – several hundred of them by 1915, according to a reference work of the day, *Titled Americans*: forty-two American-born princesses, sixty-four baronesses, one hundred and twenty-six countesses . . . In 1956 Grace Kelly came to Monaco in a Hollywood adaptation of that old tradition.

What distinguished Grace was her wholesomeness. She looked wholesome, she talked wholesome – she had developed her own, wholesome, rounded, theatrical accent – and, so far as most people knew, her behaviour was thoroughly wholesome as well. She epitomized a highly cherished element in America's identity, particularly in the 1950s – the years of President Eisenhower. Grace Kelly went with country clubs, malted milk and *Reader's Digest* – though, like *Reader's Digest*, her formula included a healthy ration of sex. Nice sex, giggles-in-the-back-of-the-car sex, but sex which, in 1950s terms, was actually rather daring. In her great film roles Grace played the adventuress, a single woman who was experienced in some unspecified way and who

3

carried her nightgown in her handbag. She was the sort of girl who enjoyed the sauciness of a double entendre, and who kissed Cary Grant first and passionately, rather than waiting to be kissed.

Grace knew how to do it with a smile and sleight of hand that made it all quite respectable. She managed to be naughty while appearing very nice. Alfred Hitchcock, who coaxed the finest and most tantalizing film performances out of her, liked to compare Grace Kelly to a snow-covered volcano. Working closely with her on three films, he had witnessed the eruptions of sexuality that she usually managed to conceal behind her virginal exterior. The contradiction was one of the major issues of Grace's life. The public at large saw only the snow on the top of the mountain – perhaps that was all they wanted to see. But the truth about Grace Kelly was that she was, in some very important respects, quite the opposite of what she seemed.

Performance. Performance. Where did the acting stop and real life begin? Did Grace forsake fantasy when she said goodbye to Hollywood? Or did she sign on in Monaco for a role that was even more unreal?

She always was a dreamer, and this was, in many ways, the key. From her earliest years, Grace Kelly was marked by the curious certainty that she could make her dreams come true – as a successful model, as a television actress, as a movie star, and then finally in her princessly calling. It was Grace's particular gift to dream and to become, and this lent her a magic that fascinated people in a non-religious age. Through the course of her fifty-two years, she came to be a sort of talisman to her generation, a saintly figure, venerated and almost holy. Perfection may be a fantasy, but that is what Princess Grace symbolized for millions. She was an international icon, one of the untouchables. So people could not believe she was only mortal when death came to her before her time, following a car crash.

This book has taken two years to research and write, and is based on press coverage, personal letters and papers, and upon interviews with many of Grace Kelly's closest colleagues and friends. It contains the first detailed account of the police investigation of her death, and reveals how she had love affairs both before and after her marriage to Prince Rainier of Monaco. It also examines the controversial medical decisions taken in her final hours. With different medical handling, might Princess Grace be alive today?

It is not, perhaps, surprising that Prince Rainier and his family declined to be interviewed for this book, for it presents a portrait of Grace – and her family – which is very different from the image cultivated by them and by their public relations experts. The conventional picture of Grace Kelly, Princess Grace, was a beautiful illusion created for an age that liked to be deceived, and it may seem cruel to subject it to the intrusive and unforgiving analysis of the 1990s.

But the lady can take it. The truth does not destroy, it actually enhances the beauty of her illusion. Grace Kelly was a tough and courageous woman who conquered the challenges of her life and of her age with hard work, ingenuity and, yes, with great charm. She was warm and brave and loyal and human. But the myth-making started early.

PART ONE
HERO'S DAUGHTER

ONE

Father and Daughter

JULY 1935. She was five and a half years old, lithe and skinny and gap-toothed. When her father picked her up to whirl her around him, she laughed and twirled in his orbit, her feet flying out over the sand. How little Grace loved her Daddy, loved to curl in the winter against his warm tobacco-smelling coat. Now, this summer's day by the ocean, he was all hers for the moment, spinning her around him until the world was just a blur.

Jack Kelly, six-foot-two and 185 pounds, was dressed in swimming shorts with a belt and sleeveless top. The shoulder straps strained across his muscles as he turned. With his geometric, chiselled features and his dark, shiny hair, this man was the source of joy and power to his daughter as she spun. Yet even as she circled, the five-year-old knew what was expected. She could sense the instant she must look up and give her smile, and she gave it just right – as she came around with the ocean behind her. The photographer from the *Bulletin* got a perfect shot.

You had to put on a good performance if you were a daughter of Jack Kelly. In July 1935, age forty-five, he was the Democrats' candidate for mayor of Philadelphia. That was what had brought the cameraman to the seaside – to snap handsome Jack without his collar and tie, playing with his photogenic children on the sand.

One pose here, one pose there. Now, into the ocean to catch the breaking waves. So the five-year-old Grace waded into the water, stood at attention and stared straight at the photographer, smiling but serious, quite undiverted by the distractions of the spray. Her brother and her two sisters were looking left and right. They were giggling and ducking – but not young Grace. She kept looking straight ahead, always the good girl. Smile for the camera. Get it right for Daddy.

It is not unusual for a five-year-old girl to rate her father as something close to a God among men. But in the case of Grace Patricia Kelly, born in Philadelphia on 12 November, 1929, her fond opinion was also shared by a remarkable number of other people.

Her father did not, in fact, win his bid to be mayor. In the election of 1935 Jack Kelly lost by some 40,000 of the 700,000 votes cast. But no Democrat had ever done so well before, and the defeat was only a temporary setback in the career of a man who, love him or loathe him, was generally acknowledged to be one of the city's more remarkable and charismatic sons.

Born in 1890, one of a sprawling Irish Catholic family of ten children living in the poor, immigrant quarter of East Falls, Philadelphia, Jack Kelly had earned his first wages as a bricklayer. Then he started his own contracting firm, Kelly for Brickwork, and, by dint of charm, hard work and the right connections, he managed to build the business into the largest construction enterprise on the East Coast. Kelly for Brickwork had a hand in everything from the classical pillars of Philadelphia's Thirtieth Street Station to Radio City Music Hall in New York. Jack Kelly became a millionaire.

But he also won eminence in another field. In his spare time he was an oarsman dedicated to that most solitary of rowing sports, the single sculls – eight minutes or more of self-imposed torture propelling a fragile wooden shell through 2,000 metres of water – and his sculling triumphs had secured him the special status which adorns the sporting champion. Set money and brickwork aside. Grace Kelly's father was a local hero.

Rowing counts for more in Philadelphia than it does in most other places. The boathouses cluster close to the grandest boulevards of the city, just behind the art museum, linking together to form a quarter of a mile row along the eastern bank of the Schuyl-kill (pronounced 'Skookle') River. They make a surprising sight as you drive north out of downtown Philadelphia – a sudden riot of timbered gables, coats of arms, spires and turrets, with their concrete boat aprons sloping down to the water.

Penn, Villanova and other local schools train out of Philadelphia's Boathouse Row, but the essence of these ramshackle clubhouses is not varsity. Schuylkill rowing is for the regular, local, working fellow – like Kelly the bricklayer, who would rush from work every evening in the second decade of this century to get in his practice before the light left the river. He was then a single man.

In those days the members of the Vesper Club were the undisputed kings of the Schuylkill. The crews that rowed out of the club's chapel-like boathouse dominated regattas up and down the East Coast – and Vesper's best sculler was Jack Kelly. In one extraordinary spring and summer in 1919, the twenty-nine-year-old won every race in which he competed – including the US singles sculling championship.

The next logical step was for the US champion to compete in the Diamond Sculls, the world's premier sculling event, held each July at the Henley Royal Regatta at Henley-on-Thames in England. Vesper had raised money to send crews there before. But early in June 1920, with his training complete and his shell crated and ready for his transatlantic passage, Jack Kelly received a cable from Henley. The stewards had rejected his entry.

Henley's main objection was to the way in which Vesper had financed the previous sorties of its representatives across the Atlantic. The American club had put the money it raised straight into its rowers' pockets, making them professionals according to the complicated and famously stuffy rules of the Royal Regatta. A standing regulation banned all future entries from Vesper.

But the Henley stewards had a further and particular objection to Jack Kelly, deriving from his job and from their class-based view of what made for fair competition. 'Mr Kelly,' they declared in their meeting of 3 June 1920, 'was also not qualified under Rule 1 (e) of the General Rules (manual labour).' In plain language, a Philadelphia bricklayer who made his living through his own physical toil and sweat had no place in a regatta for English gentlemen.

This rule was not quite as obnoxious as it seemed. It derived from the middle of the previous century, when the River Thames was the busiest street in London, plied by husky, professional watermen who organized races of their own, and who easily out-rowed the schoolboys and college students who competed at Henley. But it was an exercise in prejudice to be enforcing this regulation two years after the end of the First World War, and Jack Kelly wasted little time showing Henley's stewards what he thought of their snobbery. 1920 was an Olympic year. The games were due to be held in Belgium. So, watched by all Philadelphia, and by a good many other non-rowing Americans piqued by this latest skirmish between the new world and the old, the twenty-nine-year-old Jack Kelly trained and raced as never before.

He packed up his racing shell again, and this time he did make it across the Atlantic – to the Scheldt River outside Antwerp, Belgium, where he won all his qualifying heats, and made his way to the Olympic final. He had guaranteed himself the silver medal. To win the gold, he had to get the better of the noted English rower Jack Beresford – fresh from Henley a few weeks earlier, and his triumph in the Diamond Sculls.

In a storybook conclusion to this storybook confrontation, Jack Kelly swept across the finishing line the clear victor, leaving Henley's champion paddling ineffectively in his wake – and, as his daughter Grace liked to recount the tale that her father told her, the new *victor ludorum* promptly packed up his battered, Irish-green racing cap and sent it off to King George V at Buckingham Palace. We do not know what His Majesty made of the worn and sweat-stained offering, but to Jack Kelly the message was very clear.

More than 100,000 Philadelphians turned out to cheer him home in the autumn of 1920. He was a national celebrity. A much-syndicated photograph showed the victorious oarsman standing beside Jack Dempsey, the boxer, and Man o' War, the racehorse – three world champions, three superb symbols of physical excellence. One newspaper named Jack Kelly 'the most perfectly formed American male', and there was even talk of the handsome young bachelor going out to Hollywood for a screen test.

He was the toast of the town – literally. The quick-tongued Kelly became the speaker Philadelphia wanted at every benefit and roast, and from his celebrity followed power and money. He won election as a City Councilman and became Chairman of Philadelphia's Democratic Party. His vigorous New Deal campaigning won him the gratitude of President Roosevelt – and that counted for a lot in these difficult years when the Federal Government was the fountainhead and only dispenser of construction work. The Federal Courthouse, Philadelphia, the Federal Office Building, Philadelphia, the handsome US Post Offices sprinkled around Philadelphia's suburbs – Kelly for Brickwork got the best government contracts.

But no one was heard to accuse the new party boss of profiteering or corruption. Though Jack Kelly's broad shoulders were now encased in elegant, double-breasted suits, he never lost his aura of the straight blade in the water – the solid handshake, the bluff, open stare. When he did use his pull, it was to help put deserving kids through college, or to find temporary work for husbands and fathers who had fallen on hard times. Kelly for Brickwork did jobs at cost price, or less, for the Catholic church – as well as for synagogues, chapels, and just about any good cause that could sidle up to the boss's generosity. Kelly's friends would tell you how he knelt beside his bed every night to say his prayers, and of 'Dreams', the poem that he kept framed in his study:

> *Never by many are marvels wrought,*
> *By one or two are the dreams first caught . . .*
> *The dreamer must toil when the odds are great,*
> *Must stand to failure and work and wait . . .*
> *Must keep his faith though he stand alone,*
> *Until the truth of his dream is known.*

'Dreams' was by Edgar Guest, the bard of middle America in the 1930s and 1940s. Syndicated in newspapers all over the country, Guest's singsong rhymes lauded the ethic painted by Norman Rockwell and set to song by Rodgers and Hammerstein – if you climb every mountain, you will surely find your dream.

The hours of lonely toil and training which underpinned Jack Kelly's success on the river provided him with his own great metaphor for life, and of all his children, none took it more to heart than his middle daughter, Grace. The legend of the bricklayer and the Diamond Sculls, the straight blade who ran for mayor — these were the formative myths that shaped the thought patterns and ambitions of a little girl who would, one day, far eclipse her father's somewhat provincial fame. The other young Kellys performed better in sporting contests, but it was Grace who assimilated the lesson where it counted most. Like a champion sculler, she knew how to hide the pain and keep on going. There was a sense in which Grace Kelly's entire life was a race for which her father had trained and coached her.

Jack Kelly was not a soft or indulgent trainer — rowing coaches never are — and there were moments when Grace was bitterly to rue the supremacy exercised over her by this inspiring, driving, impossibly demanding man. It is no simple task to be the offspring of a hero, particularly if you admire him and are caught up in his spell. Indifference or rebellion offers the easiest escape route from under the shadow of greatness, and those are the roads that the children of great men often choose.

But it was Grace's choice to try to please and win the approval of her father — to try to live up to the legend in her own fashion — and years after his death she was to acknowledge his primacy in curious ways. Invited at the beginning of Monaco's prestressed concrete building boom to christen one of the principality's new apartment towers, she chose 'Le Schuylkill', a name whose spelling and pronunciation perplexes the locals to this day. Then shortly before her death, aged fifty-two, and basking in the undiluted admiration of just about the entire world, she was asked if she was contemplating writing her memoirs.

'No,' replied the Oscar winner and princess. But she revealed that she was thinking of writing her own sort of double biography – the story of her father's life, with her own life serving as its postscript.

TWO

3901 Henry Avenue

GRACE KELLY grew up on a hill overlooking the genteel but threadbare neighbourhood of East Falls, Philadelphia, two miles north of Boathouse Row. A former mill town, East Falls was a cluster of faded grey row houses nestling in a valley that was dampened by the mists which came floating off the Schuylkill River. The only landmarks of any note were the deserted mills that had once employed the town, and the rising spire of St Bridget's, the Roman Catholic church.

It was in this humble and faintly depressing community that Jack Kelly spent his youth and first made his mark, but by the time his daughter Grace was born in the winter of 1929, Jack's days of manual labour were already far behind. He had won at the Olympics. He had started his own business, and the measure of his success was the grand brick home that he had built for himself and his family at the top of the hill above East Falls – 3901 Henry Avenue.

Henry Avenue was where the bigwigs lived. One of its grand mansions had once housed the Dobsons, the English family who owned the looms that had drawn the Kellys and thousands of other poor Irish immigrants to East Falls in the middle of the nineteenth century. But by 1929 the looms

17

were shut down. The Dobsons were gone, and it was the bricklaying son of one of the lace-curtain families who now lived in style on Henry Avenue. Three storeys high, with mullioned windows and broad chimney towers, the seventeen-room Kelly mansion was a palace in comparison with the modest wood and tar-paper villas down by the water. It stood in its own grounds, surrounded by trees. A curved, U-shaped drive led up to the Colonial-style front door. There was a tennis court, a cook, a companion-secretary, a supply of maids – and a black chauffeur-gardener to care for the flowers.

It was tough for most people to survive in East Falls in the 1930s. Grace entered the world three weeks after the great Wall Street crash, and she grew up through the darkest years of the Depression. But these events had very little impact on her life. Her father had never believed in the stock market. He had avoided debt, and put his spare money in government bonds. With his New Deal connections, Jack Kelly sailed through the Depression like a king.

So life up at 3901 Henry Avenue was a comfortable and almost dreamlike sequence of activity and fun. The basement downstairs was decked out like a Bavarian ratskeller, complete with panelled bar. At Christmas a giant train set ran through a model landscape of hills, trees and waterfalls. In winter the tennis court was flooded for ice hockey and skating parties. In summer a truck from Kelly for Brickwork delivered a huge metal cement-mixing container that was filled with water and served as a swimming pool. In the 1940s 3901 Henry Avenue boasted East Falls's first domestic television set, and neighbours still remember coming around to gaze in wonder at the test pattern flickering on the nine-inch screen.

The Kellys were a showcase family, a handsome sight as Fordie the chauffeur-gardener drove them down the hill to

18

St Bridget's on a Sunday morning. They made a grand entrance, well dressed and upstanding as they trooped in line to their pew, and after the service the priest was especially attentive as he paid his respects. In later years, newspaper stories often played up the lowly character of East Falls, the impoverished township that produced its own princess. But East Falls was only the backdrop to Grace's childhood, and the role that she played in front of it was definitely young lady of the manor.

Grace was the third of the four Kelly children, arriving after Peggy, born in September 1925, and Jack, Jr ('Kell'), born in May 1927. Grace was the youngest child until her sister Lizanne completed the family in June 1933, and she very much enjoyed her four years as baby of the household. She was never quite reconciled to being the daughter in between.

'My older sister was my father's favourite,' she recalled in later life, 'and there was the boy, the only son. Then I came, and then I had a baby sister . . . I was terribly jealous of her.'

It was fortunate for Grace's brother Kell that he was a strong and athletic character, for as the only boy of the brood, he was the child charged with a sacred quest. Defeating Henley's champion and winning the Olympic gold medal in 1920 had not been enough for Jack Kelly. He would not have settled his accounts finally with the English, in his mind, until he could see the name of Kelly inscribed on the trophy of the Diamond Sculls itself, and he had no hesitation in charging his only son with the accomplishing of that mission.

The moment Kell was old enough, his father took him down to the Schuylkill. The kid started off as a cox, graduated to double sculls with his father, then went off on his own. Mornings and evenings saw the boy out on the water, skimming between the arches of the grey stone railway bridges. Kell enjoyed football at school, but his father warned him that the risk of injury would jeopardize his rowing. He grew pudgy and indolent in his early adolescence. Two brisk years away at military school snapped that out of his system – and when the weather was too dirty for working out on the Schuylkill, Kell could be found in his gymlike bedroom on the second floor of the family home. In the centre of the floor sat a rowing machine.

Even in an age that was not much given to psychologizing, Jack Kelly's obsessive channelling of his son's life into the path of his own ambition struck some people as unhealthy. Relatives and the closer family friends mumbled about it forebodingly. But Jack Kelly was not a soul who could be easily diverted from his chosen purpose, while Kell, for his part, was an amiable and biddable boy, the epitome of good nature. He had the physical build for the river, and he seemed quite happy to be indentured to his father's dream and to the Schuylkill.

'Kell was the boy lying on the couch doing exercises to strengthen his wrist,' remembered Charlie Fish, a friend of the family who grew up in nearby Germantown.

Angular and crew-cut, Kell revelled in the knowledge of the special hopes and dreams that he carried for his father – and for the whole family. But the boy was not bright. It was Peggy, the eldest daughter, who had inherited her father's quickness of wit. She was the Lucille Ball of the clan. Tall and slender, with long grasshopper legs, Peggy Kelly was funny and outgoing, always ready with the snappy retort. Her nickname was Baba. She had a combination of good looks, athleticism and spirit which her father considered just about perfect.

'The sun, the moon, the stars, they all rose and set on Baba,' remembers Alice Godfrey, who lived around the corner and was a playmate of Grace's. Peggy had been just six months old when her father carried her proudly over the threshold of 3901 Henry Avenue – the first child he had made, moving into the home that he had made for her. It was a memory that Jack Kelly often recalled with pleasure, and it formed the basis of the particularly close relationship between the father and his eldest daughter.

Lizanne, the baby of the family, was tough and foursquare – bigger-boned, once she had grown for a year or so, than either of her elder sisters. She manoeuvred robustly to find her own niche, shaking off Grace's attempts to bring her under her wing. When Grace had been the infant of the household, she had been quite happy to play dutiful younger sister to the brilliant Baba, fetching and carrying and following her instructions in games. But Lizanne was not taking orders from anybody.

'Why aren't you nice to me,' Grace would complain, 'like I was nice to Peggy?'

By Kelly standards, Grace had a feeble side. She was by far the least forceful of the four Kelly kids – quieter and more withdrawn, almost waiflike. Grace was the one with the colds and allergies, the child who was always falling over in the playground. When the Kellys sat round the dinner table for their roast, it was not Kell the rower or Lizanne the baby who got the essence from the meat. The juice went to Gracie with the scabs on her knees.

'Grace was always sniffling,' remembers Gloria Otley, whose father, Jess, was Jack Kelly's estimator and principal partner in Kelly for Brickwork. 'We were always saying, "Gracie, blow your nose," "Gracie, stop your sniffling," "Gracie, here's a handkerchief." '

The sniffler would spend long hours apart from the other children, playing with her dolls. 'She was always very good at being alone,' remembers Maree Frisby, a childhood friend who was to stay close to Grace throughout her life. Grace would lose herself in the little dramas that she dreamt up for

21

her dolls. She made up her own language for them, creating a private world of formality and make-believe that she could share with these wood and plaster friends. One cherished piece of Kelly lore relates how Lizanne, in a fit of temper, locked her elder sister in a closet. It was hours before Grace was discovered – unconcerned and quite self-sufficient, happily at play with her dolls, babbling the private code of endearments that she reserved for her own little family.

In adult life Grace Kelly was to prove something of a chameleon. Grace the sensible, Grace the sensuous, Grace the frivolous – she had a whole range of personalities, and she flung herself into each with rare energy and commitment. It was not a matter of superficial posing. She passionately believed in every role in which she cast herself, and it was her skill to isolate and insulate her various selves from each other with such success that people often swore they had met a totally different person. Grace Kelly was not naturally endowed with the tricks and techniques of the actress – she always had to work hard at her craft – but she did have conviction, an absolute belief in the part she was filling at that minute. 'I've always liked to make-believe,' she told the Hollywood columnist Sidney Skolsky in 1954.

Grace's infant world of fantasy illuminated another streak in her character. In later years her sister Lizanne was rummaging through some closets in the palace at Monaco, when she came upon a compartment that was stuffed with Grace's childhood collection of dolls. At first surprised by her sister's sentimentality in preserving her family of inanimate friends and transporting them all the way to the south of France, Lizanne then reflected on how remarkably clean and unbroken the dolls all seemed. Grace had usually preferred to play with somebody else's toys if she could. She liked to keep her own dolls out of harm's way, saving them for best.

22

So the waif with scabby knees had not, perhaps, been quite as helpless as she seemed.

There was always a certain element of detachment in Grace. When her childhood friends recall her early years, they dwell almost enviously on the richness and excitement of life at 3901 Henry Avenue – the playhouses and the Christmas trees, the dynamic people shuttling to and fro. But Grace herself never felt entirely part of it. 'I was terribly shy when I was young,' she recalled in one interview in 1974. 'I almost crawled into the woodwork I was so self-conscious.'

'We were always competing,' she added two years later, developing the theme, 'competing for everything – competing for love.' Grace felt like an outsider in her family of triers and tusslers, the third of four children, and lost in the shuffle. 'I was always on my mother's knee, the clinging type,' she remembered. 'But I was pushed away.'

Grace's mother subscribed to the energetic and elbowing Kelly ethic as completely as her husband. Margaret Majer came of stern and purposeful German Protestant stock – her family had owned a featherbed business in Baden-Württemberg – and she spoke nothing but German until the age of six or seven. She had first met Jack Kelly at a swim meet in 1913, and one of the principal reasons why the couple did not marry for nearly eleven years was Margaret's insistence on first accomplishing the goals that she had set for her own life. Jack Kelly had left school in eighth grade, but Margaret Majer graduated from Temple University with a degree in physical education, then worked as a phys ed teacher at the Women's Medical College of Pennsylvania, a pioneering institution which was for many years the only all-female medical college in the United States. Margaret also found time to coach the University of Pennsylvania women's swimming team, the first woman ever to be entrusted with the task.

A striking blonde with well-shaped cheekbones and a firm jaw, Margaret Majer was a handsome woman. She never worked as a professional model. That would not have been dignified. But she did pose in the 1920s for the cover of *The Country Gentleman* magazine, the very picture of refined and healthy beauty – with a distinctly Nordic tinge. When Margaret married Jack Kelly in 1924 she converted to Catholicism, but she remained unmistakably Teutonic.

'I wouldn't say that Mother is a Nazi,' remarked Kell in later years. 'But sometimes I do refer to her as, quote, "That old Prussian mother of mine".'

'Ma' Kelly had the overlarge, practical hands of the hausfrau. She never wore coloured nail polish, and she brought up her three pretty blond daughters to present themselves in the same unadorned style. She had their fine hair cut straight and simple across the brow, and she actively discouraged them from getting fussy over clothes. Frugal to a fault, Ma recycled her girls' dresses systematically, so that Grace's clothes were more old than new. If the children failed to hang their clothes properly, their mother fined them a nickel from their twenty-five cents per week pocket money, and she was not averse to enforcing her discipline with a sharply wielded hairbrush or with the back of her hand.

Ma Kelly was the day-to-day, hands-on technician who kept the Kelly household functioning. Parsimonious and purposeful, she inspired a deep and lifelong awe in all her children – and that awe was shared by their friends from a respectful distance. ' "The Boss" was what she used to be called,' remembered Grace's friend Charlie Fish. 'She ran things pretty good.'

Ma Kelly's particular passion was the raising of funds for her beloved Women's Medical College of Pennsylvania, and she volunteered her children's energies for fashion shows and benefits as imperiously as her husband put his only son out on the river. One year she got the kids to organize a circus in the back garden. Kell, age eight, did a strongman act. Peggy, then ten, was the ring-master, while the five-year-old Grace did a tightrope act dressed in a little ballet costume. The children sold tickets to all their rich Henry Avenue neighbours.

'Everything was for Women's Medical in our life,' remembered Peggy. 'We stole flowers. I would tell my little sister to go up and steal all the flowers from next door . . . I would send her up there, and she would pick those violets and then sell them back to the lovely ladies.'

Ma Kelly had the same striving tunnel vision as her husband. A Kelly cause was a good cause, and normal rules could be waived in the achieving of it. Grace's focus never strayed far from her charismatic father, but her mother influenced her in ways that were equally profound. There were the physical attributes – the Teutonic blondness and features that contributed so much to Grace's astonishing adult beauty, as well as the oversized and sometimes ungainly Majer hands. More important was the willpower and the sense of purpose, the sheer busy-ness with which Ma Kelly tattooed her girls' spirits.

'We were never allowed to sit with our hands empty,' Peggy told the author Gwen Robyns, many years later. 'We just knew we were expected to knit. We had to knit and to crochet from the time we were three or four years old. We had to because we were German girls . . . Honey, we just had to. It was expected of us, and we just did it.'

Peggy herself felt that she had managed to avoid most of the maternal Germanness. A fey and carefree spirit, the firstborn Kelly child saw herself as incorrigibly Irish. 'I'm my father's daughter,' she used to say with pride. It was middle sister Grace who turned out to be the German

25

daughter, in Peggy's opinion. Grace was the good girl who knew what was expected of her and just did it.

Grace's mother needed all her backbone to manage the task of being married to the dashing and romantic Jack Kelly. Ma Kelly ran the household and handled so much of the discipline at Henry Avenue because her husband was away from home so often – and the usual, painful reason for his absence was that he was off romancing other women.

Handsome Jack took full advantage of his reputation as America's most perfectly formed male. There was the telephone girl at the office, and a secretary. On many an afternoon his car was to be seen outside the home of Ellen Frazer, a divorcée who lived in Chestnut Hill and who was his escort to baseball games. February was Jack Kelly's month for a jaunt to Florida without his wife and family – and one December the Elizabeth Arden store in downtown Philadelphia got a glimpse of how very extensive his social range might be. Jack Kelly placed an order for twenty-seven identical make-up cases, each to be gift-wrapped and sent to a different lady.

This was the other side of Jack Kelly the hero. Fame went to his head. He cultivated his image as the showcase father of a showcase family, but his philandering suggested that the show might be more for his benefit than for theirs. There is a sense in which the 110 per cent sportsman denies adult life, retreating into a world in which play is a value beyond any other, and when it came to women, Jack Kelly's values were those of a playful child, tied up in himself and totally oblivious to those he might hurt. He would have left his wife and family for Mrs Frazer, Germantown gossip asserted, if the lady had not been too canny, realizing how a woman had to maintain her independence from a man like Jack in order to avoid total subjugation to his will.

'I don't think there was one good marriage in the entire

Kelly family,' commented Charles Kelly, a nephew of Jack's. 'The Kellys had a tendency to take over.'

Jack Kelly could annihilate you in a sculling race, and he could annihilate you in real life, exhibiting an unblushing indifference to the feelings of other people. When in later years his son Kell became a father himself and confessed his disappointment that his first child was not a boy but a girl, Jack Kelly told the young man who had laid his whole childhood on the altar of the Diamond Sculls, 'Don't worry, son. My greatest joy in life has been Peggy.'

Ma Kelly coped with her inspiring and enraging child-husband, all agreed, with real dignity. His infidelities might even have suited her Germanic and slightly masculine style. Like Mrs Frazer, she carved out her own territory and protected it, making sure that she remained in charge of her own life. 'It's very difficult to be married to a Kelly,' she would acknowledge.

Margaret Majer had not married for passion. She had always had her own, unusually woman-centred goals to achieve, and these assumed more importance as she resigned herself to her husband's errant ways. With Jack in Florida, February was Ma's month for a grimly savoured shopping spree, and she threw herself more fiercely than ever into the raising of funds for her beloved Women's Med. She endeavoured, above all, to hide her marital problems from her children.

In this she temporarily succeeded. The Kelly clan stayed looking good. Peggy, Kell, Grace and Lizanne did not learn directly about their father's womanizing – or of the pain inside their mother – until they were all adult. But what they did learn, and from an early age, were the ways in which a family manoeuvres around a problem whose existence it does not acknowledge. Keep up appearances. Impress the world. Don't talk about what is really bothering you, and –

particularly in the Kellys' case – make sure that you keep on playing the game.

Sport can provide most helpful training for the game of life. Jack and Margaret Kelly believed that fervently. It was one subject on which they were very happily united, and a typical Saturday or Sunday for the Kelly family involved long hours of working out together, parents and children, in the gym and pool of the Penn Athletic Club on Rittenhouse Square. After long hours of training, Peggy and Lizanne, the eldest and youngest Kelly girls, both became outstanding competitive swimmers.

But sport becomes a form of sickness when it turns into obsession, and it is difficult to think of another word for the way in which three of the Kelly children came to dedicate their childhoods to the pursuit of sporting excellence – Kell sculling after the spectre of his father on the river, Peggy and Lizanne seeking to win his attention as their mother had done, in the swimming pool.

The exception was child number three, the sensitive one. Grace was no slouch at athletics. She was as nimble as Peggy or Lizanne, and as she grew older she easily won her way on to her school teams for field hockey. But the reflective little girl who wove dramas around her dolls was looking for more than physical exertion and competition – and she found it in a family elder who provided a very different role model from either of her charismatic parents.

George Kelly, Grace's uncle, lived just around the corner from Henry Avenue, in an elegantly bohemian set of rooms in the Alden Park apartments. 3901 Henry Avenue had a spartan feel with its displays of sporting trophies. But Uncle George's bachelor apartment was altogether more relaxed, for Uncle George was a creative spirit – an actor-turned-playwright who had once been a big name on Broadway. Outside Philadelphia, in fact, George Kelly was better known in many circles than his younger brother Jack. In 1926 George had won the Pulitzer Prize for his play *Craig's Wife*, the harrowing moral tale of a woman who marries for status, and four of his plays were made into movies that featured such stars as Will Rogers, Spencer Tracy and Joan Crawford. His satirical comedy *The Torch-Bearers* is revived and played to this day as one of the classic treatments of the backstage misadventures that can befall an amateur dramatic company.

The bricklaying beginnings and energetic self-publicity of Grace Kelly's father have fostered the impression that Grace's acting talents sprang, somewhat against the odds, from Irish labouring roots. But there is another Irish tradition – of ballads and humour and light entertainment – and this loomed as large as bricklaying in the history and make-up of the Kellys of East Falls. Apart from Uncle George, the dramatist, there was Uncle Walter, a bill-topping vaudeville comedian, and Aunt Grace, a comic actress and mimic in whose memory little Grace was named.

Uncle Walter developed a most successful stage persona as 'The Virginia Judge'. Dressed in a baggy white suit and panama hat, he played the role of a Southern magistrate hearing the cases against a succession of Amos 'n' Andy characters who provided the pretext for a stream of unashamedly racist jokes:

Virginia Judge: 'Want to make a quarter?'

Darkie: 'No, Suh. I've got a quarter.'

Aunt Grace was more demure. Her forte was a Harry Lauder impression which she performed dressed in tartan, while enunciating her lines in a faultless Scottish accent.

Young Grace never knew her humorous and extrovert namesake – Aunt Grace died before she was born – but any child who grew up in the unconventionally talented Kelly family was provided with ample evidence of how it was possible, in the words of the author Steven Englund, 'to make a career not from bricks and mortar, but from make-believe'. Uncle Walter, fat and jolly and smelling of cigars, entranced the children at family gatherings. He could always be counted on for a large and enjoyably frivolous present when birthdays came around – and he was also a reminder of how make-believe can make bricks and mortar possible, since it was a $5,000 loan from Walter, with a further $2,000 from George, the playwright, that had launched their younger brother's company, Kelly for Brickwork, in 1919.

Uncle George took great pleasure in correcting the Jack-centred, rags-to-riches version of Kelly history that was propagated by his younger brother. It was true that the Kellys, like thousands of Irish-Americans, had fled from Ireland during the potato famine of the 1840s. But by the time Grace's grandparents, John and Mary Kelly, were established in East Falls half a century later, the family was by no means without resources. Old John, the pater-familias, was making a decent living from his own insurance business, and he was able to provide quite a comfortable and solid home for Walter, George, Jack, Aunt Grace and six other sons and daughters. Two of the sons, Patrick H. and Charles, were already partners in their own successful building business when their younger brother Jack left school, and it was Patrick H. who had given Jack his first job.

So while it was technically correct to say that Jack Kelly had started his working life as a bricklayer, he had, in fact, been something of a privileged trainee, working on the payroll of his brothers' construction business – and it was his rich show-business brothers who provided the cash that enabled him to get started on his own. Uncle George liked to point out that the calluses on Jack's hands came less from manual labour than from his own decision to spend so much of his time at 'scull practice on the Schuyl-kill river'.

They were both master mythmakers, these divergent Kelly

siblings, tycoon Jack conjuring up the picture of a youth among lunch pails and work boots, while George, the playwright, talked grandly of ease and comfort, and of being educated 'privately' – a boast which played with truth and fantasy in a fashion that was oddly similar to Jack's claim to have started out in life a bricklayer. George went to the local public school, but, as a dramatist, he could fairly be said to have educated himself.

In later life the adult Grace Kelly was to pick what she wanted from the contrasting myths developed by her uncle and her father, shaping an identity for herself that embraced the striving East Falls girl who made good, as well as the serene and fully fledged Philadelphia princess. But, beyond mere ingredients, the lesson that she absorbed from the two men who dominated her childhood was the need to write her own scenario for life. Jack and George were living proof that if a person believed their own myth with enough conviction, most other people would come to believe it, too.

Grace Kelly's style in later years was to be notable for its aloofness, and this was something else that she learned from her Uncle George. Publicly remote and fastidious, George Kelly was definitely a snob. When it came to politics, he was a conservative Republican, and he hated the populist style of FDR as thoroughly as Jack Kelly adored the president. The two brothers felt so strongly about the subject that they avoided talking politics after a time, but they kept on arguing fiercely about everything else. 'He was one of the few people', Grace remembered of Uncle George, 'who ever contradicted my father.'

Worship of Jack Kelly was the organizing principle of life at 3901 Henry Avenue, and Grace was a willing devotee of the cult. But she found a safe substitute for rebellion in her attraction towards the alternatives that were offered by Uncle George. He cut a handsome figure, as tall as his brother Jack at six-foot-two, but more slender and refined – a man of standards and of subtlety. A photograph of the dark-haired George Kelly in 1924 at the time of *The Show-Off*, his second Broadway hit, displays a pair of piercing black eyes, a long aquiline nose, and curving lips that seem almost feminine.

Uncle George's sexuality was something of a mystery. Unmarried, he never had girlfriends, and though he wrote rich and challenging roles for women, the critics sometimes accused him of misogyny. He shared his life with a discreet and loyal manservant. But if George Kelly was homosexual, he gave no overt sign of it. He lived detached and sufficient unto himself – precise and a little self-righteous, like his plays. His cup of tea had to be brewed from the raw leaf, *never* from a tea bag.

'He was a very old-world gentleman,' says Dorothy Langdon Sitley, whose father, Roy, was family doctor to both the Majers and the Kellys. 'He was very continental.'

Grace loved it when Uncle George would take her out to lunch and talk to her of scripts and books and parts. 'You could sit and listen to my Uncle George all night long,' she later recalled. 'One story after another.'

George Kelly had started off in vaudeville as an actor in the dramatic one-act sketches that were a feature of many music-hall bills, and he had been drawn into writing by the need to generate his own material. Graduating to full-length plays with *The Torch-Bearers* in 1922, he enjoyed a decade of great success. But his formal drawing-room dramas lost ground to the social realism of the Depression years, and in the early 1930s he moved out to Hollywood to write and polish dialogue for the talkies. He was placed under contract by MGM, and one of his greatest themes was the importance of protecting artistic integrity against the pressures and compromises of the studio system.

'He is the most wonderful and intelligent man I have ever

known,' wrote Grace of her uncle when she was seventeen. 'Whatever he talks about, he makes you understand all its beauty and hidden meaning.'

If there was one single influence that directed Grace Kelly toward her career as an actress, it was her adored Uncle George. Declaiming long narrative passages from the nine-teenth-century poets that he loved, lecturing his young nephews and nieces on the need to correct the nasal twang of their Philadelphia accents, walking, even in old age, with the same stately posture with which he had first trod the vaudeville boards, George Kelly was the inspirational essence of dramatic art – filled to his fingertips with the magic of acting.

Talking in 1966 with Irwin W. Solomon about the com-edienne Ina Claire, and trying to describe the artfully scatter-brained way in which she had performed a scene from his play *The Fatal Weakness*, George Kelly suddenly offered a demonstration. He was in his Alden Park apartment, and he walked from the living room into the dining room. The two areas were separated by a dull green theatrical curtain that hung from a long, heavy rod with old-fashioned hoops.

'A few moments later,' Solomon recalled, 'his hand came through; he pulled the curtain apart a bit, then the whole curtain, and he walked into the room.'

The transformation was astonishing. Without make-up, costume, or even a flick of his hair, Uncle George had accomplished the miracle of the actor. Assuming the postures and saying the lines, George Kelly was no longer George Kelly – 'He *was* Ina Claire.'

THREE

White Gloves

GRACE KELLY started school just before her fifth birthday, in the autumn of 1934, at the Academy of the Assumption, Ravenhill, Philadelphia, in the parish of St Bridget's. The Jesuits boast that any child they educate becomes theirs for life. The Sisters of the Assumption could certainly claim as much of their student Grace.

Ravenhill was a grand and upstanding Victorian residence that had been bequeathed to the Catholic diocese of Philadelphia, and the Sisters of the Assumption had adapted the mansion's handsome wood-panelled walls and pink stained-glass windows into a fee-paying school that was fragrant with wax polish and piety.

'Who am I?'

'I am a child of God.'

'Why am I here?'

'I am here to know Him, to love Him, and to serve Him.'

Ninety to a hundred little girls, with a few boys in the kindergarten, were shepherded through their catechism and schoolwork by a score of nuns and their helpers who lived on the premises. The domestic, or lay, sisters did the cooking and kept the place clean. They wore black aprons with white headdresses. The more senior teaching staff wore purple and had a large white felt cross sewn in the middle of their habits. The children addressed them as 'Mother'.

The Order of the Assumption was a French teaching order whose mother house was in Belgium. Ravenhill was their first, and at that time, only North American academy, and their ethic was purposefully European. If you wrote 'color' in an essay, you lost a mark. The correct spelling was 'colour'. Everyone who mattered in the convent's hierarchy spoke with a foreign accent, or in clipped and precise Oxbridge English in which you heard every consonant. 'I didn't have a native American teacher until I was in sixth grade,' remembers Mary-Ellen Tolan, a Ravenhill schoolmate of Grace's.

There was a vivid sense of being part of an international community. Each issue of the Ravenhill school magazine dwelt lengthily on the adventures in the thirty or more Assumption colleges around the world, and these became very real as the Second World War approached. Children from threatened sister houses were sent to America for safety. Among Grace Kelly's fellow students were the singing children of the Von Trapp family, fresh off the Alps in their native costumes, and bringing Ravenhill's concerts alive with the sound of music.

The mothers and sisters of the Assumption laid great emphasis on manners. Each Ravenhill girl kept three uniforms in her locker – one for everyday wear, one for sports, and one for special holy days. She also had to bring her own white, embroidered linen napkin to lunch, where one of the staff patrolled the tables, correcting the girls who did not hold their knives and forks in a proper fashion.

'Any kind of rudeness was taboo,' remembers Mother Dorothy, who was one of Grace's teachers. 'We explained how we are all a body of Christ, and how disrespect and rudeness to each other is rudeness to Christ. We stressed that very much.'

Mother Dorothy remembers Grace as a girl who asked excellent questions. 'She asked in a nice way, like somebody who was interested personally, and who wasn't looking to pick flaws. She was always very positive.' Sister Francis Joseph recalls that Grace was 'an average girl intellectually – pretty matter-of-fact.'

Grace Kelly was no brainbox. Ravenhill used the innovative teaching techniques of the Montessori method, but it was not conventional schoolwork that made the impact on Grace's mind. Her maths was particularly weak. She attended Ravenhill for nine years, from the time she was four until she completed eighth grade at the age of thirteen-and-a-half, and what she brought away was less academic accomplishment than an all-embracing and quite unshakable faith in the Catholic religion and its relevance to every detail of her life.

A different spirit might have rebelled against it – the rules, the bells, the curtseyings to Reverend Mother, the lines of white-veiled little girls filing silently to the chapel. But Grace was always a conformist, on the surface at least, and in the absence of her attaining any particular classroom distinction, religion offered an area in which she could excel. She enjoyed the pageantry and the certainty, and she felt comfortable taking her cues from authority figures.

Grace also encountered a tenderness at the convent that she did not find at home. The Kelly household was an environment of considerable material comfort, but it was tough in emotional terms. Grace found the cosseting she needed in the Mothers and Sisters of the Assumption. There was something otherworldly about them. Vanishing from lessons on a regular basis in order to fulfil their prayer vows eight times a day, Ravenhill's teachers were gentle and naïve

– and also slightly mysterious. They lived in their own forbidden areas of the mansion, and they were never seen to eat. But after lunch they always smelled of oranges.

The Order of the Assumption attached particular importance to the drama and liturgy of the Catholic faith, and the sisters introduced this to new arrivals by having them act out the ceremonies of the mass, with the kindergarten boys playing the part of priests, dressed in little paper vestments. God and human mortality were not remote or complicated prospects. Once a girl could write with any fluency, she was given a small black book to note down the questions she would like to ask her heavenly Father when she met Him face-to-face.

Grace's parents were by no means unquestioning Catholics. As a former Protestant, Ma Kelly had particular problems with the doctrine of the Virgin birth. She found the idea of Mary getting impregnated via an angel quite ridiculous, and she did not hesitate to express her scepticism on this and similar topics when family table talk turned to religious matters. But Grace drank down everything the sisters taught her. They had the same mixture of class and delicacy that she found so attractive in Uncle George. She took her first communion at the age of seven in the Ravenhill chapel, dressed all in white for her entry as a full member into the Body of Christ. The evening before, she made her first confession, kneeling in the darkness of the curtained box that stood inside the chapel door, whispering her sins through the screen to Father Allen, who came up to the school every afternoon from St Bridget's.

What sins could a seven-year-old girl find to confess? ' "I hit my friend," perhaps, or, "I told a lie," ' explains Mother Dorothy, who would prepare the girls before they went to the confessional. 'Just that little lack of cooperation with what the Lord wants from us.'

Grace's friends remember quite a mischievous little girl who got the giggles during Benediction. 'Something would start her going,' remembers Alice Godfrey. 'She would try to hold it in, and then her whole body would be shaking.'

Away from the intense and coercive Kelly environment, the sniffler became a snickerer. The Assumption sisters were not fierce disciplinarians, and Grace felt able to stretch out a little, revealing a definite friskiness. Her place at lunch was by the window, and she would help friends jettison unwanted food into the bushes when the patrolling sister was not watching. Beyond the bushes were the convent gardens and a grotto that was the rendezvous for all sorts of naughtiness.

'Grace Kelly,' remembers Glenna Costello Millar, 'was the girl who taught me how to smoke.'

It was at the Academy of the Assumption, Ravenhill, around the age of nine or ten, that Grace began to manifest the intriguing dualism that was to become the central feature of her adult character – the prime and proper Goody Two-Shoes inside whom lurked a wild and often reckless spirit. This was not a simple matter of hypocrisy. Whatever her failings, Grace was never a sly or deceitful person. It was her genuine and wholehearted wish to be a good girl and to do the right thing. But this did not stop her from puffing on a cigarette behind the convent grotto. Grace the naughty was absolutely as authentic as Grace the good, and it was the appetizing tension between these conflicting personalities that was to provide the essence of her appeal as a film star – the outwardly reserved and cool girl who hinted at such wildness underneath.

Roman Catholicism, of all religions, addresses the conflict between virtue and indulgence with particular practicality. The priest in the confession box represents the most tangible acknowledgment that we cannot possibly hope to eradicate sin and must therefore find a mechanism for living with it on a permanent basis. It is a dogma which positively embraces the basic schizophrenia that is the human condition – and it may be that the young Grace was drawn so strongly to the Catholic faith because it offered her some sort of rationale and solace for the conflicting impulses that she could already feel battling inside her.

The Academy of the Assumption, Ravenhill, no longer exists. The sisters later transferred their ministry to the Philadelphia ghetto. But Ravenhill remains a treasured memory for Grace's school friends – the remembrance of a different and rather innocent world, now more than fifty years past. On holy days the entire student body would participate in *cache-cache*, a massive, school-wide game of hide-and-seek. Every day after school, when sports were over, the girls would be served with *goûter*. One of the cooking sisters would emerge from the kitchen, bearing a tray piled high with fresh-baked pastries.

Grace's mother and father took her away from Ravenhill at the end of eighth grade because Jack Kelly felt that the convent's sporting programme was inadequate. Pastries after training certainly did not sharpen the competitive edge. But Grace's early brush with the compelling power of faith and idealism stayed with her all her life. From the year she left, she kept in touch with the sisters, sending them Christmas cards and writing long, newsy letters to her favourite teachers. It was as if she saw them as parents. Sometimes, as an adult, she would turn back to her childhood mentors for advice.

'The sisters were quite remarkable women,' says Alice Godfrey. 'I remember being struck by their sense of obligation and social duty. It was quite compelling. It affected us all, I think.'

Alice Godfrey has a particular memory of Sister Inez, a young nun from central America who took her final vows while Grace and Alice were her pupils: 'Grace loved her. She was the most beautiful woman you ever laid your eyes on, with the biggest brown eyes and the creamiest skin. Grace and I talked about it. We just couldn't believe that this gorgeous creature was giving her whole life to God.'

With her friend Alice, the nine-year-old Grace was one of a small group who were invited to witness Sister Inez's solemn submission and induction into the order: 'The ceremony was just unbelievable – the music, the chanting. The sister lay prostrate on the floor, and they covered her. The cardinal was there. If you could have seen the mothers and the sisters in their long white veils, coming in and kneeling at the prie-dieu, all bowing down and touching the marble floor . . . Grace said to me afterwards that she would never forget it. I mean, there was a moment in that ceremony when we both felt quite certain that God had come down and was right there beside us.'

Grace was nearly fourteen years old when she transferred from Ravenhill to the Stevens School in Germantown, a private establishment for girls that had been founded in Civil War times by a Miss Susie Stevens. This lady was said to have fallen down the stairs on hearing the news of her fiancé's death in battle, and to have devoted the rest of her life, from her wheelchair, to the education of refined young ladies. Miss Stevens's staircase was still there when Grace went to the school, the striking and dramatic centre-piece of yet another old, wood-panelled mansion that had been converted into an academy with an accent on decorum. The former stable house at the back of the courtyard had been remodelled into a sort of practice salon, where the girls were instructed in the etiquette of how to serve, and how to take, afternoon tea.

Grace completed her high school education at Stevens, and it was during these last four years of schooling that she started going out with boys. But she did not, initially, meet with great success. 'There was one period when she was between fourteen and sixteen,' her mother later recalled, 'when she was nothing but a giggly somebody with a high, nasal voice. She always had had trouble with her nose . . . That gave her the peculiar voice. Her enjoyment of food gave her a little extra weight. And she had been nearsighted for several years, which made it necessary for her to wear glasses.'

Grace had matured early and looked older than her years, but she suffered from a crippling lack of self-confidence. 'I was terribly shy when I was young,' she later remembered. 'I almost crawled into the woodwork I was so self-conscious . . . I was so bland, they kept having to introduce me again and again before people noticed me. I made no impression.'

Grace conjured up these painful memories in 1974, when she was nearly forty-five years old, one of the most famous women in the world and universally revered as an example of poise and self-assurance. But the ache was clearly still there. For all her beauty and apparent serenity, the princess retained a core of insecurity that dated back to her childhood years. It was as if she still held inside her the plain and gawky little girl that nobody noticed.

The teenage Grace had a particular anxiety about her breasts, which, she felt convinced, were not large enough. 'She had a complex,' remembers one of her school friends. 'She was forever massaging them, hoping to make them bigger.'

Flat-chested, overweight and wearing glasses. 'Grace was not really known as a beauty queen in those days,' remembers Jim 'Butch' McAllister, who knew Grace down in Ocean

41

City, New Jersey, where the Kellys had a summer home. As Grace's mother crisply put it, 'She was nobody's Princess Charming.'

At the time, Ma Kelly felt sorry for her shy and gawky fourteen-year-old. She was reminded of the withdrawn and waiflike child who had always seemed to require more babying than her extrovert brother and sisters. But later she came to wonder whether some of the survival techniques that Grace developed in her ugly-duckling years were not a source of her successes in later life. 'I always wanted to protect Gracie,' she said. 'She must have struck men the same way she struck me. Every man who knew her from the time she was about fifteen . . . wanted to take care of Gracie.'

Even as a successful and stunningly beautiful adult, Grace Kelly had the knack of getting people to coddle her. 'She always had a way of getting people to do things for her,' her sister Lizanne once explained. 'You really thought she needed help, but she did not need help at all. You'd find yourself thinking, "Oh, I'd better go over and help her." And she didn't need help at all. She gave that impression.'

The streak of fantasy that had taken the baby Grace into her own safe world of dolls ran strong as ever. 'When she was eight, nine, ten,' remembers Alice Godfrey, 'we used to sit and we'd open up the *Esquire*, or whatever magazine was at the house, and we'd turn the pages, and she would make up a story about it – "Now, that's my home, and that's my car. There's my husband, and they're our children, and there's this, and oh, yes, there's where we're going on our honeymoon." '

Grace's social confidence might falter from time to time, but she could fantasize with rare conviction. In the winter of 1940–41, when she was eleven, she went to a matinée of the *Ballets Russes* and was entranced with its star, Igor Yous-kevitch, the Baryshnikov of his day. She decided that she would become a prima ballerina. So she took ballet lessons until she was told that she was too tall – when she moved on to Ginger Rogers with equal enthusiasm. Maree Frisby, the new best friend she had made at Stevens, remembers Grace phoning her reproachfully from the modern dance class in which they had both enrolled. 'I was not that keen on it, and I remember getting calls from Grace on Saturday morning – "Maree, where are you? You promised you'd be here." '

Grace had acted in plays from an early age. After serving her apprenticeship as angel and shepherd in the annual Ravenhill Christmas pageants, she had graduated to the role of the Virgin Mary. But it was during her gawky years that Grace's passion for acting really started to take root, as she discovered how, on the stage, she could fashion herself into what she wanted with a style she could not yet master in real life.

A visit to a production by the Old Academy Players, a small East Falls amateur dramatic group, lit the spark. Grace rushed home from the play, which had featured her mother's brother, Uncle 'Midge' Majer, to tell her father that she wanted to be an actress.

Jack Kelly was not impressed. 'He just looked up at me from his desk for a long time,' Grace later remembered. 'Then he said: "All right, Grace, if that's what you want to do . . ." '

The Old Academy Players were one of the many 'little theatre' groups of amateur enthusiasts that flourished in Philadelphia in the 1930s and 1940s. They had converted an old East Falls schoolhouse into a theatre, and it was in the plain but functional setting of this 'old academy' that Grace Kelly made her stage debut in 1942 at the age of twelve. 'I remember the first time on stage as a nice feeling,' she recalled in

Hollywood a dozen years later. '[It] was nice to feel an audience respond.'

The play was *Don't Feed the Animals*, and Ruth Emmert, who directed it, was struck by Grace's professionalism. The young actress was always on time for rehearsals, and she never forgot her lines. She also displayed a commendable willingness to raid her mother's wardrobe for the costumes and props that the amateur company needed.

By the time she was a teenager, Grace was an amateur dramatic mini-star. She was a juvenile stalwart of the Old Academy Players, cycling down the hill for rehearsals with the same commitment that Kell was displaying about rowing. The boy was starting to win at regattas. Grace's equivalent was to win the leading roles in the productions at Stevens. She played Kate in *The Taming of the Shrew*, she was a dazzling Peter Pan, and she was the star of the school dancing classes. She brought the Stevens field day to a halt one year with a strangely erotic interpretation of a ritual fire dance, all jerks and drama, performed barefoot.

Her Stevens schoolmates had no doubt about her acting and her dancing abilities. The 'prophecy' section of her final school yearbook envisioned a future for Grace Patricia Kelly as 'a famous star of screen and radio' – though this was not to suggest that her friends considered her stagy or self-important. In the yearbook's composite portrait of the 'Perfect Senior', Grace was listed as a model of a popular student.

'She had a real sparkle about her,' remembers Jane Porter, who was several years behind her at Stevens. 'She was just fun!'

When Jane Porter first went to Stevens, she found that she had been assigned to Grace as her 'little sister'. Older girls were given newcomers to take under their wings, and Grace carried out her responsibilities more thoroughly than most. 'She was one of the few girls who had her own car,' remembers Jane, 'a convertible, a Plymouth, I think. It was light blue – zippy. Every day we'd have to go down for hockey practice, and because I was her little sister she'd say, "Come on, Jane!" '

Jane Porter has horrified memories of Grace shifting the light-blue convertible into 'drive', jumping onto the top of the back of the driver's seat – and then steering the car with her toes. The frolics of the convent schoolgirl now had an adolescent tinge. Grace was the centre of an effervescent, bobby-socked group of girls at Stevens who shared her weakness for giggling and fun. They would meet Saturday mornings in Germantown for milk shakes and sundaes at the Dairy Maid.

Evenings found them at the Bandbox, the Orpheum, or the Colonial, one of the local movie houses, where Grace would swoon over the composed good looks of Alan Ladd, who was her favourite male film star. Her favourite film actress was Ingrid Bergman. Hopelessly sentimental, Grace did not like to leave the theatre without a good cry. Alice Godfrey remembers her friend dissolving into tears at Mickey Rooney's memorable line in *Boys Town*: 'He's not heavy, he's my brother.'

And then there were the boys . . . Some time before Grace was sixteen, these were no longer lacking. A year or so of development, the chemistry of the Kelly–Majer genes, and the self-confidence that had grown with Grace's adolescent acting success had all come together to produce a real stunner. Grace was now a beauty.

'She had the most wonderful complexion,' remembers Teddy Hughes, a friend and schoolmate of Kell's. 'Her colouring was fantastic – sort of fresh and clear. It was her best feature – and it never showed in the photos.'

All the Kelly kids had luminosity. With their geometric good looks and their mouthfuls of perfect teeth, they exuded an aura of happy destiny that was comparable to that of Boston's Kennedy family, another high-profile clan of Irish-Americans who were marching in these years to the drumbeat of a dynamic father. But Grace's facial features clicked together with a symmetry and charm that her siblings could not quite match. Kell's looks were so regular he was almost bland. Lizanne was on the tough side, Peggy a trifle coy. Only Grace was blessed with the balance that got the mixture just right – a near-perfect combination of the physical traits that her handsome parents had brought to their marriage. Good looks which seemed to shout out pedigree were the cornerstone of Grace Kelly's adult fame, and the same was true of her beauty as a teenager.

3901 Henry Avenue acted as a kind of clubhouse for all the friends of the four Kelly children. Everybody gathered there. So it was not surprising that Grace's first serious boyfriend was a schoolmate of her brother's – Charles Harper Davis, the son of the local Buick dealer. Harper Davis belonged to the Trident Society, the elite fellowship of senior boys at Penn Charter School. Penn Charter was quite elite itself, the second-oldest school in America, having been founded in 1701 by William Penn, and it was a social focus for middle-class teenagers in the Germantown area. The school's various clubs and societies held a series of dances through the winter, the high point being the Trident dance, and Grace went through a happy season on the arm of one of the biggest men on campus. The romance between the 'Buick salesman's son and [the] bricklayer's daughter' was serious enough to rate a mention in the Penn Charter Class Diary.

In 1944 Harper Davis graduated from school and enlisted in the Navy. The war was drawing to an end, and he was anxious to follow in the steps of his father, a Navy man. But two days after Harper told Grace he would be joining the service, he came to his friend Teddy Hughes, ashen-faced and shaken. Grace had suddenly dropped him. Their romance was off.

At the time Harper said Grace had given him no real reason for her decision, and Grace never talked about it even with her closest friends. But it soon became clear that Papa had been involved. Jack Kelly considered it his paternal right and duty to regulate the love life of his daughters. He had forced Peggy, his beloved Baba, to break off her relationship with Archie Campbell, a young man who was too pasty-faced and non-athletic for Jack Kelly's taste, and he was to prove equally interfering – though ultimately he surrendered – when it came to the wish of his youngest daughter, Lizanne, to marry a Jew.

The paterfamilias was surprisingly relaxed when it came to casual dating. The more boys the merrier was Jack Kelly's point of view. He seemed to take it as a compliment that such crowds of eager young men should flock to the house in pursuit of his beautiful daughters.

'There were so many of us he could not remember our names,' recalled Charlie Fish. 'So he'd just grin and call each of us "Son." '

It was when things threatened to get serious that Jack Kelly intervened. That was when his daughters became his property. As he put it bluntly to one of Grace's teenage suitors: 'You can take her out as much as you like. But don't think you're going to marry her.'

This was the prospect raised by Harper Davis's imminent departure for the war. There was the likelihood of the love-struck young couple being drawn towards fantasies of engagement or marriage – and the equal possibility that, engaged or not, Grace might feel impelled to proffer her brave companion the ultimate going-away present, as many a romantic young virgin did in those tense and stirring wartime years.

Either option was unthinkable for Jack Kelly. He disliked Harper Davis's father, the Buick dealer – and the Davises were not Catholic. Grace was too young. Whatever way you looked at it, the relationship had to end.

Grace bent obediently to the imperious will of her father. She said goodbye to Harper Davis, and replaced him with a succession of handsome young men – the more the merrier, just as her father wanted. Grace had a wonderful time. She played the field with enthusiasm – though it seemed to her friends that she was seeking to bury some sort of pain or guilt in her busy and almost promiscuous programme of self-gratification.

The boys about Germantown recorded their clambering up the sexual mountain in code. 'Bra' meant inside the blouse, but outside the support system. 'B.T.' meant bare tit. 'F' stood for finger, from which you advanced to the jobs, hand and blow. It was an age in which full sexual intercourse was still regarded as a special and almost sacred event, not the routine commonplace of a teenage Saturday night. 'Petting' was the coy name for the coy explorations of buttons and zips and the soft flesh at the top of the stocking. Each sweaty advance was ungraciously bragged of as the boys compared notes in the locker room, and it became quite common knowledge how far each girl would go.

In her post-Harper Davis years, Grace Kelly became known for her generosity. 'I am sure she was still a virgin when she graduated,' says one of her dates. 'But I reckon that she had done just about everything else.'

Grace would laugh about it herself when she got older. Charlie Fish was one of her regular dates while she was still at Stevens. He used to take her out in his old blue Ford roadster, and she would ask fondly after the car in later years.

'I hope it's safely in the scrapyard,' chuckled the Princess of Monaco. 'Just think of the tales that backseat could tell!'

But Grace was never laughed about, or scorned as cheap or easy. She waltzed through the rituals of perpetual foreplay with nonchalance and pleasure, but she was never available to just anyone. She was discriminating about whom she dated, and she worked hard at being a good companion.

'She didn't talk too much,' Howard Wikoff explained to Gwen Robyns. 'Instead of showing off and chattering all about herself like most teenagers, she was attentive to her dates. She made each escort think he was King Bee.'

'If you wanted to sit, she'd sit,' remembered Jack Oechsle. 'If you wanted to dance, she'd dance. And if you took her to a party she wouldn't float off with another fellow. She was your date, and remained your date.'

By the time Grace was seventeen and coming to the end of her years at Stevens, the streaks of Kelly poise were clearly showing through. Grace was developing a very firm sense of who she was.

'It's like her father when he would row,' remembers Alice Godfrey. 'He would look at the rest of the group and say, "I wonder who's coming in second?" There was something of that about Grace.'

Inside her own close circle, Grace was impish and extroverted – zany even. Teddy Hughes remembers a crowd of friends discovering her padded bra under the seat of her convertible. Grace seemed to find it as amusing as everyone else, and joined in the mêlée with gusto, fighting fiercely for her falsies and flinging them cheerfully around the car. Yet she also had a sterner face. Jack Kelly and Uncle George each had their own ways of shrivelling people with a look – scornful in Jack's case, more brittle and aloof in George's – and Grace developed her own rapier glance that was a combination of the two. It could be devastating. If you chanced to earn Grace Kelly's displeasure, you were left in no doubt that you had offended a member of the royal family of East Falls.

This chilly side was to become another of the prominent elements in Grace Kelly's public persona in later life. It seemed to go neatly with her cool good looks, and it dovetailed with the plausible but mistaken assumption that was commonly made about her wealthy background – that she came from the aristocracy of Philadelphia. The Kellys were rich and royal by East Falls standards, but that was very different from making any kind of an impression on the serious society of Philadelphia itself.

The Philadelphia Assemblies Ball is the oldest and most exclusive social gathering in North America. George Washington attended. Held continuously since 1748, with only a few years' break in times of war, the ball draws Philadelphia's most ancient families together every winter for a glittering evening of dancing, display, and celebration of the comforting feeling that – at least by their own standards – everyone present has come out of the very top drawer. The men dress in white-tie and tails, the women in their finest and most flowing ball gowns.

The Assemblies Ball provides the arena in which some of Philadelphia's best-born débutantes create their first social splash. The girls and their escorts parade down the marble staircase of the receiving room to the grand ballroom of the Bellevue-Stratford hotel, an elegant cascade of white silk and chiffon. One by one, each débutante curtseys to the reception line of matrons from the leading families. Then she prepares for her first dance in grown-up society – for which, custom ordains, she must keep wearing her elbow-length, white kid gloves.

It was one of the dreams of the teenage Grace Kelly to 'come out' as a débutante, according to her friend and bridesmaid, Judy Kanter, to whom Grace disclosed the fantasy in later years – and Grace would surely have provided a marvellous sight, sweeping down the marble staircase, eighteen years old and dazzling, in her white dress and white gloves. But this was not a fantasy of which Jack Kelly or his circle of friends approved.

'You want to "come out"?' Grace's Uncle Bill Godfrey asked his daughter Alice, who shared her friend Grace's fancy for a glamorous evening in white. 'Well, I'll hold the door open for you!'

This robust, man-of-the-people attitude masked a certain pique. 'Jack Kelly always resented the fact that he was never in the Blue Book,' said Phil Klein, a friend of Kell's – or as Jack himself preferred to put it, 'I'm aiming for the *Do* Book, not the Blue Book.'

With his charisma, wealth and political connections, Jack Kelly could have made it to the top of almost any other city in North America. In Washington, people manage it with votes and influence. In New York you can buy your way into the most prestigious social function. But when it comes to Philadelphia, one has to be *born* into the Assemblies.

Trying to explain it to outsiders, Assemblies members tend to talk in terms of history and of old friends sticking together – who got off the boat with William Penn and all that. But the bottom line is social and ethnic. This is old blood, and old money, literally the clique for whom the word WASP was invented, since it was while analysing the social context of the Philadelphia Assemblies that Professor Digby Baltzell was driven to seek some easy abbreviation of the classification he found himself using most frequently – White Anglo-Saxon Protestant. Philadelphia's charmed circle is Old Guard and no apology about it – no blacks, no Jews, no Catholics, and no *nouveaux riches*. There is no room in this picture for self-made Irish bricklayers or their daughters, however slim and elegant.

In her extraordinary career as an actress and princess, Grace appeared to the outside world to be the very epitome of Philadelphia class and breeding. She played aristocratic roles, and she successfully conveyed the impression that she was reared in the elite Assemblies environment of white gloves, white dresses and fluttering débutantes. But in reality, Grace never attended the Philadelphia Assemblies Ball. She never paraded down the Bellevue-Stratford staircase as a débutante. Her manners and her sense of etiquette came from the Stevens School and from the Sisters of the Assumption in the parish of St Bridget's, and for all her eminence in her own particular corner of Philadelphia, she could never make it in the society that really counted.

Grace Kelly was an outsider, an excluded observer of a world that was held to be the ultimate in terms of class and privilege – which may be one reason why she made such a good job of mimicking the style and customs of that world in her later life.

In May 1947, Grace graduated from the Stevens School. She was seventeen and a half, and she had no idea what she was going to do next. She had assumed she was going to Bennington, then a women's college in Vermont. 'I wanted to be a dancer,' she later remembered, 'and Bennington had a wonderful four-year course in all forms of dance.'

But Bennington had entry standards for mathematics that Grace could not match. Ever since her earliest Ravenhill days, maths had been her weak suit.

Her parents did not really focus on the problem. The priority at Henry Avenue in the summer of 1947 was the boy of the family, Kell, whose years of pain and training on the Schuylkill were poised to reach their intended climax – capture of the Diamond Sculls at Henley. Grace's college plans had to take a back seat to the preparations for the Royal Regatta that July – getting the shell packed up safely, and ensuring the young athlete a reliable supply of frozen steaks to supplement the austere and rationed food supplies of postwar Britain.

At the end of June 1947, the family set sail for England. Kell had gone to Henley the previous summer, and had failed to bring home the coveted trophy. He had crossed the line in second place and had collapsed where he sat, folding into himself, almost comatose. His hands had gripped the oars so tightly that it took two strong men to pry them off, finger by finger.

Now, on 5 July 1947, with his parents and younger sisters looking on, Kell made no mistake. Wearing a replica of his father's famous green racing cap, he was the easy winner of the polished antique box that enshrined the world's premier sculling trophy. When he brought it back to America, he was honoured with a victory ride through the streets of Philadelphia, sitting in an open car in the company of his laughing father. The Mayor gave a testimonial dinner in his honour. Only just twenty, and still three years from graduating at the University of Pennsylvania, Kell had already achieved his purpose in life. It was difficult to see what he, or any other member of the family, could possibly accomplish that would add further lustre to the Kelly name.

Not until all the rituals of celebration were concluded did the further education of the champion's second sister resume its place on the family agenda. Ma Kelly set about organizing a tour of women's colleges in the Northeast, and she set off with Grace at the beginning of August 1947. But they were far too late. Everywhere they went the entry rolls were full, and the middle of the month found mother and daughter taking gloomy stock in the New York apartment of Marie Magee, an old friend of Ma Kelly, who lived just off Broadway on West Fifty-fifth Street.

'We can't get into any college,' Mrs Kelly reported. 'What are we going to do?'

'Well,' replied Mrs Magee, 'what do *you* want to do, Gracie?'

'Aunt Marie,' said Grace, 'I wonder if I could get into the American Academy of Dramatic Arts?'

Marie Magee had been an actress herself, and her own daughter had been a student at the American Academy, which, as its name implied, was one of the country's leading private drama schools. In 1947 the American Academy was located in the studios above Carnegie Hall, only two blocks away from Broadway and Fifty-fifth Street, and Marie Magee wasted no time. She made an appointment for Grace to see Emil Diestel, the administrator of the school, who was also in charge of admissions.

'Mrs Magee, I can't take her,' was Diestel's discouraging opening line, according to Marie Magee's memory of the episode. 'Our registration's closed . . . We don't have one spot in the school for her.'

Mrs Magee asked Grace to wait outside.

'Look, Mr Diestel,' she explained, 'this child's father and George Kelly are brothers.'

The name of the famous playwright got results. George Kelly was a revered figure to Diestel's generation, and he also stood for the traditional, four-square form of drama which the American Academy favoured. 'I'll see what I can do,' Diestel said, and gave Grace thirty pages of Uncle George's *The Torch-Bearers* to read and prepare for another meeting the next day.

The handwritten audition book of the American Academy of Dramatic Arts records that Grace Patricia Kelly of

Philadelphia appeared in front of Emil E. Diestel on 20 August 1947. She weighed 126 pounds and stood five foot six and a half inches in her stocking feet. Her colouring was described as 'blond', her proportions 'good', and her nationality as 'American-Irish'. The entry was headed by the significant notation – 'niece of George Kelly'.

Grace had spent what she remembered as a sleepless and anxious night in the apartment of Aunt Marie, but she rose to the occasion splendidly. Emil Diestel rated her reading as 'intelligent' and her temperament as 'sensitive'. Her dramatic instinct was awarded a solid 'Yes'. Diestel's only criticism was of her voice. It was 'not placed' – but that could be fixed. The director of admissions was quite won over. 'Lovely child,' he noted. 'Good and promising youthful symptoms. Should develop well.'

Quite against the odds, Grace had accomplished the goal she did not know she had six months earlier when she had applied to Bennington to pursue a career in dance. Grace Patricia Kelly was registered for entry at the American Academy of Dramatic Arts for the semester beginning in October 1947.

There was just one other piece of business to get tidied away. Reminiscing in later years to a lover whom she met at the American Academy, Grace recalled how she had lost her virginity shortly before she went away to New York.

'It happened very quickly,' she related. 'I went round to a friend's house to pick her up, and I found that she wasn't there. It was raining outside, and her husband told me she would be gone for the rest of the day. I stayed talking to him, and somehow we fell into bed together, without understanding quite why.'

Grace did not sleep with the man again, though she stayed on polite terms with the couple. The episode for her was a rite of passage, a secret and only incidentally passionate matter that she had to take care of as she said goodbye to childhood and made ready for the big city. Ever since the ending of her relationship with Harper Davis she had been playing with sex, seeing what it felt like when separated from true commitment, and this was just the conclusion of the game. Little Gracie was moving on.

Jack Kelly had always been patronizing towards his daughter's acting ambitions, and he did not rate her nick-of-time entry to one of America's leading drama schools as one of the major Kelly accomplishments of 1947. 'Oh, no, no!' had been his reaction when his wife had returned to Philadelphia and told him the outcome of the last-minute college-fishing trip. 'I don't think that is quite the place for her,' he said.

'Let her go now,' cajoled Ma Kelly. 'She'll be back in only a month, dear. You know she's very timid.'

But brother Kell, who was basking in his glory as the hero of the moment, knew Grace rather better, and he came to appreciate what his younger sister managed to achieve. Asked in later years why Grace had 'turned out differently' from the rest of the family, he replied without hesitation, 'she got away from home early.'

Kell, of all people, realized what a victory that represented for a child of Jack and Margaret Kelly. 'None of the rest of us,' he explained, 'managed to do that.'

PART TWO
ACTRESS

FOUR

Dramatic Beginnings

IN 1947 THE American Academy of Dramatic Arts seemed as bohemian and artistic as a drama school could be. Packed into the attics above Carnegie Hall, it was a maze of wood-floored studios, with high, arching windows, exposed pipes and echoing fire-escape staircases. Creaky and dusty, the place positively reeked of 'backstage'.

'You could see, smell and touch theatre,' remembers Rachel Taylor, who was a fellow student of Grace's. 'It was as if you could hear the voices of actors past. You felt you were part of a real and creative activity that lifted you above ordinary things.'

The inspiration of the American Academy was Charles Jehlinger, one of the founding fathers of the modern American theatre. A pint-sized, white-haired and ferociously concentrated German Jew, Jehlinger had been a student in the very first class of the Academy in 1884, and he had been the director of instruction since 1890. 'Jelly', as he was known behind his back, focused particularly on the students who were approaching graduation, but his ideas set the tone for the whole school. Aristide d'Angelo, one of his principal lieutenants, used to welcome his students to their first-year studies with an apparently banal exercise that took them straight to the heart of the matter.

A volunteer would go out of the room while a pencil was hidden, and would return to be guided toward its hiding place by his fellow students calling out 'cold', 'warm', or 'hot' in the manner of the party game. Then the pencil would be left where it was, and the volunteer would have to repeat the search with an equal display of doubt and confusion – now knowing full well where the pencil was, but giving a performance that was convincing enough for him to keep commanding the help of the rest of the class.

D'Angelo was illustrating the fundamental challenge to every actor. The audience knows, rationally, that the play has been rehearsed many times before, that the movie is just patterns of light that are being projected through a roll of celluloid that lives in a can. But it is the actor's job to suspend disbelief so that this rational truth is never actually registered with the audience, even for an instant.

For Charles Jehlinger, acting was a grand and mystical version of conjuring. 'The Actor', he wrote in the high-flown and occasionally incomprehensible prospectus to his Academy, 'is, all that is, at will.' But, like the best illusionists, Jehlinger knew that the secret of successful conjuring lay in such strictly practical matters as hard work and rehearsal – the battery of skills that he liked to call the 'firm foundation'. So his students found their lives consumed by hours of exercises and drills that sometimes took them a long way from Hamlet. 'We would be assigned to go to the Bowery and observe a drunk and then come back and act out a drunk,' Grace later remembered, describing a class that went by the name of 'Pantomimic Expression: Life Study'.

'We would have to pretend that we were an ape,' remembers Bettina Thompson, who was a friend of Grace's. 'So we would all walk around the studio with our backs straight,

our fanny tucked in, and our arms dangling along the floor.'
Murr Sinclair, another friend, remembers complicated and
painful classes in how to fall down stairs.

Jehlinger and his Academy were considered hopelessly
technical and old-fashioned by the avant garde in the American theatre. The vogue in the years after the Second World
War was for the 'Method' school of acting, as developed in
America by Lee Strasberg's Actors Studio, and later brought
to the popular audience by the moody performances of James
Dean and Marlon Brando. Stage 'business' was scorned as
artificial. It was *feeling* that mattered. The key to the 'Method'
was the idea that the actor should reach back into his own
personal experience to locate authentic expressions of joy,
shame, anger, or whatever emotion his part required.

But Jehlinger, like Strasberg's many critics, felt that
'Method'-style introspection produced self-obsessed performances which often meant more to the actor than they
did to the audience. It was the job of the actor to entertain,
and Jelly had no time for mumbling or stumbling. He saw
his job as the imparting of a professional code of acting
techniques and behaviour to his students – from 'the habit
of consulting the dictionary' to the style in which his charges
presented themselves to the world, both offstage and on.

'The actor and actress should know how to dress with
fitness, good taste and sincerity,' read his prospectus for
1947–48. Jehlinger's pupils might be artistic and even
bohemian, but they were also expected to remain young
ladies and gentlemen. 'There were guest lectures,' remembers
Murr Sinclair. 'People like Helen Hayes would come and
talk to us, and then the girls were expected to dress up
properly, in hats and little white gloves.'

Yet again, Grace Kelly's education was set in a structure
where manners and etiquette were taken very seriously. The
American Academy's roster of famous graduates included

Spencer Tracy, Katharine Hepburn, Kirk Douglas and Lauren Bacall. In the year that Grace joined the Academy, Don Rickles and Jason Robards were the stars of the graduating class. None of these actors or actresses could be described as overmannered in their professional style. But it was the traditional and formalistic element in Jehlinger's teaching that seemed to strike a chord in Grace. She loved the school's old-fashioned 'Fencing and Stage Duelling' lessons, and she always credited the Academy with her upright posture and eerily regal gait. 'I was a "swayback",' she would relate. 'When I was lying as flat as I could, this teacher used to get down on the floor and would say, "I can see air." This meant that I'd have to try and lie even flatter.'

'Technique, technique,' remembers Rachel Taylor. 'That was what the Academy was all about. I remember one exercise where they would throw open those big windows onto Fifty-seventh Street and tell us to breathe. And I thought, "I am coming to New York to learn how to breathe?" It was thanks to the Academy that we all fell in love with the theatre, but we also came to realize that the only way to learn how to act – to really act – was to go out and do it.'

Grace Kelly certainly came to feel this herself. Blessed and cursed by her father's demanding and perfectionist nature, she was always asking more of herself and of her own personal command of her craft. Her career as an actress turned out to be a constant process of learning, much of it accomplished in the years after she left the American Academy. But it was during her months in the musty studios above Carnegie Hall that she acquired several of the components of her dramatic persona, and the most important of these was the voice that was to become her trademark – the Grace Kelly accent.

'It takes a trained ear to detect all errors of pronunciation, accent and emphasis,' read the Academy's prospectus for 1947, 'but by careful and persistent criticism, the dialects of

Pennsylvania or New England, of Canada or the South, are at last dethroned.' Aristide d'Angelo was the voice coach in charge of dethroning, aided by Edward Goodman, a short and elegant Englishman who carried a silver-topped cane containing a phial of ready-mixed Martinis of which he partook regularly. Goodman spoke with a perfectly modulated Oxbridge accent, and he did not mince his words. He listened to Grace just once, then delivered his verdict without hesitation: 'You have got to get rid of that *terrible* twang!'

Pitch and diction were the elements that Goodman attacked in the revoicing of Grace. He had an elaborate relaxation exercise that he got his students to perform while sitting in a straight-backed chair. This lowered Grace's voice, correcting her tendency toward squeakiness, while she also worked through a series of vowel and consonant drills that taught her how to isolate the components of every word that she said.

'The effect of these classes,' boasted Jehlinger's prospectus, 'is sometimes little short of magical' – and so it proved with Grace. By the time her Academy voice tutors were finished with her, her professional stage and screen accent was a triumphant confection – high class and bell-like, with the precise enunciation of those grand English actresses who end up as Dames. When Grace Kelly pronounced the word 'rotten' you could hear every single 't' and a few more beside, while her vowel sounds, tugged firmly away from East Falls by the example of Edward Goodman, had ventured out across the Atlantic to hover remarkably close to the British coast.

The credit for Grace Kelly's astonishing good looks had to go to the happy accident of her Irish-German ancestry, but her voice was very much the creation of her own hard work and her powerful homing instinct for what she wanted to be. Part Jane Austen, part Mary Poppins, Grace's voice breathed tutored and well-bred vulnerability. If Marilyn Monroe's voice said 'Squeeze me', and Mae West's said 'Screw me', then Grace Kelly's said, 'Please hold my hand'. Augmenting the instruction she received at the Academy, Grace took private voice lessons from Mario Fiorella, an operatic tenor who was the boyfriend of Aunt Marie Magee, and she would also spend long hours doing voice exercises with a clothes peg attached to the end of her nose. 'It was a deliberate thing,' remembers her old friend Dottie Sitley. 'She put on the clothes peg to lower the register of her voice, and to pull it down into her throat.'

If you paused more than a second to analyse the components of Grace Kelly's professional accent it sounded quite ridiculous – and that was how it seemed to her family and friends when she first returned to Philadelphia. 'We went to a cocktail party,' remembers Jane Porter, her young friend from Stevens. 'Grace came in, and I thought, "I don't believe it!" She had such a thick British accent.'

The Kellys called it 'Gracie's new voice'. 'They teased her unmercifully,' remembers Alice Godfrey.

'I must talk this way – for my work,' Grace responded huffily, and, for the time being, the family held its peace.

Jack Kelly had only consented to his middle daughter going off to New York on the eve of her eighteenth birthday if there was a safe and suitable place for her to stay. The Barbizon Hotel for Women at Sixty-third Street and Lexington somewhat allayed his anxieties – an all-female establishment in the heart of Manhattan where three references of respectability were required to become a guest, and where male visitors were not allowed beyond the ground floor. 'It was exactly like a very posh boarding school,' remembers Murr Sinclair.

The Barbizon was legendary as the New York nest from which many a beautiful fledgling had first taken flight. Joan

Crawford, Gene Tierney and Lauren Bacall had all lodged in the Barbizon's pink and green rooms, with the bathroom and lavatories situated inconveniently down the hall. In her novel, *The Bell Jar*, Sylvia Plath renamed it 'The Amazon' – a place 'for women only . . . with wealthy parents who wanted to be sure their daughters would be living where men couldn't get at them and deceive them'.

For this very reason, however, the Barbizon was something of a magnet for young men about town. They cruised the lobby, joking with the burly female lift operators who came on duty in the evening with the mission of protecting the virtue of the upper floors. Murr Sinclair lived further uptown with a group of fellow Academy students in a pension-apartment under the watchful eye of a landlady, and she can remember envying the clusters of suitors and the relative freedom of the girls who lived in the Barbizon. 'They had a wonderful time. It was not very difficult for them to do just as they wished.'

This was certainly the case with Grace. Mark 'Herbie' Miller, a fellow student of hers at the Academy, has vivid memories of the Barbizon. 'We would go up to the thirteenth floor. There was a recreation room, with part of it roped off. So Grace and I would go into the roped-off part, and just smooch. 'Necking,' we used to call it in those days – a lot of kissing and stuff. We were like young little puppies, throwing ourselves at each other.'

Herbie Miller had met Grace on his very first day at the Academy. 'I saw this angelic creature. I just fell madly in love with her at first sight – and I suppose that she did the same for me.'

Breezy and genial, with the build of a football quarterback, Herbie Miller was one of the best-looking males that the Academy recruited in 1947. His style was matinee idol, with the collar of his polo coat always stuck up at a rakish angle. Working under the professional name of Mark Miller, he subsequently starred in a number of TV series, among them *Please Don't Eat the Daisies*. But in 1947 Herbie shared an accent problem with Grace. 'You'll be playing cowboy movies all your life,' Mr Goodman told him, 'if you don't get rid of that Texas accent.'

The voice tutor made this diagnosis in the same class in which he had jumped upon Grace's Philadelphia twang. 'So we did our voice exercises together almost every night,' remembers Miller. ' "How – now – brown – cow", that sort of thing, backward and forward to each other, three or four times a week for over a year.'

Herbie and Grace made an attractive and purposeful young couple, working together on their craft and making a point of catching the latest European art movies that were screened once a week at the Museum of Modern Art. They were devotees of the understated British style of Alec Guinness. Bettina Thompson, who shared a room with Grace at the Barbizon, remembers more frivolous outings. 'We went to see a Fred Astaire movie one night,' she recalls, 'and afterwards we all did pirouettes and dance steps up and down the stone steps of St Patrick's Cathedral.'

Grace's was a clean and joyous New York that did not know of muggers or drug dealers – or parking meters. 'We might be sitting around in the evening in our pyjamas drinking coffee,' remembers Murr Sinclair, 'and someone would say, "Let's go see such-and-such a movie." So we'd throw on our raincoats, jump into my convertible, which I kept outside in the street, unlocked, and go off to the theatre – still in our pyjamas.'

Grace fitted perfectly into this giggly and artless companionship, in which wickedness was measured by your ability to smuggle curling tongs into your room at the Barbizon, where electrical appliances were strictly banned. She was exuberant, extroverted, fun – in no way the timid girl that Ma Kelly had expected to see come running back to Henry Avenue. 'Mother,' Grace wrote home after just a few weeks in New York, 'this is exactly the place I have always wanted to be!'

In her new circle of friends Grace was a grown-up version of the little girl who had jettisoned unwanted lunches out of the window at Ravenhill and organized smoking parties behind the grotto. Her Barbizon companions recall Grace, clad only in the skimpiest underwear, performing her exotic dances in the hallway, then skittering back into her room when the lift approached.

Unlike some of her lovers, Herbie Miller is reluctant to discuss the physical side of his relationship with Grace. 'Let us just say we were sweethearts,' he says. 'We stumbled on each other when we were children, basically. I just know how much she loved life, and how much she loved romance. She was a very romantic person, not cold or chiselled in granite or marble – the total opposite of that. She was an incredibly warm and earthy and fun-loving girl.'

Grace did not introduce her New York boyfriend to her parents, but Herbie did meet the fabled Uncle George – 'he was a very swishy old guy, very elegant' – and he also met her sisters. 'It was really strange, because she was in total awe of her big sister. She idolized Peggy. I'd say, "C'mon, Grace. You're much prettier than she is." And she'd say, "Oh, no, I'm not." For some reason she felt totally inferior to her.'

This hangover from the childhood praise heaped upon the brilliant Baba was reflected in Grace's appearance when she was feeling shy. 'There were times when she was anything but a glamour girl,' remembers Murr Sinclair. 'She wore tweed skirts, an old cardigan, and heavy, horn-rimmed glasses.' When Grace was in her dowdy mode, it was as if she were actually striving for a schoolmarm look. Friends recall her eating dinner on her own at the Barbizon, sitting straight-backed and rather forlornly alone at her table, wearing her glasses and reading a book – the model of a bluestocking spinster.

Dick Coons, a young banker just starting in New York, took Grace on a few dates soon after she moved into the Barbizon, and his memory is of a young woman who still seemed to be searching for herself, with her uncertainty reflected in her clothes. 'One night,' Coons remembers, 'she appeared in a very elegant black dress, with her hair up. She was statuesque and sophisticated. Next time she was the farmer's daughter in a calico skirt and blouse. And the third time she came down wearing a tweed suit and looking preppy – the standard Smith girl. It depended on her mood. It seemed to me that she was trying on different personalities for size.'

Grace got the chance for more role-playing when she went to Connecticut one weekend. 'I was doing a modelling job,' remembers Herbie Miller, 'and we were staying together at the house of the photographer. But the guy never looked at me. He only had eyes for Grace. "Do you mind if I take a picture of your girlfriend?" he asked me. "I have a cover for *Redbook* coming up." '

Grace made the cover of *Redbook* – and the covers of *Cosmopolitan, True Romance* and *True Story* – all within the course of the next year. Without really trying, she suddenly found that she was a model. It came naturally to her. She had been posing for photographs all her life, from her father's political campaigning to the fashion shows and benefits that her mother organized for Women's Med. Now Grace flashed her wide and even-toothed smile for Old Gold cigarettes ('for a TREAT instead of a TREATMENT') and even held up a can of insecticide for the Bridgeport Brass Company. 'I used to do what they called "illustration",' she later remembered. She started posing for lingerie advertisements, until she came home one weekend and asked her old teachers at Ravenhill for their advice.

' "Who are you, Grace?" ' Sister Francis Joseph remembers asking her. ' "Who are you?" Well, I let her give me the answer. I let her tell me why she shouldn't be posing for those kinds of pictures – and after that she didn't.'

Grace had always been photogenic. All the Kellys were. But dashing to photographers' studios between her Academy classes, Grace rapidly discovered just how much the camera loved her. Her good looks became something extra when translated into silver nitrate. She was not sufficiently hollow-cheeked and starving to get regular work on high-fashion assignments, but she was wholesome and handsome, a dreamy and glamorous version of the girl-next-door.

Carolyn Scott, a friend across the hall at the Barbizon, was already earning good money as a model, and she encouraged Grace to start doing the rounds of New York's advertising agencies on a systematic basis. Toothpaste, skin cream, soap, beer, vacuum cleaners – Grace promoted them all, at rates that ranged from $7.50 to $25 an hour ($70 to $230 in early 1990s dollars). She did not do very well at conventions. She could be decidedly frosty with the businessmen who considered the models on the display stands fair game for a squeeze. But she commanded good fees for her television commercials. Back at 3901 Henry Avenue, dinner was disrupted more than once as the family decamped to the television room to watch Grace posing with the latest offering from Electrolux.

Grace's modelling career proved remarkably lucrative. Old Gold paid her $2,000 for one session (more than $18,000 today). But Grace did not go wild with the money. The frugal Ma Kelly had taught her kids well. Brother Kell kept his money in a strange little clip-topped change purse of the sort that a woman might carry. He was notorious for his reluctance to open it, and Grace was similarly careful. Her friends used to joke about the dangers of sharing a cab ride with her. Somehow she usually managed to drift off, smiling and vague, when the meter got clicked, leaving someone else stuck with the fare.

It was the old syndrome of the girl who appeared to be fey and helpless, but who was taking very good care of herself. At the core, Grace was all business. It was what her father expected of a Kelly – and Grace made sure that her father got the point. She did not spend her modelling income on an extravagant new collection of shoes or clothes. The first instalments of the money went straight to Daddy to pay off the tuition and her bills at the Barbizon.

This was Grace's decision, not her father's. 'She wanted to be self-sufficient,' remembers Maree Frisby Rambo. 'She wanted to make it on her own, without her father taking the glory for himself.'

By 1948 Grace's brother, Kell, was a world-famous oarsman, thanks to his father, while Peggy was married and living with her new husband close to Henry Avenue in a home which Jack Kelly had built and furnished at not inconsiderable expense. Grace wanted to step away from that. As Peggy herself later said, 'She did it all herself. She paid her rent. She paid her tuition. Mother and Daddy never sent her a penny.'

Grace's sudden success as a model provoked some envy among her fellow students. She was 'a candidate for Miss Rheingold [beer],' remembered John Lupton, who was in her class. 'There were big billboards all over the place. You looked up at the top of a five-storey building, and there was a picture of Grace Kelly's face.'

Grace was well liked within her own particular circle of friends. She was warm and close with them. Life along the upper corridors of the Barbizon was a succession of high-spirited giggles and japes. But she could be distinctly off-hand with people whom she did not know well, and this earned her a reputation as 'snotty'.

'She was a loner,' said Mary Woolverton, another Academy student, talking to James Spada in 1985. 'She looked like a model who came in, did her thing, and left. There were students who were in awe of her because of her beauty and that distant quality she had . . . I'll never forget when she got dressed for exercise class. We had to get into our leotards and Grace was absolutely exquisite. She was *so* beautiful. But I always thought she was kind of cold.'

It was the apparent effortlessness of Grace's success that got under people's skin. 'She always seemed sort of swanlike,' remembers Murr Sinclair. 'I can remember Anna Italiano, who later became Anne Bancroft. She was at the Academy with us. She was earnest and intense. Certainly not rich, and not very social. She brought her own sandwiches to the cafeteria. She had these big, fierce, dark eyes. There was no doubt that Annie was heading to be an actress with a capital A. But Grace always seemed to be cruising.'

Champion scullers relate that there are moments of such pain in a tough practice or race that you feel you are driving into a black cave of rage and despair. But betraying even a hint of your agony is the surest way to upset the fragile poise that keeps your shell on the top of the water. Jack Kelly raised his children never to reveal their weaknesses. It was not Kelly-like to reveal the slightest acknowledgement that you feared you might fall. So Grace was always adept at concealing her effort and ambition. Unlike the young Anne Bancroft, she disclosed the purposeful, striving side of herself to very few.

When Grace first met Alex D'Arcy at a Park Avenue party in 1948, she did not even tell him she was training to be an actress. She said only that she was a model. She was excited about a booking she had just secured modelling hats – a definite step upward from vacuum cleaners and bug sprays. This reticence was surprising, because Alex D'Arcy was an established and successful actor with more than twenty movies to his credit. The Academy of Motion Pictures *Players' Directory* for 1938 ranked Alexandre D'Arcy alongside Gary Cooper, Cary Grant and Clark Gable as one of Hollywood's leading men.

'I'd love to take you to dinner,' D'Arcy told Grace.

'All right,' she replied. 'Call me.'

For their first date, he took her to El Morocco, where the owner, John Perona, greeted the couple warmly and came to sit and chat at their table. This would have been gratifying in any establishment, but it was particularly flattering on the part of a host who was notorious for developing the concept of 'Siberia', that back area of a New York restaurant room to which are relegated the unchic, the unfamous, and the requesters of doggie-bags. For their second date, D'Arcy and Grace went to the Stork Club, where, by coincidence, the owner, Sherman Billingsley, treated them with equal solicitousness. 'I think she was impressed,' remembers D'Arcy.

Hailed as 'the new Valentino' when he made his film debut in 1928 in the *Garden of Allah*, D'Arcy was a well-liked figure in café society. In a 1940s photograph of him nightclubbing with his friend Errol Flynn, it is difficult to tell which man is which. Both have the same dark, slicked-back hair and thin pencil moustache – and both were driven by the same consuming interest in life. 'Girls were my hobby,' says D'Arcy frankly today. 'But I never, never went to bed with a girl unless she wanted to. I'd say, "Look, darling, if you want to – fine. If you don't want to – that's fine, too." '

D'Arcy's 'dahling' was articulated in a husky and seductive

French accent. He had been born in Egypt of French parentage, and he was in his mid-thirties when he met Grace Kelly. He was almost twice Grace's age, and – not for the last time – she found the appeal of an older man with a French accent quite irresistible.

'We were going home in a taxi,' remembers D'Arcy. 'I had known her about ten days, and we had been out several times. She was a nice date, a shy girl from a good background. She was always shy, that's why I liked her so much. She dressed very conservatively and very nicely. She didn't dress as the sort of girl that would jump into bed with you.'

Just the same, D'Arcy thought that he might try a gentle approach. He reached out and touched Grace on the knee in a casual fashion. He was amazed at the response. 'She just jumped into my arms,' he remembers. 'I could not believe it. She was the very opposite of how she seemed.'

There was no need for D'Arcy to deliver his 'if you want to, if you don't want to,' routine. Grace happily came up to his apartment at 140 East Fifty-third Street and spent the night with him.

It was the first of several nights of passion that, nearly half a century later, still leave Alex D'Arcy awed and respectful at the appetites and energy of his new young friend. 'She was a very, very, very sexual girl,' he remembers, 'very warm indeed as far as sex was concerned. You would touch her once, and she would go through the ceiling. It was very obvious she was not a virgin. She was certainly experienced.'

Looked at in one way, Grace seemed quite a simple girl to D'Arcy. Her sexual needs were so straightforward and direct. But when he reflected on the difference between the tigress that he went to bed with, and the proper and demure girl that he escorted in every other context, he came to feel that part of Grace Kelly must be very complicated indeed. 'Basically, she was shy,' he remembers. 'But physically, she was not shy. With sex, everything would come out. Maybe it was something she was hiding. She was like a different person.'

Grace's living arrangements in the Barbizon were not an obstacle to her relationship with D'Arcy. The hotel did a good job keeping men out of the bedrooms, but had no system of checking whether their lady guests actually spent the night in their own beds.

Grace also went on seeing her fellow drama student, Herbie Miller, who did not realize the extent to which his girlfriend was two-timing him. 'There were these guys who would call for her,' Miller remembers today. 'I would be thinking that I'm the only love in her life, and some stud would arrive at school. So I'd ask her, "Who's that guy?" and she'd say, "Just some guy I know. He's crazy about me." She would laugh about it and brush it off, like she was just sort of doing the guy a favour. I never gave it too much thought. I was very naïve, I suppose.'

Grace and Alex D'Arcy said their goodbyes when the actor had to leave New York for some work in Paris. Shortly before he left, Grace did mention the fact that, aside from her modelling, she had hopes of becoming an actress. But she did not make much of it, and she certainly did not pump her older lover for the useful advice and contacts that a well-connected movie actor might be able to offer a girl who was just starting out on her career.

'In this business, it's ninety per cent phoney,' says D'Arcy, who went on to make sixteen more movies, among them *How to Marry a Millionaire*, with Marilyn Monroe and Betty Grable. 'Grace was not a phoney. She was a very warm and wonderful girl. I do not look back on the month I spent with her as a cheap adventure. I felt it was a real friendship. It was precious to me, a rather beautiful fragment of romance.'

Just over a dozen years later, in the early 1960s, D'Arcy

found himself on the beach at Monaco, sitting in the cabana of some French friends who were members of the Monte Carlo Beach Club. Their tent was about thirty yards away from that of the princely family, and suddenly D'Arcy saw his former girlfriend, now a world-famous princess, stepping out elegantly on to the sand. Grace seemed more demure than ever, and D'Arcy's first instinct was to look away, to avoid any embarrassment. But Grace had caught sight of him, and she started to peer hard across the beach, straining her eyes in her shortsighted fashion to try to recognize this face that she evidently thought she knew.

D'Arcy was hit with a flash of panic as he realized that the memory bank was going into action. It was more than likely that he was quite forgotten after all the years. Or was he, perhaps, too well remembered, so that he had put himself in line for a right royal blank?

Suddenly the Princess of Monaco recognized who her old friend was. Her face lit up with her magical smile, and she threw him an affectionate wave in which the actor felt he could glimpse just a little of the warmth and companionship that he had enjoyed in his brief time with the young Grace.

'I did not go over to talk to her,' says D'Arcy. 'Not with her family there. That would not have been right. But I still have that memory of her, the shy girl who was modelling hats when I met her, smiling and waving to me across the sand.'

FIVE

The Arms Around Her

IN OCTOBER 1948, on the eve of her nineteenth birthday, Grace Kelly moved into her second and final year at the American Academy of Dramatic Arts. This was no small achievement. A gruelling obstacle course of tests and grading reports often eliminated as many as half the Academy's students before the end of their first year. Charles Jehlinger wanted only the tough and the talented in his graduating class.

It was the Academy's policy to treat its final-year survivors less as students than as young working actors and actresses. They were organized into acting companies under the supervision of professional directors, and Grace was assigned to the group working with Don Richardson, a thirty-year-old protégé of Jehlinger's who had been a student at the Academy, and who already had several groundbreaking professional productions to his credit. He had recently directed Burt Lancaster's début on Broadway.

Richardson was an intense and voluble young man, dark-haired and dark-eyed, with a gypsy look about him. Born Melvin Schwartz, he had worked as an actor in radio and theatre, but had changed his name after a producer denied him a role in a Christian drama on the grounds that he was

Jewish. Richardson's training was evident in the ringing tones he used to declaim his directions to his students, and he was a fierce knight-errant on behalf of Charles Jehlinger's battle against the self-absorption of the 'Method' school of acting.

Now in his seventies and living in California, Don Richardson continues to teach the deft and creative acting techniques that he absorbed from Jehlinger. After an award-winning career in television drama, he is a lecturer at the University of California, Los Angeles, and he cannot today recall any particular contribution that Grace Kelly made to the American Academy acting group that he was assigned in the fall of 1948. She was not the red-meat style of actress that he preferred. It was an incident that occurred outside the classroom that drew the pupil to the attention of her drama instructor.

One winter evening, Richardson was coming down in the lift after class, when he noticed a slim, blondish girl standing in the corner, with a scarf tied over her head. 'She did not seem terribly pretty,' he remembers. 'She was fragile-looking, about nineteen years old, very well dressed, with a camel coat.'

The girl seemed oddly distanced from her classmates in the lift – half shy and half aloof – and sensing this, one of them began to tease her. Richardson knew this young man as the class clown. The boy was something of a bully, and he happened to be holding a puppy in his arms. He thrust this puppy into Grace's face, and instead of laughing, she burst into tears.

'I bawled the guy out,' remembers Richardson. 'Then everybody left, and I was alone with the girl. When she finally stopped crying, we were standing by the exit to the street.'

It was snowing outside, and after twenty minutes of vainly trying to hail Grace a cab so that she could get home to the

Barbizon, Richardson suggested that they might warm up in the Russian Tea Room next door. 'Her eyelashes were frozen,' remembers Richardson. 'Then she went to the john to dry her hair, and when she came back and had taken her scarf off, I noticed that she was actually much prettier than she had seemed in the lift.'

The Russian Tea Room was still quite a bohemian hangout in the years after the Second World War. You could eat there inexpensively, and you could nurse a cup of tea for hours. But when a waiter came over to the table, Richardson realized to his horror that he only had a few cents in his pocket. So it was out into the snow again to search for a taxi – with Grace sniffling and sneezing rather pitifully, and giving every indication of developing a severe cold.

'Grace was never a great actress,' says Richardson today. 'I was her teacher, and I should know. But she had some fantastically advantageous attributes, and one of them was getting people to feel that they should do something to help her. There were times when she seemed so pathetic and helpless. You had the feeling that if you left her alone, she would die. She would be destroyed. Seeing her sniffling there, I felt very drawn toward this girl – and, believe me, it was in no way sexual.'

With no taxis in sight, Richardson suggested an alternative – a bus ride down to Thirty-third Street, where he lived. He could pick up some cash there, and they could go out together for a hamburger. Richardson lived in a small, unheated apartment in an old converted brownstone. Many of the nearby shops were occupied by Armenian rug dealers, and it was Richardson's practice to gather his firewood from the crates and packing cases that the dealers had discarded in the street. Grace joined in with the fuel-gathering as her drama teacher walked her along through the slush from Broadway. 'Here was this pretty girl in a camel-hair coat, stooping down in the snow to pick up those boxes,' he remembers. 'It was somehow *La Bohème*.'

The couple went upstairs to Richardson's bare and arctic apartment, where he knelt down to kindle the fire. 'I got the fire going,' he remembers, 'and went out to make some coffee. When I came back into the room, she was waiting for me on the camp bed. She had taken all her clothes off and had pulled up the bed so it was alongside the fire. I never saw anything more splendid. We had no introduction to this. There was no flirtation. We both had a desperate need, like two people on a lost island. We were in bed, and when I came up from this miracle, I couldn't believe it. Here was this fantastically beautiful creature lying beside me.'

From the moment he had noticed her in the lift, Richardson had been idly analysing Grace's features with the eye of a professional. Her jaw, he had considered, was perhaps rather strong and square — her nose just a little too small. But suddenly the drama coach had no reservations. 'Her body was stunning. She was like something sculptured by Rodin. She had the most beautiful, delicate figure — small breasts, small hips — and her skin was almost translucent. She was the most beautiful girl that I had ever seen naked. So I was lying there and discovering that I was in love, that this was not just getting laid. I felt involved with this girl. I was in love with her wrists. I was in love with her ankles. I was in love with the blood flowing through her fine, transparent skin. I felt that I had to look after her, that I had to protect her — and she seemed to be madly in love with me. So that night was just sheer ecstasy. She didn't go back to the Barbizon at all.'

Next morning Richardson suffered a severe attack of remorse. 'I realized that I had done something dreadful. I was this girl's teacher. It was like a psychiatrist having an affair with a patient.'

So the affair had to develop furtively. Grace and Richardson tried to pretend not to notice each other when their paths crossed at the Academy, where Grace continued seeing her student boyfriend, Herbie Miller — without telling Richardson about it. 'Herbie was definitely Grace's "steady",' remembers Murr Sinclair. 'We did not find out about Don until later.' If anybody thought twice about Grace's relationship with the young director, it was in the context of her acting career. 'When I saw them together,' remembers Rachel Taylor, 'I remember thinking, "Oh, so she's already in with the professional crowd." '

Most weekends Grace would sneak down to Thirty-third Street to spend Saturday night with Richardson in his austere and scruffy bachelor quarters. 'We made love in this broken-down place with this horrible furniture,' remembers Richardson. 'Raskolnikov's lair in *Crime and Punishment*! The setting was anything but romantic.'

Grace Kelly brought the romance with her, in the form of 78 rpm records to which she would dance after they had made love — Hawaiian melodies when she was just playful, 'The Great Gate at Kiev' when she was in a martial mood. 'The Great Gate' was a classical composition by Modest Musorgsky, its music grand and imperious, conjuring up visions of fur-coated Cossacks as they processed insolently through the great gate. Drums and trumpets, clashing cymbals — Grace would sway around the room as the music reached its climax. She was the Eastern princess, the dancing princess, a sensuous queen of angels glorying in her nakedness in the flickering light of the fire.

'When she was modelling,' recalls Richardson, 'she used to wear a Merry Widow corset with a cinch to pull her waist in. People liked that kind of pinched look then. So she would strip down to nothing but her Merry Widow and run around the place, cooking and cleaning and all that, with her buttocks only barely covered. She was marvellously endowed in that department.'

Grace's workdays were patchworked with her professional modelling engagements, and sometimes, between photo sessions, she managed to steal away to Thirty-third Street. 'I would have hot Campbell's vegetable soup waiting for her,' Richardson remembers. 'I would feed it to her out of the can, and then we would go to bed and make love. Afterward she would jump up again, put on her clothes, and go back to model. She used to say that it put lights in her eyes.'

Richardson never discussed religion with his new girlfriend, but he soon discovered what a devout Catholic she was. 'She always wore a crucifix,' he says. 'It was a tiny little gold crucifix, and on Sunday mornings, when we spent the weekend together, she would jump out of bed to go to church. She would throw her clothes on, run and make the mass, then come back. I'd still be asleep, and she would jump right back into bed beside me, naked with the crucifix.'

Grace told her lover of her sexual initiation in Philadelphia – the rainy afternoon encounter with the husband of her friend – and she also told him that he, Richardson, was only the second man that she had been to bed with. 'I do not now believe that,' says Richardson. 'I mean, a girl who was as busy in bed as she was . . . I am not saying that she was a nymphomaniac. During my life, I have known two of those, and they both had this characteristic of never being satisfied. They would get desperate and sad. They needed to go on and on and on.

'That was not Grace. She was happy in bed, and she always knew when she'd had enough. We were young, and after, say, four times, well, that was just fine for her. She was perfectly normal. She had her orgasms, and she enjoyed them. But, though this may sound strange, I do not think it was sex that she was doing it for. There was something else.

'If you read *After the Fall*, Arthur Miller has his Marilyn Monroe figure say something like, "Just lie on top of me. You don't have to do anything." And I think that is the key. Grace wanted somebody's arms around her – the security. That is what she really craved. She enjoyed getting laid, all right. But I think that for her the truly important part was the arms around her.'

Richardson diagnosed a similar need in himself. His wife had recently left him for an older man, and he was bogged down in a divorce. His normally robust self-esteem had been in tatters until Grace's arrival. 'I was desperate for affection,' he says. 'We were both lost souls when we met – two devastated people.'

Clear in his own mind about the nature of his problems, Richardson started to analyse what might be wrong with Grace, and he could not help noticing how vague and reticent she became when talking about her close family, and about her father in particular. She had lots to say about her show-business uncles – Uncle Walter, the Virginia Judge, and Uncle George, the playwright, so stylish and theatrical. But there was a deadness when it came to Jack Kelly. Grace seemed to lose her focus, getting vague and changing the subject, and Richardson concluded that this must reflect some component of her father's attitude towards her. 'Grace was just a chip in his game, as I saw it,' says Richardson. 'So that meant she was always looking for somebody with a father image, somebody who could replace Papa.'

Don Richardson was very happy to try to play that role himself. The Svengali in him was entranced by the idea of making his girlfriend a star. 'She seemed just magical,' he remembers. 'She was a marvellous blank canvas on which anyone could paint their own picture.'

As Grace worked with Richardson at the Academy in his acting company, she began to develop her own fantasy about the future – that she and Don would start up and run a stock theatre together in Philadelphia. She would be the leading actress, Don would be the director – and Uncle George would write the material. 'Making her mark in Philadelphia and getting accepted. That always mattered a lot to her,' remembers Richardson, who did not see himself as an out-of-town repertory manager.

Richardson had quickly registered the direction of Grace's ambition from some of her mannerisms – the aristocratic voice that she had constructed for herself, with her posture to match. 'She *marched*,' he remembers. 'She did not walk. She had begun to take a great interest in sitting up straight, in being almost regal. She clearly had this notion of what she wanted to be. When she danced the Great Gate, she was actually pretending that she was a mid-Eastern princess. She told me so. She said it was her fantasy. I thought nothing of it at the time, but now I can see that she was already working on building the mythical Grace Kelly.'

Richardson had a major problem with the high hopes he was nursing for his girlfriend's theatrical career. When he looked at Grace's abilities with the fish-eyed scepticism of an impresario, he had serious doubts as to whether she had the technical armoury to make it on the stage. 'I never felt that Grace had more than minimal acting talent,' he says today. 'Great looks and style, yes, but no vocal horsepower – no voice projection. She would never have had a career in the theatre.'

Then one day Richardson went to the local drugstore to pick up some photographs he had recently taken of Grace, one of them a head and shoulders that he had shot in the apartment without any special light. 'That night, when she wasn't there, I sat down and studied this picture, and I noticed something miraculous. It came out in the photograph – the difference between what she was in reality, and the way that she imagined herself to be. You could see it there in the print. When you looked at that picture, you were not looking at her. You were looking at the illusion of her, which is another way of putting that old Hollywood thing, that the camera loved her. And the thing about Grace was, the camera did more than love her. It was insane about her – just like I was. When I looked at that photograph, I knew that her future would have to be in pictures.'

That weekend Richardson escorted Grace to Penn Station. She went home to see her parents at least once a month, and Richardson would go along to kiss her goodbye. 'She was crying,' he remembers. 'Worrying about going home, worrying about her career, and playing that game I came to recognize, winding me up to help her. She seemed such a waif, sitting there on the bench in her white gloves, sobbing, saying that she would never make it, that she wasn't getting anywhere. So I promised that next week, when she got back, I would take her to meet an agent.'

Richardson brought his drugstore photograph along when he took Grace to the office of Toni Ward at the William Morris Agency in Radio City. Ward represented some major Broadway talent, and Richardson went straight into action. ' "Toni," I said, "I have a girl sitting outside who is going to be a very important movie star!" '

'Bring in this paragon!' responded the agent, who had clearly been treated to this style of introduction before. Ten minutes later Grace was outside in the corridor again, sobbing. Toni Ward had not been impressed.

Undeterred, Richardson took Grace on to the offices of MCA, where his contact was another powerful agent, Edie Van Cleve – and this time his technique got results. 'Edie had a perception about feminine beauty,' he recalls. 'When I brought Grace in, I knew that I had struck something. I could see it in Edie's eyes.'

It was half an hour before Grace came out of Edie van Cleve's office – and this time she was smiling. 'She wants to be my agent,' she said.

'That's marvellous,' said Richardson.

'I'll have to ask my father first, of course,' said Grace.

The climax of every student's career at the American Academy came toward the end of their second year when they played a leading role in a production that was known as their graduation play – and Don Richardson knew exactly the role and the play for Grace. Philip Barry's *The Philadelphia Story* had been a Broadway hit in 1939 and had been made into an equally successful movie the following year, with Katharine Hepburn playing the heroine, Tracy Lord, on both stage and screen. Tracy Lord was based on a real person, Hope Montgomery, a pretty, young Philadelphia socialite, and Richardson felt that Grace was ideal for the part. 'She was too young for it really. She was only nineteen, and Tracy Lord is getting up toward her thirties, just ending one marriage and planning a new one. Hepburn was the right age when she acted it. But it all played so well to Grace's dreams and illusions – everything from the white gloves to the camel-hair coat. Grace had the look of the part.'

Grace's graduating performance was held in the little theatre under Carnegie Hall, in the presence of the entire student body of the Academy, with the faculty headed by Charles Jehlinger. Jack and Margaret Kelly came up to see their daughter's mimicking of a Philadelphia socialite, and this might have been an ideal moment for Grace to introduce them to the handsome and accomplished director of her graduation play. But her affair with her teacher was still supposed to be a secret.

'On the day of the play, we went to lunch together,'

Richardson remembers, 'several blocks away from the Academy, to an Automat where nobody went. Then I wished her luck, and she went to the back stage to get ready.'

Grace was reluctant to give her parents any clue about her relationship with Don Richardson – but she had not reckoned on a mother's intuition. Margaret Kelly had been noticing the change in her daughter in recent months. 'Whenever she came home on weekends,' she later related, 'her mind seemed to have remained in New York.'

Ma Kelly recognized the symptoms. 'Gracie,' she asked her daughter, 'there's a man, isn't there?'

'Yes,' Grace replied, 'there is.' And out it came tumbling, the story of the young director at the Academy, his faith in her, his plans for her career, their hopes of getting married.

So Don Richardson found himself, reluctantly, in the spring of 1949, on the train to Philadelphia. 'I did not want to go,' he says today. 'I could sense there was only grief ahead. But Grace would not hear of it. She said that her parents were really very nice, that they could live with my being Jewish, that they would not even mind my being in the process of a divorce – though she had not told them that detail. She kept telling me that they would be understanding.'

Grace's brother, Kell, later recalled the preparations that he made to welcome his sister home with her first potential fiancé. His mother had briefed him ahead of time about Don Richardson. 'She asked me to bring over three of my bigger and better-looking friends on the Friday night,' he told author Gwen Robyns. 'One was the Olympic Butterfly champion, and looking a bit like Kirk Douglas, and the other was a big-looking guy, a weight-lifting type, who was my partner in rowing races and was also in the life-guards at Ocean City. There was another chap also, a big, tall, swimming type.

'I gave them the word that this fellow was a bit of a creep, which I had deduced from my mother's description. When they came into the room they gave Grace's guy the grip, and in a second had him on the floor.' Younger sister Lizanne, another member of the Kelly family welcoming committee, hotly disputes this picture of the three muscle men jeering down at the wimplike director on the floor, and Richardson supports her recollection. He has no memory of Kell's buddies engaged in any physical assault. They were engaged in a more sly attack. 'They had this Jewish routine,' he remembers. 'Jewish jokes, Jewish accents, and so on. I was sitting there horrified. I couldn't believe this was going on.'

Richardson was downstairs in the Henry Avenue ratskeller taking the measure of his girlfriend's good-looking family. 'They were stunning,' he recalls. 'When I walked into that den, they all looked like models in an advertisement. Her father was a gorgeous man. He really looked like a Greek god. They *all* looked like Greek gods. The mother was handsome. The older sister was ravishing. The youngest sister was still a child. The brother had a thick neck, Sylvester Stallone-style – and Grace was sitting in the corner, kind of removed from the group. She was the real model, and yet she was the one person who did not look like a model. She said nothing at all. She had disappeared into this thin, silent, frightened little person – like the girl I had met in the lift that first night.'

Jack Kelly asked his guest if he would like a drink, and, not to seem impolite, Richardson accepted. 'So then there was this performance with keys and locks. There seemed to be locks on everything. He poured me a Bourbon and water, then he locked everything up again, without taking a drink for himself. So there I was, the only person holding a glass, looking like some sort of alcoholic.'

Richardson did not have to suffer long, for scarcely had Jack Kelly handed him the glass than he took it away from him again, and replaced it on the bar. 'Time to go to the club,' he said.

Grace shyly took her boyfriend's hand as they followed the other Kellys out to the car. 'When we got to the front door, the oldest sister's husband had shown up. So we went round to look at their house, which was close by, and the father walked us around like an inspection party, touching everything and saying that it had held up pretty well, indicating that he had made it, or bought it.'

Jack Kelly repeated this performance three times on the way to his country club. 'The cars stopped outside various churches,' remembers Richardson, 'and we all had to get out and study the brickwork. He was showing off what he had built, and we all stood there nodding respectfully. Grace was saying nothing, and I was thinking, "How weird! How fucking weird!"'

Things got weirder still when the family sat down to dinner – father, son, and the athletes at one end of the table, Richardson with the women at the other. Ma Kelly inquired of the drama teacher how Grace was doing at the Academy. 'Mrs Kelly,' Don Richardson replied, 'I have to tell you that I think your daughter is going to be a very important movie star.'

Margaret Kelly appeared to choke on what she was eating. 'What's going on down there?' Jack Kelly called.

His wife took a sip of water to compose herself, then responded in astonishment. 'This young man says that our Gracie is going to be an important movie star!'

The entire table collapsed in laughter. 'Don't worry,' called out Jack Kelly, laughing as heartily as the rest. 'She'll get over *that*.'

Don Richardson looked across at his girlfriend. Grace's head was down, and she was looking at the table, saying nothing. 'They just didn't understand him,' Lizanne told

James Spada in 1986, in defence of her parents' treatment of Don Richardson that night. 'He was just so different from the boys she had dated at Penn Charter, the friends of my brother – little athletes and so on. All of a sudden, this sophisticated man arrives from New York.'

'That dinner,' says Richardson, 'was one of the most horrible experiences of my life. I was a grown man. Apart from my work at the Academy, I had just started directing Helen Hayes in a play in New York. But it meant absolutely nothing to them. When we finally got back to the house, the father stood at the foot of the stairs, watching to make sure that I went to my room, and that she went to hers. The last thing he said was, "We're going to church in the morning. Do you want to come?" As if he did not know that I was Jewish.'

Next morning Richardson rose to find the house deserted. Everyone was at church. When the family returned, the women went into the kitchen to prepare breakfast, while the men sat down with the Sunday paper. 'The father split up the sections and handed them around. He took the financial section for himself, the brother got the sports pages, and I got the theatre. As he handed it to me, he noticed an ad for *Death of a Salesman* that was playing locally. "Why do they put on these Communist plays?" he asked.'

Jack Kelly was a 'Reds under the bed' man, a keen supporter of the House Un-American Activities Committee, and shortly to become a voluble Philadelphia champion of Senator McCarthy. 'After breakfast, Grace took me upstairs to see the trophies,' Richardson remembers. 'It was like a shrine, all lined with black velvet. There were these cups and medals that the men had won, and there were some pictures of the mother as a model. It was the first time I had heard about the rowing Kellys of Philadelphia. But the thing

I noticed was that there was absolutely nothing there to do with Grace – no pictures, nothing.'

The morning took a turn for the better when Grace drove off with her boyfriend to visit Uncle George. 'He was a wonderful man,' says Richardson. 'Very gentle and kind, and very sensitive. My impression was of a man who was a total contrast to the whole family. He was much more like Grace. She adored him, and he was very affectionate towards her. He was like mother and father. You could tell that his home was the home of an intellectual, and that he was an art lover. He was happy that we were in love. He thought everything was splendid. He encouraged her and he was interested in her career. He was the only sunlight in that whole terrible weekend.'

After about an hour with Uncle George, Grace gave Don Richardson a tour of the neighbourhood, driving him around East Falls and her other childhood haunts in Germantown and Chestnut Hill. She showed him where she went to school. It was the first time that the couple had been alone together with a chance to talk, and they discussed the previous evening, and how badly it had gone. Richardson felt angry and humiliated, and Grace did not know what to tell him. 'She just kept saying the same thing – that they were really wonderful people once you got to know them.'

When Grace and Richardson got back to Henry Avenue, there were no cars in the circular driveway, and the house seemed deserted – with the exception of Ma Kelly standing in the hallway, radiating grim rage. The dark cloud over her head was almost visible. 'Gracie, go to your room,' she snapped, and Grace went upstairs meekly, no questions asked – 'like a little child,' thought Richardson as he watched his girlfriend disappearing up the stairs.

'As for *you*,' said Ma Kelly, turning to Richardson with

unconcealed distaste. 'I want you to leave this house immediately.'

Richardson went upstairs, partly relieved, but totally mystified – until he reached his bedroom, and saw the contents of his suitcase strewn all over the bed. 'Everything was laid out,' he remembers. 'She had not made the slightest attempt to hide what she had done. There was a letter I had just received from my lawyer about a hearing in my divorce. That was lying there, opened, by the envelope. And beside that there was a packet of condoms I had brought, in case Grace and I had the chance to get laid. Grace always left that side of things to me.'

At a stroke Ma Kelly had discovered that her daughter was involved with a married man – and that her nineteen-year-old Gracie was no longer a virgin. When Richardson left the house in a taxi a quarter of an hour later, there was no one downstairs in the hall. He did not see Grace, and he had no idea what she was feeling.

But later that day Maree Frisby came round to Henry Avenue – to find Grace up in her room, lying on her bed, red-eyed and weeping. Grace told her friend the story of the nightmare weekend, and of her parents' fury at their discovery of her affair with Richardson. The Kellys were talking of banning Grace from returning to New York, and had lectured her severely on her immorality. But Grace would not admit defeat.

'I hope I *am* pregnant,' she sobbed defiantly.

SIX

Letting Go

'I CRIED SO MUCH ... Hell just can't be much worse than what I went through.' Three days after Don Richardson's catastrophic visit to Henry Avenue, Grace described the details of the weekend and its aftermath in an emotional, eight-page letter to Prudy Wise, her Barbizon room-mate. After Don had left for New York, she wrote, her parents had summoned her to Ma Kelly's room for a serious talk. They said they had some frank questions to ask, and that they expected frank answers. Was Grace secretly married to Richardson?

The Kellys confronted their daughter with the divorce letter that Ma Kelly had discovered, though they did not mention the condoms. Her father was beside himself – ready 'to blow a fuse' – while her mother tried a more moderate, woman-to-woman tack, asking Grace to talk about what she saw in Richardson. 'The fact that I could fall in love with a Jew,' wrote Grace, 'was just beyond them.'

The inquisition went on and on. Grace was crying so much, she told Prudy, that she could not remember all the details, but she had no doubt about how she felt – 'They ... made me so mad.'

It was the first time that Grace had ever seriously crossed

her parents. As a young teenager, she had bowed obediently to her father's wishes and had ended her romance with Harper Davis. Collegeless in the summer of 1947, she had meekly allowed her own life to be placed on hold when the family rules ordained that Kell and his rowing should be the priority. But now the good girl had become a bad girl – for the moment, at least. 'It was when I went away to New York,' she later said, 'that I had my rebellion.'

Grace was no longer willing to function as a mere accessory to her family, and she felt so angry that she could barely bring herself to speak to them. 'For a month we ate in silence,' remembered Kell, describing the chilly domestic atmosphere that spring.

But Jack and Margaret Kelly were equally resolute. Their style was unapologetically Victorian. When Peggy and her friends had got drunk down in the Henry Avenue ratskeller one Saturday night, Peggy had been compelled to pay for the damage, and Jack Kelly had locked up the booze. That was the reason for all the bars and bolts that had attended the serving of Don Richardson's bourbon and water. Now Jack Kelly essentially locked up his middle daughter. Grace was banned from New York. She was allowed to go up once, for the day, to close down her room at the Barbizon and bring home her things on the train. She had no more classes and she had done her graduation play at the American Academy. Then she was sent down to the Kelly summer home at Ocean City, where the family took turns at keeping an eye on her. It was several weeks before Richardson heard from his girlfriend again, and when she phoned she was puffing and panting. She told him she had had to give her sister Peggy the slip and run several miles down the beach in order to find a pay phone.

Her other Barbizon friend, Bettina Thompson, heard the whole story when Grace came to New York. 'She told me that she had been to bed with Don,' Bettina remembers. 'That came as news to me. I was horrified. I had no idea. I told my mother some of what had happened. I was living in my mother's New York apartment at the time, and I asked if Grace could, perhaps, come and share my room there. My mother just looked at me. "Sometimes," she said, "parents know better than children." '

But Grace's defiance had its limits. When it came to the ultimate loyalties, she was her father's daughter. She did not really hope that she was pregnant by her drama coach. That no more fitted into her nineteen-year-old vision of what lay in her future than it appealed to her parents. It was Grace's delight to surrender to her emotions when she wanted, to live out events romantically, as if real life were a role that she was performing on stage. But something inside her always stayed in control. She had a very calm centre – and in the summer of 1949, with her drama training now at an end, she had some serious professional work on her plate. Two of the best students in the American Academy's graduating class were picked every year to join the company of the prestigious Bucks County Playhouse in New Hope, Pennsylvania, and in 1949 Grace Kelly was one of those selected.

The Bucks County Playhouse was a converted barn on the border of New Jersey and Pennsylvania, not far upriver from the spot where George Washington made his historic crossing of the Delaware. It was a comfortable, arty place, set in beautifully rolling and wooded countryside, a pleasant summer evening's drive from Philadelphia and Manhattan. Audiences would dine at a local inn, then stroll to the playhouse for a couple of hours of light drama. Bucks County was a propitious spot for Grace's very first professional engagement, and she had no difficulty learning the words for her opening role. She was cast as Florence McCricket, the ingenue in Uncle George's *The Torch-Bearers*.

George Kelly was delighted that his niece's career should get off to such a notable start, and he arranged for Gant Gaither, an actor-producer friend, to watch Grace's performance with a view to booking her for some future engagements. But the playwright spurned Gaither's suggestion that the two men might go to watch the performance together. 'See one of my plays performed by a summer-stock company?' he exclaimed to Gaither. 'Never!'

Summer stock was the means by which aspiring actors and actresses put their training into practice in the years before television. It was the equivalent of English seaside repertory. 'You rehearsed for a week, and you played for a week,' remembers Natalie Core O'Hare, who played Bucks County with Grace in the early 1950s. 'By Friday you felt that you were beginning to give a really good performance. Then you had two more shows, and it was over.'

In the absence of any previous acting credits for Grace, the caption to her photograph in the Bucks County playbill said little about her career and concentrated instead on the exploits of her father, brother Kell, and Uncle George. But Grace acquitted herself like a professional. 'For a young lady whose previous experience was slim,' wrote one of Philadelphia's leading critics, 'Miss Kelly came through this footlight baptism of fire splendidly . . . From where I sat, it appeared as if Grace Kelly should become the theatrical torch-bearer for her family.'

Still furious and untrusting after the Richardson weekend, Grace's parents would not allow her to find lodgings near the playhouse. She had to base herself in Henry Avenue for the two weeks of rehearsals and performances. Grace drove the thirty-five miles to New Hope every morning, and drove all the way home again each night. But public recognition made a difference to the senior Kellys. By the time it came to opening night, Jack and Margaret had decided to put the past behind them. Their daughter was on parade, and they sat in the very front row at Bucks County to cheer her on. Jack Kelly positively glowed. Grace's achievement was family achievement, and he brought along a contingent of friends to share in the celebration. His unpromising middle daughter had done something very right – and there was more to come. Grace had won herself a part in a production of Strindberg's tragedy *The Father* starring Raymond Massey. It was an ambitious project in which the venerable actor was planning both to act and to direct himself. He had cast Grace for the role of his tortured daughter. After opening in Boston, the play was scheduled to transfer to New York before the end of November 1949 – when Grace would reach her twentieth birthday.

Grace could hardly do all this from her bedroom in Henry Avenue. Even for Jack and Margaret Kelly, it was scarcely feasible to 'ground' a grown daughter whose name was scheduled to share the canopy with a major star on Broadway. Financially, Grace was quite independent of her parents, in any case. She could command solid fees as a model, and she was also now earning good money as an actress. It was her time to go, and her parents conceded the fact. Jack Kelly had been one of the contractors involved in the building of Manhattan House, a massive and monolithic grey-brick apartment building that covered a full New York City block on Sixty-sixth Street, just up Third Avenue from Bloomingdale's. Manhattan House had all the charm of a workers' apartment complex outside Stalingrad, but for Grace it came to represent adult freedom. On her word of honour that she would not see Don Richardson again, her father installed her there in an apartment which Ma Kelly furnished.

'Grand Rapids furniture,' remembers Richardson. 'It was really ugly. Crude, dark, heavy wood, all slabby – like you were in a cabin at summer camp.'

Grace broke her promise to her parents the very first day she got back to New York. She went straight to Don Richardson's apartment on Thirty-third Street and made love. It was a passionate reunion. There were no preliminaries of wood-gathering or fire-lighting. Richardson was delighted to have his beautiful young girlfriend back, while for Grace the resumption of the affair represented the best defiance of her parents she could manage. She was going to make her own decisions about the allegiance of her body at least.

Don Richardson could not help noticing, however, that the allegiance of his partner's mind remained fixed as firmly as ever on her father. Grace did not welcome her boyfriend's attempts to discuss the dreadful weekend and what it meant, and she remained unwilling to entertain the slightest criticism of her parents. Richardson ventured a couple of negative comments about her father, and never tried it again. 'It was like running into a brick wall,' he says. 'It was a subject that just could not be discussed. Her parents could no more be criticized than you could question her Catholic faith. It was something you just believed in and never questioned.'

Soon the couple were seeing each other as frequently and as ardently as before. But the shadow of Jack Kelly hung over them. Grace was terrified that her father would discover her deception, so the lovers would meet, out of prudence, in Greenwich Village. They spent so many hours in the Granados café there that they came to consider the seats by the espresso machine their own. They would go to Thirty-third Street under cover of darkness and would peek around the curtains to make sure they had not been followed. The fear of discovery became something of a game that added spice to their assignations – and then, one day when Richardson was on his own at home, the nightmare came true in an unexpected fashion.

'The doorbell rang,' remembers Richardson, 'I opened it,

and there was Daddy standing in the hall. He looked absolutely enormous. He was terrifying. He was wearing a dark overcoat, very well dressed, with a tie and suit, the whole thing, and as I opened the door he took a step into the apartment without being invited. He was huge.'

The front door opened directly into the kitchen of the apartment, and Richardson was half intimidated, half amused by the spectacle of the immaculately dressed businessman staring disdainfully at the dirty dishes and the worn and broken fragments of furniture. The two men looked at each other. 'Would you like a Jag?' Jack Kelly asked.

The young director was confused. 'The only meaning that I knew of a "jag" was to go out with some buddies and have some drinks. So I thought, "My God! We're making up! We're going to be friends!" Then he said, "Any colour you like." And I thought, "It's an object?"'

'So then I made this enormous, stupid, emotional speech in which I said that I did not want anything from him, that I loved his daughter, and that I was not interested in a payoff. He did not stay to listen. He walked out of the door.'

Soon after that the phone calls started. 'They'd happen around two o'clock in the morning,' remembers Richardson, 'from the brother. He never said he was the brother, but he would say things like "Hello, you son-of-a-bitch. I'm gonna break every bone in your fucking body! You stay away from my sister, or you'll be paralysed for life." That kind of thing.'

When Richardson told Grace about the phone calls, she would look puzzled and hurt. 'All she could say was that they were really lovely people, and that I would get to understand them one day, and that once everyone understood everybody, then everything would be just fine.'

It was the same passivity Grace had shown during her weekend with Richardson at Henry Avenue. When confronted by her father she became a little girl again. Her adult brain processes shut down. Her placid acceptance of the male Kellys' right to interfere in her life made explicit a loyalty that she would never surrender, and though she and Richardson went on seeing each other for another two years, the threatening phone calls and the bizarre offer of the Jaguar proved a watershed in their relationship. They saw each other less frequently. When they did meet, their passion was not as overwhelming as it once had been, and Don Richardson was not really surprised when he eventually discovered that he was far from being the only object of Grace Kelly's affections.

Claudius Charles Philippe was not a conventionally good-looking man. With his long hooked nose and thick round glasses, he had the air of a startled owl. Nor did his position as Banqueting Manager of the Waldorf-Astoria Hotel obviously mark him as the sort of man that Grace Kelly was likely to date. But Philippe of the Waldorf was a character of extraordinary charm and magnetism. He had the drive of a Napoleon. Many women found him quite irresistible, and when it came to café society, he was a very prince of New York.

Philippe made his name as an assistant to the legendary René Black, a professional Frenchman whose Central Park restaurant, the Central Park Casino, pioneered the concept of restaurateur as showman – Cherries Jubilee, the hand-prepared Caesar salad, and the other table-side mummeries of flame and chafing dish. Philippe brought this panache to the Waldorf-Astoria, where he elevated the unpromising business of private banqueting into a consummate and immensely profitable art form. His supreme creation was the April in Paris Ball – which he organized in October to fill a hole in the banqueting year – and to which he attracted, with the help of his friend, Elsa Maxwell, every social luminary of the day: the Duke and Duchess of Windsor, Marlene Dietrich, Gypsy Rose Lee, the Winston Guests, the Drexels, the Vanderbilts, the Cabot Lodges.

If part of Grace Kelly was drawn to the nonconformist and bohemian style of Don Richardson, she was equally attracted to the social gloss and connections of a Claudius Charles Philippe. Alex D'Arcy had discovered this side of Grace when he introduced her to his important friends at the Stork and El Morocco. Once she had found her feet, the girl from East Falls was very impressed to be in New York and to find that her charm and good looks could open all sorts of doors that were closed to her in Philadelphia.

Philippe wooed Grace with champagne. He dispatched Martin Riskin, a young assistant in the banqueting department, with magnums for the attention of Miss Grace Kelly, Manhattan House, and Riskin bore them to the young actress's door. 'She was definitely cool,' Riskin remembers. 'She seemed rather haughty. And she had something that I considered an affectation. Sometimes, indoors, she would be wearing sunglasses.'

When she was with Don Richardson, Grace played the ardent and aspiring young actress. With Claudius Philippe, she played the great lady. Tom Hogan, another of Philippe's assistants, remembers Grace being distinctly standoffish when she stayed at Philippe's weekend farm at Peekskill in the Hudson valley. Guests were supposed to compete and collaborate in the preparation of Sunday brunch, diving out into the garden to dig up salads and vegetables. You might find Victor Borge and Maurice Chevalier racing each other in the peeling of potatoes. Grace held back from the general merriment – though Tom Hogan liked his boss's girlfriend, and did not think that she was affected. He put her distance down to shyness.

It was when Grace was spotted wandering without make-up through the upper floors of the Waldorf in the middle of the afternoon that the banqueting assistants really started to talk. 'You could play all sorts of games in the towers and various suites,' remembers Martin Riskin, 'and not be caught in the act.' There were quite lengthy periods when Grace was something of a fixture at the hotel, stationed for long hours in Philippe's outer office, patiently waiting for him to complete his daily barrage of solicitations and phone calls. The pretty young actress seemed more like a wife, at times, than a girlfriend. Grace was clearly under the spell of the forty-year-old Philippe, and he appeared to reciprocate the infatuation. Under her influence, Philippe softened his habitually hard-bitten style, and his much terrorized assistants were pleased to note some sentimental chinks in the armour of the iron man.

Charles Ohrel, Philippe's principal assistant and confidant, began to get worried about the time and attention that his boss was devoting to Grace. 'We would take a little rest period in the evenings while the banquets were going on,' remembers Riskin. 'We would sit in the office with a glass of champagne and some supper, and Charlie would begin to talk. "Poor Philippe," he would say. "He doesn't know what to do about Grace." '

Philippe of the Waldorf was the kind of man for whom Grace so often fell – mature and experienced, with a pronouncedly flamboyant streak. He offered the dictatorial control and guidance to which her childhood had addicted her, blended with a sense of fantasy and ambition that was curiously similar to her own. Brought up in London by French parents, Philippe had devised a way of talking to match the pseudo, self-bestowed title in which he gloried. 'His accent was most indicative of the man,' remembers George Lang, no mean showman himself, and one of the several successful restaurateurs who served their apprenticeship under Philippe. 'There were French overtones and English overtones, with American bits and pieces, all blended together by his artifice to form a basic sauce.'

Philippe introduced Grace to the world of fine food and finer wines, a continuation of her delicate lunches with Uncle George. Ma Kelly's Henry Avenue cuisine had been hearty and simple, with something of a German farmhouse touch. Blood sausage with fried apples had been one of Grace's childhood favourites. Now she learned about pâté and fine claret. Along with the champagne, Martin Riskin reverently bore to Manhattan House bottles of Château Margaux and other *premiers crus* that he himself could only dream of tasting.

Don Richardson picked up hints of his girlfriend's crash course in high living from her sudden familiarity with smart names and with the price of things. He found it unattractive, and he sneered dismissively at 'Grace's maître d' ', He could not believe that her relationship with Philippe could amount to anything serious. But up in the banqueting office at the Waldorf, over the late-evening suppers, Charles Ohrel was telling it differently. 'He's truly in love,' he told Martin Riskin. 'They want to get married.'

Philippe was on the rebound. He had just broken up with his second wife, the food writer Poppy Cannon, while Grace, for her part, was suddenly less enamoured of the idea of a theatrical partnership in Philadelphia. Marriage to Philippe promised an enticing role as a social queen of New York, sharing confidences and the society columns with her new friend Elsa Maxwell, entertaining the likes of Cole Porter and the members of Philippe's elite Lucullus Circle, the private dining club that he organized for the occupants of the Waldorf Towers. It was no bad thing for an actress to have a polished and metropolitan social dimension.

But Grace's father would have none of it. 'It's the old man,' reported Charles Ohrel in one of his late-evening briefings. 'He just won't allow it. He's giving poor Philippe a terrible time.' It was quite out of the question for Jack Kelly to surrender his daughter to a twice-divorced man who was a banqueting manager. He angrily refused to countenance any notion of marriage – as George Lang heard it, Jack Kelly went 'absolutely bonkers' when he was told of the idea – and that was the end of Grace becoming Mrs Claudius Charles Philippe, though she did go on seeing Philippe, following the pattern in which she continued to date Don Richardson, hoping for the best and trying not to lose a friend. Congenitally nonconfrontational in her personal relationships, Grace always found it difficult to end her romances, preferring her lover – or, more usually, her father – to make the decisive move.

George Kelly's play *The Fatal Weakness* was the story of a woman who could not resist going to weddings, and there must have been moments when Jack Kelly wondered whether his daughter Grace did not suffer from a variety of the same affliction. It was not just that Grace seemed to fall for men so readily. It was the fact that she wanted to marry them – and that the men themselves were so obviously not husband material. By his own admission, Don Richardson was anything but the settling kind, while Claudius Philippe's reckless and hard-driving ways were to propel him rapidly through two more marriages (bringing his total to four), a number of notably unsuccessful business ventures, and a conviction for tax fraud that prompted his ignominious departure from the Waldorf in 1959. It is difficult to see how marriage between Grace and the banqueting manager could have ended in anything except disaster, and in the light of Philippe's subsequent misadventures, Jack Kelly's refusal to let go of his daughter could very reasonably be seen not as meddling but as prudent and very necessary parenting – protecting his naïve and impulsive daughter from herself.

But what was a pretty girl to do in New York? In the winter of 1949, the dashing young Shah of Iran arrived in America on an official visit, met Grace Kelly, and fell instantly in love with her. Thirty years old, slim, dark and single, Mohammed Reza Pahlavi had ruled Iran since 1941, in name at least, and he had come to the US to cultivate the ties that were to help him to absolute power in 1953. After talks in Washington with President Truman, the Shah had come up to New York and was staying at the Waldorf-Astoria, as did most official visitors to the city. Grace was introduced to him at the opening reception arranged by Claudius Philippe, and the young prince wasted no time. He invited Grace out, and she was delighted to accept. 'They went out together six nights in a row,' remembers Grace's friend, Maree Frisby Rambo.

The Shah gave Grace the definitive tour of Manhattan's smartest clubs – the Stork and El Morocco – and every ballroom in the Waldorf in a dizzying succession of receptions and dinners. The reporters covering his visit were amazed by his capacity to stay out nightclubbing until two-thirty every morning, then to reappear at eight, fresh and rested, ready for another full day of official engagements. The secret servicemen assigned to the Iranian party begged for mercy. 'Miss Kelly,' one of them pleaded with Grace one day, 'could you please stay home tonight?' One evening Grace accompanied the Shah to the opera and encountered the heady experience of a packed auditorium rising to its feet, fifteen hundred faces turned upward in homage. 'It was her first taste of it,' remarked one of Grace's friends to Sarah Bradford.

The relationship between the blonde actress and the handsome Shah was hard for the gossip columnists to miss, and one newspaper noted that the visiting ruler had presented Grace with some expensive items of jewellery. New York news was Philadelphia news, and the moment Jack and Margaret Kelly found out about the jewellery it was action stations again at Henry Avenue. A handsome young head of state represented a definite improvement on a penniless drama director or a hotel banqueting manager, but the Shah's expensive gifts were simply not respectable. Ma Kelly got on the first train from Philadelphia and by ten-thirty a.m. she was in New York, knocking on the door of her friend, Marie Magee. 'That jewellery – did you see about that jewellery?' she exclaimed to Marie. 'Get her on the telephone! Tell her I want to see her right away.'

Marie Magee described the episode more than thirty years later to Sarah Bradford. 'Gracie! Where are those jewels?' Ma Kelly demanded as soon as her daughter arrived.

Grace tried to play for time. 'They're three pieces of jewellery.'

'You mean you took pieces of jewellery!' Ma Kelly's indignation knew no bounds. A bunch of flowers, a book, or a box of candy – that sort of gift was respectable. But jewellery was something else entirely. 'You go get them,' she instructed her daughter.

'Oh mother . . .' said Grace, balking.

'I said, go get them,' repeated Mrs Kelly, 'and I am sitting right here till you return. Get in a cab and come back and bring them. I want to see them. Your father says they have to go back.'

So Grace took a taxi back to her apartment and soon returned with her presents from the Shah – three extravagantly bejewelled confections whose every detail was etched into the memory of Marie Magee: a solid gold vanity case about eight inches long, with thirty-two large diamonds in the clasp; a gold bracelet watch, whose face was covered with a dome of pearls and diamonds; and a gold pin in the form of a birdcage, with a delicate barred door that opened and closed on a minuscule hinge; inside the cage, on a swing, sat a diamond bird with pavéed wings and eyes made of bright-blue sapphires. The gifts were worth tens of thousands of dollars.

Ma Kelly needed only one look. 'You've got to give them back,' she said.

'Mother,' Grace replied, 'I can't give those back.'

'Well, you've got to,' repeated Mrs Kelly. 'I'm going to sit here till those jewels go back to that Shah. Your father says they've got to go back. I say they've got to go back.'

'Mother,' Grace replied, 'one does not refuse a king . . .'

Grace did not tell her mother that there was one offering from the Shah which she had refused. The young prince was on the lookout for a bride. He had recently divorced his beautiful first wife, Fawzia, King Farouk's sister, and in the course of his six nights on the town he had invited Grace to take her place. The three items of jewellery were tokens of infinite treasures to come.

Grace confided this extraordinary news to her student boyfriend, Mark 'Herbie' Miller, on the telephone one day. Grace and Herbie had ended their romantic relationship by mutual consent when they came to the end of their time at the Academy, but they had kept in touch as old friends. 'He's asked me to marry him!' Grace told Herbie in astonishment, recounting the upshot of her action-packed week.

For Grace the prospect of becoming Empress of Iran was something of a joke. Her heart might be hasty, but it was not that easily captivated. Her cool head could tell the difference between a week of fun and a lifetime of commitment, and whatever her social-climbing fantasies, Grace was far from abandoning her dreams of acting glory. She did not love the Shah, and she told him so politely.

But that did not stop her hanging on to his jewels. Grace kept the three exotic pieces in the top drawer of her dressing table, showing them off delightedly to her girlfriends, and joking that the gems were only rhinestones. Then, on the eve of her marriage to Prince Rainier in 1956, she handed them out as gifts to her bridesmaids. Judy Kanter, the daughter of the president of Paramount Pictures, was amazed to be offered the sapphire-eyed bird in the delicate gold cage, still in its original Van Cleef & Arpels container, and she told Grace that she could not possibly accept so rich a present. Grace must keep it for herself, she insisted.

'I can't,' Grace replied without elaboration. And on that particular subject, the normally talkative bride-to-be had no more to say.

One day in the early 1950s, Richard Waterman, a young Philadelphia businessman, found himself seated at a table next to Grace Kelly. They were both guests at the marriage of Anne Levy to Herbie Siegel, two old friends and neighbours of the Kelly family on Henry Avenue. Anne Levy had been a student at the Stevens School with Grace.

The Levys were mega-rich and extraordinarily well connected. In partnership with William Paley – to whom they were related – Ike and Leon Levy had built up CBS, the Columbia Broadcasting System. Showbusiness people were forever passing through the Levys' Henry Avenue home. 'It was the sort of place', remembers Richard Waterman, 'where you would ring the bell, and Van Johnson would answer the door.' For the marriage of Anne Levy, the entertainment was by Frank Sinatra.

Grace Kelly was quite a minor figure in this company. She was only just starting to make a name for herself, and Richard Waterman did not find her looks particularly appealing. 'She was a thin and bony creature,' he remembers. But it was Grace's manner which Waterman found still less attractive: 'She was so aloof and remote. She scarcely spoke a word to anyone at the table, and all through the wedding she had her eyes fixed on this one man, Manie Sacks. He was old enough to be her father.'

Emanuel 'Manie' Sacks was an old friend of both the Kellys and the Levys. As head of Columbia Records (then part of CBS), he had advanced Frank Sinatra the money he needed to buy out his contract with the Tommy Dorsey band. Manie Sacks was always there when people needed him. 'He met me at the dock when I came back from winning the Olympic championship,' Jack Kelly said of his friend. 'He sat beside me when I was licked for Mayor and consoled me.'

Manie Sacks had helped Grace secure some of her earliest modelling assignments through his rag-trade contacts in New York. With strong, chiselled features and curly black hair, he was a well-liked and very attractive man. But Grace's interest in Manie Sacks struck Waterman as excessive: 'She did not take her eyes off him. She followed him everywhere he went. She craned her neck. She seemed oblivious to anything else. I don't know if she was having an affair with him, if she wanted to have an affair with him, or whether she was just obsessed with a powerful man in her business. I have no way of judging. But it was quite extraordinary. She had no time for anyone else. "Now, *that's* a cold drink of water," I thought.'

It does not seem likely that Grace Kelly would have had an affair with one of her father's best friends, and even less likely that Sacks, a solid and widely trusted character, would have succumbed to it. But Waterman had caught a revealing glimpse of the calculating side of Grace in action. Her sex drive and her sense of ambition were curiously similar. Grace

Kelly was never casting-couch material. She did not exploit sex crudely to get herself a job. She was at some pains, indeed, to choreograph her love affairs as grand romances.

But unlike many who daydream, Grace Kelly actually got the job done, and she accomplished this thanks to the steely, almost obsessive determination that betrayed itself to Richard Waterman. 'It was always there underneath,' says Don Richardson. 'When I first met her I had thought she was helpless, but I came to realize that she was about as helpless as a Patton tank.'

It was Richardson's full realization of this that finally put an end to the romance in his relationship with Grace. 'She had invited me over to her apartment for dinner,' remembers Richardson, 'and afterward, when we were both in bed together, she said, "Do you want to see some lovely things?" Well, for me, the sight of her naked was the most lovely thing that I could think of. But she started to do a fashion show for me, coming out in all these expensive clothes. Gown after gown – I could not imagine where she got them from. And then she came out, stark naked again, wearing nothing but a gold bracelet that had several emeralds around it, and she waved the bracelet at me. Well, I knew where *that* bracelet came from.'

Richardson had known a couple of girls who went out with Aly Khan, the playboy who was famed for his sexual technique. 'When he first had a date, he would give them a cigarette case with one emerald in it,' says Richardson. 'When he fucked them, he'd give them the bracelet. Well, that was it. I was heartbroken. I put my clothes on, and said that I was leaving. I just didn't want to see her any more. She asked me if the bracelet had anything to do with it, and I said it had everything to do with it.'

Richardson had long been aware that his love affair with Grace was dying. He himself had enjoyed a number of romantic adventures, so he could hardly complain at the evidence that Grace had been playing the field. But suddenly he realized that there must be many more men in her life – and that his girlfriend's strange fashion parade, culminating in the revelation of the bracelet, was her oblique way of telling him that.

'She had become a career carnivore,' he says. 'She was rapacious about getting famous and being important. She'd already talked to me about some of the men she'd been dating, how they helped her to make social contacts, and were teaching her things she needed to know. I decided I had had enough of it.'

As Richardson said goodbye to Grace, he dropped the emerald bracelet contemptuously into her fishtank. He put on his clothes, and when he reached the door of the apartment, he turned for a farewell glance. He had evidently made the correct decision, for his girlfriend was not crying. There were no hands outstretched, no pleadings for him to come back. Grace was still naked and beautiful, but she was not thinking of her lover. 'Her hand was in the water,' Don Richardson recalls. 'I shall never forget the sight of her. She was fishing for the bracelet in the goddamn tank.'

SEVEN

Fire and Ice

GRACE MADE HER Broadway debut on 16 November 1949, four days after her twentieth birthday. Raymond Massey had plucked her straight from the American Academy for his production of Strindberg's harrowing tragedy *The Father*, and the young actress justified his confidence. 'Grace Kelly gives a charming, pliable performance as the bewildered, brokenhearted daughter,' wrote Brooks Atkinson in the *New York Times*.

But the production as a whole was not so well received. 'Only the novice Grace Kelly,' wrote George Jean Nathan, 'convincing as the daughter, relieves the stage from the air of a minor hinterland stock company on one of its off-days.' Massey's gentlemanly rendering of Strindberg struck the highbrows as thin-blooded, while the play's gloomy theme – the tale of a malevolent wife who deliberately drives her husband to insanity – was not what the mass audience fancied at Christmas time. *The Father* closed in the early weeks of 1950, after only sixty-nine performances. Grace Kelly was out of work, and it was two years – and the best part of forty unsuccessful auditions – before she made it back to Broadway again.

'I read for so many plays, I lost count of them,' Grace

111

told an interviewer in later years. 'People were confused about my type, but they agreed on one thing: I was in the "too" category – "too tall', "too leggy", "too chinny".'

That was the kindest thing that some people said. When John Foreman became an agent at MCA, and took Grace to lunch to see what he could do to help the beautiful young protégée of Edie Van Cleve, Grace turned up in gloves, a hat and a little veil. 'This is a strange, dead-assed girl,' thought Foreman, disconcerted by her shyness and by her odd formality.

Don Richardson's gloomy assessment of his girlfriend's dramatic potential was borne out by the tough and unforgiving standards of the Broadway market-place. Grace did not have the voice or the more general character projection to make it on stage. She was personally endowed with ample quantities of grit. She was willing to prepare for part after part, to trudge the round of the rehearsal rooms, and to submit unflinchingly to the pain of scrutiny and rejection. But she did not yet know how to expose her inner steel in a dramatic fashion. Her stage personality lacked the timbre – the sheer guts and swagger – to reach out and grab the hearts of several hundred people in a live theatre. As the director Sidney Lumet put it, 'She has no stove in her belly.'

Fortunately for Grace, however, live theatre was not her only option. John Foreman, the MCA agent who had been so unimpressed with her hat, veil and gloves, specialized in the rapidly developing field of television drama, and Grace's delicacy took on a different dimension when it was projected on the miniature screen. Even before *The Father* closed, she had played the lead in NBC's Philco Playhouse production of *Bethel Merriday* by Sinclair Lewis. That was broadcast on 8 January 1950. Less than three weeks later, on 23 January, she was on CBS in a Studio One production of *Rockingham House*. Then it was back to NBC for *Ann Rutledge*, in which she played the lead again – as Abraham Lincoln's legendary sweetheart.

Television had only just started its invasion of the American home. It was still a heavy, rather lumbering device, and the plays that the networks started putting out regularly in 1948 had a similar character – worthy and stilted productions, with an emphasis on costume drama and an excess of false moustaches. But there were innovative directors and writers who were experimenting with the new medium, and Grace found herself in the midst of a heady and creative hurly-burly of young acting talent. Rod Steiger, Walter Matthau, Lee Remick, Eva Marie Saint, Anthony Perkins, Lee Marvin, James Dean, Jason Robards, Steve McQueen, Jack Palance and Charles Bronson all got their start in television in New York in the years around 1950.

It was an electronic version of the summer-stock company – with more money at stake, less time to rehearse, and everything riding on the success of a single, live performance. Videotape was not yet an option. Rita Gam, a young actress who met Grace through television and became a close friend of hers, compared it with shooting the rapids: 'You only had one chance.'

Grace herself said it was like working on the edge of a precipice. 'Ten minutes before you go on,' she later remembered, 'they change the script. They say "Don't sit down. Play it all standing up by the fireplace." '

Television was where Grace Kelly learned the basics of her craft as a working actress. From 1950 to 1953 she appeared in over sixty television shows – an average of more than one a month. *Lux Video Theatre, Kraft Television Theatre, Hallmark Hall of Fame, The Prudential Family Playhouse, Philco TV Playhouse, Goodyear TV Playhouse, Robert Montgomery Presents* – Grace played them all. Some of them were productions of real quality. Many were no better than melodrama. Her appearances for *Lux* were some of the original tear-jerkers for which the term soap opera had recently been coined.

Grace accepted parts at short notice, absorbed her lines in a matter of days, and learned how to look good on camera after only minimal rehearsal. She did not stand on her dignity. For Ed Sullivan she donned fishnet stockings and did a spirited job as a chorus girl. When Cary Grant found himself playing opposite the young and still comparatively inexperienced actress in 1954 in *To Catch a Thief*, he was amazed at her mastery of dialogue and asked her the secret. 'Dozens of soaps,' she cheerfully replied.

Dominick Dunne, the writer, was working as a television stage manager in those days. It was his job to arrive at rehearsals before everyone else and to mark out the floor with grey tape to show where the furniture and scenery would be positioned 'on the night'. The rehearsals often took place in rented West Side dance halls. These were drab and seedy establishments in the cold light of day, and Dunne can remember the glamour that Grace would bring to a thin winter's morning, sweeping in off the street in an elegant mink coat: 'She was one of the most ravishing creatures you ever set eyes on. Always friendly and always very professional. She just lifted the spirits.'

'She was no Eleonora Duse,' said Ted Post who directed her in two episodes of *Danger*, a popular mystery series. 'But Grace was very determined . . . She listened to you, and she applied what you said.'

Much early television drama was lifted straight from the live stage, so Grace got a chance between soaps to play some of the roles to which she aspired, but which she could not capture for herself on Broadway. One of these was *The Swan*, Ferenc Molnar's hit drama about a young princess torn between the passion of her dashing young fencing instructor and the courtship of the moody prince whom her family expects her to marry. Grace Kelly topped the bill in *The Swan* on CBS on 9 June 1950.

Grace became so busy with her TV work that she decided to give up her modelling. She also became something of a resource centre for other young actors who hoped that her commercial success might rub off on them. One day Elia Kazan asked if she could spare time to help a young man who was rehearsing for a particularly important audition. He was only free on weekends because he had to work for his father during the week and had a young family to support.

'I tried to find a kind way of letting him know that he wasn't going to make it,' Grace remembered more than twenty years later. 'I explained how difficult it was to get work, and reminded him that most actors in New York were hungry most of the time. I advised him to keep his job so he could support his wife and child – and maybe act as a hobby, in amateur productions.'

This became a favourite story of Grace's, and her punch line was the identity of the inexperienced young man whom she, the seasoned TV professional, had considerately consigned to amateur dramatics. The actor's name was Paul Newman.

Every summer in the years of 1951, 1952 and 1953, Grace went back to the Bucks County Playhouse, and she accepted work in any summer stock that Edie Van Cleve could book for her. Making it in live theatre remained her most immediate ambition, and she turned down television engagements for any stage work that she could get. Grace enjoyed the texture of a live appearance, the hush from the audience as the curtain went up – and, as ever, she was also seeking the approval of her father.

'Mr Kelly loved the theatre much more than he did

films or television,' remembers producer Jean Dalrymple. 'He didn't want her to do films at all.'

Dalrymple was the impresario and general inspiration of City Center, a municipally subsidized theatre which staged low-budget productions of classic revivals in the Mecca Temple on Fifty-fifth Street in Manhattan. She had gone backstage to congratulate Grace after her first, brief Broadway appearance in *The Father*. Dalrymple saw Grace as the ideal Roxanne in a *Cyrano de Bergerac* that she dreamed of staging, and Jack Kelly encouraged her. If his daughter had to be an actress, he much favoured her appearing in serious and respectable classics.

'He had heard terrible things', remembers Dalrymple, 'about how the girls had to sleep around in Hollywood in order to get good parts. And he hadn't heard anything like that about the theatre – well, only for chorus girls, perhaps.'

By 1951, when Grace went back for another summer at Bucks County, she was a television drama star by any measure. But taking her cue from her father, she did not count this as any particular distinction. In her eyes, the veterans of the summer-stock company were the real actors. 'You probably don't remember me,' she said shyly to Sara Seegar, one of the senior Bucks County players, who remembered Grace very well and had watched her quite frequently when she appeared on television. 'I'm Grace Kelly and I played in *The Torch-Bearers*.'

The 1951 Bucks County production of *Accent on Youth* cast Grace opposite Jerome Cowan, a minor movie actor who had enjoyed his heyday in the 1930s, and who made no secret of his envy of Grace's television success. 'She's twenty-something, and she doesn't know anything,' he complained to anyone within earshot – Grace included.

'He treated her abominably,' remembers Natalie Core O'Hare, who was playing in the same production. 'He scared her to death, and she just had a terrible time learning her lines. So I would take her off in the corner, and I would cue her. "Don't let him frighten you," I would tell her. "He's slipping in his industry, and he's jealous of everybody. Hang in there. This is a good test of what you can do." Well, of course, on opening night she came on stage looking ravishing, and the audience went, "Ahhhh!" She remembered her lines and she got all the reviews. He could have killed her.'

It was the beginning of a fast friendship between Grace and Natalie, who joined the group of regular visitors to the Kelly apartment, a merry circle of girls who brought the Barbizon atmosphere to the Stalinist severities of Manhattan House. There was Prudence Wise ('Prudy'), the friend Grace had made at the hotel; Grace's former Barbizon room-mate, Bettina Thompson; Carolyn Scott, who had helped Grace get started in modelling; and Sally Parrish, a Southern girl who, like Grace, had wanted to go to Bennington, and had ended up at the Academy.

Sally Parrish was actually living in Manhattan House, sharing the apartment's single bedroom with Grace. This had been at Mrs Kelly's request. Grace had reached the age of twenty-one in November 1950, but, according to Sally Parrish, Ma Kelly still 'wanted her to have some French companion, or someone to give this aura of respectability.'

Mrs Kelly was horrified when she saw the disarray of the girls' shared sleeping quarters. 'Oh, Grace,' she exclaimed, 'I hope when you get married you have someone to pick up after you!'

'I hope so, Mother,' Grace replied.

Pride of place among the Grand Rapids furniture went to a large, round table of black Formica, which doubled for dinner and drinks. The table operated on a spiral. It was swivelled up for food, then spun down again eighteen inches for the coffee and tea afterward. Natalie Core O'Hare remembers a meat and potatoes dinner prepared by Grace, who cooked hearty and ate hearty: roast leg of lamb, vegetables, and Grace's own, home-baked lemon pie for dessert – with games and charades to round the evening off.

Grace and her friends would sit up late into the night, sharing jokes and confidences. Men were a constant source of entertainment. Grace got rid of one unwanted admirer by borrowing Sally's mother's engagement ring, and doing a love scene with an actor friend who was in on the joke. To dampen the ardour of another suitor who seemed incapable of taking no for an answer, the girls draped themselves in sheets and cooked up a fake séance.

'The lights were out, and everything was pitch black,' recalled Sally Parrish. 'The furniture had been pushed on one side . . . A candle was burning, and this man walked in, and she pretended that this was all very serious and all very much part of her life. Well, that got rid of *him*.'

The séance was rather more than a joke, for during her Manhattan House years Grace developed quite an interest in table-moving, Ouija boards and the occult. She was a Scorpio herself, and throughout her life she could discourse learnedly on the Scorpio characteristics as she saw them – efficiency, creativity, stubbornness, sensuality and passion. 'She got terribly astrologically minded,' remembers June Sherman, who socialized with Grace in the early 1950s. 'She was such a romantic. Having her palm read or studying her chart was like buying jazz records or going to French movies. It was all part of the excitement of being young and untethered in New York.'

'Most of us didn't have very nice places to live,' John Foreman remembered twenty years later, talking to Gwen Robyns, 'and Grace had a wonderful place. So a great many people used to congregate at her apartment. Everyone was young and we were sure we were going to take over the entertainment business. There was a party atmosphere. Late in the night there would be improvisational dancing by everyone. I remember Grace doing a flamenco once to rival Ava Gardner in *The Barefoot Contessa*. She was heavy into ballet lessons. She had no genuine talent, but she still went every day because that was the way she was. She was a disciplined girl.'

Her other friends remember the same dedicated, purposeful Grace behind the giggling. 'When she had something to do, she didn't make a big fuss,' recalls Bettina Thompson Gray. 'She just did it. This was a very determined woman.'

Grace Kelly was not pushy, but she was forever pushing forward, and as her friends got to know her more intimately and became familiar with her extraordinary family, they came to a fairly unanimous view as to the sources of her drive and ambition. 'It was her father,' says Natalie Core O'Hare. 'She was forever striving to get that recognition – the good, kind words at home.'

'She had this drive to win his attention,' agrees William Allyn, an actor who played *Ring Round the Moon* with Grace in Ann Arbor, Michigan, in May 1951, and who became another firm friend. 'She once said to me, "I am going to be the greatest film star that Hollywood ever saw," and I do not think that she said that out of ego. "My father and my brother were Olympic oarsmen," she said, "and my uncle was a Pulitzer Prize playwright. Whatever the Kellys do, they have to do well." ' As Don Richardson put it, 'Grace had to make a bigger splash than a pair of oars.'

It weighed heavily on Grace sometimes, the duty of being a Kelly. Working in Albany in the snowy January of 1951, she seemed particularly stiff and serious to some of the cast who were trying out in Lexford Richards's new play *Alexander*. Then, at the end of the two-week run, someone brought an electric guitar to the closing-night party. Music always had a way of loosening Grace. It unlocked the sensuality inside her. As the electric guitar began to play, the stuffed shirt clicked dramatically into life, throwing off her high-heeled shoes and dancing barefoot, her full skirt whirling as she turned. 'She ran her fingers through her hair,' remembered Gant Gaither, 'and as it fell to her shoulders, the pins flew in all directions.'

'There it is!' exclaimed Ernestine Perry, the stage manager. 'I've said all along there was fire beneath that surface of ice!'

To her friends, Grace was a fundamentally warm and natural girl who also happened to be blessed with a very cool head. To strangers she was the opposite – an aloof and rather forbidding young woman who only occasionally betrayed the passions that were waiting to be released.

It was love that kindled the passions, and love was never difficult for Grace to find – with her mother and father doggedly shadowing her every move. The drama coach, the banqueting manager, the Shah of Iran – who would she fall for next? In the summer of 1951, Ma Kelly went out to Denver, Colorado, where Grace had secured a summer engagement with the prestigious Elitch Gardens stock company, and it did not take her long to work out that her daughter's affections were committed once again.

It was an emotional time for Grace. Her earliest teenage sweetheart, Harper Davis, was dying of multiple sclerosis. He displayed the symptoms of the disease in 1946 soon after he returned from the wartime naval service that had provoked their separation, and by 1951 he was almost totally paralysed. He was living in the Veterans Hospital in Wilmington, and whenever Grace came home to Philadelphia, she would get Charlie Fish to drive her down to see him. She would sit by Harper's bedside for a full hour, though he could no longer move or speak, and when she got back to Henry Avenue she was always in tears.

When Grace Kelly, film star, was giving interviews in later years, she would invariably be asked if she had ever been in love, and her standard reply was the story of Harper Davis: 'We were childhood sweethearts,' she would relate, 'and he died of multiple sclerosis.' The clippings repeat the story half a dozen times or more, an affecting tale that supplied the apparently intimate 'love life' paragraphs that the reporter needed, while politely cutting off inquiry about any current and more embarrassing romance. The tactic was pure Grace – elegant, dignified, and very convenient. But her mourning was genuine for all that. Harper Davis was the first in a long line of men whose love Grace had renounced in obedience to her father's wishes.

In Colorado, her new boyfriend was Gene Lyons, a strutting and poetic young actor with reddish-blond hair. Like Grace, he came from Pennsylvania and was of Irish descent. But while Grace had grown up in the comfort of Henry Avenue, Gene Lyons came from poverty in Pittsburgh, and was proud to label himself 'shanty Irish'. Lyons was handsome, complicated, unexpected, and very charming. 'Mother,' confided Grace, 'I think I'm in love.'

Gene Lyons appealed to the bohemian side of Grace. He was a step back from the gilded salons of the Waldorf, towards the carpet dealers of Thirty-third Street, and he shared her passion to make it on the stage. 'He not only knew how she felt, but he felt the same way,' remembered Mrs Kelly. 'He kept telling her that they could be stars in the theatre together, that they would stimulate each other to success and fame.'

Mrs Kelly had heard this sort of thing before, and when Gene Lyons's ex-wife was thrown in, the handsome young actor added up to a package which was not that different from Don Richardson. Mrs Kelly felt about him in much the same way. 'He was not the stable sort of young man I'd hope Gracie would marry . . .' she said. 'I had real reservations toward her marrying someone in her profession . . . "Gracie," I said, "Please be absolutely sure before you do anything as final as marriage." '

In the event, Grace's work priorities dealt with the dilemma, as they had done before. Although Edie Van Cleve had booked Grace into Elitch Gardens for a succession of performances through the summer of 1951, the agent had also been working on another, very different project for her young client – and on 10 August it finally came through. Grace received a telegram in Colorado from the movie producer Stanley Kramer in Hollywood: 'Can you report 28 August, lead opposite Gary Cooper. Tentative title *High Noon*.'

EIGHT

High Noon

GRACE KELLY had been to Hollywood once before. Twentieth Century-Fox had flown her out for a few days in the summer of 1950 to film one of the vignettes that made up *Fourteen Hours*, a worthy and vaguely experimental production based on the true story of a young man who had spent fourteen hours threatening to jump from a New York hotel ledge in 1938.

Grace's appearance had been so brief that her character was not given a name. She was listed as 'lady in lawyer's office', her role being that of an elegant young society woman who catches sight of the would-be suicide across the street as she confers with her attorney about her forthcoming divorce. It was a small part in the original script, and it was even smaller by the time the editing room had finished with it. *Fourteen Hours* was not a commercial or a critical success. But Grace's few days of work earned her enough for her to treat herself to her first mink stole, and she was offered several long-term studio contracts – all of which she refused.

It was standard practice in the early 1950s for Hollywood studios to offer seven-year contracts to promising young actresses, guaranteeing them a thousand dollars or so a week in return for taking charge of their destiny – the right to change a girl's name or hair-style, to get her teeth capped, and even to supervise her choice of boyfriend or husband. This paternalism was exercised in the name of career development, but in practice the studios' care of their charges amounted to what the film critic Richard Schickel has described as the 'cafeteria' system – placing all sorts of tasty morsels in front of the audience, 'then sitting back to see which of them the public hungers for most deeply'.

Grace Kelly did not see her future in the ranks of the studio starlets. 'I wasn't interested,' she later said. 'I could earn more modelling.' Grace knew what her father thought of Hollywood, and her Uncle George had imbued his niece with a horror of the gilded slavery of the studio contract. George Kelly had experienced it himself in the 1930s, when he went out to Los Angeles to work as a studio script doctor, and he felt it was the death of artistic independence. Grace took his lectures to heart. One of the keynotes of her Hollywood career was her ability to be intelligently choosy. She proved to have an instinct for landing work in the very best company – the best scripts, the finest direction and the most glamorous co-stars – and she hit upon all of these in the autumn of 1951, when she left Colorado summer stock to join the cast of *High Noon*.

The team of Stanley Kramer, producer, Carl Foreman, writer, and Fred Zinnemann, director, had already produced *The Men*, a powerful drama about wheelchair-bound war veterans. Shot in the stark, black-and-white, 'semirealistic' style that was Fred Zinnemann's trademark, the film had not proved good box office. But undeterred, Kramer and Foreman moved on to a Western, the story of a sheriff who tries to rally the inhabitants of his small town against a bunch of desperadoes. Every able-bodied citizen, from the judge to the pastor and his upstanding congregation, finds their own good reason for turning their back on the sheriff in his hour of need – which is scheduled for noon, when the train is due, bearing the villains.

Carl Foreman wrote the script while under subpoena to appear in front of the House Un-American Activities Committee. Years previously he had been a member of the Communist Party, and he knew how many friends he could count on once he admitted that allegiance in a town and an industry that was running scared. '*High Noon*,' he later said, 'was about Hollywood and no other place but Hollywood.'

Grace was picked to play Amy Kane, the marshal's young Quaker wife whose pacifist principles prompt her to join the town's general disavowal of her husband. Under the stress of events, Amy changes her mind and returns to his side, firing the crucial shot that saves him. It was the pivotal role in the plot, but Grace could take no particular credit for landing it. 'I wanted somebody unknown opposite Gary Cooper,' remembers Stanley Kramer. 'I couldn't afford anybody else. So I signed her.'

Kramer was an independent producer, raising his money wherever he could find it. One of his investors was a lettuce grower from Salinas. Kramer put together his own combination of stars, director, supporting cast and production crew, then sold the finished movie to a studio. This system of 'packaging' is the way in which virtually all Hollywood movies are produced today, but in the days of the studio production line it was revolutionary – and it offered a particular advantage to Grace. 'As an independent, Stanley didn't require any studio contract,' explains Jay Kanter, the young colleague of Edie Van Cleve at MCA who got Grace the job with Kramer. 'She didn't want to sign the long terms.'

When Grace arrived in Hollywood at the end of August 1951, she went to the set to meet her new director. All that Fred Zinnemann knew about the young actress was that she had been playing summer stock, and that she came at the right price. 'She was wearing white gloves,' remembers Zinnemann, 'which seemed rather out of place in the small studio where we were working, which was rather a dump. She was beautiful in a prim sort of way. But she was very tense. She seemed definitely inhibited.'

Zinnemann's eloquence lay in his film-making rather than in his powers of conversation. 'I am very bad at small talk,' he says, 'and she wasn't very good either. So she answered most of my questions with a "Yes" or "No". It was a very, very quick discussion.' The director felt a certain relief as he shook the actress's white-gloved hand and sent her on to the office of Carl Foreman. She did not seem promising material, but as he reflected on the work that he had to do with Grace, he realized that she was exactly how he imagined the marshal's young wife should be.

'Sort of boring, and thin-blooded,' says Zinnemann today, 'the image of virginity in a colourless sort of way. She was a Quaker girl from the East who suddenly found herself among all these wild people in this crude Western town. She was *supposed* to be inhibited and tense. She was type-cast. She just had to play herself. The fact that she was really not quite ready as an actress made her that much more believable.'

Just playing himself was what made Gary Cooper's performance as Marshal Kane so memorable. The fifty-year-old actor was unhappily separated from his wife, Rocky, and did not seem to be deriving much joy from an affair with the actress Patricia Neal. He was suffering from arthritis, back pain and a stomach ulcer – and he discovered after the filming ended that he was also in need of a hernia operation. The word around town was that Coop was on the way out. His last two pictures had been flops, and he had dropped his fee considerably to work for Stanley Kramer.

'I told him, "Just look tired," remembers Fred Zinnemann, 'and he did it wonderfully well.'

Grace could scarcely believe she was working with one of the stars over whom she had swooned on Saturday nights with Maree and her other girlfriends at the Orpheum in Germantown. 'Did you kiss him?' Peggy asked her sister the moment that Grace got back to Henry Avenue.

'Yes, I did,' replied Grace giggling.

'How many times?' Peggy wanted to know.

'Oh,' said Grace, frowning, 'about fifty, I guess.'

The gentle and charming Gary Cooper was a prime candidate for one of Grace's romances. He was a handsome and polished older man who found her entrancing and who was anxious to help her career. He was the classic father figure. But he had more than enough woman problems in September 1951, and it does not seem likely that he was ever more than a friend. The shooting of *High Noon* was compressed into a busy twenty-eight days, and throughout that time Grace was chaperoned by her younger sister, Lizanne.

'The presence of your sister Lizzie would be very well received by the family,' Ma Kelly had declared severely when Grace first announced her intention of going out to Hollywood, so the youngest of the Ocean City watchdogs was deployed to the Hollywood hills. Eighteen-year-old Lizanne roomed with her sister throughout the time Grace was working on *High Noon*, driving her to work in the morning, hearing her lines at night, and sometimes spending the days on the set with her as well. When Coop took his pretty young female lead for a drive in his beloved silver Jaguar in search of a good steakhouse, the not-so-photogenic younger sister would squeeze herself firmly into the back.

Neither Kramer nor Zinnemann saw any obvious clues of a romance. 'Grace was odd,' remembers Kramer. 'She was separate from everybody.'

'She kept her own counsel pretty much,' agrees Zinne-mann. 'In twenty-eight days there wasn't a lot of time to get into anything personal.'

Zinnemann was struck, in fact, by what an unhappy person Grace seemed. Anything but the careless romantic, she appeared tense and introspective as she stood on the threshold of opportunity. 'She was insecure,' remembers the director, 'very busy sorting herself out. I now feel that I was knowing her before she had really developed as a human being.'

Zinnemann also worked in these years with the young Audrey Hepburn – he is the only film-maker to have directed both women – and he found that Grace was by far the more fragile of the two. 'Audrey had enormous self-confidence,' he says today, 'while Grace, so far as I could see, was not self-confident at all. Certainly not at this stage. She was her own problem, so to speak. Instead of looking out at the world, she was looking inward, into herself, a great deal.'

Zinnemann wished he could have given Grace more help with her acting. He had come to movies by way of his superb camerawork, not as someone who specialized in working with actors and actresses on the stage. But even in the tough and compressed shooting schedule for *High Noon*, the director could sense what lay ahead for the young actress who played Amy Kane: 'In some shots, she could look surprisingly average. But then in certain angles, and with a certain lighting, she looked just magical. She *looked* like a star.'

Gary Cooper won an Oscar for his role in *High Noon*. His performance was both human and heroic, and it helped elevate the movie to the status of a classic. The grainy, newsreel-like camerawork, the tension generated by the remorselessly ticking clock faces, Dimitri Tiomkin's forlorn and dramatic theme song, which also won an Oscar – every ingredient clicked. Only Grace Kelly was a failure – by her own estimation, at least. She delivered the uptight and stilted role that her producer and director had wanted, but it left her profoundly dissatisfied. 'You look into his face and see everything he is thinking,' Grace said of Gary Cooper's performance. 'I looked into my own face and saw nothing. I knew what I was thinking, but it didn't show.'

More than twenty years later Grace remained mortified by the woodenness of her first significant screen performance. 'When we graduated from the Academy, we would sit and practise how we were going to sign our autographs,' she told the author Donald Spoto in 1975. 'It was only a question of time – we were right there. There was nothing between me and stardom except a few city blocks. After I saw *High Noon* I thought, "God! This poor girl may not make it unless she does something very quickly!" I was horrified. I was miserable.'

The American Academy had given Grace a foundation of dramatic technique and her very particular accent. Television had improved the fluidity of her dialogue. But she knew that she still needed more. Somehow she had to locate and unlock the extra resource that would put real heart and soul into her acting. Her life was abubble with emotions. The question was how to release those emotions dramatically, and Grace turned for help to Sanford Meisner, one of the great gurus of American drama who was then teaching at the Neighborhood Playhouse on Fifty-fourth Street in New York. The moment she got back from Hollywood, Grace enrolled in his professional class.

Sanford Meisner had been one of the original developers of the 'Method' school of acting in the 1930s, but he had broken with Lee Strasberg over the concept of 'emotion memory', the idea that the actor should look back into his own past to discover the feelings that he needed on the stage.

There were many possible sources of authentic feeling in Meisner's view – pure imagination and fantasy not least among them. 'What you are looking for is not necessarily confined to the reality of your life,' he argued, inviting his male students, by way of example, to imagine what might happen in an encounter between themselves and Sophia Loren. 'Your imagination is, in all likelihood, deeper and more persuasive than the real experience.'

The way to find yourself, according to Meisner, was not to look inside but to look out. Acting, as he saw it, was a process of getting connected to the other actor, thus bringing life to the dramatic exchange of feelings that constitute stage dialogue, and ultimately bringing life to yourself. Meisner trained his pupils to generate this life through dialogue drills that they practised in pairs, two actors working together – talking, listening and reacting to each other intensely:

'I'm staring at you.'

'You're staring at me.'

'You admit it?'

'I admit it.'

'I don't like it.'

'I don't care.'

Meisner suggested the starting point. It was for the actors to develop the exchange of words and feeling that followed, guided by their sensitivity to their partners and to their own inner selves. 'One moment will lead to the next,' Meisner would explain. 'You have to learn how to trust. Eventually the line will come right out of the heart of you.' Only when this final stage, the ultimate goal of the course, had been achieved did Meisner move his students on to scenes and dialogues from actual plays.

Starting in the late autumn of 1951 and working solidly, between her stage auditions and TV work, for more than a year, Grace Kelly practised her way through Meisner's tough and sometimes obscure-sounding dialogues, fiercely alert for her own feelings, sensing her reaction, and then shooting it straight back to her partner, trying not to pause for reflection. It was the very opposite of the watch-your-manners, think-before-you-speak gospel of Henry Avenue. 'Repetition leads to impulse,' Meisner taught. 'You have to learn how not to think any more, and how to act before you think.'

'Her attitude was so impressive,' says Meisner's assistant, James Carville. 'She had played leading roles on television. She had had success in Hollywood and had been offered a contract. But she put it all on hold. She said she was not going back until she had studied and learned to act properly – and that was after she had already spent two years at drama school.'

Meisner, a lean, ascetic and bespectacled man, did not tolerate fools gladly. His favourite quotation, framed and hung on the wall of his office, was from Goethe: 'I wish the stage were as narrow as the wire of a tightrope dancer, so that no incompetent would dare step upon it.' There was a significant drop-out rate from his classes, and he had been known to dismiss pupils in mid-exercise, telling them never to return because he felt there was nothing they could learn from him. 'Thinking has no part in this process,' he would explain. 'Work from your *instincts*. Good acting comes from the heart.'

Grace followed his cue. Progressing through the intense tit-for-tat of her teacher's dialogues, she pushed her acting through the inhibiting barriers of convention and thought-fulness toward the stage that Meisner described as 'self-betrayal' – 'the pure, unselfconscious revelation of the gifted actor's most inner and private being'. Love and sex had already taken Grace through those barriers. Now she began to learn how acting could yield up the same joy. 'Grace was astonishing,' commented Cary Grant in later years, marvelling at the Meisner-taught intensity that Grace was able to bring to a dramatic sequence. 'When you played a scene with her, she really listened. She was right there with you. She was Buddha-like.'

Sanford Meisner today is eighty-seven years old, crippled by a cruel series of accidents and illnesses. He has lost his voice box, and he can only speak with the greatest difficulty, holding an amplifier to his jaw. He has very few words to spare, so when asked for his verdict on the pretty and hardworking actress whom he taught for twelve months in 1951–52, he searches carefully for the accolade, and mouths it out precisely. 'Grace had good emotion,' he says.

NINE

Romancing the King

WHEN GRACE got back to New York from the filming of *High Noon*, she picked up the strings of her summer-stock romance with the dashing Gene Lyons. 'They were very much in love,' remembers David Swift, the producer-director, who was then writing for television and had dated Grace himself a few times.

Gene Lyons was now in New York working in TV and trying to improve his own acting technique. He had enrolled in the Actors Workshop on Sixth Avenue, and he spent long evenings at Manhattan House, working with Grace through their respective dialogues and exercises. Romance, work and mutual encouragement – it was very much the pattern that Grace had shared with Herbie Miller and Don Richardson.

Early in February 1952, Grace and Gene appeared together on television, playing the leads in *The Rich Boy*, a Scott Fitzgerald story. 'From the beginning,' intones the narrator, 'they were in love with each other.' But the love in the story turns sour, since the rich boy of the title, played by Lyons, has a drinking problem which proves fatal to his affection for the rich girl, played by Grace. They go their separate ways in the drama – and so it proved in real life.

'He loved his Old Bushmills,' remembers actress Lee

Grant, who had enjoyed a romance with Lyons shortly before he met Grace. 'He was a really great, attractive Irishman, very complex and poetic. He loved saloons and to have his foot up on the bar. He was wonderful company. He had an enormous talent. But it was the whiskey that killed him. He had a very quick slide after Grace.'

Hobbled by his drinking, Gene Lyons never fulfilled his potential as an actor. In his later years, he played a supporting role in the TV series *Ironside*, and he died, comparatively young and hopelessly alcoholic, in 1975 – another would-be husband whose subsequent life and misadventures lent confirmation to the doubts that Grace's parents had come to harbour about their daughter's impetuous heart.

Grace's stage career was still showing no signs of getting airborne. In the spring of 1952, straight after her appearance in *The Rich Boy*, she was cast in a minor role in *To Be Continued*, an unexceptional drawing-room comedy that closed after only a few weeks on Broadway. But by April 1952, *High Noon* had won its Oscars, and Hollywood was taking a second look at the shy, blonde young actress who had played Amy Kane. Gregory Ratoff, the director, called Grace in for a screen test for *Taxi*, a movie he was due to shoot for Twentieth Century-Fox. Grace had prepared for the part, but the summons to the screen test took her unawares. She was just leaving Manhattan House for one of her classes with Sanford Meisner when she got the call, so she had no chance to dress up or to put on her white gloves. She turned up at Fox's New York office in an old skirt and shirt, wearing no make-up, with her hair all dishevelled. 'Perfect!' cried Gregory Ratoff.

The outer office was full of coiffed and polished young actresses, but Ratoff was looking for someone to play the role of a simple, immigrant Irish girl, and Grace appeared to fit the bill exactly. 'Can you speak with an Irish accent?' he asked.

'Of course,' Grace replied. To prepare for the test, she had had an Irish friend read her three days' worth of newspapers.

Ratoff's wish to cast Grace as his colleen was overruled by his Hollywood superiors. The *Taxi* part went to a Fox contract actress. But Grace's unconventional screen test was seen by John Ford, the great director of *Stagecoach*, who had been hired by MGM for a remake of *Red Dust*, the early thirties hit that had starred Clark Gable and Jean Harlow in a romance set against the backdrop of a Malaysian rubber plantation. Clark Gable wanted to play the lead again in the remake – shifted to Africa and retitled *Mogambo* – and a big budget spectacular was envisaged. There would be several months filming on location in East Africa, followed by a month or so shooting the interior scenes in MGM's studios in England. It was an opportunity that no young actress could pass up. But the price of the part was now inescapable – signing a seven-year contract with MGM.

Lucille Ryman Carroll, the head of talent at the studio, remembers the young actress agonizing in her office in the autumn of 1952. Grace had flown out to Hollywood and had been offered the part of the second female lead. She was promised third billing after Clark Gable and Ava Gardner. But even that prospect could not break down Grace's resistance to the prospect of seven years of indentured servitude. 'I am not interested in a contract,' she told Lucille Ryman Carroll, 'because once you get into a contract you don't have any options.'

Mrs Carroll found Grace's spirit and intelligence a welcome change from those of most of the pretty young women who passed through her room. 'So many of them,' she says, 'didn't have anything up there.' On the right-hand side of the talent director's office was a lush couch on which many a would-be star had reclined provocatively. But Grace had ignored the couch for a small hard chair on which she sat straight in front of the desk, upright and businesslike, firmly gripping her folded white gloves. 'Just what does a contract mean?' she asked after Mrs Carroll had made it clear that there was not the slightest chance of her acting on the same bill as Clark Gable and Ava Gardner unless she signed for MGM.

The talent director explained that Grace would start out at $750 a week, for a guaranteed forty weeks' work per year – an annual salary of $30,000 (the equivalent of $190,000 today). Mrs Carroll did not tell Grace that, as MGM's biggest star, Clark Gable was on $5,000 a week, and that most young actors and actresses started out at $1,500. 'When I look back, I really insulted her by offering her only $750,' says Mrs Carroll. 'But I knew she wasn't in great demand, and the money did not seem a problem. She had other priorities.'

Grace knew exactly what she wanted. She had worked out her conditions for signing with MGM – the right to continue living in New York, a schedule which required no more than three pictures a year, and the freedom to do stage plays from time to time if she wanted.

'None of those things were really a problem,' says Mrs Carroll. 'We didn't mind where she lived between movies, and it was hardly likely that we could fit in more than three movies into a year. As for appearing on the stage, I told her that it sounded a good idea. "We like that," I said, "because it increases your popularity, and makes you better known." '

So Grace became a Hollywood contract player after all. But she did get the special conditions that she asked for, and she was starting several layers up from the bottom of the heap. 'Sit down, catch your breath, I have some wonderful news,' she wrote to her friend, Bill Allyn, mimicking the style of J. D. Salinger's *Catcher in the Rye*, which Allyn had recently given her. 'I am going to do a picture in Africa with Old Clark Gable!'

When Donald Sinden, the young British actor who was cast as Grace's husband in *Mogambo*, arrived in Nairobi at the end of November 1952, he found that Gable and Kelly were already fast friends. Sinden joined the couple for dinner that night in the grill room of the New Stanley Hotel. 'She ordered the entire meal for the three of us in Swahili,' he remembers. 'From the moment she heard she was due to be working in Kenya, she had been swotting up on the language.'

The logical off-camera pairing was between Gable and Ava Gardner, the two major and fabled American screen idols, who were each in a class of their own. But Ava Gardner was preoccupied with the complications in her recent marriage to Frank Sinatra. Soon after her arrival in Africa she discovered she was pregnant, and she interrupted her filming for a journey to London for an abortion. Ava found, in any case, that Clark Gable's affections were already firmly engaged.

'As far as romance went,' she later wrote in her memoirs, 'Clark's eyes were quite definitely on Gracie, and hers, for that matter, were on him. They were both single at the time, and it's very normal for any woman to be in love with Clark.'

Clark Gable was twenty-eight years older than Grace Kelly, and he had false teeth. He was so inarticulate that, as Ava Gardner famously remarked, if you said, 'Hiya, Clark, how are ya?' he was stuck for an answer. But he could still twist his moustaches into the lopsided smile that captivated Scarlett O'Hara, and he had not the slightest difficulty in winning Grace's heart. She had come to Africa to play with the 'King' of Hollywood, and she did precisely that. Solid and easygoing, Clark Gable was Jack Kelly without the intimidation. Gracie liked to snuggle up to him and call him 'Ba' – the Swahili word for 'Father'.

The couple made no pretence. 'They were together', remembers Donald Sinden, 'most of the time.' In his amusing autobiography, *A Touch of the Memoirs*, Sinden recalls stumbling into Gable's darkened room one night, to find the 'King' sitting up in bed with a girl – 'both of them starkers'.

So was the young lady Grace Kelly? Sinden, a friend of Grace in later life and now one of the greying elders of the British theatre, grows gentlemanly and vague. 'I've often wondered that myself,' he says.

Grace would get up early on days when she and Clark were not needed for filming and would go driving for hours with him, bumping through the bush in an uncomfortable old jeep. In a letter back to Prudy Wise, her Barbizon friend who was now working as her secretary, she described stripping down to her underwear to go 'skinny-dipping' with Clark in Lake Victoria. The pair were totally relaxed together, flopping down side by side on their chairs between takes, both wearing their glasses, as unconcerned with impressing each other as any old married couple. When shooting was over, they would adjourn to Clark's tent, where Grace would try to help him demolish the bottles of hard liquor of which both he and Ava Gardner were so fond – though Grace soon discovered that she did not have the capacity of her famous co-stars.

'She was never much of a drinker,' remembers her school friend, Maree Frisby Rambo. 'When we used to try rum and Coke at parties, Grace could only manage one drink. Hard liquor didn't seem to agree with her.'

Ava Gardner noticed the same. 'Her little nose would get pink,' she wrote, 'she'd get sick, and we'd have to rescue her. Or she'd get easily hurt and do my trick and run off into the darkness. Clark would catch on after a few seconds and say to me, "Sugar, where's she gone? This is Africa. She can't just run off in Africa." So I'd go off and find her and bring her back before the lions ate her.'

One evening Donald Sinden was sitting outside his tent, writing a letter home by the light of a hurricane lamp, when he thought he saw something white flash past him in the darkness. A minute or so later there was another flash of white, which came, and went, and scurried around, and finally turned into Ava Gardner in her nightdress. 'Don,' she asked, 'did you see Grace? We can't find her.'

Seizing his flashlight, Sinden strode out into the bush, to locate his overwrought co-star, also in a nightdress, huddled behind a bush and weeping. 'Go away,' hissed Grace. 'I want to be alone.' So Donald Sinden stayed with the young actress, putting his arms around her until she had calmed down, and he could lead her back to the safety of her own tent.

On location near the Indian Ocean, Gable returned from a day's shooting without Grace, and was told that she had gone down to the beach. He went looking for her himself and found her sitting on some rocks, with a book open on her lap, sobbing her eyes out. 'Why are you crying?' he asked.

'It's the most beautiful thing in the world,' replied Grace. 'I'm reading Hemingway's *Snows of Kilimanjaro* about the leopard in the snow, and I looked up and I saw a lion walking along the seashore.'

Finally beyond reach of the most tenacious Kelly chaperone, Grace was free at last to indulge her immense capacity for sentimentality. Swooning over Hemingway, hitting the liquor, romancing the great white hunter – it was as if she were making her own private movie: 'What I did in Africa!' Cut off from the world in the most definitive fashion, she did not have to hide her wilder instincts in the sort of secret life that she had created in New York. She could take a few risks and enjoy the sensation of being marginally out of control.

Yet, ever the striving Kelly, Grace was also living out, in classic drama-school style, the character that she would have to play in her first major movie role. Consciously or not, she was giving an off-camera rendition of her screen role as Linda Nordley, a refined and straitlaced young Englishwoman who loses her bearings under the romance of the dark continent. On safari with her earnest anthropologist husband (Donald Sinden), she falls for the rough and roguish Clark Gable, who has been hired as their guide, but who is already half-involved with Ava Gardner, a good-time girl who has come to Africa looking for a maharajah.

Like the best Hollywood plots, *Mogambo* made less sense on paper than when projected in Vistavision with swelling background music, and it was filmed in the grandest Hollywood tradition. An army of cooks and servants catered to the stars in their luxuriously appointed canvas pavilions. An electrical generator the size of a locomotive provided power for the 300-tent encampment whose entertainment marquees featured table tennis, darts, and twin sixteen-millimetre film projectors that showed a different movie every night. When Christmas came around, a chartered DC-3 flew in bearing turkeys, champagne, and Frank Sinatra, who provided company for Ava Gardner and sang for everyone else at the New Year's Eve party.

As the principal actor from England, Donald Sinden frequently caught the rough side of his director's tongue. John Ford was a gruff Irish-American, who cultivated an immense contempt for both the English and for Italian-Americans, and he took the opportunity to indulge both prejudices when he introduced Ava and Frank Sinatra to the British Governor of Uganda at a reception. 'Ava,' he said, 'why don't you tell the Governor what you see in this one hundred and twenty-pound runt?'

'Well,' replied Ava, who was seldom at a loss for words, 'there's only ten pounds of Frank, but there's a hundred and ten pounds of cock!'

Far from being shocked, Grace revelled in the company of such spectacularly uninhibited grown-up children. It took her back to the teenage Gracie who flung her falsies around in the car, and she became a close friend to Ava Gardner, particularly in the painful weeks surrounding Ava's abortion. Gore Vidal recounts an anecdote told him by Sam Zimbalist, the producer of the movie: 'The location was full of these tall Watusis, beautiful warriors who had been hired as extras, wearing their breechclouts. The girls were walking along, and Ava said to Grace, "I wonder if their cocks are as big as people say? Have you ever seen a black cock?" . . .

'With that, she reached over and pulled up the breechclout of one of the Watusis, who gave a big grin as this huge cock flopped out. By then Grace had turned absolutely blue. Ava let go of the breechclout, turned to Grace, and said, "Frank's bigger than that." '

Inspired by the collegial saltiness, Grace was moved to treat her fellow actors to a little bawdiness of her own. Her very best story, it was decided, was her tale of how she was going to a Broadway rehearsal one day in all her finery, when she saw an old wino picking a piece of chicken skin out of a trash can and slipping it between two mouldy bits of bread. He caught her eye. 'Wanna a bite?'

Grace sniffed disdainfully, and walked on by. 'No chance of a fuck, then?' the wino flung at her retreating back.

The frolics came to an abrupt halt in the new year when the cast got back to civilization. Rumours of romance had preceded them, and reporters looked eagerly for clues as the company arrived in England for a final month of shooting at MGM's studios at Borehamwood. Grace and Gable were billeted in two of the grand River Suites overlooking the Thames at the Savoy Hotel. 'On their trek back to London,' Sidney Skolsky reported in the *New York Post*, 'the "Mogambo" troupe dispersed three ways: Ava Gardner took one plane; director John Ford and his brother-in-law took a second plane; Gable and Grace Kelly a third!'

Hedda Hopper got on the line, transatlantic. 'Tell me about Grace Kelly?' she asked Clark Gable.

'I can't hear you,' replied Gable, who had been able to hear every question of the interview with perfect clarity till that point.

The Queen of Hollywood gossip could not be shaken off that easily. 'I hear you two made Africa hotter than it is,' she persisted.

'Oh, good God, no!' said the King.

'I'm old enough to be her father,' was Gable's response to one British inquiry about his relationship with his younger co-star, and that report joined the others reaching the American newspapers. Grace's friends in New York were abuzz at the stories. The young men in the Manhattan House set all carried not-so-secret torches for Grace, and here she was, hooked up with the ultimate man.

'I remember being vitally pissed off,' recalled John Foreman, talking to Gwen Robyns in 1975. 'We were always jealous of men that Grace saw, all the rest of us guys, and it took me some years to decide – if indeed it did happen – that she had every justification. Who wouldn't have gone to bed with Clark Gable, I had to ask myself? And the answer is, *everybody* would go to bed with Clark Gable.'

The reaction at Henry Avenue was not so philosophical. Ma Kelly could sniff the smoke at 3,000 miles, and she was on the next plane to London. 'I was only too well aware,' she later wrote, 'of the emotions that our Gracie could arouse in men.'

Ma Kelly's firsthand diagnosis once she reached London was that Grace's feelings for the star added up to nothing more serious than 'a schoolgirl crush' – but she decided to stick around just to make sure. The concerned mother remained three long, cold, February weeks in London to keep her twenty-three-year-old daughter company. Admitting a weakness of her own for Clark Gable, Ma Kelly took great pleasure in chaperoning Grace and Gable on at least one of their dates. 'It was very interesting,' she reported of their dinner *à trois*, 'to hear the various experiences they'd had in Africa.'

Grace was quite accustomed to the mechanics of weaving a love affair in and around her mother's intrusive curiosity. That was how the Kellys operated. They were a family without frontiers. But it was not Clark Gable's cup of tea, and the arrival of Mrs Kelly in London was his cue to beat a courteous retreat. Henry Hathaway, Grace's director in *Fourteen Hours*, happened to be staying at the Savoy with his wife, Skip, and they witnessed the end of the affair.

'He had a guard put at the top of the stairs to keep her out,' remembers Skip Hathaway. 'The guard was there the whole time we were there. She was very persistent.'

The Hathaways were old friends of Gable. 'He just told her, "Out, out,"' says Mrs Hathaway.

The Hathaways' impression was that Gable was trying to phase romance into friendship. After four marriages and more than thirty years of travel and location liaisons, the older man knew a fling when he had had one. But Grace could not accomplish the switch so easily, and her letters home to Prudy grew flat and miserable. 'I'm not speaking to Clark these days,' she wrote. ' . . . Am terribly depressed and anxious to get home.'

'She was just devastated,' recalls Maree Frisby Rambo. 'I remember her telling me how he would not answer the phone and would not return her messages. "When we got back to London, he was suddenly on display," she said. "He was Clark Gable, and I was just nobody." '

Clark Gable was several cuts above the average heart-breaker. He was genuinely fond of Grace. His public professions of fatherly affection were more than just camouflage for what had happened in Africa, and in later years he was to accompany Grace quite regularly to Hollywood galas and public functions as a loyal supporter and friend. It took Grace some time, however, to see Clark Gable that way. When the young actress's London filming assignments were over, Gable escorted her to the airport to bid her a smiling goodbye. It was a public relations 'opportunity' designed to put the rumours to rest, but Grace could not pretend. In front of the assembled reporters and cameramen, she burst uncontrollably into tears.

Grace's screen performance in *Mogambo* displayed the dividends of her year of training with Sanford Meisner. Her acting still could not match the casual expertise of Clark Gable and Ava Gardner, but, as in *High Noon*, the part was in the prissiness. Grace's representation of painfully corseted passion had the quality of real life, and on the strength of her performances as Amy Kane and Linda Nordley, she was hailed by *Look* magazine as the Best Actress of 1953.

This somewhat extravagant nomination was the work of Rupert Allan, a young film publicist who represented *Look* in Europe. Allan had met Grace in London, where he was preparing a story for *Look* on the forthcoming coronation of Queen Elizabeth II, and he had become an instant friend. Discreet and homosexual, Rupert Allan was to become one of Grace's most intimate confidants, and he was to spend much of his life deploying his charm and contacts for the benefit of her career and public image.

Only slightly less of a fix was the 1953 Academy Award nomination that Grace received as Best Supporting Actress for her role in *Mogambo*. Her nomination in this subordinate category was traditional Academy showcasing of a pretty and promising newcomer with a powerful studio behind her. Her role was to ornament the early part of the awards evening, and no one was surprised when her name was not the one drawn out of the envelope.

But Hollywood had clearly taken note of Grace Kelly. She was a pretty face – an incredibly pretty face when she was photographed well – and she filled a particular niche that had been vacant since the departure of Ingrid Bergman. Throughout the 1940s, Bergman had reigned as Hollywood's cool and enigmatic blonde, most notably in *Casablanca*. But in 1950 the sexual vulnerability that the Swedish actress projected on the screen had overwhelmed her real life disastrously, when she fell in love with the Italian director Roberto Rossellini. Pregnant by Rossellini, Bergman eloped with him to Europe, leaving her daughter and apparently blameless physician husband behind.

The scandal rocked the entire motion picture industry. The actress was denounced as 'a free-love cultist', and 'Hollywood's apostle of degradation' on the floor of the US Senate, and Senator Edwin Johnson of Colorado actually called for legislation to license the movie business and to have its morality supervised by the Department of Commerce. The early fifties star billings given to sex bombs like Lana Turner, Jane Russell and Marilyn Monroe only seemed to prove the Senator's point.

Virginia McKenna and Deborah Kerr were possible Bergman substitutes, but they were too cut-glass and schoolmistressy. It was Grace who had the correct and intriguing mixture of fire and ice. She embodied the ambiguity which had provided the tension in Ingrid Bergman's creamy presence on the screen. Grace was blonde and, thanks to her Teutonic genes, she even had Bergman's Nordic cheekbones. The physical resemblance was quite striking – and with her white gloves and Philadelphia origins, Grace Kelly also came with a social veneer. 'It has been quite a few years,' remarked the gallant Gary Cooper, 'since we had a girl in pictures that looked like she was born on the right side of Park Avenue.'

Grace Kelly struck a timely chord. After only three slight roles, she could offer Hollywood the casting equivalent of the Biblical and classical epics that the studios were churning out to prove their respectability in the early 1950s. She was the very opposite of the sweater girls. 'We are sick of flamboyant, bouncy, flashy sex,' wrote Edward Linn in *Saga* magazine. 'Grace Kelly is all the more exciting for her quality of restraint.'

With her cool good looks and restrained public style, Grace appeared to be virginity personified – the very essence of pedigree and purity. But this, of course, was not quite all the story.

TEN

Snow Princess

*

ALFRED HITCHCOCK enjoyed toying with a recurring fantasy – that he was alone in the back seat of a taxi with a beautifully formed but chilly blonde, whose inhibitions suddenly melted in a flailing of arms and legs and the slithering of silk underwear. 'Anything could happen to you with a woman like that,' the director declared, mentally licking his lips on one of the several occasions that he divulged his imagined encounter with what he liked to describe as a 'Snow Princess'. 'The Englishwoman or the North German or the Swedish can look like a schoolmarm, but, boy! When they get going, these women are quite astonishing . . . It is more interesting to discover the sex in a woman than to have it thrown at you.'

The basis of Hitchcock's disturbing and extraordinarily successful films was that things are never quite what they seem. Wickedness à la Hitchcock could pop up in the most unexpected circumstances, and the portly impresario selected his heroines to embody this element of surprise. From Virginia Valli, the female lead of his first silent movie in 1925, to Ingrid Bergman, who played in three of his 1940s thrillers, Hitchcock's heroines acted out the intriguing ambiguities of beauty and seduction – the alchemy which transforms apparently chaste purity into flaming passion. Grace Kelly fitted the profile precisely.

The director's first glimpse of Grace came in *High Noon*, in which he pronounced her performance 'mousy'. This, in fact, was a compliment when it came from the master of the unexpected — 'mousy' was an arousing concept for Hitchcock — and when he was shown Grace's dishevelled screen test for Gregory Ratoff, his imaginings were still more powerfully stimulated. Hitchcock had a mystery movie planned for production in the autumn of 1953. *Dial M for Murder* was a detective thriller which the British writer Frederick Knott had adapted from his successful stage play. The action was set in a claustrophobic London apartment, and Hitchcock saw Grace as the wayward but ultimately naïve English heroine — *Mogambo*'s Linda Nordley as she might carry on back in North Kensington.

'An actress like her gives the director certain advantages,' Hitchcock later explained. 'He can afford to be more colourful with a love scene when it is played by a lady than when it is played by a hussy. Using one actress, the scene can be vulgar. But if you put a lady in the same circumstances she can be exciting and glamorous.'

Hitchcock asked to meet and inspect Grace personally when she got back from filming *Mogambo* in the spring of 1953. She was so nervous at the prospect of meeting the great man that she could scarcely speak. 'In a horrible way it was funny to have my brain turn to stone,' she later said. Fred Zinnemann and John Ford had been great directors, but Hitchcock was something approaching a legend — the only Hollywood film-maker, with Cecil B. DeMille, whose name on a movie usually occupied a billing above that of its stars. *Psycho* and *The Birds* still lay ahead, but Hitchcock had already trade-marked his macabre blend of humour and suspense in such ground-breaking successes as *The 39 Steps, The Lady Vanishes* and *Saboteur.*

Hitchcock took an instant liking to Grace. Her shyness and deference appealed to an artist who gloried in manipulating every component of his creation, and he offered her the female lead in *Dial M for Murder,* playing the faithless wife of Ray Milland. Grace was the only female in the cast. Since Hitchcock was making the film for Warner Brothers, he had to negotiate a 'loan-out' of the actress's services from MGM, who charged him $20,000 for her six weeks' filming, thus netting themselves a tidy profit. This was standard procedure in the days of the studio system – and it carried dividends for Grace. Along with second billing to Milland, she got a rise in salary to $1,250 a week.

It was good going for a twenty-three-year-old actress with only two half-significant movie roles to her credit. But before Grace started work on *Dial M for Murder,* she had one remaining television commitment to fulfil – playing the wife of the pioneering naturalist and bird painter John James Audubon, opposite the debonair French actor Jean-Pierre Aumont.

Jean-Pierre Aumont was a natural candidate for Grace Kelly's affections. Forty-two years old, a widower and a war hero, the handsome Frenchman delivered his lines in an elegantly fractured accent. Aumont was a younger, leaner, and more predatory version of Maurice Chevalier – a definite ladykiller. He had already played opposite such stars as Ginger Rogers and Eva Gabor, and when NBC hired him early in 1953 to play Audubon in the Goodyear Playhouse production of *Way of an Eagle,* he asked about the actress who had been cast to play his wife. ' "She's a very young and beautiful girl," they told me, "and she's just finishing a film in Africa with Clark Gable and Ava Gardner." '

Aumont was not expecting white gloves and horn-rimmed spectacles when he reported for his first meeting with Grace Kelly in the off-Broadway ballroom that NBC had hired for rehearsals. But Grace was operating in her frosty, arm's-length mode. She had just arrived back from London, and she was still suffering from the abrupt let-down in her relationship with Clark Gable. She did not intend to get picked up and dropped again. 'She was giving out a feeling of great austerity,' Aumont remembers. 'She was certainly good-looking, but she was also very, very strict.' This lady, Grace made clear to her handsome French co-star, was not for killing.

The leading man assumed that he could at least address his leading lady by her Christian name: 'In Hollywood, in our profession, everybody calls each other by their first name from the very first minute.' But Miss Kelly was not even willing to be that casual. 'It was "*Mr* Aumont" all the time. She kept on calling me that for two or three days.' The Frenchman took note of Grace's chilling ability to turn her blue eyes to steel at a moment's notice.

Aumont deployed every ounce of charm at his disposal to no avail – until he noticed on the wall a sign that had been posted to foster good fellowship when the ballroom reverted in the evenings to its designated function. 'It said, "Ladies, be kind with your gentlemen. After all, men are human beings too." So I said, "Miss Kelly, will you read this, please?" And she looked and she laughed, and the ice was broken. We became the best of friends.'

They also became lovers. 'Neither of us was a virgin,' says Jean Pierre Aumont, who, as a 200 per cent Frenchman, is amazed at the notion that a relationship between two attractive, single adults should not include a healthy ration of sex. Through the summer of 1953, Grace and her co-star enjoyed a warm and happy New York romance, playing Mr and Mrs Audubon offscreen as on. Arch ornithological exclamations

– 'Look, my dear, a crested flycatcher!' – became a running joke in their conversations.

When autumn came, they went their separate ways, Grace to take up her filming engagement with Hitchcock in Hollywood, Aumont returning to pursue his career in France. 'I loved her,' says the Frenchman today, 'because she was so lovely.' So why does he think that Grace Kelly first presented herself to him with such severity – only to succumb to him totally thereafter? 'The day that I can explain how women work,' replies the actor with a shrug of Gallic insouciance, 'is the day that I'll be sanctified.'

Jean-Pierre Aumont was a man of action when it came to the opposite sex. Alfred Hitchcock was very definitely a man of theory. Imprisoned inside his gross and pendulous body, the Englishman's hyperactive mind was that of a voyeur, flickering with the fantasies of lust and violence that inspired his art. 'Hitchcock filmed scenes of murder as if they were love scenes,' observed the French director François Truffaut, 'and love scenes as if they were murder.'

Dial M for Murder was a melodrama of those two elements, with Grace playing the lady who was the inspiration for both. Caught out by her unlikeable husband (Ray Milland) in a love affair with a visiting American writer (Robert Cummings), Grace's character, Margot Wendice, becomes the victim of an elaborate murder plot. In staving off the assassin hired by her husband, Margot kills her attacker with a pair of sewing scissors, whereupon her husband manipulates the evidence to get her convicted of murder and sentenced to death.

Hitchcock decided he would film the play virtually as it had been performed on stage, using the single set to create an enclosed and psychopathic feeling. When Grace arrived in Hollywood in August 1953, she found that her director had been at work for weeks. 'Hitchcock planned out everything ahead of time,' remembers Mel Dellar, who was the assistant director on the movie. 'I have never worked with anyone who was so meticulous.'

Hitchcock put particular effort into the choreographing of the murder struggle, which was the one piece of action in an otherwise static and somewhat wordy drama. Grace was to writhe and moan in a nightgown, arching her hands beseechingly into the audience, her bare white legs thrashing in the yellowy-green darkness of 'Warner Color'. It was a scene that needed a real lady to moderate its evident sexuality, and Hitchcock could not wait to shape the performance of the young actress who, he felt sure, would prove to be a 'snow-covered volcano'.

Even the master of the unexpected, however, was not prepared for the sort of volcano that Grace turned out to be. A cool professional on the set, she conducted herself as a completely different character when the camera stopped rolling, fulfilling Hitchcock's fantasies to a degree he could scarcely have imagined. 'That Gryce!' he reminisced in his cockney accent to the screenwriter Bryan Mawr a few years later, recalling the havoc that his not-so-virginal young star wrought among the attractive males on the set of *Dial M for Murder*. 'That Gryce! She fucked everyone! Why' – and he said this with a certain amazement – 'she even fucked little Freddie, the writer!'

Bryan Mawr, himself a writer of only moderate physical stature, could not help taking the great man's surprise a trifle personally. 'The snow princess!' Hitchcock chortled, relishing the irony of it, and looking more devilishly cherubic than ever. 'Gryce Kelly, the snow princess!'

Himself a Catholic who struggled vainly with carnal desires – sheer gluttony, most of all – the director was fascinated by the ambiguous behaviour of his leading lady. Arriving in Hollywood for her first leading role, Grace had totally abandoned the distant demeanour in which she had tried to set her professional relationship with Jean-Pierre Aumont. She could scarcely have surprised Hitchcock more if she had played out his back-of-the-taxicab scenario. 'All the men fell in love with Grace on *Dial M*,' remembered her sister Lizanne. 'They were around her in scores – Tony Dawson [who played the murderer] and Frederick Knott [the author of both the play and screenplay] really fell for her.'

Lizanne was sharing a room with Grace in the Chateau Marmont, the shabby lodging-house hotel that loomed over Sunset Boulevard like a decaying Gothic castle. The younger sister was playing chaperone as she had done two years earlier during the filming of *High Noon*, but this time she found herself overwhelmed. 'The whole cast seem to fall in love with her,' she remembered. 'Everyone was sending flowers. At one point I said, "This place looks like a funeral home." I ran out of vases . . . Every day another bouquet would come.'

Chief among the bouquet senders was the star of the movie, Ray Milland, toupee'd, smooth and glib, and twice as old as Grace. He was known to his intimates as 'Jack'. Born Reginald Truscott-Jones in Neath, South Wales, in 1905, Milland had switched from light comedy to serious drama in 1945 when he played an alcoholic in Billy Wilder's film, *The Lost Weekend*, a harrowing performance which Grace had seen back in Germantown. It had won Milland an Oscar.

Grace was greatly flattered that one of her schoolgirl heroes should be dropping in on her at the Chateau Marmont. 'After the shooting,' Lizanne remembered, 'we'd all sit around there, and he would come over. He wasn't living with his wife, and one thing led to another . . . It was pretty serious.'

'They made no attempt to conceal it,' remembers Mel

Dellar. 'You would see them together after work having a meal or whatever.'

When Joe Hyams went to interview Ray Milland for the *New York Herald Tribune* that autumn, the star answered the door dressed in nothing but a towel, and the journalist got the clear impression that Milland was not alone. 'Grace appeared after a time,' remembers Hyams. 'She was dressed, but she had had time to dress. She was cool as a cucumber. She was very patrician.'

Lizanne had to abandon the pretence that she could do very much to safeguard her sister's virtue. She knitted a pair of argyle socks for Milland, as if he were already her brother-in-law, and she offered him her ear as his confidante. 'We had a long talk,' she recalled of one plane trip that she shared with Milland. 'He really was, seriously, very much in love with her.'

Grace returned Milland's feelings. Put on her guard by the outcome of her relationship with Clark Gable, she had played wary with Jean-Pierre Aumont. But the Frenchman had relaxed her, and she positively blossomed in the adulation she received as the only woman on the *Dial M for Murder* set. Suddenly she was a star – and she was in love with a star. She did not care who knew it.

Conducting a love affair in Hollywood, however, was rather different from romantic indiscretion in the African bush. Grace had not reckoned with the power of gossip in a closed and jealous community – nor with the fact that Milland's wife, Mal (short for Murial), had many friends and was generally well liked.

'Grace Kelly was a conniving woman,' says Skip Hathaway, who was particularly close to Mal Milland. 'She almost ruined my best friend Mal's marriage. Grace Kelly fucked everything in sight. She was worse than any woman I'd ever known. She knew how to lead a man on.'

It was not long before the papers started hinting at the story. In the early 1950s the established gossip columnists still disseminated their scandal in the oblique and code-like staccato perfected by Walter Winchell, rushing from nudge to wink and back again so rapidly that their mischief was softened in a miasma of slightly confusing innuendo. Only one magazine went for the jugular in the style of the modern muckraking tabloid. *Confidential* was a scandal sheet that employed private detectives to trail stars who checked into hotels with companions to whom they were not married. The magazine was not scared to broach such taboo subjects as the homosexuality of Liberace, and when it got wind of Milland's romance with Grace it did not hesitate:

> After one look at Gracie, he went into a tailspin that reverberated from Perino's to Ciro's. The whole town soon hee-hawed over the news that suave Milland, who had a wife and family at home, was ga-ga over Grace. Ray pursued her ardently and Hollywood cackled.

In the 1990s such a story could expect to get picked up and republished throughout the tabloid media, swallowed down into the electronic databank to reappear in talk shows, magazines and even in newspapers of record. In the 1950s *Confidential* stood alone, and was regarded as a pariah. Even popular newspapers did not quote from it. There was shame attached to the repeating of gossip, an old-fashioned feeling that if you peddled scandal you were not much better than those who committed it. America still operated on the presumption that there was a moral national consensus which it was a journalist's job to support. This was an attitude that fostered hypocrisy, but it also generated tolerance and even kindness of a sort.

Hollywood could forgive almost anything in those whom

it loved. The long-standing affair of Katharine Hepburn and Spencer Tracy, the male lovers of Rock Hudson, the sexual adventuring of Marlene Dietrich – such private areas were considered out of bounds even by the journalists who made their living from gossip and from personality profiles. When Rupert Allan wrote a sun-filled story for *Look* magazine about Ava Gardner's flawless marriage to Frank Sinatra, Allan told only his closest friends that he had interviewed the actress while sitting at her bedside in a London abortion clinic.*

Such discretion depended upon the stars themselves making a certain amount of effort to be discreet. There were rules to the game. You had to keep up appearances if you wanted appearances kept up, and the penalties were savage for those who thought they were above the system. Charles Chaplin and Ingrid Bergman had both, in their different ways, chosen to flout the proprieties of the industry which made them great, and each had had to pay for their carelessness: 'Do not fool yourself,' the producer Walter Wanger had cabled Bergman as she paraded her extramarital pregnancy in Italy in 1949, 'that what you are doing is of such courageous proportions or so artistic to excuse what ordinary people believe.'

Grace was courting the same danger in her relationship with Ray Milland. An off-camera romance was one thing. An unconcealed affair leading to the destruction of a long-standing marriage that had been sanctified by years of studio press releases was quite another. Grace was sailing close to the wind. Her affairs with the young Shah and with Clark Gable had been hinted at by conventional newsstand publications. Her most recent loveblitz had attracted the attention

---

*In her old age – and in the climate of a different era – Ava Gardner wrote openly about her abortions in *Ava: My Story* (1990).

of more than Alfred Hitchcock. 'Grace Kelly, who stars in it, and Frederick Knott, who wrote it, are hand-holding after *Dial M for Murder* hours,' reported Sidney Skolsky in the *New York Post* on 8 September 1953. Now *Confidential's* story about Grace and Ray Milland could not help but hasten the possibility of full disclosure.

For a girl who was so concerned with looking respectable, Grace Kelly conducted her private life with extraordinary recklessness. When it came to sex, she had the same buccaneering streak as her father, pursuing physical and emotional impulses that were in total contradiction to the moral and religious principles to which she subscribed. Surrendering her virginity to the husband of a friend, meeting a man in a lift and going to bed with him that night – a number of episodes in Grace's life suggested a curiously hollow moral core. The moment that she dared to untether herself from the firm constraints of her Catholic ethic, she had a terrible tendency to run amok. It was as if she was actually inviting the heavy-handed rescue missions that her parents had to organize so frequently.

For her father's part, Grace's affair with Ray Milland justified Jack Kelly's worst fears about Hollywood – and it also showed that he knew a thing or two about the psychology of his impetuous middle daughter. Anticipating some sort of problem, Jack Kelly had already spoken to 'Scoop' Conlan, an old friend who was a professional PR man, asking him if he would 'keep an eye on Grace'. When news of the *Confidential* revelation reached Philadelphia, Mrs Kelly embarked on yet another of her emergency flights to her daughter's side and took the publicist along. 'She and Scoop sat down and talked things over with Grace,' Jack Kelly related later. 'They found her willing to listen.'

Submissive as ever when confronted by the formidable will of her parents, Grace agreed to stop seeing Ray Milland.

'Divorce was just something you didn't do in our family,' remembers Lizanne. 'Going out with a married man or a divorced man was a no-no.' According to sister Peggy, their father ordered Grace to leave Hollywood the moment she had finished filming with Hitchcock. Jack Kelly wanted his daughter back on his side of the continent, and he suggested she look hard for some work in New York.

According to Skip Hathaway, Mal Milland decided to get tough with her husband: 'She finally got the courage. She finally said, "Out! I have all her letters, and I can sue you both." . . . Well, he got down on bended knee. I wouldn't have taken him back, but she did.'

Mal Milland told her friends that the few weeks of her husband's affair with Grace Kelly were the most bitter and wrenching of her entire life. But Grace emerged from the trauma feeling equally battered. 'It was a bad mistake,' she later admitted to Judy Kanter, the wife of her agent.

'I really thought that the marriage was over,' Grace related to Gwen Robyns many years later. 'That is what he told me. I did not know that he had many affairs, and that I was just one of them.'

So Grace Kelly, at the age of nearly twenty-four, had allowed herself to be the plaything of an inconstant character who was under the thumb of his wife. She had come within an ace of wrecking her reputation – and she had had to be rescued from the whole mess by her parents. Grace fled from Los Angeles the moment that the filming of *Dial M for Murder* was completed. 'At times I think I actually hate Hollywood,' she said.

Back in New York, Grace set about following her father's advice – just at the moment that Jean Dalrymple was finally realizing her dream of getting *Cyrano de Bergerac* staged at the City Center theater. José Ferrer had agreed to repeat his successful Broadway portrayal of Cyrano for her.

It seemed the ideal opportunity, a chance for Grace to play the female lead in a New York production of a classic. But Ferrer did not share Jean Dalrymple's confidence that Grace Kelly would make the perfect Roxanne – 'She's an amateur,' he said dismissively – and it was only with some difficulty that Dalrymple prevailed on the actor to let Grace at least read for the part. Dalrymple then persuaded Mel Ferrer (no relation) to coach Grace for the audition. Mel Ferrer had directed the original Broadway *Cyrano* in which José Ferrer had starred, and Grace worked with him every day for a week.

'She was up and fine and marvellous,' remembers Jean Dalrymple. 'Then, on the day of the audition, José and I were sitting out in the theatre, and Mel came out and said, "I'm awfully sorry to tell you that Miss Kelly is not in good voice today. She has a bad cold." José sort of snorted, "An amateur!" And I said, "Please, now, you promised." So Grace came out, and we were in the first row in the orchestra and we just couldn't hear her. José said, "Maybe we're too close." He actually wanted to give her a chance. So we moved back, and she was worse. The poor thing! Between fried nerves and a bad cold, she really couldn't speak. It was embarrassing and terribly sad – and also a little funny.'

By the time Grace's voice was back in speaking order, José Ferrer had found himself another heroine. Grace used to laugh over the episode in later years, but her untimely attack of laryngitis proved to be a turning point. She had done her best to mould her career according to her father's wishes, but her audition for *Cyrano de Bergerac* was the last chance she had to make it on the stage.

★

As filming had drawn to an end on *Dial M for Murder*, Alfred Hitchcock had started telling Grace about his plans for his next movie. Paramount had already started building the film's massive and unique set – a rabbit warren of no less than thirty-one apartments as seen from the rear window of another apartment in Greenwich Village. Temporarily confined to a wheelchair by an accident, a normally active young photographer scans the details of his neighbours' lives through the telephoto lens of his camera, and he happens upon a sequence of comings and goings in one particular apartment that arouses his suspicions. His Park Avenue girlfriend, a stylish young fashion publicist, shares his suspicions, and together they identify and solve a murder mystery.

Early in October 1953, Jay Kanter phoned Grace to tell her that Hitchcock definitely wanted her for *Rear Window*. She would play female lead to yet another of the great stars of Hollywood, James Stewart. But the agent had received a rival offer that was equally interesting. Sam Spiegel was putting together *On the Waterfront*, a raw and angry drama about longshoremen that would be filmed in New York with Elia Kazan as the director. Grace was being considered for the female lead opposite Marlon Brando.

Grace read the two scripts and liked them both. Twenty-two years later she told author Donald Spoto of her indecision: 'So I was sitting with these two scripts. My agent said, "I have to know by four o'clock this afternoon." I said, "I don't know what to do. I love them both. I'd rather stay in New York, but I love working with Mr Hitchcock. I just don't know what to do." He said, "I'll call you back in an hour, and I have to know." So I said, "Well, okay . . ." '

Spoto did not press Grace to explore the personal reasons that led her to choose *Rear Window* rather than *On the Waterfront*, but her decision spoke for itself. Passing up the chance to play an underprivileged child of the tenements (the role eventually portrayed by Eva Marie Saint), Grace plumped for the part of a self-assured and moneyed girl-about-town. She went for Technicolor over black-and-white, she picked the comfortably ageing James Stewart over the prickly young talent of Marlon Brando, and when it came to directors, she also opted for the father figure.

For all her frequently expressed ambitions to be a serious actress, Grace seldom took any risks. She knew her limitations. She never strayed away from the safely middlebrow, in the way that even a traditional star like Elizabeth Taylor went out on a limb to play Tennessee Williams or Shakespeare. Grace felt most at ease when portraying her own vision of herself. In *High Noon*, *Mogambo* and *Dial M for Murder*, she had played women who contained striking elements of her own character, and now, in *Rear Window*, Hitchcock was inviting her to play a glossy and tomboyish Barbizon girl. The character was called Lisa Fremont, but she was no one else but Grace Kelly.

Back in Hollywood again by the beginning of November 1953, Grace lent herself once more to Hitchcock's cheerfully warped showcasing of what he was later to call her 'sexual elegance'. On the opening day of filming the director devoted half an hour to the filming of a close-up of her shoes. 'Where does that fit in?' asked Herbert Coleman, the assistant director, who had not seen the shot mentioned in the shooting script.

'Haven't you heard of the shoe fetish?' replied Hitchcock gnomically. The shot was never used. Alfred Hitchcock's biographer Donald Spoto makes a persuasive case that the director had fallen deeply, if unconsciously, in love with Grace. Spying on the world through his lens to uncover secret nastiness and desiring his blonde goddess with a passion that he could not consummate, the wheelchair-bound James Stewart looked suspiciously like a slim and handsome surrogate for Hitchcock – particularly when the director insisted on supervising twenty-seven takes of Grace planting a kiss on Stewart's forehead.

Edith Head, the costume designer, was struck by the way in which Hitchcock personally selected what Grace would wear in every scene. 'There was a reason for every colour, every style,' she remembered, 'and he was absolutely certain about everything he settled on. For one scene, he saw her in pale green, for another in white chiffon, for another in gold. He was really putting a dream together in the studio.'

In later years the director's obsession with an actress would take an overt and ugly turn, when he made direct physical advances to Tippi Hedren. But with Grace, Hitchcock's feelings only revealed themselves in curiously repetitive remarks about her sexuality: 'I exploited the fact that she had sex, but not obvious sex'; 'the perfect "woman of mystery" is one who is blonde, subtle and Nordic'; 'I've never been very keen on women who hang their sex round their necks like baubles.' Hitchcock also resurrected around Grace the fantasy he had once constructed around Ingrid Bergman: that he had discovered the perfect actress, with whom he could work in every single future film that he might ever make.

Grace, for her part, took the doting Englishman's professional care for her at no more than its face value. 'Mr Hitchcock', 'Miss Kelly' – the actress and the director worked together with all the formality of participants in an English tea party, playing to Grace's comfort with protocol, while tickling Hitchcock's pleasure in the contrast between what can be seen and what remains hidden.

'Are you shocked, Miss Kelly?' the director inquired on one occasion when she had overheard him talking dirty to an actor – a trick that Hitchcock regularly employed just as the cameras were about to start rolling in order to inject a sense of surprise into a scene. 'No,' replied Grace demurely.

'I went to a girls' convent school, Mr Hitchcock. I heard all those things when I was thirteen.'

Hitchcock's scabrous relish of his own sexual imaginings, which were blended with a crude line in toilet humour, stemmed from a sheltered youth. Directing a beach scene in one of his early films, he could not understand why one of his actresses was refusing to go into the water. When an aide explained the female menstrual period to him, the director was astonished. 'I was twenty-five years old, and I had never heard of it,' he later confessed with defiant pride. 'I had had a Jesuit education, and such matters weren't included.'

By the end of 1953, when he was directing Grace Kelly in *Rear Window*, Hitchcock's education had progressed:

> At the rehearsal for the scene in *Rear Window* in which I wore a sheer nightgown [Grace later recalled], Hitchcock called for Edith Head. He came over to her and said, 'Look, the bosom is not right. We're going to have to put something in there.' He was very sweet about it; he didn't want to upset me, so he spoke quietly to Edith . . . We went into my dressing room, and Edith said, 'Mr Hitchcock is worried because there's a false pleat here. He wants me to put in falsies.'
>
> 'Well,' I said, 'you can't put falsies in this, it's going to show – and I'm not going to wear them.' And she said, 'What are we going to do?' So we quickly took it up here, made some adjustments there, and I just did what I could and stood as straight as possible – without falsies.
>
> When I walked out onto the set, Hitchcock looked at me and at Edith, and said, 'See what a difference they make?'

Learning how to manipulate an authoritarian male, if only occasionally, increased Grace's self-confidence, and she blossomed as an actress under the warmth of Hitchcock's obsessive devotion. She had found a Svengali who wanted nothing from her beyond what she could give on the screen, and her leading man was equally professional. James Stewart later scoffed at the notion that Grace was a cold dish of tea – 'If you ever played a love scene with her, you'd know she's not cold.' But Stewart was happily married, and his off-screen relationship with Grace never prompted the slightest whiff of scandal.

The great challenge facing Hitchcock in *Rear Window* was to iron the stiffness out of Grace's acting performance. It had not mattered much in *Dial M for Murder*. Stiffness had been part of the role – as it had been an integral part of the inhibited women that Grace depicted in *Mogambo* and *High Noon*. But Lisa Fremont was nothing if she was not carefree, a will-o'-the-wisp who could enliven a sick boyfriend's evening by contriving to spirit dinner and a bottle of Montrachet away from the '21' Club – along with a red-jacketed waiter.

Grace had the looks for the part. Statuesque and regal, she was a natural model for all the clothes that Hitchcock chose for her, draping them off her finely contoured shoulders with rare elegance and style. Now Hitchcock had to animate the mannequin with some of the lust and vigour that he had so much enjoyed witnessing off-camera during *Dial M for Murder*.

'Sometimes he merely wears [his actors] down,' wrote Grace twenty years later, trying to explain what it felt like to be directed by the great man. Hitchcock told her jokes, did extra takes, shocked her, cajoled her, challenged her, flattered her as the very centre of his creative life – and finally got the performance that he wanted. As Lisa Fremont, Grace Kelly was frisky, lighthearted and enchanting. 'A pre-view of coming attractions,' she twinkled to her incapacitated boyfriend as she drew a negligee out of her handbag, encapsulating all the innocence-with-sexual-promise which fascinated Hitchcock and which he correctly identified as the essence of the Kelly appeal.

Rear Window was the first of the classic and inimitable Grace Kelly movies, stirring up the special magic that was hers and hers alone. Grace had been right to turn down *On the Waterfront*. Her gift did not lie in impersonating other people. Her talent was to impersonate her fantasy of herself. She had sensed how Lisa Fremont was her own dream, the very model of that sort of girl who would glitter at the April in Paris Ball. It was the direction in which Grace was pushing her own life, mustering the bouncy self – assurance she needed to buoy her very needy inner child, and Hitchcock helped her to accelerate the process. *Rear Window* was Grace Kelly's in the sense that a movie starring Katharine Hepburn was a Katharine Hepburn movie, a creation whose essential excitement sprang from the personality of its leading lady – which meant that Grace Kelly, like Katharine Hepburn, had now to be considered as nothing less than a star.

Rear Window opened to near unanimous critical acclaim in the summer of 1954. With its lively jazz music, its kaleidoscopic set, its puckish sense of humour and its love scenes that were considered daring in their day, the movie was a box-office sensation. In view of all the fuss, Don Richardson thought that he should take a look. Richardson's enduring memory of his ex-girlfriend was of Grace scrambling for her emerald bracelet in the fish tank two-and-a-half years earlier. Now he was presented with a new image – and it was one that gave him a great deal of pleasure. 'She was luminous on the screen,' he remembers. 'When she was bending over Jimmy Stewart and kissing him, this was the girl in the illusion. This was not the timid girl I knew. Hitchcock had turned the dream into a reality, and I was sitting there overwhelmed.'

Grace Kelly as showcased by Alfred Hitchcock was a captivating and wondrous creation – light, breezy, clean and wholesome. But the irony of the laughing Snow Princess was that words like light, clean and wholesome were the very last to describe the imagination of the stout maestro who had first seen the vision and had given it life.

PART THREE
STAR

ELEVEN

The Country Girl

THE CHURCH of the Good Shepherd, Beverly Hills, is known to the irreverent as 'Our Lady of the Cadillacs'. The only members of the congregation below the super-tax bracket are the maids. Whenever Grace Kelly was in Hollywood, she liked to start off her Sunday at the altar rail of the Good Shepherd – which was how Dominick Dunne happened to bump into her early one Sunday after mass.

It was the autumn of 1953 and Grace was approaching her twenty-fourth birthday. Dunne had just arrived from New York, having given up his job as a television stage manager. He was feeling a little lost, and Grace immediately invited him to accompany her to a première later that week.

'Grace looked absolutely ravishing,' says Dunne, recalling the excitement of their evening together under the lights. 'She had done her movies with Cooper and Gable. She was just finishing *Dial M*, and she knew that Hitchcock wanted to use her again. It was a very busy and promising time, but the extraordinary thing was that the photographers paid virtually no attention to her. We went to the opening of *The Band Wagon* with Fred Astaire and Cyd Charisse, and nobody in the crowd had any idea who she was. There was none of that buzz – no flashbulbs or autograph hunters. We just walked in like anyone else going to the movies. Many years later I reminded her of that evening. "I think that was just about the last time," she said.'

Dunne had caught Grace Kelly in that rare and delicious moment of presuccess that is almost more exciting than success itself. As 1953 drew to a close, she could cherish and savour the anticipation of great things about to happen. But Hollywood soon got in on the secret. Word spread quickly among those who saw the rough cuts of *Rear Window,* and industry insiders picked up the scent of dollars and distinction. 'It won't be long', predicted Billy Wilkerson, owner and editor of the *Hollywood Reporter* in a signed column, 'before this attractive kid will be the Number-One Box Office attraction in the world.' Towards the end of 1953, *Life* magazine had started preparing a special feature on Hitchcock's young blonde discovery, and when it appeared the following spring, Grace's photograph was on the cover, with the article inside predicting that 1954 would be 'the year of Grace'.

It was gratifying for Grace, and it was energizing for those around her. When Judy Kanter, the wife of Grace's agent, Jay, accompanied Grace to Philadelphia for a special screening of *Dial M for Murder*, she was bubbling over with what would come next. But the agent's wife encountered a strange reaction when she tried to share her enthusiasm at 3901 Henry Avenue. The three pretty Kelly sisters were sitting side by side on the sofa, talking and joking together, when Peggy said something that made Grace whoop aloud with laughter.

'Baba's a sketch!' said Jack Kelly to Judy Kanter, looking toward his eldest daughter with obvious pride.

'Isn't it exciting what's happening with Gracie's career?' responded the agent's wife, knowing that her husband had been talking to Grace's father about the tempting film offers that were starting to flood in. The smile faded from Jack Kelly's face. 'I don't understand why she'd want to be an actress,' he shrugged. 'Never did . . . I told her she could go to New York when she asked because I couldn't think of anything else she could do. Not even getting into college . . . Oh, well,' he sighed dismissively, 'I'm glad she's making a living.'

When Jack Kelly's son won a sculling race in England, the achievement was celebrated with a parade through the streets of Philadelphia. When his daughter made the cover of *Life* magazine, she was rewarded with a shrug that was not much better than a sneer. Jack Kelly later said that he did it out of concern and care for Grace – trying to prevent her head from getting swollen by the fickle nature of show-business fame. But his remarks to Judy Kanter had an edge that suggested more – that he was actually jealous of his daughter, and that, somewhere not too deep below the surface, he resented her for daring to prove that she could do very well in life without him.

It would not have mattered very much if that had actually been the case – if Grace had been able to acknowledge and act upon her impulse to blaze her own trail. She was entranced by the insolence and rebellion articulated by Holden Caulfield in *The Catcher in the Rye*, but that, for her, was just a book. It did not represent an attitude that she could imagine applying to her own life. Grace came of the generation that first made it fashionable to blame parents for the woes of children, but she did not dream of rebelling against her background, or even of turning her back and walking away. She wanted to stay on the Kelly team.

So at the very moment Grace found herself in a position to begin to enjoy herself and her achievements, she was torn in two directions. The adult half of her knew how to cherish and savour her years as a star – the love and adulation, the sheer power and the fun of it all. 'She enjoyed her stardom, as far as I could see,' said John Foreman, describing this side of Grace. 'She wasn't embarrassed by it. She had earned it and she enjoyed it.' But Grace's other half remained the uncertain and anxious daughter, her eyes perked up perpetually for approval, oscillating among all the different strategies that could provide the comfort she craved – the little girl lost, the ingenue, the woman who was desperate in her search for the love and reassurance of older men.

The one constant which had seen Grace through to this point was her drive to succeed, and this remained her talisman. Grace Kelly, film star, was still the Patton tank, steaming steadily forward. Her career eye was fixed firmly on the main goal, even if her personal vision remained clouded and immature. Grace's instinct for working with Hollywood's best was a reflection of this tough and perverse form of adulthood, and when she finished filming with Hitchcock on *Rear Window*, she moved on to collaborate with a filmmaking partnership who, in the early 1950s, commanded equal respect.

William Perlberg and George Seaton were an Oscar-winning director-producer team whose movies included such classics as *Miracle on 34th Street* and *The Song of Bernadette*. At the end of 1953 the two men were at work on *The Bridges at Toko-Ri*, a film based on James Michener's documentary novel of the Korean War, and Grace was cast as the enterprising Navy wife who evades regulations to see her husband on the eve of what proves to be his final mission. William Holden played her husband.

At thirty-five, William Holden was the youngest leading man with whom Grace ever acted in Hollywood, and he was also the most openly flirtatious. Nicknamed 'Golden Boy' after the title of the 1939 movie that made him an overnight star, he had the dash of a man who had seldom encountered rejection. He seemed to get more handsome as he grew older, and his acting was similarly blessed. When Holden's career as a heartthrob seemed on the slide in the early fifties, Billy Wilder had cast him in *Sunset Boulevard* and *Stalag 17*, which won him an Oscar, and he went on giving sterling performances to the end – most notably in *The Wild Bunch* and *Network*.

William Holden was to die a broken and embarrassing alcoholic, literally too drunk to save his own life when he fell and cut his head open at the age of sixty-three. But his drinking was not an obvious problem when he started work with Grace Kelly on *The Bridges at Toko-Ri*. As an actor, he generated fire and excitement in the style of Gene Lyons. The intensity of his performance was, in some way, his own exorcism of his demons within, and with Grace he turned a cliché – a married couple saying their farewells on the eve of battle – into a puzzled and rather moving reality. *Toko-Ri* was the first Grace Kelly movie in which she was featured wearing a bathing suit, and the only one that ever showed her in bed with a man. The couple were chastely clothed in pyjamas, and, thanks to the rules of Hollywood's still powerful Motion Picture Production Code, they did not touch. The sequence was all talk from opposite sides of the bed. But by the standards of early 1950s movies the scene was definitely intimate, and even a little shocking.

The couple's off-screen love affair carried straight on from what they developed on set. As sister Lizanne put it: 'If a lovely girl and a handsome fellow have to "play" at being husband and wife all day, they're bound to have problems switching off when the show is over.'

Holden was married to the actress Ardis Ankerson Gaines (known as Brenda Marshall during her brief screen career), but he had betrayed Ardis quite openly during an affair he conducted with Audrey Hepburn in the early months of

1953, and he was no more discreet with Grace. 'It was a heavy romance,' remembers Mel Dellar, the assistant director, who was an old friend of Holden's from his Air Corps days. According to Holden's psychiatrist, Michael Jay Klassman, Grace was so serious about her new boyfriend that she took him home to Philadelphia. 'We fell head over heels in love with each other,' Holden told Klassman. 'We couldn't help our feelings.'

Michael Klassman was Holden's therapist for an intensive four months shortly before the actor's death, and it was a breach of ethics for him to reveal the details of his client's sessions. But the therapist asserted that this was Holden's wish – the actor had wanted the world to know the details of his alcoholism, Klassman said – and his rendering of Holden's memories of Philadelphia had an authentic ring. 'Cold and hostile,' were the words Holden chose to describe the welcome he found waiting for him at 3901 Henry Avenue.

Holden's recollection of Grace's father was particularly unpleasant. Jack Kelly had been quizzing Grace about the nature of her relationship with her latest co-star. He suspected his daughter of having another affair with a married man, and Grace had kept denying it. So Jack repeated the accusation to Holden's face, 'shaking his fist', as Holden remembered it, in his anger. Equally angry to be treated as an errant teenager, the star abandoned politeness, telling Jack Kelly to go to hell and stalking out of the room in fury. 'I thought he might take a swing at me,' Holden remembered. Outside in the hall he found Grace, 'tears streaming down her face'.

'We kept falling in love with all the wrong men,' remembers Rita Gam, ' – the married ones.' An old colleague from the TV merry-go-round in New York, Rita Gam was sharing a small, two-bedroom apartment with Grace in those early months of 1954. It was on Sweetzer Avenue in West Hollywood, an eccentric and run-down neighbourhood of cottages and low-rent apartments, some of them occupied by hookers who would be returning from work around the time that Rita and Grace were leaving for their six o'clock make-up calls. The British photographer Cecil Beaton could not believe that two glamorous young actresses could be living in such seedy surroundings – 'a modern apartment project,' he recorded in his diary, 'where, rather like a reformatory, the inmates lived in cubicle apartments built around the courtyard.' The only gesture to Hollywood was a cracked and overchlorinated, kidney-shaped pool.

Sweetzer Avenue provided a thrifty and unpretentious background to Grace's affair with William Holden. The star would pick her up there for dates, but it was no setting for romance. Grace and Rita had a bedroom each, and the sofa in the small living room was occupied by Prudy Wise, who was now established as Grace's full-time assistant. In these cramped surroundings, Grace lived as frugally as ever, her one extravagance being the splits of champagne that she kept in the fridge to drink, as Rita Gam remembered it, with just about everything.

Grace never drank champagne, however – or any other form of alcohol – on a night before she had to work. During her modelling days a photographer had once told her that he could pick out the models who had had a drink for lunch. He would not work with them for the rest of the afternoon, he had said, and his warning had impressed her greatly. 'He said that it tells in your eyes,' she used to explain with solemnity.

Grace loved her champagne, but she loved her looks still more, and she came to develop something of an obsession with her alcohol intake. She was regularly going on and off the wagon, observing Lent like a good Catholic, and also abstaining, in her later years, during the months that led up to her birthday in November. It was a running theme in her letters – 'only one week to go,' she wrote to Prudy Wise in 1956, 'and I will be swizzling away' – and when extracts from her correspondence with Prudy were published in the spring of 1994, this provoked headlines that Grace was an alcoholic.

Her close friends are unanimous that this was not the case. 'In more than forty years,' says Maree Frisby Rambo, 'from our rum-and-Coke days onward, I never once saw Grace have too much to drink. Giggly – yes. Drunk or out of control – never.'

Grace was a drinker, but she was not a boozer. The alcoholic in the Kelly family was sister Peggy, whose drinking sprees were already a problem, and Peggy's excesses may have been another reason for Grace's preoccupation with keeping her own drinking under control. Jack Kelly would regularly lecture his daughters on how unbecoming drunkenness was in a woman – and Grace's ultimate worry was the havoc that drinking could play with her weight, since staying slim went with keeping her looks.

Slimming was a major concern in Sweetzer Avenue in the early months of 1954. Grace, Prudy and Rita were forever on a diet. Gayelord Hauser, prunes and exercise provided the cornerstones of their weight-loss programme and it stimulated a sisterly closeness. In their eagerness to cut calories, the young women had worked out a ritual that involved the three of them bumping energetically round the room together on their bottoms.

Grace was now twenty-four, and it was a measure of her growing independence that she had finally shaken off her family chaperones. Rita Gam had already been married and divorced and had lived openly for a time, as the saying went, 'in sin'. A catlike young woman with dark almond eyes, the brunette actress was an unconventional spirit, a hippie before her time, and the way she lived and talked about her own experiences helped Grace towards some deciphering of her own emotional life. 'I have been falling in love since I was fourteen,' Grace admitted candidly to her friend, Judy Kanter, 'and my parents have never approved of anyone I was in love with.'

Grace went on seeing William Holden in secret. It was uncanny the degree to which she was repeating the pattern of her romances with Don Richardson and Claudius Philippe – and in the end it was Holden who called it all off. 'I walked out of her life,' he told Michael Klassman, 'although I loved her very, very much.' The actor had come to realize that there was no point. In the battle with Jack Kelly for his daughter's ultimate allegiance, even the Golden Boy had to concede defeat.

In later years Holden confided to friends that he had loved Grace to a degree that surprised him. She was a warm, vivacious and satisfyingly solid woman in many ways – but he came to feel she had an innermost emotional core which he could only diagnose as immature. Wrestling one day with the question of how they might overcome the problem of Grace's Catholicism and Holden's existing marriage in order to get married themselves, Grace came up with an answer which, she thought, solved it all. Her priest had told her, she said brightly, that if Holden became a Catholic, his previous marriage would be considered invalid – so she and Holden could get married in church. It would all be quite respectable!

In the days when she had been hoping to marry Don Richardson, Grace had come up with a similar proposal as a route around her parents' objections to Richardson's divorce, and Richardson had laughed in her face. Holden's reaction was similar. 'I'd be damned,' he told Broderick

Crawford, 'if I'd let any church dictate what I could do with my life.'

Grace's eager reliance on the literalism of Catholic doctrine demonstrated the difficulty that she had in making grown-up moral decisions. The priest was another father figure whose blessing offered the validation that she could not give herself – and who also absolved her of the need to think through her problems as a mature and responsible adult. Either it was wrong to break up William Holden's marriage or it wasn't. Only Grace could know – and she had to decide for herself – whether she really wanted him sufficiently to face all the consequences. The idea that Holden's becoming a Catholic would wipe away all the difficulties created by their mutual attraction was fairy thought – trying to wave a magic wand over real problems and real people. Grace's 'falling in love' was still an adolescent and ultimately selfish process in which she took refuge from the responsibilities of real life.

The Bridges at Toko-Ri ranked marginally above *Fourteen Hours* in the canon of Grace's movies. Her brief, fifteen-minute appearance was just an interlude in a drama whose primary focus was on men doing the nasty business of war. It scarcely advanced her career with the critics, who could find little to discuss beyond the pleasure of studying her for the first time in a bathing suit. But linking up with William Perlberg and George Seaton did prove to be a shrewd career move. The two men had recently secured a property which they, and most of Hollywood, knew would make a marvellous movie, and just as Hitchcock had spent the filming of *Dial M for Murder* discussing his plans for *Rear Window,* so Perlberg and Seaton's energies during the making of *Toko-Ri* were largely centred on their hopes and plans for *The Country Girl.*

Clifford Odets's play, a massive Broadway hit in November

1950, was one of the countless productions for which Grace Kelly had auditioned and been rejected in her years as a struggling actress.* It was a drama, wrote Brooks Atkinson, 'that practically burns a hole right through the theatre'. A once great actor touches bottom, brought down by drink and depression, but is put back together by his equally depressed but tougher wife, 'the country girl', who battles against her husband's weaker side in order to redeem his career.

Uta Hagen had won rave reviews and numerous awards for her searing performance in the title role, and when the great ladies of Hollywood heard that George Seaton was at work on the screenplay, their agents and publicity men went into action. The part offered dramatic fireworks of a sort that seldom came a film actress's way. Jennifer Jones got ahead of the field with some behind-the-scenes help from her husband, the mogul David Selznick. But then, early in 1954, Selznick phoned Perlberg and Seaton with the news that his wife was pregnant. The two men were well into the making of *Toko-Ri*, and were only weeks away from starting on *The Country Girl*.

'George and I don't tear our hair out,' Perlberg later remembered, talking in the historic present favoured by his friend Damon Runyon. 'We just look at each other. We're both thinking the same thing at the same time – *Grace Kelly*.'

The trouble was that Perlberg and Seaton were working for Paramount, and in her fifteen months under contract to MGM, Grace had so far made only one MGM movie. After *Mogambo*, her career had been built through films made for other studios. MGM had turned tidy profits through the

*Grace had not auditioned for the title role in the original Broadway production of *The Country Girl*. In 1950 she was trying for an ingenue role that was written out of the movie.

loan-out arrangements they had made with Warner Brothers (*Dial M for Murder*) and Paramount (*Rear Window*). For *Toko-Ri*, they had charged Paramount $25,000, and paid Grace only $10,000 in salary. But the time had come for the studio that had originally found and signed Grace Kelly to capitalize properly on her growing appeal. MGM had seen the rough cut of *Rear Window*, and they had heard the jungle drums. Dore Schary, MGM's head of production, said no to their young contract actress's leaving the studio yet again. 'We have big plans for Grace,' he told Perlberg and Seaton.

That should have been the end of the matter, for it was a breach of studio etiquette for producers to solicit the services of artists at rival studios, particularly once a loan-out request had been made and had been rejected. But Perlberg and Seaton wanted Grace badly for *The Country Girl*, and somehow they made sure that she saw a copy of the script. 'No court on earth can make us tell how she got it,' Perlberg later said coyly. 'Just say that I suspect Seaton, and he suspects me.'

Grace was regularly reading the scripts submitted to her by MGM, and regularly turning them down – *The Cobweb*, a love triangle with Robert Taylor and Lana Turner; *The Long Day*, a romance of the early West; and *Green Fire*, a thriller about emeralds set in South America. Seaton's screen treatment of Odets's play was in a totally different class, in Grace's opinion. 'I just *had* to be in *The Country Girl*,' she later said. 'There was a real acting part in it for me.' It infuriated Grace that Dore Schary's 'big plans' should be such low-level potboilers by comparison, and, according to Hollywood legend, she stormed into the production chief's office and told him so: 'If I can't do this picture, I'll get on the train and never come back!'

But such an upfront attack was not Grace's style. Occasionally frosty, more usually effusive and charming,

Grace was almost never direct in her aggressiveness. She had been trained to hide her anger, not to flaunt it. Her toughness had to be implied from her actions, deceptively hidden below her creamy exterior. 'I never said any such thing to anybody,' Grace later commented on her alleged showdown with Dore Schary. 'I couldn't, even if I wanted to. My agent handled the whole matter.'

In the end, it was nothing that money could not fix. Paramount agreed that they would pay MGM $50,000 – double their previous loan-out price for Grace – while Grace agreed that she would go to work on one of MGM's pot-boilers the moment that *The Country Girl* was finished. *Green Fire*, the emerald adventure, seemed the least undesirable, since it promised some location shooting in the jungles of Colombia, where her old school friend Maree Frisby had recently moved following her marriage.

The one remaining negotiation involved Grace's scheduled co-star in *The Country Girl*, Bing Crosby. Crosby's movie contracts gave him leading-lady approval, and he remained to be convinced that Grace Kelly was the serious actress that the part called for. 'He had heard tales,' reported Louella Parsons in May 1954, 'that she was flirtatious and set out to capture the heart of every man with whom she worked.'

Arthur Jacobson, assistant producer on both *Toko-Ri* and *The Country Girl*, was at the Palm Springs house party that William Perlberg arranged so that Bing and Grace would meet: 'Bing had been playing golf, and he came in, and Perlberg said, "Hey Bing, I want you to meet Grace – Grace Kelly." And Bing, with the pipe in his mouth, which he never took out, just said "Oh, hi!" and walked on out of the room.'

Grace knew what a significant meeting this was – she had brought Prudy Wise along for moral support – and she was knocked backwards by Crosby's reaction. 'She was crushed,' remembers Jacobson, 'because she knew this was important in her life. Meeting a man who could say no. She didn't know what to think. I saw a few little tears starting to glisten in her eyes.'

When Jacobson cornered Crosby later that evening and asked him for his verdict, the star responded as if there had never been a problem. 'Fine!' he said. 'Good for Bill? Good for George? Good for you? Who the hell am I to judge?'

The strange behaviour of the singer stemmed to no small extent from Crosby's personal anxieties about the challenge with which *The Country Girl* confronted him as an actor. Playing Frank Elgin, the depressed and deceitful drunk who was married to the country girl, demanded a bleak and unglamorous performance that was light-years away from *White Christmas*. Seaton and Perlberg had boldly decided to cast both their hero and heroine against type. Hedda Hopper and Louella Parsons, the witch queens of Hollywood gossip, had been perfectly correct about Grace's tendency to mix romance with serious work on the set, and it was difficult to see how such a stunning young beauty could be dressed down and generally flattened to play Elgin's dreary and cheerless wife with any conviction.

Arthur Jacobson was present at the first costume try-out to see if the dressing-down of Grace could possibly work. Edith Head, the costume designer, was brought in to execute the opposite of her normal job of glamorizing young starlets. 'We looked at twenty-four sweaters,' remembers Jacobson, 'before we settled on the one that looked dowdy enough. Edith found this drab dress, and we gave Grace some heavy spectacles and we pushed them back on her forehead. By the time the hairdresser had finished with her and we had her standing by an ironing board with a basket of washing, she looked like a different woman.'

'Grace, I didn't think we could do it,' exclaimed Edith

Head with delight, 'but you look truly depressed! I congratulate you.'

Flat, dull and listless, Grace's performance as Georgie Elgin demanded a 180-degree change of direction from the breeziness of Lisa Fremont, *Rear Window*'s girl-about-town, and Grace accomplished the change with remarkable skill. As the downtrodden wife, she had to pull out emotions she had never displayed before – sarcasm, bitterness, and a rather frightening despair, which she portrayed with convincing bleakness. There was a dead soul somewhere deep inside Grace, the little girl who bowed her head submissively whenever her father disapproved, and Grace located her in the way that Sanford Meisner had taught her, by listening hard to the lines and by reacting instantly from her gut. 'Never let me open my big mouth again,' said Bing Crosby after a few days working with Grace. 'This girl can really act!'

Grace's surprising dramatic backbone helped the singer in his own struggles with his part. Locked for many years in a marriage that all Hollywood knew to be unhappy, Crosby had been a heavy drinker himself, and the story of *The Country Girl* eerily shadowed his own life. Frank Elgin is an apparently affable singer-dancer who blames his drunken lapses on his demanding wife, just as Bing Crosby, the happy-go-lucky crooner with the pipe, liked to present himself in Hollywood society as a cheery innocent whose wife, Dixie Lee Crosby, was a drunken shrew. In reality, it was Crosby who started the heavy drinking in his marriage, and when his wife was stricken with ovarian cancer in 1952, he left her to face the ordeal alone. For most of her final months, Dixie Lee Crosby had to do without her husband, who was away in Europe on a leisurely schedule of filming and exhibition golf which got him home just a few days before her death.

Knocked sideways by grief and guilt, Crosby was shocked

into a sort of moral stock-taking, and by the time he was filming *The Country Girl* sixteen months later, he felt able to discuss the parallels between himself and Frank Elgin. 'It was so like his own life,' Grace later recalled, 'he would remark about it when he did a scene.'

Fifty years old, remorseful, and seeking to make a new start, Bing Crosby found himself drawn to Grace's combination of strength and tenderness. He had already started looking for a new young wife, and it seemed to him that Grace would fit the bill nicely. He made tentative and respectable advances, which were all the more respectable for his being a widower and a Catholic. 'He would take us to church on Sunday,' remembered sister Lizanne. 'Then we'd go to Alan Ladd's for brunch and swimming.'

Grace responded to the courtship. When she liked a man and trusted him, she could act with a warmth that could sometimes be misleading. At the wrap party for *The Country Girl* she suddenly threw herself into Arthur Jacobson's lap and gave him a hug. 'There's the man who was so nice to me,' she giggled kittenishly. Mrs Jacobson was not amused. When Grace abandoned the reserve that she was cultivating against the hazards of her increasing celebrity, she reverted to the loose and comfortable Gracie who would stage a fake séance to get rid of an unwanted suitor. Bing Crosby's attentions were not unwelcome, and the couple started dating in a decorous fashion.

The only complication was that the second male lead on *The Country Girl* – the actor playing the stage director whose production is threatened by Frank Elgin's alcoholic moodiness – was none other than Grace's most recent beau, William Holden. As one of the foremost actors on the Paramount roster, Holden normally worked for nothing less than top billing, but, like Grace and Bing, he knew a good acting role when he saw one. With one of the magnanimous gestures for which he was famous, Holden proposed himself for third billing in *The Country Girl*, below the still comparatively unknown Grace – and when it came to romance, he also yielded the field. Crosby broached the subject, according to Holden's biographer Bob Thomas, one evening after filming.

'This Kelly girl,' he said. 'She's a knockout, isn't she?'

'She sure is,' Holden agreed. 'I've never known a young actress with so much know-how.'

'I'm talking about her as a person,' said Crosby, somewhat embarrassed. 'I don't mind telling you, Bill, I'm smitten with Grace. Daffy about her. And I was wondering if . . .'

'If I felt the same way?' Holden responded. 'What man wouldn't be overwhelmed by her? But look, Bing, I won't interfere.'

Holden was already looking for the way to walk out of his relationship with Grace, and he elegantly bowed to the ardour that Crosby made so little attempt to conceal.

'Bing was mad for her,' remembers Lizanne. 'Absolutely mad for her.'

The couple started being seen together more and more about town – Scandia, a restaurant on Sunset Boulevard, not far from Sweetzer Avenue, was a rendezvous that Crosby particularly favoured – and since both Grace and the singer were single, the columnists did not hesitate to report on the relationship and speculate on its prospects. The headlines proclaimed it 'Hollywood's Newest Romance'.

Ma Kelly's reaction was remarkable for being so positive. 'Crosby was unquestionably eligible,' she later remarked in the horse-breeder style that marked her approach to the mating of Grace. 'He was widowed, and he was going out with any number of girls.' Ma Kelly flew to Hollywood to meet the singer, and decided that she liked him. Working hard at his eligibility, Bing took Mrs Kelly and Grace to lunch and a film preview in the company of William Holden and his wife. 'He was very nice,' said Mrs Kelly of Bing, 'and we had a lovely time.'

But perhaps this departure from the usual pattern of parental disapproval made Bing Crosby rather too bland and easy a conquest for Grace. 'He really wanted to marry her,' remembers Lizanne. 'She called me up one night, and said "Bing has asked me to marry him." But I don't think she was in love with him at all.' Romance without adversity was romance without spice. 'Grace loved him,' explained Lizanne, 'but she was not *in love* . . . There is a difference.'

In later years Grace was discreetly forthcoming with close friends about some of her Hollywood romances – 'What else is there to do,' she would ask, 'if you're alone in a tent in Africa with Clark Gable?' But the idea that she had gone to bed with Bing Crosby, or had even considered him as a serious suitor, used to irritate her intensely. 'Perhaps he was the one who spread the word,' says the author Gwen Robyns. 'He would probably have liked to think that it was true.'

'Whatever quality she had, she should have bottled it and made a fortune,' commented sister Lizanne. 'There was something about her that men just went ape over. It was amazing to see these big names just falling all over themselves.'

When Grace moved straight on from *The Country Girl* to the filming of *Green Fire* in fulfilment of her promise to MGM, her leading man was as handsome as any that she had worked with before. Stewart Granger, forty-one years old, six-foot-three and British, was MGM's slightly flat-footed answer to Errol Flynn. He was best known for swash-buckling his way around costume epics like *Scaramouche* and *King Solomon's Mines*. But he did not impress Grace one bit. 'I don't think,' she later confided to a friend, 'that I have ever met anyone who was quite so conceited.'

Grace could not hide her scorn at the banality of the material that she was being called upon to act, and it did not help that her chum Maree Frisby was not in Colombia, as she had expected. For three weeks the *Green Fire* company rattled around a succession of depressing and poverty-stricken jungle locations – 'a wretched experience,' Grace later said. 'It dragged on in all the heat and dust because nobody had any idea of how to save it.'

Stewart Granger's memories of his weeks with Grace suggest why the actress might have been less than impressed with her co-star. 'She was very nice to kiss,' the heartthrob confided in his memoirs, also confessing that he was 'tempted a bit' by her coolness and beauty – and that he took a particular fancy to her bottom. 'Our last scene was played in a torrential downpour,' he wrote, 'and when the final kiss came we were both soaking wet, which accentuated that fabulous behind. To save her embarrassment I covered it with both hands. She was so delighted at finishing the film that she didn't even object, but if you look closely at that kiss, you'll see Grace give a start as those two eager hands take hold.'

When *Green Fire* was eventually released, MGM chose to advertise the movie on Broadway with the gigantic billboard of a green-garbed model with Grace Kelly's face grafted on top of the unsubtly busty body. For Grace the montage symbolized the crassness and commercialization of the entire enterprise. Long before she returned from South America, she resolved that she would never again lend herself to such a run-of-the-mill venture, and the moment she got back for the filming of *Green Fire's* nonlocation sequences in Hollywood, she went into battle to ensure that her next movie reflected her own judgement and not that of some studio mogul. Alfred Hitchcock wanted Grace for his next project. He had invited her to play the lead opposite Cary Grant in

To Catch a Thief, a romantic thriller set in the south of France, and she was determined to accept, even though it meant yet another fight with MGM.

Grace was asking for her fifth loan-out in only eight months. It was unheard-of for a hot actress to secure so many releases. It would be the fourth time that Paramount had to ask MGM to release Grace, but Grace herself was unperturbed. 'No matter what anyone says, dear,' she told Edith Head, who was in charge of the costumes for *To Catch a Thief*, 'keep right on making my clothes.' She hired herself a French tutor, and took language lessons in the intervals between filming on the set of *Green Fire*. The twenty-four-year-old actress could handle her professional life with a decisiveness she had yet to demonstrate in the transactions of the heart. Grace knew that MGM was nursing a production for which they wanted William Holden as badly as Paramount wanted her, and in the end the two studios came to terms. Little more than six months previously, in the autumn of 1953, Paramount had paid $25,000 for Grace Kelly's services in *Rear Window*. Now they were prepared to give MGM $50,000 *and* William Holden as well.

It was a triumphant conclusion to an autumn, winter and spring that had been packed with the most intense work and negotiation – not to mention some equally tangled love life – and Grace's schedule was hectic to the final minute. 'I finished *Green Fire* one morning at eleven,' she later recalled. 'I went into the dubbing room at one – and at six o'clock I left for France.'

TWELVE

To Catch a Thief

WHEN GRACE KELLY arrived in Paris in the spring of 1954 she was exhausted. She had made five movies in just eight months, and Alfred Hitchcock was waiting for her down in Cannes, ready to start another. Grace had only a few hours in the French capital between her morning arrival by plane and her evening departure on the famous Blue Train for the Riviera, and by rights she should have caught up on her sleep. But she could think of better things to do in Paris on a bright spring day. Grace went shopping.

'Let's go and buy some gloves,' she said to Edith Head, who was travelling with her. 'The nicest gloves in the world are at a place called Hermès.'

'And so we went in there,' Edith Head later remembered, 'like two little girls who must go and have an ice-cream soda, and, of course, she fell in love with the gloves, and the people in the shop fell in love with her, and at the end they presented her with a package and a bill that was astronomical. Grace said, 'I haven't got that much money.' So we put both our money together, and we still didn't have enough. In the end we had to get some cash from the hotel.'

Edith Head had been a ringside spectator and semi-participant in Grace's most recent struggles with MGM, and she was full of admiration for the young actress's willpower and sense of purpose. 'There is a lot of solid jaw under that quiet face,' the designer used to say. 'I have never worked with anyone who had a more intelligent grasp of what she was doing. But she still has this rather charming childish quality – the exuberance of a child in a candy shop.'

Grace had gone through some tough times in her long hard winter of film-making, and now she was set to have some fun. She had stumbled upon her previous romances more or less haphazardly as she went along, and she wanted something special for the south of France. At the same time that she had been involved with Ray Milland, William Holden and Bing Crosby, she had had another love interest dancing attendant in the background. This suitor had been courting her – and she had been teasing him – all through the winter, and now the time had come to advance the drama. Enter front stage centre the most baroque, inventive and amusing of all Grace Kelly's gentlemen, Oleg Loiewski-Cassini.

Cassini had first met Grace in 1953 towards the end of her bird-watching romance with Jean-Pierre Aumont. The couple were having a quiet dinner, tête-à-tête, in the Veau d'Or restaurant on East Sixty-sixth Street, when Cassini strolled up to their table. The Russian-Italian designer was not yet the household name he became in the early 1960s with the pillbox hats and the simple, geometric dresses that he created for Jackie Kennedy, but he was already a successful couturier with quite a high profile in Manhattan society. Cassini knew Jean-Pierre Aumont, and by one of the strange coincidences to which Cassini attached great significance, he had just come from the movies, where he had seen *Mogambo* and had been knocked sideways by the beauty and elegance of the still comparatively unknown Grace Kelly.

'I'm going to meet that girl,' he had proclaimed to his companion as he left the theatre.

'You're out of your mind,' responded his friend. 'What makes you think she'd be interested in you? What makes you think she's not already in love?'

'Such prosaic questions,' Cassini later recorded in his auto-biography. 'I don't care,' he told his friend. 'That girl is going to be *mine!*' '

Less than half an hour later Cassini found himself talking to Grace, and he went straight into action: 'I didn't tell her that we had just seen her in *Mogambo*, or acknowledge her profession in any way . . . I sensed the direct, frontal approach would not work. I wanted only to establish a beachhead, to create an agreeable presence in her mind.'

'Every woman has a sweetness somewhere inside her,' says Giancarlo Giannini in the film *Seven Beauties*. 'She may seem bitter on the outside, like a cup of coffee when the sugar has settled to the bottom. She needs stirring to bring the sugar to your lips.' Oleg Cassini knew how to stir the coffee. He delighted in it, and from the night that he first shook hands with Grace in the Veau d'Or, he devoted himself wholeheartedly to her pursuit and conquest.

'This was not the sort of girl you simply called for a date,' he realized. 'A programme of action was needed, a plan – something outrageous, romantic, even silly – to pierce her reserve.' Next morning he had a dozen red roses delivered to Manhattan House, followed by a dozen the day after, and the day after that, for ten successive days, each vase bearing the same enigmatic card: 'the Friendly Florist'. It was not until Grace's apartment was awash with roses that Cassini picked up the telephone. 'This', he said, 'is the Friendly Florist calling.'

'There was a pause, and then that charming little laugh

of hers, and I knew I had won. As Napoleon said, "A woman who laughs is a woman conquered." '

The conquest only extended to Grace's agreeing cautiously to lunch. For their second date she brought along her sister Peggy, a ploy to which Cassini responded by paying slightly more attention to the older sister. Cassini considered himself a five-star general on the battlefields of love, but he found himself up against an equally wily strategist. He was just congratulating himself, on their third date, on having such a soft and beautiful woman in his arms on the dance floor of El Morocco, when Grace smiled demurely. 'I have two little surprises for you, Oleg,' she said. 'One, I happen to be in love. Two, I'm leaving for California tomorrow.'

Grace at first refused to tell Cassini the object of her affections, then relented and gave him some clues: an actor who was an Englishman and who was very handsome; his initials, she said, were 'R. M.' The next day Grace left for California.

R. M. – Ray Milland (technically, not an Englishman but a Welshman). Cassini was not greatly worried about him. If Grace were really in love with the man, the designer reasoned, she would not have agreed to go out with him once, let alone three times. But courtship at three thousand miles' distance did pose some difficulties, and the challenge induced Cassini to intensify his campaign, sending Grace notes to Sweetzer Avenue every day and calling her regularly on the phone – briefly, lightly and, above all, amusingly. It was an axiom of Oleg's always to keep his ladies laughing.

Oleg Cassini was the son of exiled Russian nobility who settled in Italy, and his first and very happy memory was of his red-haired nanny Nina, who would stroke his penis when he was a baby to lull him to sleep. The product of another age and culture might consider this formative childhood experience something to be bemoaned on confessional television. For Cassini, quite to the contrary, it provided a delightful starting point to a lifelong fixation on the fairer sex. Women yielded him both pleasure and his livelihood as a designer, and their wooing became, in many ways, his entire identity. 'I loved women,' he wrote in his memoirs of his earliest years, 'the way they looked and moved . . . I would always be interested in women, how to make them look good, how to please them.'

In the spring of 1954, Cassini flew out to California. He had business there, and he took advantage of it to pursue his courtship at firsthand. Grace was in the midst of filming *The Country Girl*, and Cassini today recalls seeing absolutely no sign that she was romantically involved with either of her costars, Bing Crosby or William Holden. Grace was keeping her *cavaliere servente* at arm's length. She was as offhand as ever. Cassini found that he had many an evening to himself, and he seized the opportunity to escort such beauties as Anita Ekberg and Pier Angeli to Ciro's, where he made sure that his presence was noted in the social pages. Even an evening away from his intended could be harnessed to the long-term purposes of his campaign.

'I don't understand you,' said Grace to him after she had read the mentions in the gossip columns.

'It's very simple,' Cassini replied. 'You are busy. It seems I'm not very important to you. I like to dance, I enjoy pleasant company . . . and also I have a reputation to maintain.'

Romance as practised by Oleg Cassini had more in common with chess or poker than with courtship in the conventional sense, and after six months of duelling, Grace found that she was rather enjoying the contest. She turned down Cassini's suggestion that he should accompany her to the jungles of Colombia. But she did keep responding to his overtures – his almost daily letters and phone calls – and on the very eve of her departure for Paris, she sent him a postcard bearing just seven words: 'Those who love me shall follow me.' The lady had decided to join in the game.

Cassini's first attempt to join Grace in France was foiled by his own incompetence. He arrived at the airport to discover that his passport had expired. So it was nearly a week before he found himself sitting opposite his quarry in the dining room of the Carlton Hotel in Cannes, sipping Kir Royals, and embarking on a multicourse dinner that opened with *mousse de trois poissons*. Two bottles of Dom Perignon later, the couple were happy and laughing, but Grace was not giving Cassini the opening that he had been looking for. As he later described it, 'Our relationship was still distressingly platonic.'

Cassini went to his own room, resolving that he would give it just one more try. He had started his campaign in the autumn, and it was now beyond spring. He had travelled halfway round the world by plane and train. He had reached the moment of decision. Grace had another free day before filming started, so lunchtime found her with Oleg, a picnic of cold duck, and a bottle of Montrachet '49 in a romantic cove beside the Mediterranean. Out on the clear blue water floated a swimming raft, and it was on the deck of this raft, beneath the warm June sun, that Cassini made his final pitch. He spoke to Grace of his long pursuit and of the minuet that they had danced together. He told her that he cared for her deeply, that his months of persistence and devotion should surely be the proof of that. His fate, he told her, now rested in her hands. 'There is no need,' he concluded, 'for artifice any longer.'

'She said nothing,' remembered Cassini, 'but she was looking at me in such a way that I knew I had won.'

The couple went back to the hotel and put the looks into action. 'We seemed to float there,' Cassini later wrote, 'glowing, mesmerized by the intensity of our feelings. She smelled of gardenias, at once exotic and very pure. There was a translucent, pearl-like quality to her; everything about her was clear and fresh and fine – her skin, her scent, her hair. I was enraptured, aware only of the transcendence of the moment.'

In the roll call of Grace's lovers, Oleg Cassini must be rated at or near the very top. This is not a verdict upon his beddability. For a charmingly boastful man, he was charmingly modest about the physical consummations of his elaborately hatched campaigns of bewitchment. 'The actual mechanics of love,' he wrote, 'were never as interesting to me as the events that led up to it. The art of seduction was always far more fascinating than the ultimate result.' But this was part of the reason why Cassini's tireless courtship of Grace finally captured her heart. He was different from any other man she had met. Everything he did had a twist of artifice and thought. He was prepared to be tested by time, and, as a result, a flirtation which seems to have started as something of a game on both sides turned into the longest, most soundly rooted and, for a time, the most publicly acknowledged romance Grace had ever enjoyed.

Oleg Cassini was not a conventionally handsome man. With his large nose and pencil moustache he was curiously reminiscent of Philippe of the Waldorf, a resemblance made stronger by his busy, European accent, and by his readiness to kiss ladies' hands. Cassini had the bohemian dash of Don Richardson, the fire and pugnacity of Gene Lyons. He did not have the sheer, naked fame of Grace's film-star lovers, but he did have a subtle celebrity that was all his own. People who mattered knew who he was. Oleg was fun. It was one of his working principles, when in female company, always to talk more about his companion's concerns than about his own, while the nature of his work, designing elegant clothes for elegant women, gave him access, as he put it, to 'a form of knowledge that most men don't even know exists. I had the power to envision women as they wanted to be seen – to help them create fantasies about themselves.'

Cassini had already designed some outfits for Grace – subdued, patrician dresses that enhanced her inherent classiness. They gave her the look of a pale and delicate English rose. But Oleg had more than fashion to offer. He gave Grace confidence, a feeling of comfort inside her own skin. The pressures of being her parents' daughter were lifted. Cassini's twinkle-toed provocations brought out the playfulness in her. She was once more the giggly girl in the candy shop whom her friends knew so well, but whom she tended to hide from her more intense lovers.

This was a tonic that would have been welcome at any time, but Grace needed it particularly in June 1954, as she got ready to play the part that Hitchcock had designed for her in *To Catch a Thief*. After the black-and-white solemnities of her two movies for Perlberg and Seaton, she was back in glorious Technicolor, all froth and bubbles, playing Lisa Fremont again. *Rear Window*'s feisty and independent girl-about-town was renamed Frances Stevens. The character was transplanted to the south of France. She was on holiday there with her lavishly bejewelled and mildly dotty mother, and she was given all the naughtiness and sense of adventure that a healthy trust fund can encourage. The wealthy and wilful Miss Stevens was just the sort of girl who would send a man a postcard reading, 'Those who love me shall follow me.'

For Alfred Hitchcock, Frances Stevens represented another stage in the defrosting of his beloved Snow Princess. *To Catch a Thief* did not have much plot. It was a succession of improbable capers in picturesque south of France settings. The dramatic electricity was generated by Frances Stevens's remarkably aggressive pursuit of John Robie (Cary Grant), a debonair Riviera jewel thief who has paid his debt to society by joining the Resistance and performing heroic feats during the war. As the movie opens, Robie is suspected of going back to his old tricks as a cat burglar, and this fascinates Frances Stevens. Half of her is drawn to play detective and catch the thief single-handed, using her mother's jewels as bait. But her other half desperately hopes that her suspicions are wrong, that Robie has been maligned, and that she can win the heart of this dashing and mysterious man.

Hitchcock was toying once again with the tension generated by the two faces of his favourite actress, the contradictions that he liked to call Grace's 'incongruity'. Ten minutes after her first appearance in the movie, at the end of an evening spent rather formally with John Robie, Frances Stevens unexpectedly interrupts the jewel thief's gentlemanly goodnight by stepping forward and kissing him long and passionately on the lips. The thief stands astonished, his composure quite gone. 'It was as though', Hitchcock later said with relish, 'she'd unzipped Cary's fly.'

The director saved his subtlety for his film-making, spicing Grace's sexuality with some dialogues of extraordinary double entendre:

KELLY: [*Offering cold chicken at a picnic lunch*] Do you want
    a leg or a breast?
GRANT: You make the choice.
KELLY: . . . Tell me, how long has it been?
GRANT: How long has what been?
KELLY: Since you were in America last.

The action moves to Frances Stevens's hotel suite, where she has invited Robie for a view of the fireworks in Cannes harbour:

KELLY: If you really want to see the fireworks, it's better with the lights off. I have a feeling that tonight you're going to see one of the Riviera's most fascinating sights. [*She is wearing a strapless, low evening gown.*] I was talking about the fireworks . . .

GRANT: May I have a brandy? . . . Would you care for one?

KELLY: Some nights a person doesn't need to drink . . . Give up, John. Admit who you are. Even in this light I can tell where your eyes are looking. [*Close-up on her chest and necklace and generous décolletage.*] Look! Hold them! Diamonds – the only thing in the world you can't resist . . . [*The fireworks shoot upwards in the background as she kisses his fingers one by one, and places his hand beneath the necklace. Cut to close-up of the fireworks.*] Ever had a better offer in your whole life? One with everything! . . . Just as long as you're satisfied. [*Fireworks again.*]

GRANT: You know as well as I do this necklace is imitation.

KELLY: Well, *I'm* not. [*They kiss. Cut to the shooting fireworks that mount to a climax. End of scene.*]

The verbal sparring of *To Catch a Thief* was deliberately tightened and edited by Hitchcock to enhance its suggestiveness, and it illustrated what the director had said about his first use of Grace in *Dial M for Murder* – that a lady could help him get away with things he would not dare attempt with a hussy. It was as if people were so mesmerized by Grace Kelly's wholesome aura, they could not believe that a nice girl would really have said those things – or perhaps they were swayed by the sheer exuberant joy with which she said it. You knew exactly what she meant, but she smiled so sweetly. How could you possibly take offence?

Grace enjoyed herself making *To Catch a Thief*. For the first time in her filmmaking career she had an escort whom she could acknowledge openly, without complications. Cary Grant had brought his wife Betsy Drake on location, so with Alfred and Alma Hitchcock, Oleg and Grace completed a natural and merry six-some, dining out in hill villages and in the great restaurants of the Riviera. Hitchcock would never eat in a restaurant rated less than three stars. He would send for the menu ahead of time, and would then proceed to direct every detail of the repast, from soup to cheese. Grace enjoyed the *Mogambo*-like camaraderie of being away from home in an exotic location, and she was no longer the greenhorn of the party. With eight movies to her credit, she reckoned herself a pro, and her colleagues accepted her as such.

Grace fell in love with the south of France – the dusty roads, the dark-green cypress trees, the villas on distant hill-sides. Several of the movie's sequences were set in and around the little Principality of Monaco, and people later remem-bered how Grace happened to glance down from the hills onto what seemed to be a secret garden, small and mysteri-ous, surrounded by ancient fortifications.

'Whose gardens are those?' she asked.

'Prince Grimaldi's,' replied John Michael Hayes, who had written the movie's script. 'I hear he's a stuffy fellow.'

People were also to remember how appallingly Grace handled the sports car that she had to drive in some of the film's most scenic passages. The plot called on her to pilot Cary Grant around the notorious bends and precipices of the Corniches, and she steered the car so close to the edge at one point that, as she recalled in 1982, she caused her co-star 'to turn dead white under his tan'. It seemed a great joke at the time.

Grace did not have an affair with Cary Grant. It was not

in the cards. Though Grant was the epitome of the suave and mature Grace Kelly man, he was in his wife Betsy's company, as Grace was paired with Oleg Cassini. But that did not stop Alfred Hitchcock from dwelling on the sexual interplay between his stars with his customary obsessiveness. The director had his publicist compute how many hours the couple spent kissing each other under his supervision. When the endless takes and retakes were added up, the total came to two and a half working days – twenty hours of solid kissing – and Hitchcock released the figures proudly to the press.

Cary Grant was impressed by the solidity and self-assurance of his young co-star. 'Grace acted the way Johnny Weissmuller swam, or Fred Astaire danced,' he later said. 'She made it look so easy. Some people said that Grace was just being herself. Well, that's the toughest thing to do if you're an actor.'

Grant was amazed that such a beautiful and spectacular young actress should not display the slightest hint of the prima donna. 'We had a scene where I had to grab her arms hard while she was fighting me,' he remembered. 'We went through that scene eight or nine times, but Hitchcock still wanted it again. Grace went back alone behind the door where the scene started, and just by chance I happened to catch a glimpse of her massaging her wrists and grimacing in pain. But a moment later she came out and did the scene again – she never complained.'

Oleg Cassini suffered from his girlfriend's unflinching professionalism. Even at the height of her romance with him, she would refuse to go out if she was working next day, or had a scene to prepare. But there were enough free days when Grace was not working, and one evening toward the end of the location filming, she and Cassini slipped away for a little dinner on their own, in a simple fish restaurant on a pier by Cannes harbour. The company was due to trek back to Hollywood a few days later for six weeks of studio shooting, and Grace grew serious at the approach of reality.

'Well, here we are, Mr Cassini,' she said, looking out at the boats bobbing on the water. 'You've been following me all over the world. What do you have to say for yourself? Isn't there anything you want to say?'

It was the equivalent of the raft scene six weeks earlier, but now it was Grace who had got Oleg in a corner.

'I think I would be happy to continue as we are right now,' Cassini responded, frankly expressing his first preference, 'or to take this in any direction you want' – he could sense that more was wanted – 'including marriage. What do you wish?'

He had uttered, with a little prompting, the line that Grace wanted to hear. 'I want to make my life with you,' she responded quietly and movingly. 'I want to be your wife.'

'You've got it,' said Oleg Cassini.

The couple ordered champagne. They went off to the casino to dance and gamble, and Grace even won a little at the tables. 'It was an altogether magical evening,' remembers Cassini. 'I was filled with pride and love, and was entirely enraptured by her.' But as the celebration progressed, the designer was alarmed to see Frances Stevens, the self-assured and sophisticated girl-about-the-Riviera, transform herself into Gracie Kelly from East Falls, talking excitedly about the preparations for their marriage – the dress, the church, all the mundane details of the wedding reception. The globe-hopping polish of Oleg Cassini's film-star girlfriend was quite overwhelmed by 'the flushed enthusiasm of a typical American Junior Leaguer'.

Cassini was confronted by what he had not seen, or had not wanted to see, before – the square and conventional side of Jack and Ma Kelly's daughter. Part of Grace was a very free spirit indeed – the girl who had imagined her life with such out-of-the-mainstream characters as Don Richardson or Philippe of the Waldorf. This was the Grace who had coaxed Cassini to the south of France and had lain with him on swimming rafts. But now Grace had to return to the world of rules, and her mind flipped straight to the rule-makers.

'I want to write home immediately and let them know,' she said. 'Mother will be on my side in this, I'm sure of it . . .' But here was another troubling note. 'There may be some difficulties with Father. You're not exactly his type . . .'

Thinking about it later, Oleg Cassini realized that his relationship with Grace was never quite the same after those words had been uttered. The happy couple shared their joy with the Grants and the Hitchcocks, and more champagne was consumed. But when the time came to arrange their journey home, Grace said she thought that they should travel separately. Oleg should fly straight to New York, she said, while she took the boat with the rest of the company. It was important to preserve the appearance of propriety if her parents were to be won over.

Cassini kissed Grace goodbye at the boat, consigning her to the care of the Grants and the Hitchcocks, then flew alone to New York – where he discovered, as he later put it, that 'the world had turned'. The success of *Rear Window* at theatres across America had made Grace Kelly the most talked-about star in the country, and the rumours of her romance with Cassini had reached all the gossip columns. Louella Parsons and Hedda Hopper were both predicting marriage – though with a significant twist. No longer was Grace the mysterious and unknown predator who repre-sented a danger to happily married stars. Her spectacular new fame had made her the innocent heroine, while the comparatively obscure Cassini was now the figure from the shadows – a marauding playboy whose claims on Grace's affections aroused the suspicions of both her studio and the press. Why, of all the attractive men that were available, wondered Hedda Hopper, had 'the ethereal Miss Kelly' picked on the 'devilish' Cassini?

The couple's reunion in Grace's cabin in New York harbour proved stilted and awkward. The careless rapture of the Riviera had quite disappeared. Grace's two sisters were there, along with a reception committee that seemed to include every press agent and film executive in Manhattan, and reality intruded still more harshly when Cassini took Grace and her mother out for a meal to get acquainted.

'Well, here we are,' smiled the designer nervously, as he sat with the two ladies in the back of a taxi – 'the unholy trio.'

'You, Mr Cassini, may be unholy,' responded Ma Kelly, not missing a beat. 'I can assure you that Grace and I are not.'

Mrs Kelly's jibe was not unwarranted. Age forty-one in the summer of 1954, Oleg Cassini was, by religion, a less-than-practising member of the Russian Orthodox Church, and had been twice divorced. His first marriage to Merry Fahrney, a cough syrup heiress from Chicago, had lasted only a matter of months. He survived longer with Gene Tierney, a promising Hollywood actress who had burned out in the 1940s, but the marriage had not ended much more happily. Refined and well-bred, of wealthy Irish-American parentage, Gene Tierney had some eerie similarities to Grace, and the failure of her union to Cassini did not provide a happy precedent. Ma Kelly was quite frank.

'We do not consider you good marriage material, Mr Cassini,' she said bluntly over lunch. ' . . . We believe Grace owes it to herself, to her family, and to her parish to reconsider.'

Oleg Cassini never took an insult lying down. He had fought duels in his youth in Italy, and he gave Ma Kelly as good as he got. Yes, he conceded, he had been divorced, but he remained on good terms with Gene Tierney and his children. He was wealthy enough, through his own efforts, not to be suspected of fortune-hunting, and he was not ashamed to be known as a man who was attractive to women. 'There is no attractive man – including your husband – who has not been popular with the opposite sex,' he retorted. 'Why do you penalize me for success?'

Oleg Cassini was the first of Grace's lovers ever to stand up and try to slug it out with her parents. But it did little to advance his case with Mrs Kelly. 'We propose a six-month moratorium,' she said. 'We don't think you should see each other for that time . . . Grace will be able to see if it was just Europe, or your charm, or this pursuit you put on her . . .'

Twenty-four years old – only weeks away from being twenty-five – Grace sat limp and cowed through this exchange, silent as her lover did all the fighting in their battle against the enmity of her parents. Cassini had not seen this childlike, spiritless side of Grace before, and he could not believe it. If she truly loved him as she said she did, it was surely her job to explain to her parents why she wanted to marry him.

But later in the week Grace phoned from Ocean City. She had been doing some thinking. She was guest of honour at the Miss America Pageant that was due to be held that weekend in Atlantic City, just up the coast, and she wanted Oleg to be her official escort. It would serve as her own, local, hometown endorsement of their relationship. She had also been talking to her mother, and had managed to get Ma Kelly to soften just a little. Her father remained hostile, but working together, mother and daughter had secured Jack Kelly's grudging consent to Cassini's coming to stay for the weekend.

The designer discovered how grudging that consent was as soon as he arrived at the Kellys' Ocean City beach house.

The bedroom to which he was shown was a cubicle-like enclosure a few yards down the hall and within obvious earshot of the bedroom of the senior Kellys. 'I was trapped there at night,' he recalls. 'My movements were easily monitored.'

But the more extraordinary thing was the way in which both the male Kellys, Jack Senior and Kell, absolutely declined to speak to their guest or even acknowledge his presence in their home. They might allow the man through the door, but that was only to demonstrate the extent of their scorn and dislike of him. 'They actually refused to say a word to me,' Cassini remembers, 'even in response to questions. At one point Grace and I were swimming, and she said, "Try and talk with my father." But whenever I attempted a conversation with him, he looked right past me. He would not say a word.'

Jack Kelly's cold shoulder was comparatively benign. When his wife had first broached the subject of Oleg Cassini coming down for the weekend, he had exploded. The dress designer, he sneered, was a 'wop', a 'dago', and a 'worm'. He would kill the man if he dared to walk through the door.

Grace and Ma Kelly had modified that threat, but this was slight consolation for Oleg Cassini, who felt utterly humiliated by his treatment at the hands of Grace's family. He sat through whole meals disbelievingly trying to make conversation, and receiving not one male word in response.

The designer could not help remembering a similar occasion at the Tierney home a dozen years earlier, when Gene Tierney had come to his defence. 'You can't treat him this way!' she had screamed at her parents. But Grace was saying absolutely nothing. It seemed to Cassini that she was deliberately standing back, watching the drama as an outsider, not as the person who had created it. It was sad to see a beautiful, successful and apparently mature woman whose reactions were so totally frozen by her parents. Grace seemed very much a victim.

Seen in another light, however, Grace's behaviour to her boyfriend had been almost sadistic. What had she expected to happen? Don Richardson, Claudius Philippe, Ray Milland, William Holden, and now Oleg Cassini – she had placed all her lovers in the same arena, enlisting them to her banner in the full knowledge of the impossible challenge that they faced as men who were either married or divorced. It was like the fairy stories of the princess whose father will only yield her hand to the suitor who can solve some insoluble riddle or perform an impossible feat of arms. In terms of Freudian theory, it was classically oedipal behaviour. Grace was toying with a variety of suitors in order to affirm her tie to the male who mattered most.

When Oleg Cassini left Ocean City he was deeply depressed. His suffering had been for nothing. The Kellys would never accept him, he felt quite sure, and Grace was too craven ever to do battle on his behalf. The situation seemed quite hopeless.

Yet as the weeks went by, Cassini discovered that his girlfriend had more spirit than he had suspected. It was true that Grace felt obliged to abide by what she described as 'this silly moratorium'. When she got back to New York, she was reluctant to go out too often to restaurants or night-clubs, or to occasions where there was the risk of her being photographed on Oleg's arm. She still felt compelled to stick by her parents' version of the rules.

But, at the same time, she continued to consider herself as committed to Cassini. She did not date anyone else. The couple saw each other constantly, dining in Grace's apartment together almost every night. They would take it in turns to do the cooking in a cosy and domestic fashion, and one evening Grace was stirred to a moving declaration of independence. The phone had been ringing repeatedly all night, with an insistence and regularity that suggested someone parental at the other end of the line. One could almost sense the steam rising in Philadelphia.

'Aren't you going to answer that phone?' asked Cassini.

'No!' replied Grace. 'If it's personal, then I don't want to hear from anyone, because I am with the one person who I care about the most. There is no one else I'd rather be speaking to. On the other hand, if this is business . . . they will call again.'

The defiance would have been braver if issued directly to her parents instead of to a ringing phone, but it was better than nothing. When Grace went out to Hollywood to complete the studio scenes of *To Catch a Thief*, she rented herself a house, but she lived for the most part with Oleg Cassini. In New York they would spend discreet weekends at the Long Island homes of Cassini's friends like Sherman Fairchild. Avoiding the world, the couple recreated together the cocoon of romance and fantasy they had shared in the south of France. The rejection they were living through pushed them closer together, and as they put the memory of Ocean City behind them, they began to speculate and fantasize again, thinking of the future. One day Cassini got a phone call from Grace. 'I don't care what my parents think,' she said. 'I miss you. Let's get married anyway.' A few days later, a letter arrived:

'Darling —

I . . . can't wait to see you, now that I know I want to marry you. We have so much to learn about each other — there are so many things I want you to know about me. We must be patient with each other and go slowly without wanting results too quickly. But we need each other and we must be completely honest, at all times. I feel for the first time ready to approach love and marriage in an adult way.

Last November [at the end of her romance with Ray Milland], *I hit rock bottom and never thought I could be capable of thinking and feeling this way. Thank God I had my work to help me through that period, and thank God for you. But in this last year, six pictures have taken so much from me physically and emotionally that it will take a while to recover. Please, darling, try to understand and to help me – I love you more every day and I hope you feel that way too. One time you said to me that you couldn't love me any more than you did then. That upset me terribly, because I so hope that we shall never stop growing and developing our minds and souls and love for God and each other, and that each day will bring us closer. I love you and want to be your wife – .*

Grace

Solemn and determined – and not afraid to invoke the name of God – Grace was taking a remarkable stand. She was ready, finally, to break the rules and to defy her parents, not quite directly, perhaps, but in the best way that she knew how. She had reached the turning point, and she was looking to the daring and impertinence of her lover to help her achieve the independence that was her right by the age of twenty-five. Both of Cassini's previous marriages had been romantic, runaway matters, and now Grace wanted him to arrange a third.

Cassini found a priest in Virginia who was willing to accept him into the Roman faith. This would wipe out the impediment of his divorces in the same fashion that Grace had proposed to Bill Holden. The couple could then get married in church. It would be a small, secret wedding – an elopement, to all intents and purposes – and Grace and Oleg started working out the details. But as they confronted together the hard realities of what added up to a sensational scandal – the virginal Grace Kelly running away to marry a twice-divorced fashion designer – their courage failed them. 'We both hesitated,' Cassini remembers, 'and the moment was lost.'

Looking back today, Cassini is inclined to lay the blame for the indecision at his own door. Elopement had not brought happiness to either of his previous marriages, rather the opposite. His stealing away of Gene Tierney had led to a bitter and draining ordeal as the couple fought off the hostility of parents, press and studio, and he could see the same thing happening again.

Grace had hoped for so much of the sprightly knight errant who had opened his courtship with red roses. It was her postcard that had lured Cassini to the south of France. She was the one who manoeuvred him into marriage over their fish dinner on the dock in Cannes harbour. Back in America, she got him telling home truths to her mother, going head-to-head with her father, and planning the stolen, Romeo and Juliet marriage which, his résumé suggested, he was ideally qualified to arrange.

But it was Cassini's own painful experience of runaway romance that shut off the escape route Grace was looking for. Her lover had tried the fantasy twice himself, and he had discovered that it was not all that it promised. If Grace really wanted her freedom, she would have to learn how to free herself.

THIRTEEN

Oscar!

THERE WERE those who disapproved of Grace Kelly kissing Cary Grant so firmly on the lips. *To Catch a Thief*, they felt, featured a lady who had become altogether too saucy and adventurous. 'There has been a growing tendency', complained Carson Kerr in the *Toronto Star*, 'to overplay the sexy side of her portrayals.' 'I wonder,' queried Sidney Skolsky in *Photoplay*, 'if Grace Kelly knew she had so much S.A.' – an abbreviation which, in itself, demonstrated the era's unhappiness with overt displays of sexuality. S.A. stood for sex appeal.

But sexiness, sauce and adventure were integral components of Grace Kelly's appeal. Without them she was June Allyson or Jennifer Jones. It was Grace's knack to incorporate the primness of these models of propriety with the naughtiness of Jane Russell and the sweater girls. Lisa Fremont and Frances Stevens were characters who were simultaneously innocent and experienced, and the dynamic of Grace's screen persona came from the tension that these contradictions generated.

The conformist, country-club side of Grace played perfectly to the female role model of the 1950s, the smiling and competent middle-class spouse in the suburbs, her life made a joy by the endless array of labour-saving appliances that were the fruit of postwar affluence. Television portrayed this paragon serenely pushing the vacuum cleaner in her pearls. Though she lived on the outskirts of a big city, her values were essentially those of small-town America; and when she went shopping, it was to small-town stores grown large – her local Hudson's, Bullock's or Sakowitz.

But to this suburban prototype, Grace Kelly added a touch of the cosmopolitan. She came from Philadelphia, a city that was still thought of as a major and trend-setting metropolis. She did her shopping at Saks Fifth Avenue, and there was something about her taste and demeanour that hinted at more. The archetypal fifties housewife was still regulated by the confining values that had produced victory in the previous decade – discipline, structure, discretion, self-control – and these remained at a premium in the age of the Cold War and the hydrogen bomb. But the sexual revolution was at hand. Alongside *Betty Crocker's Cookbook*, one of the best-sellers of 1954 was Alfred Kinsey's *Sexual Behavior of the Human Female*, an academic study that detailed clinically, but all the more shockingly, the wide extent of premarital and extramarital sexual experimentation among American women – a disproportionate number of them middle-class and college-educated. The mind and body of the suburban female, according to Kinsey's painstaking interviews, were preoccupied by a great deal more than Little League and station wagons.

Grace, of course, mirrored this ambivalence precisely in her own life. Attracted to sexually experienced older men, she was forever trying to fit her freewheeling impulses into the old-fashioned parameters of parental approval and the wedding ring. As her friend Judy Kanter later remarked, it was unthinkable for a nice girl to admit in the early fifties that she might do 'it' for purely casual or pleasure-loving reasons. Good girls waited until their wedding night – or lied about it. When Judy Kanter surveyed the virtue of her closest friends, she reckoned she would be hard-pressed to raise a quorum for a Board of Virgins, but she was only guessing. Sex was something that other people did, and that nobody talked about.

Still subject to the heavy hand of the Motion Picture Production Code by which Hollywood censored itself, the movies reflected this reticence. Sexual relations could only be depicted in the context of marriage, and that in the most indirect form. Marlon Brando and James Dean were two male stars who embodied the rebellious sexuality that was to shatter the conformity of the Eisenhower years, but they had no female equivalent. Stars with big boobs had no brains. The sex bombs stuck to the old-fashioned stereotypes. In the absence of a philosophy for the independent and intelligent woman, female aspirations had to focus on comparatively tentative modifications to the familiar role models – and this was where Grace Kelly came in. She was the forces' sweetheart of a generation that was only just starting to discard its mental uniform. The spouse in the suburbs did not yet imagine that she might be dissatisfied or unfulfilled by her lot, but she did rather like the idea of being a Park Avenue girl. Katharine Hepburn had represented several firm steps in this direction, but, independent and quirky, she was always ultimately Katharine Hepburn – someone who was difficult to imitate. Grace Kelly was a woman whom a lot of other women imagined they really could become.

'She was a new thing,' remembered her friend and television agent, John Foreman, 'and there was no one to compare her to before or since. She set a style that was right for its time.' Though Grace's vibrance, polish and self-assurance were in a well-established movie tradition, her implied sexuality was something new. She was clearly experienced in some way that was only hinted at, but this had not been at the cost of her freshness or respectability. She was no virgin, but she was no slut either, and in squaring this particularly difficult circle, she spoke to the shy and mysterious questings in the hearts of women across the land. Grace Kelly was hardly a role model for the bra burners of a later generation, but she represented as much liberation as the decade of Pollyanna could take. Even the swinging sixties had its problems with Jane Fonda.

The trouble was that Grace's employers at Metro-Goldwyn-Mayer did not demonstrate the slightest awareness of all this. Grace Kelly for them was the latest blonde starlet to make it big, and they offered her the same range of roles they had been offering their female leads for thirty years – Westerns (*Jeremy Rodock* with Spencer Tracy), costume dramas (*Quentin Durward* with Robert Taylor) and, after some grumbling and cogitation, the ultimate concession to the star who took her acting rather too seriously, a worthy bio-pic (the poet Elizabeth Barrett Browning in *The Barretts of Wimpole Street*).

Grace could not get excited about any of these roles. It was not that she could articulate exactly who or what she was. Alfred Hitchcock, after all, had been the principal visionary in the shaping of the heroines of *Rear Window* and *To Catch a Thief*. But Grace knew she was on to something different. 'Hollywood has overworked the word "sexy",' she remarked to the British journalist Donald Zec in March 1955. 'It really takes them by surprise when they see it displayed in a new way.'

The details of this new way were more a matter of instinct than calculation on Grace's part. But she certainly knew who she was not – and that included the watery heroine of *Quentin Durward*. 'All I'd do would be to wear thirty-five different costumes, and look pretty and frightened,' she explained to one reporter, setting out her reasons for her rejection of that part. 'There are eight people chasing me, from an old man to the head gypsy. The stage directions on every page of the script read, "She clutches her jewel box and flees".'

Grace was entitled to a break. The filming of the interiors of *To Catch a Thief* had come to a riotous and unforgettable conclusion in Hollywood on 13 August 1954. This was Hitchcock's birthday, an occasion on which, by time-honoured tradition, his cast and crew were expected to produce champagne and a massive birthday cake. The director would invariably greet this demonstration of affection with expressions of modest surprise, but in 1954 the surprise contained an extra ingredient. 'Ladies and gentlemen,' announced his precisely spoken English secretary with all-too-perfect enunciation. 'Would you all come into the other room, please, and have a piece of Mr Hitchcake's cock?'

Grace spent the autumn in New York seeing a great deal of Oleg Cassini, then going down to Philadelphia on her own to play the role of dutiful – if deceitful – daughter. There was a sense, remarked Judy Kanter, in which the well-bred fifties girl never left home. These were the months in which Grace took up, then abandoned, the options of elopement or pregnancy. She could express her independence and maturity very clearly when it came to her dealings with MGM, but her parents, as ever, were a harder nut to crack.

She settled for moving out of the beautiless slabs of Manhattan House to acquire her own, elegant, high-ceilinged apartment just across Fifth Avenue from the Metropolitan Museum of Art. Her mother offered to help her decorate her new home, but Grace politely declined. She hired George Stacey, a fashionable Manhattan decorator who specialized in the French antique style that Claudius Philippe and Oleg Cassini had taught her to appreciate. Faded silk rugs, polished Louis Quinze pieces, instantly old-looking curtain treatments that infused a room with a feeling of haze and duskiness – the George Stacey package delivered class and subtlety conveniently ready-mixed. When you walked into the place you got the feeling that Grace Kelly must have been living on Fifth Avenue for ever. Grace's new home was Kelly-like in its excellence, but, as with her career, its style and sensitivity reflected her own contribution to the equation.

Just before Christmas 1954, the world outside Hollywood got a chance to see Grace's performance in *The Country Girl*. Ten months after shooting finished, the movie was released in New York on 16 December, to a near-unanimous chorus of critical approval – 'as close to theatrical perfection,' declared *Cue* magazine, 'as we are likely to see on-screen in our time.'

Bing Crosby won particular praise for his depiction of the self-pitying Frank Elgin, but the unexpected power and poignancy that Grace displayed in the title role was equally acclaimed. 'Kelly extends her range down to the bottoms of un-glamour, dead-faced discouragement,' wrote Archer Winsten in the *New York Post*. 'She gives it everything a great actress could.' In the *New York Times*, Bosley Crowther described Grace's acting as 'intense' and 'perceptive'. She had made a major contribution, the critic wrote, to a 'trenchant, intense, and moving film . . . one of the fine and forceful pictures of the year'. The movie was released just in time to be eligible for the following spring's Oscar awards, and in January 1955 the New York Drama Critics' Circle provided a most promising omen. They presented Grace with their award for Best Actress of 1954.

By now there was scarcely a magazine that had not done its cover story on Grace Kelly, though the writers often found fresh material difficult to gather. Grace would not allow MGM's publicity department to give out her vital statistics, and she declined to answer questions that she considered too personal – 'What do you wear in bed?' being at the top of the proscribed list. (Marilyn Monroe's memorable answer – 'Chanel No. 5.') Extracting a personal anecdote from Grace Kelly, complained one reporter, was 'like trying to chip granite with a toothpick'. 'A Grace Kelly anecdote?' cheerfully agreed an unnamed friend. 'I don't think Grace would let an anecdote happen to her.'

But Grace's inscrutability became the story itself, and this served to enhance her image of intelligent refinement. 'A person has to keep something to herself,' she said, 'or your life is just a layout in a magazine.' She was not cultivating mystery for the narcissistic reasons of a Dietrich or Garbo. Her rationale smacked of modernity and thorough good sense, and if a writer worked hard enough, Grace would come up with the goods. When she spoke to Hedda Hopper, she was positively loquacious:

> I have a phobia about telephones, and will avoid them if it's possible. As a little girl, I used to run so I wouldn't have to answer the phone . . .
> *Do you have any eccentricities?*
> I hate to drive a car . . . I am not a good driver. That's probably why I don't like to drive . . .
> *Why don't you drink when you're working?*
> I have a tendency to put on weight quickly, so I don't take anything during the week . . .
> *Do you think an actor would make a good husband?*
> No. But also I don't think someone outside of the business would make a good husband either.

Would you be willing to give up your career for marriage?
I don't know. I'd like to keep my career. I'll have to wait, and make that choice when the time comes.

The cover of *Time* magazine provided the ultimate accolade. 'Grace Kelly – Gentlemen Prefer Ladies,' ran the cover line on 31 January 1955, below a handsome photograph of Grace. The magazine had some shrewd things to say about the nature of Grace's appeal – 'she inspires licit passion' – and it corrected the common misconception about her wealthy Philadelphia background: 'She is neither Main Line nor a debutante.' The piece was almost totally admiring, and it was only the Kelly family who could not think of a nice thing to say. 'We'd hoped she would give it up,' said her mother of her acting. 'Those movie people,' added her father, 'lead pretty shallow lives.' 'I don't generally approve of these oddballs she goes out with,' remarked Kell with reference to Oleg Cassini. 'I wish she would go out with the more athletic type. But she doesn't listen to me any more.'

Kell spoke truer than he knew. Grace was not paying the slavish heed she once had done to being on the Kelly team. Spending more and more time creating a life for herself, she could stand a little sniping from Henry Avenue, for she had bigger battles to fight. 'Last week,' reported *Time*, 'MGM's Production Boss Dore Schary summoned Grace to Holly-wood to propose a new picture . . . After two days of talk, Grace was still noncommittal: she would wait, she said coolly, until she could see the completed script.'

It was nearly six months since Grace Kelly had made her last movie, and her employers' patience was beginning to wear thin. Dore Schary was only recently installed as MGM's head of production in succession to the great Louis B. Mayer. His producers were constantly bringing him projects that they considered right for Grace, and it was embarrassing that he could not deliver the services of the studio's hottest property.

The question of yet another loan-out to a rival studio brought matters to a head. Early in 1955, Hollywood's most talked about project was the Warner Bros. production of *Giant*, due to be directed by George Stevens and featuring James Dean. MGM had already agreed to loan out Elizabeth Taylor for the female lead. But she was recovering from the Caesarean birth of her second son, and it was uncertain that she would be well enough to begin filming in April. Grace was George Stevens's favoured substitute, and Grace herself liked the part. 'Could it be', speculated Sidney Skolsky in his column of 23 February 1955, 'that Grace Kelly is holding out with MGM because she wants to be loaned to George Stevens for *Giant*?'

Louella Parsons put the question directly to Dore Schary, and she got a very sharp response. 'We are not going to loan out Miss Kelly for *Giant* or any other picture,' declared the production chief firmly. 'She's coming back to MGM very shortly. We've already agreed to loan out Elizabeth Taylor, and that's that. We feel Miss Kelly has certain obligations to us. After all, we were the first to give her a chance. All of her offers came after *Mogambo*. She has a contract, and she has only made two movies for us.'

The MGM scripts which were currently in front of Grace were *Jeremy Rodock*, the Western starring Spencer Tracy, and *Something of Value*, a screenplay based on a forthcoming novel about the Mau Mau uprising in Kenya. Neither was by any means a demeaning vehicle, but Grace wanted her next project to be more than just good enough. Kellys went for the best. Grace was not willing to be pushed along somebody else's production line, and if she was still wrestling with how to cope with this problem in her private life, she now knew how to deal with it in her career. 'I don't want to dress up a picture with just my face,' she declared with a definite fieriness. 'If anybody starts using me as scenery, I'll do something about it.' Grace was willing to admit that both *Jeremy Rodock* and *Something of Value* contained their strong points. But she had quite definitely decided, she announced in an interview in February 1955, that neither of them was 'right for me personally'.

It might have been different if Grace had been living in Hollywood and had made her decision public after a long and earnest meeting with Dore Schary. But she remained adamantly in New York, supervising the decorating of her new flat, and passing out her none-too-flattering opinions of MGM's taste in the interviews she was giving to promote her Hitchcock and Perlberg/Seaton movies for Paramount. Grace had developed a definite edge since her travails with her parents over Cassini. Nor was her respect for MGM increased by the bosomy, green-draped lady that was currently looming over Broadway advertising *Green Fire*. 'The dress isn't even in the picture,' she remarked with scorn.

MGM responded in kind. On 26 February 1955, Loew's Inc. (MGM's parent company) informed Grace by telegram that she was 'instructed' to report to the office of Sam Zimbalist, Jr, the producer of *Jeremy Rodock*, at MGM's headquarters in Culver City – and when the star failed to appear, another telegram followed. At the beginning of March 1955, Loew's notified Grace that her contract with the studio was suspended. She would no longer be paid, nor could she make a motion picture anywhere in the world, at the risk of legal action.

Grace went through the motions of distress. She was 'bewildered and disappointed,' she confessed. But she did not sound too brokenhearted. 'I'm afraid,' she said, 'I'll have to stop decorating my new apartment for the present.'

Ten years earlier Grace's suspension could have constituted

something close to catastrophe. Ten years later suspension did not exist, for her disagreements with MGM were played out in what proved to be the twilight of the old studio system. Built around different packages of independent acting and production creativity – Hitchcock for one project, Perlberg and Seaton for the next – Grace Kelly's career foreshadowed the free-for-all of modern Hollywood in which the studios serve as bankers for competing syndicates of talent. In these syndicates, agents are the brokers and stars are the kings – and in March 1955, Grace Kelly was a star. MGM needed her more than she needed them.

A sudden flurry of front-office meetings and memos in Culver City showed that the studio had belatedly woken up to this. A valid disagreement that was really quite resolvable had somehow got out of hand. It was not unusual for studios to discipline their stars for unprofessionalism – fits of temperament, laziness, arriving late on set. But no one could accuse Grace Kelly of that. She was a byword for her reliability and her capacity for hard work. The dispute arose, in fact, because Grace took her profession more seriously than MGM did.

The studio's biggest mistake was its timing. In February Grace had been nominated for an Oscar for her role in *The Country Girl*, and the awards ceremony was due to be held in a few weeks' time. The word around the Academy was that Grace had a very good chance in her category. So there was every possibility that, before March was over, MGM would turn out to have suspended the Best Actress of 1954.

Bernie Thau, the studio's head of talent, moved quickly. Grace still had not given a final 'no' to *The Barretts of Wimpole Street*, he reported to a meeting of MGM executives on 18 March 1955. He proposed that they accept her refusal of *Jeremy Rodock*, while naming *The Barretts* as her provisional new project. This would save face for both studio and star, and they could discuss *The Barretts* and other projects with Grace in due course. On 21 March 1955, Dore Schary formally announced the lifting of the suspension. 'We respect Grace,' he told the press, 'and we want to do everything possible for her during this important time in her life when she is up for an Academy Award.'

It was an unqualified victory for the actress and a tribute to the stature that she had won in a very short time on her own. Now the question arose, could she win the Oscar as well? Carrying off an Academy Award is a complex equation of studio politics, popular sentiment, and the intangible chemistry of what the Hollywood herd instinct defines, that year, as being deserving. All the nominated performances are usually meritorious, so pure acting ability tends to be the least important factor.

In 1954 Grace's rivals for Best Actress were Judy Garland (*A Star Is Born*), Dorothy Dandridge (*Carmen Jones*), Audrey Hepburn (*Sabrina*), and Jane Wyman (*Magnificent Obsession*). Wyman generated the least excitement. Dorothy Dandridge was non-white, and was considered fortunate to be included among the nominees – it was another decade before Sidney Poitier became the first black to win an Oscar in the Best Actor category. Audrey Hepburn had won Best Actress the previous year for *Roman Holiday*.

That left Grace and Judy Garland as the main contenders. 'Many are backing Judy,' reported Sidney Skolsky on 30 March 1955, 'because she never won an Oscar and they say it's about time.' Difficult and unreliable though she was, little Dorothy from Kansas was one of Hollywood's own. Grace's competing claim to sentiment was that, as a hardworking newcomer who had only just established the outlines of her glamorous persona, she had been brave enough to go against type and debeautify herself as the drab and downtrodden Georgie Elgin.

Bob Hope's opening monologue, on the stage of the RKO Pantages Theater on the night of 30 March 1955, showed how Grace was already regarded by her peers as something of a trouper. 'I just wanna say,' he cracked, 'they should give a special award for bravery to the producer who produced a movie *without* Grace Kelly.'

When Grace had emerged from her limousine outside the Pantages in her ice-blue satin evening gown, she had drawn the biggest fusillade of flashbulbs of the night. It was a far cry from her première evening with Dominick Dunne only eighteen months earlier. Grace had not judged it politic to bring Oleg Cassini along, so her entourage comprised Edith Head, who had designed her dress, and Don Hartman, the chief of production at Paramount. Judy Garland was not at the theatre. Two days before the show, she had gone into labour, giving birth to a son, Joey Luft. But NBC had their cameras waiting outside her hospital room in case she turned out to be the winner.

As a dramatic occasion, the Academy Awards for 1954 fell somewhat flat. To save time, NBC decided to tidy away the lists of nominees by rolling them as a sort of title sequence at the beginning of the programme, and in their absence it became clear that the recitation of the names in each category was an essential ingredient of the suspense. But when William Holden stepped up with the envelope containing the name of the Best Actress, the tension was palpable. A gutsy but frequently charmless old stager was pitted against an equally gutsy new girl who had worked very hard at being charm personified. Holden himself made no secret of his delight as he read out Grace's name. He had a broad smile across his face, and there were cheers and spontaneous cries of 'Bravo!' from Grace's supporters in the crowd. Grace herself was quite lost for words. 'The thrill of this moment', she said, 'prevents me from saying exactly what I feel.' Then, in front of the whole theatre and a television audience of millions, the ice maiden burst into tears.

Up on the third floor of the hospital, Sid Luft, Judy Garland's husband, was frank in his disgust. 'Fuck the Academy Awards,' he said, putting his arms around his wife as the TV cameramen unplugged their equipment and started to go home. 'You've got yours in the incubator.' Judy Garland herself never bothered to hide her opinion that she had been gypped, sniffing at the thought of Grace Kelly 'taking off her fucking make-up and grabbing MY Oscar'. Judy Garland received over a thousand telegrams of condolence following the ceremony – her most treasured coming from Groucho Marx. 'Dear Judy,' he wired, 'this is the biggest robbery since Brink's.'

Forty years later, one can see what he meant. *A Star Is Born* – and *Carmen Jones*, for that matter – live on today as infinitely fresher and more original creations than *The Country Girl*, which seems ponderous and dated by comparison. Grace's thoroughly worthy performance lacks the spark of her classic Grace Kelly roles. Dare one say it? – Georgie Elgin is actually dull. When the New York drama critics voted Grace best actress of 1954 it was for her work on all three of her releases that year – *Dial M* and *Rear Window* as well as *The Country Girl* – and there was a sense in which the voters of the Academy were saying the same. *The Country Girl* was by no means Grace Kelly's finest movie, but it was her Oscar movie.

It was a wonderful night. Marlon Brando won the Oscar for Best Actor for his role in *On the Waterfront*, and success made him positively jovial. He happily posed with his arm around Grace, kissing her twenty times or more until the photographers had got all the pictures they needed, and Grace seemed to enjoy the experience as well. 'I can't believe they were saying my name,' she sobbed, breaking into tears again.

Don Richardson had just finished watching the show on television with a group of friends in New York, when the telephone rang. It was Grace calling long distance from Hollywood. 'Thank you, darling,' she said. It was an evening for celebration and good feeling, and even Jack Kelly's predictable comment wired to newspapers across the country could not spoil the euphoria. 'I can't believe it,' declared her father. 'I simply can't believe Grace won. Of the four children, she's the last one I'd expected to support me in my old age.'

'This is the one night I wished I smoked and drank,' exclaimed Grace, happily looking around the revellers who had joined her at Paramount's after-the-show celebration at Romanoff's. Brando's success had meant disappointment for Bing Crosby, the other fancied contender in the Best Actor category, but, debonair in white-tie and tails, the crooner raised his glass with Humphrey Bogart, another failed nominee, at what Bogart cheerfully described as 'the bad losers' table'.

It was the small hours of the morning by the time that Grace got back to her bungalow in the Bel Air Hotel. She was all alone, with only her Oscar for company, and she set the little metal manikin on the top of her dressing table. She lay down on the bed, she later remembered, and looked across the room at the statuette that represented so much effort and hope and sacrifice, the culmination of her life and work to that point.

'There we were,' she recalled, 'just the two of us. It was terrible. It was the loneliest moment of my life.'

FOURTEEN

Photo Opportunity

HOWELL CONANT was a rising young New York fashion photographer when *Photoplay* commissioned him to shoot a cover of Grace Kelly in the spring of 1955. It was just a few weeks before she won her Academy Award.

Photoplay was the leading American movie magazine. Its editors favoured photos in an idealized style – limelit star portraits of the sort that are framed in gilt in cinema lobbies – and Conant gave them exactly what they wanted. His *Photoplay* cover displayed Grace as an untouchable icon. Shot against a background of bright rose pink, her complexion seemed air-brushed in its perfection. She was like alabaster, an image of fantasy beyond reach.

But Howell Conant felt sure there was more. He found Grace an intriguing and rather challenging person to meet. Beneath the crispness of the professional model, he could detect daring, intelligence, and a certain vulnerability – the whole complex of contradictory impulses that made up her screen persona, and he felt certain there must be a way of capturing this personality in an image that moved beyond the traditional glossy star portrayal.

Conant soon got his chance to find out. *Collier's* magazine had commissioned him to shoot a behind-the-scenes look at the new young sensation from Philadelphia, and the photographer suggested he might follow his subject around New York, taking impromptu photos for a day.

'No,' said Grace, 'I don't like that sort of thing.'

A few weeks later, Conant discovered what she did like. The star was in Jamaica, taking a vacation with her sister Peggy, and she suggested that *Collier's* might send their man down to the Caribbean to photograph her there, snorkeling and collecting shells along the beach.

Conant had been experimenting with underwater photography, and he had an idea for a different sort of pose – Grace rising from the water wearing a diver's face mask. They tried it a few times, standing on tiptoe in the ocean to dodge the sea urchins on the bottom. Grace was wearing just a trace of eye shadow, a smear of waterproof make-up that she had borrowed from the wife of the hotel manager, and Conant suddenly realized that the rubber mask was a mistake. Her face looked better without it. So Grace ducked down and surfaced seven times just as she was – and the eighth time, bingo! Howell Conant had got the photo he was looking for.

Conant's picture of Grace Kelly's sculptured head rising damp and fresh from the waters of the Caribbean captured all the allure of the actress's ambiguous beauty. It was timeless. It could stand today on a Lancôme or Clinique counter: the swanlike neck, the drop of seawater for an earring, the staring eyes with their level look of appraisal – or is it invitation? Chastely but intriguingly enveiled by the ocean, Grace stares up at the camera, exuding wholesomeness and freshness – and a sexuality of extraordinary power.

Out of the water, Conant took another sequence of pictures, using a device that he had never tried before, the mechanical motorwind. Sports and action photographers were just starting to use this recently invented accessory, but

Conant reckoned that it might have potential for portrait work. He noticed how Grace reacted each time she heard the shutter. She was a performer to the marrow. 'She'd start to smile,' he remembers, 'and click, click, click, she would smile more and more and more. The more the camera hummed, the more she reacted.'

Howell Conant got his pictures back to New York, and he never had to look for work again. When his images of Grace Kelly appeared in *Collier's* that summer, they caused a sensation. They had a vigour and freshness that lifted them above conventional glamour photography. Statuesque in a canoe, making a speech to a peeled orange, wearing a man's dress shirt with her hair scraped back simply from her forehead, Grace came vibrantly alive – young and uninhibited, on the very crest of her own personal wave. Conant had accomplished the still-life equivalent of Alfred Hitchcock. His shots glowed with the serenity and wildness of this woman. Janet Leigh, Doris Day, Natalie Wood – the up-and-coming stars of the era – queued to have Conant work the same alchemy for them, and he became the hottest property on Madison Avenue. Advertisers from Pond's cold cream to Eastman Kodak beat a path to the Conant studio on East Thirty-fifth Street, anxious to bottle and sell the elegance, class or whatever it was that the photographer had captured in his few days with Grace Kelly on a Jamaica beach.

'Almost everything happened,' remembers Conant, 'after I became famous with Grace.' It was the making of Conant's career, and it was also the beginning of an extraordinary collaboration between subject and photographer. Whenever Grace had any say in who was to take her picture – and she developed a great deal of say as time went by – she insisted that Howell should be the one. Conant, for his part, would plan out the photo sessions ahead of time with Grace, then go through the contact prints with her afterwards, editing the images according to her wishes, and destroying any of which she did not approve. He was happy that she should have the final say, while Grace had found the man she wanted to shoot the movie of her life.

Howell Conant came from a family of portrait photographers. His father was a professional photographer, as were two uncles and his grandfather before that, operating small clapboard portrait-studios on the main streets of Wisconsin. The Conants memorialized the rituals of Midwest immigrant life – christenings, weddings, high school graduations – and from this background Conant learned the tricks of the portrait trade: throw a shadow on a bald head so it does not look shiny, shoot from above to make a square chin look round.

'Grace's jawline was the only slight problem,' Conant says today, recalling the technicalities of shooting his favourite subject. 'You didn't have to flatter Grace. She always looked good. You just had to be a little selective about the angles. Six inches this way, that way, up or down – that's all I needed to move to get the jaw right.'

Blending soft-focus glamour with hard-edged reportage, Conant's pictures made fantasy credible and graspable – the most attainable thing in the world, it seemed. His deceptively simple-sounding definition of a good photograph was a photograph that made his subject look good, which was why Senator John F. Kennedy came to the Conant studio for a session in the mid-1950s to learn about the good and bad angles of his face. The ambitious young senator spent the best part of a day being photographed in different poses, then studying the contact prints, thus helping himself to develop the dashing, sideways glance into the middle distance which came to symbolize his style – and which also hid the fact that, when seen head on, JFK's eyes were oddly close-set.

Conant did the same for Grace. To be a success, to sell yourself – to count for just about anything in the age of celebrity – you needed the right image, and though Grace herself was naturally blessed with the right ingredients and worked hard to achieve the correct blend, it was through the lens of Howell Conant that they all came so graphically together. When people spoke of Grace Kelly as one of the classic faces of her era, it was usually a Conant photograph that they were thinking of.

Since Conant personally was a well-built, tough and very attractive man, the question inevitably arose as to the nature of his relationship with Grace. Some of her friends suspected a holiday fling. A handsome young couple thrown together on a Caribbean island? How could attraction not bloom? But the photographer himself denies it flatly. 'I should be so lucky,' is his gentlemanly, if not quite total dismissal of the idea today. The intimacy that mattered to Howell Conant was the private moment of union through the viewfinder that he was to enjoy with Grace as actress and princess literally thousands of times from 1955 until her death in 1982 – that momentary yet eternal coupling of photographer and subject which holds magic for both of them, and which, in the case of Grace and Howell Conant, generated magic sufficient for millions of others to share.

From Jamaica, Grace returned briefly to New York, before setting off again almost immediately for the south of France. Being an Oscar-winning film star was really quite fun. She had been invited to head the American delegation to the Cannes Film Festival, a high-profile position with only the gentlest of duties attached. So May 1955 found Grace Kelly on the Riviera for the second time. It was exactly eleven months since the filming of *To Catch a Thief*.

By 1955 the Cannes Film Festival was already the most glamorous trade show in the world. Originally founded to compete with Mussolini's Venice Film Festival, Cannes was just in the process of eclipsing its Italian rival – thanks, in no small part, to an incident that had occurred the previous year. Arriving with his wife at the opening luncheon of the 1954 festival, Robert Mitchum had been confronted by a shapely French starlet, Simone Sylva, who walked up to him and boldly let drop her bikini top. Photographers rushed forward to record the spectacle, prompting the chivalrous Mr Mitchum to extend his hands in an attempt to shield the modesty of the anything-but-modest Ms Sylva. The resulting image – for which, some felt, Mr Mitchum kept his hands in place just a moment or two longer than duty alone could strictly justify – was flashed to newspapers around the world, and it defined the enticing perfume of sun-oil and reckless abandon which has wreathed the Cannes Festival ever since.

In 1954, however, the festival's organizers considered the incident a serious embarrassment. Most of them belonged to that school of Frenchman which regard *le cinéma* with a reverence beyond anything that normal Americans would dream of mustering for the movies, and they huffily requested Simone Sylva to leave Cannes forthwith. For 1955 they made a conscious decision to head their image for the high ground and they invited Grace Kelly to serve as the head of the Hollywood delegation. 'They thought she had class and she was regal,' remembered Grace's old friend, Rupert Allan, 'and they needed that kind of thing after what they had been through.'

Allan had been coming to Cannes for several years, helping to smooth relationships between visiting Americans and the French organizers, and as an unofficial public relations adviser to Grace, he was the ideal person to approach her on the festival's behalf. 'I called her in New York,' he remembered, 'to tell her that if she agreed to go to Cannes she could come back any time. The ticket would be open-ended, and it was spring in Europe.'

The previous spring, Grace had organized herself a Riviera love affair by inviting Oleg Cassini to follow her to Cannes. That had led to a painful eleven months trying to translate her holiday adventure into real life, and her professional life remained in continuing confusion. In the aftermath of her Oscar victory, Grace was still trying to work out some modus vivendi with MGM. Love and romance were not at the forefront of her priorities.

But they came looking for her just the same. Jean-Pierre Aumont happened to be at Cannes in 1955, and when he heard that his old girlfriend was there as well, he went off immediately in search of her. 'I found her at a dinner,' he remembers. 'There were lots of important people. But that didn't matter. It was like magic. She was so pleased to see me, and I felt just the same. It was as if we were meeting and falling in love with each other for the very first time.'

Grace was out on the swimming raft once again. Wet sand, red ochre dust, long lunches in vine-shaded, hillside restaurants – for the second time in a year she played out the delicious details of a Côte d'Azur romance. The pleasures of discovery were mingled with the comfort of reunion with an old acquaintance. Casual and easygoing, Jean-Pierre was tuned several notches lower than Oleg Cassini. He did not stand on his dignity. In his blue-and-white striped T-shirt and rope-soled canvas shoes, the Frenchman was very much the matelot. He and Grace were lovers, but they were also old friends. A press photographer caught the pair of them chatting one lunchtime, heads together, ice bucket at the elbow, fingers intertwined, and they did not give a damn. 'I am deeply in love with Grace Kelly,' Jean-Pierre stated confidently to the French journalist Bernard Valéry, and sitting beside him, Grace smiled in happy confirmation. She decided that she would take advantage of Rupert Allan's offer to extend her stay when the festival ended. She would go up to Paris with Jean-Pierre and meet his family. It was spring in Europe, after all.

There was just one chore in connection with her festival duties. Sharing confidences with Jean-Pierre one lunchtime, Grace let slip that she was planning to cancel a meeting she had scheduled the following afternoon with Prince Rainier of Monaco at his palace some ninety minutes along the coast. It was a photo opportunity arranged by the French magazine *Paris Match*. There were gardens to walk through and the princely hand to shake. But Grace had a festival reception back in Cannes quite early in the evening, and a hairdressing appointment before that. She could not fit everything in.

Jean-Pierre was horrified. 'Grace,' he exclaimed, 'you can't possibly do that! The man is a reigning prince. He has invited, and you have accepted. You can't just say "I'm going to the hairdresser." '

The photo opportunity was the brainchild of Pierre Galante, a *Paris Match* journalist who had hatched it with his editor as a variation on the magazine's standard Cannes Festival cover. Galante was a dashing, John Robie-like character, who had used his job as a reporter as a cover for Resistance work during the war, helping Jews and anti-Nazis to escape from Vichy France. Galante had recently wooed and married Olivia de Havilland, whom he met at the Cannes Film Festival, and now he used his film-star wife to create the setting in which he could sell his Monaco cover story to Grace.

Galante contrived to arrange the sleeper reservations on the Blue Train down from Paris to the Cannes Film Festival so that Grace's compartment would be in the same carriage as himself and his wife. The two women had not met before, but they had their celebrity in common. The railway follows

Image and reality. Grace Kelly at the age of twenty-three.

Smile for Daddy. Grace, age five, and her father, Jack Kelly, perform for the Philadelphia Bulletin on the beach at Ocean City, New Jersey, July 1935.

First pose. Grace Patricia Kelly, born Philadelphia, November 12, 1929.

Flower girls. Grace, age six, with Lizanne, the younger of her two sisters.

Model family. The Kellys at their Ocean City home in the 1940s. From left: Peggy, Grace, Jack, Lizanne, Margaret, and Jack Jr.—"Kell."

Childhood idol. Grace's beloved uncle, playwright George Kelly, shortly before he won a Pulitzer Prize in 1926.

Facing page: Sporting hero. Grace and her brother, Kell, on the Schuylkill River in the mid-1940s.

Far right: 3901 Henry Avenue —the Kelly home on the hill above East Falls, Philadelphia.

The Kelly look. Working as a model in the late 1940s, Grace advertised dairy products (above) and bug spray (top). Landing a few prized fashion assignments (right), she made her greatest mark (facing page) promoting cigarettes as the "Old Gold Girl," and on numerous magazine covers as a glamorous version of the girl-next-door.

"For a TREAT instead of a TREATMENT
— have an

Old Gold"

Old Gold

Early loves—Harper Davis

Alex D'Arcy

Don Richardson

The Shah of Iran

Philippe of the Waldorf

Gene Lyons

Soap opera start. Grace in 1952 as a chorus girl in one of her TV roles.

Hollywood debut. Grace in an early screen test.

Romancing the "King." Grace costarring with Clark Gable in <u>Mogambo</u>, 1952.

Quaker wife. Grace with Gary Cooper in <u>High Noon</u>, 1951.

Provoking gossip. Grace with Ray Milland in <u>*Dial M for Murder*</u>*, 1953.*

Girl about town. Grace with James Stewart in <u>*Rear Window*</u>*, 1953.*

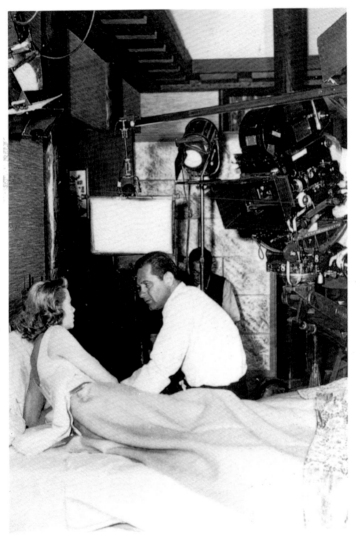

Playing husband and wife. Grace with William Holden in <u>The Bridges at Toko-Ri</u>, *1954.*

Private rendezvous. Grace lunches with Jean-Pierre Aumont in the spring of 1955.

Unofficially engaged. Grace with designer Oleg Cassini in 1954.

In the hands of Alfred Hitchcock: To Catch a Thief, 1954.

Movie in Monaco: on location with Cary Grant, a lifelong friend.

Brave transformation. Grace dresses down for <u>The Country Girl</u> (left) and wins the Oscar—Best Actress of 1954.

a picturesque route along the sea as it approaches Cannes, passing through little tunnels and beside parasol-decked beaches, and it was standing in the corridor with Grace and Olivia de Havilland, looking out at the sparkling blue waters of the Mediterranean, that Galante proposed his idea of a photo session with the Prince of Monaco. As befitted a star, Grace was politely noncommittal. She did not say yes, and she did not say no. As befitted a journalist, Galante phoned Monaco the moment he got off the train and made a definite date with the palace.

Grace woke up late on the morning of the meeting, feeling cornered. She did not particularly want to go to Monaco, but she felt that she should be a good girl. She washed her hair and plugged in her hairdryer. Nothing happened. France's electrical workers had called a strike the previous evening – which meant that there would be no power for the chambermaid to iron the wrinkles out of the elegant dress that Grace had mentally earmarked for her princely encounter. The one unrumpled frock in her wardrobe was a shiny black taffeta evening creation printed with large pink and green cabbage roses. Her friend Judy Kanter used to pull her leg about it, saying that the dress made Grace look like a pear. But it was hardly Oscar night. The photo session was only for a French picture magazine. 'It's not like,' Grace told her girlfriend when she got back to America, 'anyone will ever see those pictures again.'

Pierre Galante thought that the frock looked just fine when Grace finally appeared in the hotel lobby, but that she needed a hat. A lady could not shake hands with the prince, he explained, without wearing something on her head. So Grace dashed back up to her room to improvise a tiara of artificial flowers woven into her simply combed and still undried hair. It was one thing to look wild and wanton for a Caribbean photo shoot. It was quite another to be throwing herself together for an occasion like this. Grace had come close to dropping the whole Monaco enterprise for the sake of a hairdressing appointment, and now here she was, rushing to meet a prince with her hair scraped back unstyled – and still soaking wet.

By the time that Grace and Galante were driving out of Cannes in a large Studebaker rented for the occasion, the timetable allowed no margin for error. They had little more than an hour to get to Monaco, and they were just getting up speed when the pursuing Peugeot that contained *Paris Match*'s photographers failed to heed the Studebaker's brake lights. The Peugeot drove smartly into the back of the rental car, losing another ten minutes. The sixth of May 1955 was a day that tested the serenity and professionalism of Grace Kelly to the full.

The Principality of Monaco has a surface area of 482 acres – which is something less than one square mile. Once masters of quite a lengthy stretch of Riviera coastline, Monaco's ruling Grimaldi princes were compelled to surrender most of their territories to France in 1861, and since then they have ruled over no more than the mini-city that clusters round their picturesque harbour, with its palace on one side and the casino on the other.

Speaking French and using the French franc, Monaco has formalized its strange status under the wing of France into a complicated series of agreements and protocols with its neighbour – but on 6 May 1955, the most important aspect of that status for *Paris Match*'s speeding and dented caval-cade of cars was the absence of any border formalities that might delay their arrival for their three o'clock meeting with His Serene Highness Prince Rainier III. As they drove down towards the harbour, they could see the prince's personal banner flying from the ramparts of his pink palace on the rock.

It was already after three, but Grace was complaining of an empty stomach. She had had no proper breakfast or lunch, and she was not so awestruck by her forthcoming encounter that she was willing to go without something to eat. So Galante headed his cars for the Hôtel de Paris, Monaco's white, wedding-cake hotel beside the casino, and snatched a sandwich from the bar. Grace was munching hungrily on this snack, scattering crumbs over the car, as Galante drove the steep road up the rock, rehearsing his apologies for their late arrival at the palace.

He need not have bothered. The prince was still entertaining a lunch party at his Cap Ferrat villa down the coast.

'I think he's very rude to keep us waiting like this,' complained Grace, worrying about her early evening reception duty back in Cannes. 'Let's get out of here.'

It was a definitely testy Miss Kelly who finally shook hands with Prince Rainier III of Monaco shortly after four o'clock on that May afternoon. The photographs show a short and portly, rather unprincely-looking prince, wearing sunglasses, a boxy blue suit with patch pockets and flaps, and a most disarming smile. His Serene Highness – age thirty-one and never married – was clearly delighted to be meeting a pretty blonde film star, and he displayed not the slightest remorse at being an hour late for his appointment.

Would Miss Kelly care to visit the state apartments? The prince was unfazed to learn that his guest had already done the tour to fill in the time spent awaiting his arrival. So he led her instead through the gardens to his private zoo, where he put his arms through the bars of one of his tiger cages and fondled the beast as if it were a tabby cat.

Talking about it afterwards, Grace commented on the prince's familiarity with his wild animals. It was an exotic, curiously princely aptitude to have. It was surprising that Rainier spoke absolutely perfect, unaccented, upper-class English – he had had an English nanny and had been to a British public school – and, all things considered, the visit had ended on a considerably more cheerful note than it started.

But Grace complained to Rupert Allan that the whole business had taken far too much time and trouble for what it was worth. If she was going to do that sort of thing again, she said, then she wanted to do it properly.

'How was it? How did you find the Prince?' Jean-Pierre Aumont enquired eagerly when the lovers were reunited that evening.

'Charming,' replied Grace. 'I think he's very charming.'

Then she fell silent. What more could you say about a photo opportunity?

FIFTEEN

The Swan

GRACE KELLY and Jean-Pierre Aumont made no attempt to conceal the delight they took in love the second time around. When they went up to Paris at the conclusion of the Cannes Film Festival in the middle of May 1955, they stayed in adjoining suites in the Raphael Hotel. Hand in hand, they made a very public assault together on the sights and excitements of Paris. Jean-Pierre was on his home turf, and he took pride in introducing Grace to friends and colleagues like Jean-Louis Barrault, the Laurence Olivier of France. Impulsive, optimistic, and happily filling his mind with all sorts of ventures for the future, Jean-Pierre saw Grace as the woman with whom he would spend the rest of his life.

'When a man is deeply in love with a person of Miss Kelly's quality,' he told the press, 'marriage is obviously what one would dream of.'

Grace was scarcely less exuberant. 'It has been wonderful to discover Paris in Jean-Pierre's company,' she told reporters as she flew back to America on 18 May. She saw 'no obstacles to marrying a Frenchman,' she said. 'Love is not a question of nationality.' Noting that her boyfriend conducted his acting career on both sides of the Atlantic, she indicated that she would not be averse to doing the same herself. 'I could be very happy,' she said, 'dividing my time between the United States and France.'

The ingredients of a new scenario were shaping in Grace's head. Where there was love, there had to be marriage, particularly since Jean-Pierre was conveniently single – a widower uncompromised by any divorce entanglements. During her final days in Paris, Grace met and played happily with Marie-Christine, Aumont's nine-year-old daughter by the actress Maria Montez, who had died four years earlier. Things would certainly have been less complicated if Jean-Pierre had been Catholic rather than Jewish. 'I'd rather you married a nigger than a Jew,' old man Kelly had once told his daughter. But in the last year Grace's father had finally consented to the idea of his youngest child, Lizanne, marrying Donald LeVine, the Jewish boyfriend whom she had been dating since college days, and the wedding was scheduled for the following month. Grace was going to be one of the maids of honour, and she flew back to the United States in May 1955 with the news that Jack Kelly could look forward to the prospect of a second Jewish son-in-law.

'We got engaged,' remembers Jean-Pierre Aumont. 'It was not official, but we were committed to each other. We thought we were going to get married.'

It was an uncanny replay of the previous summer – the Riviera romance, the unofficial engagement, the dashing and unconventional Latin lover – and when Grace arrived home, she found the reaction was very much the same. The interviewers pried, the gossip columnists speculated disapprovingly, and her studio evinced not the slightest enthusiasm for her latest romantic adventure. Most serious of all – though Grace could hardly have expected otherwise – her parents created endless difficulties.

'They raised hell,' remembers Jean-Pierre Aumont. 'Both

of them were very strict. She told me that about them – especially her father.'

The couple wrote letters to each other and struggled with the delays and expense of the transatlantic telephone system. It was the autumn of 1955 before Jean-Pierre was able to get to America to see Grace again, and by then it was clear that his moment had passed. The bloom was off the rose. There were too many arguments to be won – 'I was Jewish, I had a little girl, I was French,' Aumont remembers. When the French film star took a hard look at the obstacles besetting marriage to Grace, he had to acknowledge, like Oleg Cassini before him, that he could not heave the stone uphill alone. Grace herself was not admitting defeat, but now she was home, she was no longer committed to him with her previous abandon. The situation seemed to demand some extra and ultimate signal of decisiveness from her that was not forthcoming.

'There were a lot of things,' says Jean-Pierre today, 'that were not exactly right . . . Anyhow, I was perfectly happy with how it all turned out, and she too. Finally' – he smiles philosophically – 'the best is for the best.'

'Gracie,' asked Ma Kelly casually when she heard that Jean-Pierre would be coming to America, 'shall I ask Mr Aumont to visit us in Philadelphia?'

'Mother,' replied Grace evenly, 'that's entirely up to you.'

'I knew then,' Mrs Kelly later related, 'that she was not planning to marry him. She was still waiting for her prince.'

Mrs Kelly was talking figuratively, of course – aided by a fair measure of hindsight. At the time that she discussed Jean-Pierre Aumont with Grace in the late summer of 1955, she knew only that her daughter had had a fleeting and formal meeting with Rainier of Monaco in the course of the Cannes Film Festival.

But unknown to her mother – or to anyone else – more

had come of that brief encounter than Grace admitted at the time. In 1989, in the course of interviews with the American writer Jeffrey Robinson, Prince Rainier revealed for the first time that his rushed handshaking with Grace on the afternoon of 6 May 1955 had led to a correspondence which both of them kept secret. Being a well-brought-up girl, Grace had sent the prince a thank-you letter a few days after their meeting. Rainier had been only too happy to reply to the attractive actress whose calmness and lack of movie-star mannerisms had impressed him.

'I was pleasurably surprised,' he later explained, 'because I suppose I had been influenced by what I saw on the films, and read about, and this was nothing like what I had expected.'

It was naturally polite for Grace to write back to His Highness, so by the high summer of 1955, letters were flowing steadily between the two.

Grace was a conscientious, but never a very profound, letter writer. The short, eager notes that she sprayed out to friends in her round, childish hand were testimony to genuine feeling that she could not always find the words to express. Rainier, on the other hand, was a most winning correspondent. He had a fluent command of both French and English, and while frequently cautious in his conversation, he was quite the opposite on the page – wise and quirky, with a knack for disarming honesty. Shy in real life, Rainier came alive in his private letters, which flowed long and naturally. His correspondence had the charm of making people feel that he was holding their hands as he talked to them, so it was not surprising that Grace soon came to feel that she knew her prince quite well.

The summer of 1955 was a time of personal stock-taking for Grace. Her romance with Jean-Pierre had foundered on the usual problems, while her relationship with Oleg Cassini had lost its momentum. Her Oscar had raised her professional career to a point from which it might be difficult to make much more progress – and here was a young prince come a-courting. When Judy Kanter met up with Grace that September, she was struck by her friend's strange mixture of contentment and restlessness.

Grace had invited Judy to her Fifth Avenue apartment because she said that she needed to talk – the first time in their two-and-a-half-year friendship that she had ever admitted to needing anything. Since her return from France, Grace explained, she had been trying to devote more time and energy to simple, non-career things. She was trying to focus on her family. She had helped Lizanne with her wedding. She had been enjoying long, lazy weekends down at Ocean City playing with Peggy's two little daughters, Meg and Mary Lee, and when she was in New York, she had taken to spending time with Carolyn Scott, who was now married with two little girls.

All this had set Grace to thinking. Sally Parrish was expecting. Bettina Thompson had a three-year-old. Maree Frisby's daughter, Linda, was coming up to four. Her friends were passing into a new phase. As Grace did a roll call of her contemporaries, every one of them a young mother, the tears welled up in her eyes.

'I want all of that,' she said to Judy Kanter.

Then, looking hard at her friend, as if wondering if it was safe for her to reveal something that was very, very private, she added the real problem.

'But I want more,' she said.

Grace Kelly threw herself earnestly into every new part that she played. It was a sort of therapy for her. Each new character offered her wise words to say and a fresh spirit to inhabit.

They were practical try-outs for a young woman who had encountered some difficulty in foreseeing the real-life implications of her dreams, and when she struck a dramatic note she liked, she would weave a strand of that character into her own personality.

It was a complex and interactive two-way process – the parts that appealed to her existing impulses, and the parts which helped her to locate something new in her still-developing self. But the film character that Grace was rehearsing in the late summer of 1955 as she took stock of her life and wrote letters to Prince Rainier was quite uncanny in the mirror that it held to real life. Grace was cast as Alexandra – the heroine of Ferenc Molnar's drama *The Swan* – a spirited young blonde of good family who finds herself wooed by a prince, and who is compelled to weigh the advantages and disadvantages of the royal life and to decide whether she really wants to marry him.

This anything-but-everyday dilemma struck a special chord in Grace. '*The Swan* was one role', remembers Jay Kanter, 'that she was desperately anxious to do. In fact, I think it was she who suggested it.'

Grace had played the part of Alexandra in her days as a television actress. *The Swan* had twice been a hit on Broadway in the 1920s, and now it provided a solution to Grace's long-running impasse with MGM. The studio liked the idea as well. MGM's story department and its difficult star had finally found a project upon which they could agree. Falling over himself to patch up past differences, Dore Schary said that he would take a break from his duties as studio production chief so that he could oversee the movie personally. Grace was given single top billing, the only time in her career she enjoyed that rare and exclusive eminence, and her supporting players were appropriately prestigious. Louis Jourdan was cast as Dr Agi, the handsome but penniless tutor whose role in the plot was to offer the young Alexandra romance without wealth or status. Alec Guinness played her other suitor, the wife-seeking Prince Albert, whom Guinness embellished with all the wry touches that Grace had admired on foreign-film night back in her American Academy days.

MGM decided against building themselves a backlot palace. The American fantasy of a stately home already existed in Biltmore House, the replica of a Loire château constructed by George Vanderbilt near Asheville, North Carolina, in the 1890s. Much beturreted on the outside, Biltmore House was positively monumental in its interior layout and furnishings. It laid claim to being the largest mansion in the United States, and Howell Conant went down to Asheville to shoot Grace on location there. He photographed her sitting, fresh, white and waiflike, dwarfed by the statuary of the grand staircase. He followed her through her fencing lessons as she duelled and danced time and again with Louis Jourdan – Grace had insisted on doing all the fencing scenes herself, without a stand-in. Most strangely, Conant caught the actress beside a jumble of discarded lights and filters, cut off from the rest of the production and lost in her own thoughts as she sat alone in a chair so grand and gilded that one could easily have mistaken it for a throne. It was difficult to avoid the fancy that Grace was trying on a few things for size in the weeks that she rattled round this extravagant, robber-baron dream of how a baronial home should be.

'A little too big for me!' remarked Jay Kanter wryly, shaking his head, on a visit he made down to Asheville.

'I love it!' replied Grace enthusiastically.

The Swan was not one of Grace's more memorable movies. It suffered from too many words and too little action, and its strongest lines, which explained the title and finally gave some meaning to Grace's part, were not delivered until the closing scene.

'Think what it means to be a swan,' says the prince to Alexandra, 'to glide like a dream on the smooth surface of the lake and never go on the shore. On dry land, where ordinary people walk, the swan is awkward, even ridiculous. When she waddles up the bank, she painfully resembles a different kind of bird.'

'A goose?' asks Alexandra/Grace wonderingly.

'I'm afraid so,' replies the prince. 'So there she must stay, out on the lake, silent, white, majestic. Be a bird, but never fly. Know one song, but never sing it until the moment of her death.'

This wise but rather dispiriting analysis persuades Alexandra/Grace that she should do her duty and get married to her prince. Offered the choice between a life of passion and a life of position, the heroine opts for status. She has been raised as a swan, and she decides that she must go on being a swan for ever. 'Take me in, Albert,' she says dutifully, uttering the final words of the film and putting her arm gravely through the prince's arm — no kissing — to walk with him into the palace.

It was not an ending to send audiences floating dreamily out of the theatre. *The Swan* enshrined a reality that people go to the movies to forget. But it did provide Grace with some instructive role-playing in the seriousness of life out on the lake. Professionalism, determination, composure, self-control — being a princess apparently called for qualities that were not so different from being a movie star.

Based on nothing more than one photographed handshake in *Paris Match*, European newspapers had started speculating about the possibility of a romance between Grace and the Prince of Monaco. The stories reached America, and Grace found herself having to deny them. 'There is no romance,' she told Rupert Allan indignantly. 'I've not heard one word from him – never heard one word from him, one way or the other.'

Grace's indignation was plausible. It was, on the face of it, ludicrous to suppose that there should be any romance between herself and His Serene Highness Prince Rainier III. But the fact that she felt it necessary to lie to an old friend about the letters that Rainier was now sending her on a regular basis showed the line that her thoughts were beginning to take. Real love with a real prince – might it actually be possible? Grace could not yet be sure where her secret correspondence with Rainier might be taking her, but she did know that premature disclosure and the risk of publicity could bring everything to a grinding halt. Grace the practical was taking good care of Grace the dreamer.

The filming of *The Swan* ended in December 1955 with some studio sequences shot in Hollywood, and a few days before Christmas Rupert Allan went round to see Grace for a seasonal glass of champagne. He found her packing furiously. She was due back in Philadelphia for the traditional Kelly Christmas party, and she had received news that Rainier was planning to drop in. The prince had arranged his first-ever visit to the United States. He was coming to Johns Hopkins Hospital in Baltimore, apparently for the purpose of a medical check-up, and he had asked if he could pay a social call at Henry Avenue. It seemed a curious occurrence, right out of the blue, for the Prince of Monaco to come calling at East Falls, Philadelphia, but Grace was studiedly offhand about it.

'Rupert,' she insisted, 'really, there is no romance.'

Prince Rainier wanted a wife. He was on the wrong side of thirty – 31 May 1955 had marked his thirty-second birthday.

It was a matter of dynastic necessity for him to take care of the succession, and in the eyes of some of Monaco's more influential inhabitants, it was a matter of business necessity as well.

Somerset Maugham famously described Monaco as 'a sunny place for shady people', and if anyone exemplified that Côte d'Azur cocktail of swank and scandal it was Aristotle Onassis. The Greek shipping tycoon controlled the *Société des Bains de Mer et Cercle des Étrangers*, the Sea Bathing Society and Foreigners' Club, whose quaint name belied its basic and unsentimental purpose, to extract maximum profits from Monte Carlo's famous casino and luxury hotels. The SBM was a public company, and Onassis had recently won control of it through some nimble manoeuvring on the Paris Bourse. But his investment was not living up to his expectations. The big spenders were not coming to Monaco. A decade after the Second World War, the principality had a drab and dated air. It was the fading dowager of the Riviera.

Onassis was worried about what he described as this 'legend in decline'. Monaco had lost its sparkle, he complained in 1955 to his American friend George Schlee during the cruise that he took with Schlee and Greta Garbo every summer. The place was nothing if it did not have glamour. Could not Schlee find some chic and scintillating American personality that young Prince Rainier could marry? It would attract rich Americans – and it might also put a smile on the face of the rather lugubrious prince. Onassis had all sorts of means by which he could bring a pretty girl to Monaco and make sure that she and Rainier would meet.

Schlee carried the challenge back to America to Gardner Cowles, the loquacious founder and publisher of *Look* magazine, who took great pleasure in broadcasting the story widely in later years – to the considerable irritation of Prince Rainier. The prince had not the slightest inkling of the activities of his self-appointed matchmakers, and he was less than amused by their idea of a chic and scintillating princess. Marilyn Monroe was staying with Milton Green, the photographer, not far from Cowles's home in Connecticut, and Cowles invited the star over for drinks to see how she felt about the prospect of marriage to the Prince of Monaco.

'Is he rich? Is he handsome?' Marilyn wanted to know, giggling happily at the idea of marriage to the prince whom the party disrespectfully dubbed 'Reindeer'. She had no idea where Monaco was – was it somewhere in Africa? – but she had little doubt that she could capture the heart of its retiring young ruler. 'Give me two days alone with him,' she said to Gardner Cowles, 'and of course he'll want to marry me.'

By the time Marilyn Monroe was joking over Monaco's future beside Gardner Cowles's Connecticut swimming pool, Prince Rainier was deep in correspondence with a film star who had a very different image. Struck at the start by how Grace did not conform to the normal movie-star stereotype, Rainier had felt himself increasingly drawn towards the aura of purity she evoked. He discussed her with his personal chaplain, Father Francis Tucker, an Irish-American member of the order of St Vincent de Paul, and Father Tucker took it upon himself to send Grace a little note of his own. 'I want to thank you,' he wrote, 'for showing the Prince what an American Catholic girl can be, and for the very deep impression this has left on him.'

Rainier had taken to Grace from the moment she confided in him, soon after they met, that she had not really wanted to do the photo session that brought them together. Rainier himself had felt just the same. He had been a shy child, just as Grace had been, never feeling quite adequate in the duties placed upon him by membership in a demanding and high-profile family. As adult celebrities, neither the prince nor the movie star had any intention of giving up their fame, but both were starting to betray naggings of unhappiness about it, as if they felt that their public faces did not do justice to their private selves. Grace struck Rainier as steady, constant, honest – and he also liked her sense of humour. She had the spontaneity of an American without the besetting American sin of brashness, and as she revealed more of herself to him in her letters, he came to feel he was in touch with 'someone very special'.

As a moderately good-looking prince with a yacht, a sports car and a palace on the Riviera, Rainier had never had much trouble getting girlfriends. 'My greatest difficulty', he said at the time, 'is knowing a girl long enough and intimately enough to find out if we are really soul mates as well as lovers.' Rainier's correspondence with Grace solved that problem. He later described their letters as his 'secret treasure garden' – the path that led him, step by step, towards the girl of his dreams. The challenge now was to test the dream against the reality. If Rainier and Grace were to progress beyond being pen-pals they had to devise a way to meet, some casual-but-serious context in which they could get to know each other without too much pressure – and in the summer of 1955 they received help from an unexpected quarter.

Aunt Edie and Uncle Russ Austin were Philadelphia friends and Ocean City neighbours of the Kelly family, two of the crew of loud and laughing adults who featured prominently at Henry Avenue parties. They were not blood relations to Grace, but they were 'uncle' and 'aunt' to her when she was growing up, and Uncle Russ considered the connection strong enough for him to get in touch with Rainier when the Austins arrived in Cannes in 1955. The couple were on a European summer holiday, and Aunt Edie was anxious to go to Monaco for the Red Cross Ball, the highlight of the Riviera summer season. Uncle Russ knew about Grace's meeting with the prince in the course of the Cannes Film Festival. So when the hotel concierge told them there was not a single ticket to the ball to be had by anyone on the coast – least of all by a couple of stray tourists – the Americans did not hesitate. Demonstrating all the brashness that little Grace so charmingly lacked, Uncle Russ called the palace to see if the prince could get them in.

The Kelly circle still cringes at the memory of Russ and Edie's presumption. 'We heard later that Rainier had just had his appendix taken out,' remembers Alice Godfrey. 'One of his banks [the Monaco Bank of Precious Metals] was failing, Aristotle Onassis had taken over the casino, and Uncle Russ Austin gets on the phone to tell him that *he's* got a problem.'

Uncle Russ's request ended up on the desk of Father Tucker, and the sprightly chaplain did not hesitate. He got in a car, drove to Cannes, and personally delivered two ball tickets to the Austins, compliments of Prince Rainier. The priest then sat down with the visitors, and with all the skill of a seventy-three-year-old father confessor, got them to tell him everything they knew about Grace – her parents, her local church, her family background. The Austins needed no encouraging.

Those in Monaco who disliked Francis Tucker considered him a busybody who exerted a manipulative and even sinister influence over their prince. They compared him to Rasputin, and felt their mistrust justified when his career in the royal service ended badly in the early sixties, with a scandal over choirboys. By that date, however, Francis Tucker had played matchmaker to the most spectacular and widely watched Catholic wedding service of modern times, and, as such, had more than fulfilled his mission from the Vatican, which had assigned him to the principality in 1950.

The relationship between the Catholic church and

Monaco's ruling family had been particularly close since 1858, when the local bishop had allayed the fears of Rainier's great-great-grandfather, Charles III, that the game of roulette, banned elsewhere in Europe, looked suspiciously like the immoral and forbidden pastime of gambling. In the right cause, the bishop assured the prince, gambling was no sin, and he proved it by holding a service of dedication for the new casino.

The bishop's prayers were answered in a spectacular fashion. The casino of Monte Carlo, which opened on 13 May 1858, proved the key to the modern identity of the principality, bringing prosperity to the ruling house of Grimaldi and a life without income tax for the populace as a whole. It was only right that the church should get its share in the shape of a major contribution to the construction of a grandiose white marble cathedral up on the rock beside the palace, and it was in this tradition of cooperation that Father Tucker exerted himself in 1955 to find a suitable bride for the master he referred to as 'My Lord Prince'. Russ and Edie Austin found themselves going to more than the Red Cross Ball. Father Tucker invited them up to the palace to take tea with Prince Rainier as well.

In years to come it was only natural that Aunt Edie and Uncle Russ should have come to see the contact they established with Prince Rainier and his chaplain in the summer of 1955 as the decisive moment in the romance of the century, the initiative from whose enterprise everything flowed. It was not realized at the time that Grace and Rainier were already writing to each other, and that the couple would, certainly, have contrived some way of their own to meet. But the when and the where of the meeting was definitely the work of the two Austins and Father Tucker, who, between them, fixed on Philadelphia as the first major stop on the itinerary of the prince's forthcoming trip to

America. The Austins would return Rainier's gracious hospitality by having him to lunch at their home, then they would take him over with them to Henry Avenue for the Kellys' traditional Christmas evening party. Aunt Edit took it upon herself to prime Grace for the occasion.

'He's a very nice young man,' she told her, 'and he would like to see you again.'

Edie had telephoned long distance, catching Grace while she was caught up in the shooting of *The Swan*, and the actress was carefully noncommittal on the subject of Prince Rainier.

'He's short,' she said. 'I met him' – her tone implying to her auntie that she had not been that impressed.

'Well,' persisted Edie, 'he would very much like to see you again – and I am not going to bring him along unless you promise you'll be nice to him. I don't want any of this, you know, frosty, cold-shoulder bit.' Edie had had some experience, she would explain in her retelling of the story, of how Grace 'could knock you down with a stare'.

'All right, Aunt Edie,' Grace replied, being careful to reveal not the slightest excitement. 'I'll be nice to him.'

John Pochna was Aristotle Onassis's general counsel and legal adviser. A graduate of Harvard Law School, he was a member of the bars of New York, Massachusetts and Connecticut, so when Onassis heard of Prince Rainier's plans to visit America at the end of 1955, he suggested that his attorney should go along for the ride. Pochna might be able to proffer some useful legal advice, and it would be a very good way of keeping an eye on whatever the prince and his energetic American chaplain might be up to.

Pochna had already spent some time with Rainier, and he had not been enormously impressed. The prince was a profligate golfer – he might lose as many as half a dozen balls in the course of a round – and he cut a knock-kneed figure on the tennis court. You did not often catch him in shorts. This did not sit well with Pochna, a strong and salty hunk of American physique who was not too different in build or outlook from Jack Kelly. The lawyer had been especially alarmed when, in the course of a visit to Paris, Rainier took him to a *Cage aux Folles*-style nightclub featuring drag queens. 'It was this little dingy theatre,' remembered Pochna, 'with truck drivers and all the rest of it, fondling each other.'

Pochna decided that the prince was not gay. Rainier was curious and daring – a man who stuck his arm in tigers' cages. He was also a spirit who seemed faintly bored and lost. He could be a melancholy fellow, a young man who had so many options, and nothing that he really wanted. For six years in his twenties, Rainier had had a love affair with the French actress Gisèle Pascal, living with her openly in his villa at Cap Ferrat – to the neglect of his princely duties, in the opinion of some Monégasques. Rainier himself was offhand about the liaison. 'It was fine while it lasted,' he later said, suggesting that it was never a matter of great moment to him. 'It simply ended.' But the prince did get on his boat and depart on a solitary voyage down the coast of West Africa when that 'simple' ending came about.

Pochna knew that Rainier's first-ever trip to America had something to do with the search for a mate. It was hardly a secret. One of the conditions for Monaco's strange survival into the twentieth century as a French protectorate was that the French government should approve any marriage that affected the Monégasque succession, and early in November 1955, Rainier had formally notified Paris that he would be looking for a bride in America. If things went well, he might be making a proposal.

Pochna saw the list of possible candidates drawn up by Father Tucker. Grace's name was on it, and also that of a Catholic Dupont who lived in Delaware. The prince and his priest were travelling by liner to New York, and were then planning to head south by car and train. Philadelphia would be their first stop. Father Tucker was taking a side trip to Wilmington, where he had started his career as a priest. He would be celebrating fifty years in his order, and if the Delaware inspection seemed appropriate, it could be fitted into the timetable at this point. Then the itinerary moved on southward, via Johns Hopkins in Baltimore, to finish in Florida with a scout around the wife potential of Palm Beach.

Rainier was due to embark for New York from Le Havre on 8 December 1955, and he spent the previous night in Paris. The French press had got wind of his voyage and what it might entail. A popular legend maintained that Monaco would revert to France in the event of the prince not producing an heir. In fact, the Franco-Monégasque treaty of 1918 clearly guaranteed that, in the event of the Crown falling vacant, Monaco would maintain its existing, protectorate status as 'an autonomous state'. But Rainier's daring mission for love and dynastic survival was exactly the sort of melodrama that republican France expected of its pet principality to the south, and reporters and photographers had dogged the prince most of the day.

In search of peace and quiet, Rainier took refuge in John Pochna's modest Paris apartment, a former chauffeur's quarters over a garage. The two men chatted and had a drink together, discussing the details of the coming trip. Then, as Pochna watched from an upper window, Rainier finally set out for his own lodgings, peering cautiously up and down the street to see if the coast was clear. The prince was evidently very anxious to make sure he was not observed, and when he was quite certain he was alone, he made a beeline for the nearest tree. 'He took his pecker out,' remembered Pochna, 'and he peed against the tree.'

Rainier of Monaco appeared at that moment, to John Pochna, to be a very happy prince indeed – rather like an ordinary man, in fact. The lawyer had just said a temporary farewell, since he was flying on ahead to New York to complete some other business. He would be waiting for the Monaco party when they disembarked. It was going to be quite an adventure. As Rainier zipped up his fly and stepped off into the December night, he seemed positively jaunty.

SIXTEEN

'I have made my destiny'

WHEN GRACE arrived in New York from Los Angeles on the evening of Friday, 23 December 1955, she dashed straight to Fifth Avenue, dropped her luggage with the doorman of her apartment building, then carried on out into the night. Her agent Jay Kanter was giving a Christmas party at his home in Sutton Place, and some of Grace's closest friends would be there. She was looking forward to seeing John Foreman, and also Rita Gam, who had a new boyfriend to show off.

Grace was on her most sparkling form. She chattered happily about *The Swan*, whose filming she had just finished. She talked of the Henry Avenue Christmas gathering to which she was travelling next day. Anything but jet-lagged, the actress was bubbling with energy and fun. 'I *shall* return!' she giggled to Judy Kanter as she made her way to the lift, laughing and delivering a mock salute in imitation of General Douglas MacArthur. Yet in the course of a long and convivial evening with some of her most trusted confidants, Grace Kelly gave not a hint that she had a date in Philadelphia the day after next with His Serene Highness Prince Rainier of Monaco.

The prince himself had reached New York a few days

255

previously, complete with priest and doctor – the quicksilver Father Tucker and Dr Robert Donat, a young surgeon from Nice. Donat had been in charge of the prince's appendix operation earlier that year, and now he was travelling to Johns Hopkins in Rainier's company. They made a modest entourage at their welcoming reception. 'Where's the nigger prince?' inquired Frank Cresci, the bodyguard assigned to Rainier by the New York Police Department. Like many another American, Cresci was somewhat shaky on the distinction between Monaco and Morocco. John Pochna stayed for a few drinks, then slipped off to his own family for a week. Christmas was coming, and nothing of importance could possibly occur until the new year was under way.

It was late on Christmas Day 1955 when Prince Rainier arrived at 3901 Henry Avenue in the company of his father confessor and his personal physician. The trio had had Christmas lunch with Uncle Russ and Aunt Edie, and it was getting dark as the Austins proudly escorted their unusual guests to East Falls for their long-awaited evening with the Kellys. Jack Kelly and the prince's chaplain Father Tucker hit it off at once. 'My father knew an Irish priest if ever he saw one,' remembered Peggy. ' "Father Tucker," he said, "sit down and I'll give you a cigar." '

Grace was trying very hard to be casual. She looked so cool and collected she seemed ready to deliver the 'frosty cold-shoulder bit' that Aunt Edie had feared. But her mother knew the signs. It was Grace's defence mechanism. As Ma Kelly looked at her middle daughter she could tell that Grace, in reality, was 'delightfully on edge'.

That was a considerable understatement. For the last six months Grace had been talking through her letters to this wry and often diffident man, and she had very much liked what she read. Rainier had come to occupy a special place in her own private realm of hope and imagination. But would he now stand the test of real life? Grace was a bundle of nerves. 'Christmas morning,' she later remembered, 'I was sorry I'd gone home.' Things would have been much less fraught and complicated, she reflected in a panic, if she had stayed in California. She telephoned her sister Peggy round the corner, begging her to get herself organized and to hurry to 'be over here with me'.

Rainier, for his part, had to try to forget that, personal feelings aside, he was dealing with a serious matter of state. He had given notice to the French government. He had crossed the Atlantic. As ruler of Monaco, he now had to close the deal. But if he was nervous, he managed to hide his feelings as skilfully as Grace.

'He all but monopolized her!' recalled Mrs Kelly, wondering at the charm and lightness of touch that the thirty-two-year-old prince displayed. As soon as he arrived, he jumped straight into conversation with Grace. Rainier behaved exactly as a debonair prince might be expected to conduct himself, talking and smiling and focusing all his attention upon his lady – to instant and remarkable effect. 'I've never seen Grace,' commented Bill Godfrey, 'show so much interest in any young man.'

The evening went fast. It was ten o'clock in no time, and Father Tucker had to take his train for Wilmington. But his two young companions seemed to be dragging their feet. Rainier, clearly, did not yet feel ready to say his farewells, and Dr Donat was taking his lead from his prince.

Ma Kelly came to the rescue. Would the prince and Dr Donat like to spend the night at Henry Avenue, she suggested? There were a couple of beds in the guest room, and the prince and the doctor could rejoin Father Tucker in Wilmington next day. Rainier leapt at the idea so readily that Ma Kelly knew, 'then and there, that his intentions were not just those of a smitten young man. There was purpose,' she remembered, 'in his every word and movement.'

'Peggy,' said Ma Kelly, realizing that it was time for the grown-ups to be removed from the scene, 'you must take these young people back to your place.'

So Peggy took the visitors, with Grace, round the corner to the house that her father had built for her nearby.

'We sat and played cards,' Grace's elder sister later remembered. 'Well, I ended up playing with the doctor, while Grace and Rainier were playing cards in the other room.'

It was more than cards that occupied Grace and Rainier's attention. When the pair finally emerged from the other room, sometime after two o'clock in the morning, they were happy and smiling – and the prince had black dog hairs all over his suit. Peggy lent Rainier some Scotch tape to take off the hairs, and went off into her bedroom for a whispered conference with Grace.

'I think he's very, *very* fascinating,' said Grace, who seemed to be glowing with a double wattage.

'Well, I think he is too,' said her elder sister, with thorough approval. And that, as Peggy subsequently remembered it, was just about that.

Next morning Grace and Rainier drove out into the country together for lunch, and later that day Grace made her way excitedly up to her mother's bedroom. 'She held my hand,' Ma Kelly remembered, 'as she had when she was a little girl.' Out it all poured – the nerves, the joy, the whole tumbling complex of emotions that Grace had been experiencing in the twenty-four hours since she had renewed her acquaintance with the prince. 'It was then that I knew,' said Mrs Kelly, 'that she was going to accept if he asked her.'

Grace's father already knew more than that. Jack Kelly had driven Father Tucker to the station the previous night, and as they drove, the ever-busy priest had confided in Jack the intentions of his 'Lord Prince'. This was one romance that Jack Kelly could have done very little to stop. There was such a head of steam building already. But it was shrewd of Father Tucker to invite Jack in on the game — and it was particularly clever of him to broach it as a man-to-man thing. If Jack Kelly knew his Irish priests, Father Tucker knew his Irish-American patriarchs. The young couple could count on the Kellys' blessing, declared Jack Kelly stoutly — providing, of course, that it turned out to be what Grace herself really wanted. The priest had his permission to tell the prince as much.

That left little more than the formalities to conclude. It had all come about in the blinking of an eye, but no one who had been there while it happened seemed greatly surprised. Grace and Rainier displayed their infatuation with such openness that everyone felt sprinkled by the star dust. Peggy was driving the couple through the night streets of Germantown the following evening, when she glanced in her rearview mirror. It seemed perfectly natural to see her sister with this virtual stranger, locked in a passionate embrace.

On Wednesday, 28 December, the prince and Dr Donat drove Grace the one hundred miles from Philadelphia to New York. Grace had some singing lessons to attend in preparation for *High Society*, the new film project on which she was due to start work in a few weeks' time. More urgently, she had a thrilling item of news to share with her friends. Between backseat embraces, long, loving walks, and endless, exploratory conversations, Prince Rainier had asked if she would consent to be his princess, and she had not hesitated to say yes. She had got what her married girlfriends had got — and she had got more.

'Gracie's home!' Jay Kanter told his wife Judy when they spoke on the telephone that evening. 'Call her immediately.

She's waiting to hear from you.' Kanter and John Foreman had just received a pair of curious phone calls from Grace. 'We each have to promise to meet her tomorrow morning, separately,' said Kanter mystified. 'We don't know what's going on.'

It turned out that Grace wanted to meet Judy as well – for lunch. 'It's vital,' she said, giggling happily, 'absolutely vital.' When her old friend told her that she already had other plans, Grace was beside herself. 'You must come,' she begged. 'I'm pleading with you.'

Judy Kanter did not, in fact, have any plans for lunch next day. Pretending to be busy was her ploy to coax at least a little information out of her friend, and she partially succeeded. 'I'll tell you one thing and one thing only,' said Grace. 'After I've told you the one thing, I'm going to hang up. If you call back, I won't speak to you.' She paused and her voice dropped to a whisper. 'I'm engaged to be married.' Then Judy Kanter heard the phone go click.

Over dinner that night, the Kanters and John Foreman got out paper and pencil to try to divine who Grace's fiancé might be Oleg Cassini had to be top of the list. Grace had not been seeing much of him lately – Oleg had not been amused by Grace's springtime fling in Europe with Jean-Pierre Aumont. But the designer remained her most serious long-term suitor, and he had come closer than anyone to getting Grace to defy her parents and to live her own life. Jean-Pierre himself was a distant second.

Looking at more obscure candidates, it seemed clear that something had happened in Philadelphia in the five brief days since Grace had done her General MacArthur imitation in Sutton Place. The Kanters knew that when Grace went home she would step out occasionally with a local date, Bill Clothier, the scion of a prominent Main Line family. Bill Clothier was handsome and athletic, and he had been wholeheartedly endorsed by Jack Kelly as ideal husband material. Was it possible that Grace had surrendered, that she had finally given Daddy the solid and respectable Philadelphia alliance that he had been hoping for all these years?

Judy Kanter found out at twelve-thirty the next day, in the dining room of Grace's Fifth Avenue apartment. Two green salads and some dainty chicken sandwiches sat on the table. 'I am so very much in love with the most wonderful man,' said Grace. ' . . . I am going to marry Prince Rainier of Monaco.'

For several long moments Judy Kanter did not know what to say. She shook her head to and fro in disbelief, then blurted out the only words that seemed appropriate. 'No shit, Grace!' she exclaimed. The two women looked at each other, saying nothing, then dissolved into paroxysms of helpless laughter, doubling up with such hysteria that they had to push their salads aside. They risked banging their heads on their plates.

Judy Kanter's irreverent joy summed up the reaction of many of Grace's friends in the days ahead. They were delighted for Grace and they wished her every happiness. But since no one knew anything about Rainier's letters and Grace's months of secret anticipation, they could but speculate on her motives. On the evidence at hand, she had either succumbed to a rush of foolish and impetuous passion — which was certainly consistent with her previous romances — or else she was guilty of some very cold-blooded calculation indeed. Trying to sort it all out for Judy Kanter, Grace cheerfully admitted to both.

'I love his eyes,' she gushed. 'I could look into them for hours. He has a beautiful voice . . . He is everything I've ever loved.'

More practically, however, she explained, 'I don't want to be married to someone who feels belittled by my success . . .

I couldn't bear walking into a restaurant and hearing the maître d' refer to my husband as Mr Kelly.'

For someone who liked to act carefree, Grace Kelly worried a lot. She worried about the 'Mr Kelly' problem. She worried about getting old as an actress, and finding it hard to get parts. She worried about how she could remain in the movie business and still have babies, raise a family, and lead her old-fashioned idea of a proper married life. She worried, above all, about how she could please her demanding mother and father while also gaining independence for herself with the man of her dreams – and His Serene Highness Prince Rainier of Monaco provided a single, simple and spectacular solution to all of the above. To be a princess. To be married with a bishop's blessing. To live in a castle in the south of France. To turn real life into a movie, and to live it, securely, for ever. All this, plus the love of a witty, red-blooded man with dark brown eyes into which she felt able to gaze for hours. It was far better than *The Swan* – better, even, than a medal on display in the Kellys' black velvet trophy room.

'I acted more on instinct,' Grace later said. 'But then I always have . . . We happened to meet each other at a time when each of us was ready for marriage. There comes a time in life when you have to choose.'

If it took Grace Kelly only a day or so to fall in love with the idea of becoming a princess, it seemed clear that the rest of America would make up its mind even quicker than that. 'Prince to wed movie star!' The press would go wild. It was a mingling of so many cherished fantasies, picking up where the dreams of Hollywood left off and giving them an extra twist. How to break the news to the world was the immediate question, and on Friday, 30 December, Grace organized a dinner in her Fifth Avenue apartment so that Rainier could meet some of her New York friends and talk about what came next.

Father Tucker eased the formality of the introductions with one of his famous jokes, and the prince told Grace's friends to forget his titles and call him 'Rainier'. It was a relaxed and jovial evening – until the moment when Father Tucker presented his schedule for announcing the engagement of his Lord Prince. Monseigneur (Rainier's official style of address) would return with Grace to the Kelly home in Philadelphia, the priest explained, whence the official announcement would be released. A private photographer, hired for the occasion, would record the event, and his pictures would be passed on to the newspapers. Father Tucker proposed two decorous poses – one of the happy couple on their own, and another of them circled by the smiling Kellys.

The chaplain's proposal revealed a charming but abysmal ignorance of the appetites of the American press. There was no way that America's news organizations would be satisfied without their own pictures of the couple and a chance to ask each of them some questions. But as Jay Kanter – along with John Foreman and Grace's New York lawyer, Henry Jaffe – gently tried to explain the problem, they encountered an unmistakable stiffening on the part of the prince. Rainier wanted to keep his private day private, and as the Americans tried to explain the impracticality of his wish, the atmosphere cooled perceptibly. Voices became tight. The prince became princely – and there were no more jokes from Father Tucker. Grace sat back in her seat, Judy Kanter remembered, 'as though wishing she could disappear into the sofa pillows'.

It was Jack Kelly who resolved the impasse a few days later. 'Daddy was always understanding with the press,' remembered Peggy. ' "Look, Gracie," he said, "this is going to be a big thing." He knew you have to give them their story.' Jack explained to his future son-in-law that there was no way around it. Stupid questions would have to be answered and the same picture posed for again and again. So on Thursday, 5 January 1956, the full cast of characters assembled in Henry Avenue. Reporters and cameramen crowded into the Kelly mansion. 'Was it love at first sight, Prince?' 'How many children will you have?' The photographers climbed over Ma Kelly's armchairs and stood on her piano. The pregnant Lizanne had to be escorted upstairs, out of harm's way. Rainier kept his temper to start with, and demonstrated a rather attractive concern to protect his fiancée. But well before the end he was heard to be muttering, '*I* don't belong to MGM.'

The following evening, the couple went through a similar performance in New York. It was a charity ball for which the organizers had hastily constructed a 'Royal Box' topped off with a paper crown. 'It looked particularly silly,' remembers Elliott Erwitt, one of the several dozen photographers who were desperately scrabbling for a different angle on Grace in her white Dior satin gown.

On only his second exposure to a mass photo call, Prince Rainier was showing the strain. His Serene Highness was not accustomed to being on display except on his own terms, and having put on a reasonable show at Henry Avenue, he had now stuffed his royal charm firmly back in his pocket. Conspicuously unhelpful to the photographers that he and his fiancée had summoned there, the prince struck Elliott Erwitt as 'a pudgy and rather unpleasant person'. But the evening improved when the party moved on from the ball to the Harwyn Club. Grace squeezed Rainier fondly and nibbled at his ear. As Jack Kelly's daughter, she knew how to correct an attack of the sulks. She giggled and joked, and the couple danced happily together until four in the morning.

Grace was floating on a cloud. Her engagement had unravelled so many knots, making her life suddenly simpler and lighter. But while she was pleased to be rid of her complications, she did not discard them with nonchalance. Ever the considerate one, she had sat down and written long letters to Gene Lyons and to Jean-Pierre Aumont so that they should hear of her engagement in her own words before they read about it in the newspapers.

Oleg Cassini, she decided, was entitled to a personal meeting, and she selected the Staten Island ferry as the forlorn but sentimental setting for their farewell. 'I have made my destiny,' she told Oleg, as the cold wind whipped off the grey Atlantic. With sirens sounding in the harbour and the Statue of Liberty slipping by, the only touch needed was background music for the credits to roll – an apt and somehow caring conclusion to a love affair that had always hovered on the edge of make-believe.

Grace's airy and exhilarating new world of dreams-come-true, however, was not without its complications. 'Daddy's making so much fuss about the dowry!' she exclaimed one day in anguish over the phone to Don Richardson. 'He's going to ruin everything!' Grace had been phoning Richardson from time to time in the previous year. She seemed to use him as a sounding board for issues that troubled her, and the practicalities of her engagement produced several of those.

Monaco operates under the principles of French law – the *Code Napoléon* – and the formalities of any French marriage customarily include a property contract. Like most old and monied families, the Grimaldis married under an arrangement known as the *Séparation des biens*, whereby everything that a spouse brings to a marriage remains strictly his or her own property, and this made perfect sense to Jack Kelly. He was planning to give Grace a major shareholding in Kelly for Brickwork on her wedding day, as he had done with his other two daughters, and if things went wrong with the marriage, he did not want his affairs getting tangled up with an ex-son-in-law on the wrong side of the Atlantic.

But when Father Tucker also broached the ancient aristocratic tradition of the dowry – the idea that the father of the bride should pay for the favour of having his daughter taken into a noble family – the Irish Democrat rebelled. 'I certainly told that Father Tucker,' he reported to his wife and Aunt Marie Magee. 'I told him off . . . I didn't want it, and I didn't intend to get involved.'

'Kelly reckoned his daughter was dowry enough for any goddamn suitor,' remembers John Pochna, who had heard about the engagement on the radio and had driven straight to Philadelphia to try to get back into the game. Was Monaco doing Grace a favour, or vice versa? Rainier might be 'My Lord Prince' to Father Tucker, but in the eyes of a right-thinking American he was just 'any damn broken-down prince who was head of a country over there that nobody knew anything about'.

'Oh!' Aunt Marie remembered. 'He did really carry on.'

Not until Father Tucker produced documentation which gave credible evidence that Rainier had adequate resources of his own, did Jack Kelly relent and agree to pay the dowry. How much he handed over is unknown, but it was not the only price that the bride and her family were required to pay. In the event of a divorce, Grace was informed, any children of the marriage would have to remain strictly in their father's custody. For dynastic reasons it was impossible for potential heirs to be surrendered to the care of a separated wife. There were no buts or maybes. It was Grimaldi family law – an absolute condition of a marriage affecting the succession of a semi-sovereign state.

Grace herself found this condition rather less horrifying

than did most of her girlfriends when she told them about it. The question for Grace was quite academic, since she simply did not contemplate the possibility of divorce. As Judy Kanter put it: 'If Grace worked at it, it would work. She had controlled her adult life, and, so far, had made it a series of "hits".' Her marriage would be just the same. For all her insecurities, there was a part of Grace's spirit that was borne along by the most immense self-confidence. The Patton tank in her blithely eliminated even the imagining that her marriage might fail. What agitated Grace far more was the test she knew that she would have to pass before she could get to the stage of having children – Dr Donat's medical examination to make sure that she could bear heirs for Rainier.

'They'll find out I'm not a virgin,' she worried to Don Richardson on the phone.

'Tell them you broke it,' Richardson suggested, 'while you were playing sports in high school.'

Asked about this test in 1988, Prince Rainier denied that it ever took place. Yet the Grimaldis have a long history of denying embarrassing facts that later turn out to be true. The existence of a dowry payment was denied for many years, until the prince himself produced the contract. From his notifying of the French government to the hard-bargained details of the marriage contract, Rainier's courtship of Grace was hedged about by a whole catalogue of unsentimental – and perfectly practical – conditions and precautions. It would hardly make sense to negotiate the custody of children without making sure that children could be produced in the first place.

Prince Rainier has always maintained that Dr Donat accompanied him to America in December 1955 in a purely casual and friendly capacity – to keep him company while he went through his own medical tests at Johns Hopkins.

But this is not what Don Richardson recalls Grace telling him. 'She said the priest came to deal with the religious side of it, and that the doctor was there to make sure she was fertile,' he remembers. 'She said she would have to get up in the stirrups to get poked and prodded. Her worry was not the fertility, but the virginity. Who knows what the doctor was actually looking for, but that was her anxiety.'

The anxiety was understandable. Grace's ability to play the good girl lay at the heart of her appeal as a film star, and purity was even more crucial to her image as a princess. It was unthinkable in 1956 that a princess should not be a virgin when she married. It was part of the fantasy, the still potent idea that one purpose of celebrity was to set a moral example to the rest of the world. People did not expect quite so much of film stars and entertainers, but virtue was a sine qua non of being royal or princely – and this was the new, grander category of distinction to which Grace hoped to graduate.

'They believed me!' Grace reported in relief and delight to Don Richardson a few days later. It was a major obstacle overcome. The contradiction between the reality of Grace's sexual appetite and the chastity of her public image had always been a source of strain and potential danger. The actress had had to live constantly with the risk of being uncovered, and now she could hope to resolve the problem. She was totally in love with her husband-to-be. She had been trying for years, in her own impulsive yet essentially moral fashion, to bring inclination and duty together, and with her engagement she seemed to have pulled the trick off. She was finally getting married. Grace, the princess, would no longer have to pretend, and she could reasonably expect that the embarrassing romantic mishaps of Grace, the film star, would fade into decent obscurity.

But Grace had reckoned without her mother. On 15

January 1956, only ten days after the official announcement of the engagement, the *Los Angeles Herald Examiner* published the first of a lengthy and detailed series of articles, 'My Daughter Grace Kelly: Her Life and Romances,' by Mrs John B. Kelly – 'as told to Richard Gehman.' There were ten parts to the series. It had been produced by the King Features Syndicate, and it was circulated to Hearst newspapers all over the country.

The series strung together the most astonishing and embarrassing stream of revelations. 'Men began proposing to my daughter Grace,' wrote Mrs Kelly, 'when she was barely fifteen' – which made Prince Rainier, by Ma Kelly's calculation, 'at least the fiftieth' man to ask for Grace's hand in marriage. No detail was spared, from Grace's 'nasal whine' as a gawky teenager to the fact that Ma Kelly's pet name for her future son-in-law was 'Ray' – 'He did bring a ray of light into our home.' Day after day Grace's mother plodded relentlessly through the chronology of Grace's love affairs, from the sad story of Harper Davis – ' I suppose we never knew how much it meant to her at the time' – through Don Richardson, whom she did not name, to Gene Lyons, whom she called David. 'That isn't his name, but I see no reason for making him wince at the sight of his name in this series.'

The possibility that her own daughter might find cause to wince was, to Mrs Kelly, a matter of lesser concern. Clark Gable, Ray Milland, William Holden, Bing Crosby – all the names that Ma Kelly herself had worked so hard to keep out of the papers were now paraded and their relationships with Grace discussed. Ma Kelly revealed 'these intimate stories,' she explained, 'with the hope of setting straight many false rumours.' But she rehashed each rumour with such relish that it seemed she did protest too much. 'Next in line was dress designer Oleg Cassini, and I don't mind saying that this situation had us all concerned . . . For a time we all felt that she might well go against our wishes and marry him.'

Over the years the Kelly family was frequently to complain about the way that the media treated Grace, but no journalist ever wrote anything more damning than that which the Kellys managed to produce themselves. '[It] struck Grace a terrible blow,' Prince Rainier later remembered. 'She just didn't understand how her own mother could do something like that.'

Margaret Kelly's justification was contained at the head of each of the ten instalments: 'Mrs John B. Kelly's royalties for this series of articles are being sent in entirety to the Women's Medical College of Philadelphia, the only medical college exclusively for women in the United States.' But this cut no ice with Grace, who could remember an entire childhood of homage to the sacred cause of Women's Med. 'Why couldn't she have baked some cookies?' she complained in cold rage to Maree Rambo, 'or organize a damn benefit? I've worked so hard, and now my mother's going to destroy everything overnight.'

It was the only occasion on which Judy Kanter ever heard Grace speak ill of one of her parents, or admit to any untoward wrinkles in the polished perfection of Kelly family life. Grace phoned her mother in fury when she read the articles, speaking her mind bluntly and plainly for once. She was seething – an adult for ten minutes at least – and her anger shocked her mother into offering some amends. Margaret Kelly started apologizing to friends in a halfhearted sort of way, claiming that the series had been 'rushed out of her,' and that she had not had time to check it properly for mistakes.

But anyone who knew Grace's mother and father had to conclude that both the tone and the message of the series precisely reflected the Kellys' Victorian and egotistical style.

All of their children – from Kell, the winner of the Diamond Sculls, to Grace, the princess – existed essentially to serve their parents' purposes and for the greater glory of Jack and Margaret Kelly. The fundamental intent of 'My Daughter Grace Kelly: Her Life and Romances' was to make clear that if anyone deserved the credit for Grace's spectacular engagement, it was not Grace herself – whom the articles depicted as something of a foolish virgin – but the parents who had worked so hard to keep her out of trouble, pending the arrival of suitor no. 50. One of Jack Kelly's little jokes at the engagement news conference summed it all up. 'Well, Mother,' he said, referring to the fact that Grace was the last of his daughters to get engaged, 'I guess now we're all sold out.'

Grace understood it perfectly. 'First I had to fight the studio to avoid being a commodity,' she complained to Judy Kanter. 'Now my own family trades me on the open market. Doesn't it ever end? When do I get to be just a person?'

'Never' was the short, hard answer to that. Making the particular marriage choice that she did was Grace Kelly's definitive farewell to that most basic of human comforts – being able to mind one's own business. It was particularly painful that her own mother should be the messenger, but it is the devil's pact with celebrity that famous people can never hope to be 'just a person' again.

That did not stop Grace from trying, however. Looking back over the extraordinary story of her extraordinary engagement, it was, in one sense, highly deceptive of her not to have given any advance hint to her friends and family of her developing relationship with her prince. The aim-for-the-top in Grace realized how discretion was a crucial passkey to the world she hoped to enter, and, as usual, that part of her got what it wanted. 'I knew from the start,' said Rainier shortly after his marriage, 'that I could trust the Princess. It was one of the reasons why I felt so surely that she was the person for me.'

But Grace had had another, equally powerful reason why she should want to keep even the fact of her correspondence with Rainier to herself. Though it seemed to be forgotten sometimes in the blitz of interviews and lights, there was a genuine, private reality to the engagement of the prince and the film star, and the letters that they wrote to each other had contained the real heart of that. It was not much, but it was one corner into which the world could not pry, somewhere that Grace could walk hand in hand with her prince, unwatched and undisturbed in the privacy of their secret garden.

SEVENTEEN

True Love

H IGH SOCIETY was MGM's musical adaptation of *The Philadelphia Story*, the comedy of manners that Don Richardson had chosen in 1949 as the graduation play of Grace Kelly, actress-to-be. Now, in the middle of January 1956, Grace, princess-to-be, was due to play Tracy Lord with songs by Cole Porter. It was to prove her graduation from Hollywood.

MGM had lined up a cast that glittered with singing talent – Bing Crosby, Frank Sinatra and the jazz musician Louis Armstrong – and since Grace had never sung before, the film's musical codirector, Johnny Green, took it for granted that her solid but rather artless voice could not survive in such high-powered company. 'I had spent a lot of time,' he told James Spada in 1986, 'listening to any number of samples of Grace's dialogue – the timbre, the quality of her voice and diction – and I listened to her sing informally in my office . . . I decided that she was not capable of singing her own track.'

The musical director started making arrangements to find Grace a voice double, but he had not reckoned on the ambition and willpower of the actress. 'She insisted on

273

singing her own track,' he recalled, 'and she came on like Refrigerator Perry.'

Grace had been taking singing lessons since the moment she was offered the part in the summer of 1955. She had one spoof song to sing off-key, and one to sing properly – 'True Love', a guileless and syrupy ballad that she was due to perform with Bing Crosby. It was a matter of pride for Grace that she should deliver her own song in her own voice, and when Green disagreed, she took her case to the very top. She went to see Dore Schary.

'I lost,' Green remembered ruefully. MGM did not hire a voice double, and Grace sang 'True Love' beautifully. It was smooth and simple, and it seemed to take on extra strength from the unentangled directness of her voice. Grace was a calm, dark contralto, and her serenity turned a slightly sappy tune into a classic. 'At the end,' recalled the musical director, 'she and Bing sang in *harmony* yet . . . She made a real monkey out of me, because the record didn't just go Gold, it went Platinum!'

Grace had escaped from the reporters and photographers in New York to the comparative peace of the MGM back lot, and she tried very hard to pretend it was business as usual. Rainier was due to join her at the end of January, and the actress buckled down to work with her customary professionalism. She avoided any special fuss about her engagement and coming marriage, which was scheduled for Monaco in the second half of April. Taking her cue, her co-stars and the crew politely pretended they were not sharing a soundstage with the world's most famous fiancée.

On the third day of filming, however, Grace could hold it in no longer. Several scenes in the story called for Tracy Lord to show off her engagement ring, and the studio props department had provided Grace with a ring whose centre-piece was an implausibly large, paste diamond.

'Do you think,' Grace shyly asked the director Charles Walters, 'that I might wear my *own* engagement ring?'

Walters could see the joke immediately, but he pretended to be serious. It all depended, he told Grace solemnly. He would have to see the ring to make sure that it was good enough.

'Well, next day,' remembers Celeste Holm, who was one of Grace's costars, 'she came in with this diamond as big as a skating rink. It was beautiful, just beautiful! Normally I don't care for diamonds – that terrible dead whiteness. But this one had colour. It was wonderful! It made me think of the first prism I ever saw when I was a little girl in kindergarten, it was so full of life and sparkle.'

Grace's real, emerald-cut diamond was as huge as the paste gem given her by the props department, and there was a general chorus of 'oohs' and 'ahs' as people saw it flashing on her finger. Grace coloured modestly. 'Yes, it is sweet, isn't it?' she said – and that became the joke of the set. 'We never let her forget it,' remembers Celeste Holm. 'Grace's "sweet" diamond ring! We teased her about it until the last day of filming.'

John Pochna travelled out to Hollywood ahead of Rainier to find a villa that the prince could rent. The lawyer had no difficulty finding a secluded Bel Air mansion, but he did experience some trouble getting all the prince's bills paid. After Pochna had sent out several cheques bearing the prince's signature – to the landlord and to the laundry service, among others – he discovered from the bank that the cheques had not been presented.

'Did you receive our cheque?' he enquired of each of the payees.

'Oh, yes,' he was told. 'Thank you very much. We have got it framed and hanging on the wall.'

Rainier was not treated quite so worshipfully when he

went to visit MGM. Dore Schary arranged a lunch in his honour in the cramped surroundings of the executive dining room. 'Grace was there,' remembers Celeste Holm, 'along with the prince and his father, who was a charming elder gentleman who had flown out specially to meet Grace. He reminded me of Clifton Webb.'

Celeste Holm could see that Grace was strangely on edge. 'She was white,' she remembers. 'She was so nervous, and suddenly I thought, "I've got it! If the prince and his father don't like the studio, they will never let Grace return. She won't be able to make any more movies."' Sitting beside Celeste Holm was Charles Walters, the director, who, Holm realized with horror, 'had never been heard to issue a sentence without a four-letter word in it.'

Walters behaved himself, as it happened. It was Dore Schary who committed the faux pas. 'Someone asked, "How big is Monaco?"' Celeste Holm remembers, 'and they gave us this answer in square feet, or something which sounded quite a large number. Well, then there was a pause while everyone did quick arithmetic, and suddenly Dore Schary, who could figure faster than the rest of us, said, "That's not even as big as our back lot!" I had the feeling that a giant chandelier had suddenly crashed in the middle of the table into a thousand pieces. There was this dead pause, and I knew there and then that Grace would never make another picture again.'

The decision, in fact, had already been made. From the moment their engagement was announced, Rainier and Grace had been repeatedly asked if Grace's marriage meant the end of her movie career, and they had both answered vaguely – Grace because she did not know, Rainier because he did. The prince had absolutely no doubt that Grace would have to give up her acting. He had first been attracted to her because she was *not* like a film star, and he could see no way at all that it would be either practical or dignified for his wife to keep on working as a Hollywood performer.

But Rainier was not yet certain how difficult it would be for Grace to break her MGM contract, and he had been made sharply aware that, while Grace was already a princess so far as her own culture was concerned, his own approval rating was precarious. 'He's not good enough for a Kelly,' stated a Chicago paper. 'She is too well-bred a girl to marry the silent partner in a gambling parlour.' Treading carefully, Rainier took advantage of the mêlée that followed the engagement announcement at Henry Avenue to give only vague answers to questions about Grace's future career.

But the questions kept getting asked, and the more that reporters badgered Rainier, the more his princeliness came to the fore. His Serene Highness resented the assumption that being an American screen goddess was a more important occupation that presiding over the place that he called home. When Rainier first met Howell Conant at the beginning of January, he had extended his hand in greeting, then grasped the photographer's hand with a curious combination of a squeeze and a twist that brought Conant to his knees. It was Rainier's idea of a joke, and Conant accepted it as such. But the message was clear. There was a new boss in Grace's life, and it was not the demands of Hollywood publicity.

Rainier had also discovered, through conversations with John Pochna and others, that there was not much MGM could do, in practical terms, if Grace never made another movie again. A studio might sue a contract player who tried to work for a rival, but dragging a princess out of self-imposed retirement was not a feasible prospect. So when Rainier was asked, on his arrival in Los Angeles at the end of January 1956, whether his wife-to-be would be making any more movies, he no longer bothered to pretend. 'I don't think so,' he said.

Grace herself could neither think nor talk with such brutal clarity. She was hoping, as usual, for the best of all possible worlds. In an interview that appeared in the *Los Angeles Times* on 22 January 1956, just three days before her fiancé's blunt announcement, she had talked as if she was contemplating the prospect of a long vacation from acting, followed by occasional work on really plum roles. But Grace was not inclined to argue with Rainier. She was rather pleased to have a man who took such firm charge of her life. She had been searching for such a father figure for years, and now she had got one in spades. Rainier's moods with the press did not trouble her. What was the point of marrying a prince if he did not act in a princely fashion?

By the age of twenty-six, in any case, Grace very much wanted to become a wife and mother. She had always said that she doubted whether it was possible to combine either of these responsibilities with the life of a working actress, and there was also that part of her which had never liked Hollywood – the inconstant, gypsy life, the days living out of a trailer, the combination of tension and tedium, with dozens of people all standing around and only two or three of them doing any obvious work. Legend had it that Marilyn Monroe's engagement congratulations to Grace ran: 'So glad you've found a way out of this business.'

Grace was ready to move on, and it was not as though her new life would fail to satisfy her need for public acclaim. Becoming a princess, indeed, would lift her to a new and permanent level of performance. As Alfred Hitchcock slyly put it, 'I am very happy that Grace has found herself such a good part.' Grace remained politely noncommittal in her public utterances. 'Right now,' she would tell journalists, 'I am more interested in my marriage career and too excited about it to think about any other.' But Rainier's wish was her wish. There would be no more movie-making.

MGM did not like it. Though Grace was well liked as a person, the studio had the lingering unhappiness that it had not got its money's worth from her as a company asset. At the first news of her engagement, studio spokesmen made halfhearted attempts to point out that Grace still had several years left on her contract, but by the end of January 1956, they had come to realize how counter-productive it would be to play the dog in the manger. In a storm of news reports and magazine cover stories, their actress had already been crowned and married in the popular imagination. The best that MGM could hope for was to jump aboard for the ride. So in true studio tradition, they bid to stage-manage the event, announcing that they would provide their star's wedding dress – $7,266.68 in materials and manufacture, plus the services of the designer, Helen Rose – and would release Grace's favourite studio hair stylist, Virginia Darcy (at $300 per week, plus all travel expenses), to accompany Grace to the wedding. As their contribution to her trousseau, MGM made Grace a present of all the costumes she had worn in *High Society* – and they also paid her a salary bonus of $65,166.66 ($352,000 in 1990s values), on top of her $1,500 a week retainer.

All that the studio received in concrete terms for this generous package of benefits was the exclusive right to film (though not to televise) the story of the wedding in Monaco. After mutterings that Grace might take on one more assignment after *High Society*, it was tacitly agreed that she would do no more work for MGM. Her contract was allowed to lapse. But in 1983, the year after Grace's death, Steven Englund was going through the Grace Kelly file in the then-accessible MGM archives, when he came across a strange document described as a 'layoff sheet'. For some 520 weeks after her marriage – way beyond the expiry of Grace's original contract – an unknown MGM functionary had methodically kept Grace's name on the studio roster, pains-takingly entering 'Grace Kelly' in some weeks and 'Princess Rainier' in others, as if the actress had been present all that time, hiding in some obscure commissary. In the heart of the dream factory it was evidently difficult to accept that Grace Kelly would never make another movie.

So *High Society* was her swan song, and it turned out a frothy and entertaining MGM musical in the finest tradition. Striding boldly into the character that Katharine Hepburn had shaped so firmly in the non-musical original, Grace created a Tracy Lord of her own. If her 'True Love' was a triumph, she did even better with her off-key, drunken version of 'You're Sensational' – 'I don't care if I am called the Fair Miss Fridgidaire,' she slurred as she staggered around the ballroom. At the very last moment, Hollywood discovered that the Ice Maiden could laugh at herself.

Grace played a girl falling off her pedestal and enjoying every minute of it. Though her Tracy Lord was a divorcée who, according to the bald facts of the plot, gets so drunk she imagines next morning she has been to bed with a stranger, Grace managed to float above such sordid details with the cheeriness and uplift of a Sunday school teacher. It was a final twirl of the paradoxical Grace Kelly magic. Grace was light and witty and scintillating, and her most moving accomplishment – in her acting, as well as in her brief bursting into song – was to depict the state of being in love in all its mad sentiment and folly, while also transmitting the deeper sense of destiny and purpose that is the eternal but elusive promise of true love.

On 4 April 1956, it seemed as if half of New York had clustered onto Pier 84 on the Hudson River to wave goodbye to the USS *Constitution*. The liner was bearing Grace, most of her family, three of her bridesmaids, over fifty friends, a varied assortment of journalists, and a black, wiry-haired poodle, Oliver – a present to Grace from Mr and Mrs Cary Grant – across the Atlantic to Monaco. Confetti fluttered, sirens sounded and cameras flashed. The waterfront had not seen excitement like it since the boys set out to rescue Europe in the Second World War. According to Edmond Duffy, the dean of New York's shipping news reporters, it was the harbour's biggest shipside news conference in thirty years. When the time came for the *Constitution* to sail, there were so many extra well-wishers to be cleared from the ship that the departure was delayed by forty-five minutes.

The filming of *High Society* had ended on 6 March, giving Grace slightly less than a month to organize her trousseau, say goodbye to her friends, deal with countless press requests, and supervise such details as the bridesmaids' dresses and the socks to be worn by the flower girls. (The dresses were a present from Neiman-Marcus; Grace paid for the socks at J. C. Penney.) On top of all this, she had to pack for the new life that she would be starting on the other side of the world. When Rupert Allan arrived at her apartment for their now-familiar ritual of champagne and packing, he was amazed to see, set out beside the cocktail dresses and ball gowns, more than a dozen pairs of old jeans, along with piles of faded shirts and blouses.

'For heaven's sake, Grace,' he said, 'you're not taking those with you, are you? You'll never wear them.'

'Oh yes, I will,' she replied. 'Most of the time.'

Monaco's need to see its prince married on his home territory had relieved the Kelly family of both the duty and the pleasure of organizing their daughter's wedding, but they more than made up for it in their eight days on board the USS *Constitution*. Every dinner was a special occasion, with champagne, toasts and speeches. There were organized party games, charades, canasta contests, shuffleboard contests, bingo contests, pioneer sing-songs, walks around the deck with Oliver, farewell-to-America parties, welcome-to-Europe parties. The entire voyage, recalled Judy Kanter fondly, resembled nothing so much as 'a floating summer camp'.

For Judy Kanter and the five other girlfriends whom Grace had chosen to be her bridesmaids, April 1956 was a highspot that gave six ordinary American girls the chance to share in the scarcely credible fantasy their famous friend was living through. Judy Kanter kept meticulous notes on the experience, and later wrote a 498-page book on the subject.* Maree Frisby was Grace's oldest and closest intimate, going back to Stevens School days. Bettina Thompson had been her first room-mate at the Barbizon. Carolyn Scott had helped Grace get started in modelling and was another Barbizon girl. Sally Parrish had been Grace's room-mate in Manhattan House, Rita Gam her room-mate in Hollywood on Sweetzer Avenue.

None of the bridesmaids was Catholic, two of them were Jewish, and two of them were already divorced. Maree Frisby, one of the divorcées, had brought her new boyfriend along for the trip. The French press had some difficulty understanding how this assorted group of ladies fitted into the symbolism of the solemn church ceremony, since the French term *demoiselle d'honneur* implies a state of maidenhood which all six had, clearly, left far behind. But the choice showed the priority that Grace set on friendship. She was a loyal soul. Who else should she choose as her bridesmaids but her oldest chums and confidantes, and who could provide better support and fellowship as she sailed into the unknown? As

---

* *The Bridesmaids: Grace Kelly, Princess of Monaco, and Six Intimate Friends*, by Judith Balaban Quine, 1989.

Grace reminisced with Maree and Judy and Bettina on board the *Constitution*, the old friends laughed and gossiped and shed tears. They were reliving fond memories, and they were also savouring the anticipation of what lay ahead. It scared them slightly, but they also felt sure that it would be both wondrous and unique.

This feeling transfused the whole ship. Jack Seabrook, one of the sixty-six-strong Kelly party on board the *Constitution*, knew a bit about transatlantic crossings, but he had never received so many presents before he sailed. Sending wine to an ocean traveller was the accepted way of wishing them luck on the voyage – and also of getting invited to the sailing party. 'There must have been forty cases of wine stacked in the passageway outside my stateroom by the time I got on board,' remembers Seabrook. 'There was champagne in magnums, burgundies – everything.'

Seabrook worked valiantly to drink and distribute all the wine before he disembarked in Monaco – with happy results when he sent a bottle of champagne across the dining room to a table of attractive lady journalists. One of them was the UPI representative Elizabeth Toomey, who, within six months, became Mrs Jack Seabrook. When he got back to America, Seabrook found he had been summoned to a black-tie dinner meeting of the board of directors of AT&T. Seabrook was a director of New Jersey Bell, so he swotted up desperately on local business conditions, to discover, when he arrived at the dinner, that he had been invited to entertain the board of one of America's most massive corporations with a firsthand account of Grace Kelly's wedding.

The whole country was mesmerized. On Broadway, Ethel Merman ran for months in *Happy Hunting*, the hastily thrown-together tale of a rich Philadelphia girl who is snubbed by Main Line society but finds herself happily wooed and won by a Mediterranean nobleman. Fashion magazines tried to analyse the 'Grace Kelly look'. Shops tried to sell it. NBC added Monaco time to the clocks in its Radio City headquarters, and ran a two-week series of radio and TV briefings on the history and culture of the principality. Grace Kelly had made herself America's clean and sparky girl next door, and it was only natural that the neighbours should want to join in the celebration. Grace, Ma Kelly had written in the final instalment of her ten-part series, was a 'shining example of what we in this country are, and what we believe. In a way, her story is an affirmation of the American dream. If Gracie can marry a Prince, every American girl can!'

Given the number of American girls who were nubile and single in January 1956, and the available pool of marriageable princes, this statement did not make statistical sense. Grace Kelly had, in fact, snapped up one of the few bachelor princes in the mid 1950s with any worthwhile realm to his name. But the spirit of Ma Kelly's thought flew with real wings. There is a moment in every romance when Prince Charming takes the hand of Cinderella, and this was the moment to which Grace had given tangible form. Myths are anything but false if they embody values that ring true to their believers, and Cold War America was only too happy to forget about fallout shelters and UN bloc votes to celebrate such basic human truths as hope, commitment and tenderness.

The cutting edge of that celebration, unfortunately, was anything but tender for those passengers on the *Constitution* who had to deal, day by day, with more than a dozen rival journalists and photographers cooped up on the ship, each of them searching for their own scoop to wire home. News organizations had competed bitterly to get their representatives into the limited number of berths on board the liner, and they wanted stories about more than shuffleboard contests to put on the front page. 'It was awful,' remembers

Maree Frisby Rambo. 'Some of them were quite nice, but you got the feeling they were all hanging around just waiting for Grace or someone to fall down and break a leg.'

Grace Kelly's engagement and wedding was the first modern event to generate media overkill – the concentration of reporting resources in gross disproportion to the number and importance of the facts to be reported upon – and the Kelly family had to cope with the consequences. Two days out in the Atlantic, cables from worried friends told of the sour and frustrated tone of the shipboard reports published in some American newspapers. There had been speculation about family discord based on the fact that the older and younger generations were observed to be sitting in different sets of deck chairs, along with criticism of the special areas of the ship that had been cordoned off to give Grace privacy.

Jack Kelly called a council of war. Over the rest of the trip, it was decided, Grace would have to give a little exclusive time to each of the reporters, and more effort should be made by everyone to make the press feel part of the party. Morgan Hudgins, MGM's press representative, was put in charge of coordinating the programmes of interviews and photo calls. As the days went by, the stories wired home from the ship became more friendly and positive. But there were the best part of two thousand journalists and photographers from all over the world waiting in Monaco, and Grace would not be available to give exclusive time to any of them.

As the *Constitution* passed through the Straits of Gibraltar and started to strike north towards France, the mood of the summer camp sobered. The American ocean had been left behind. The Mediterranean was Rainier's territory. The unknown was suddenly imminent.

Throughout the gaiety of the voyage, Grace had spent several hours every day in her cabin with her long baskets of letters, paying bills, sorting her papers, and writing personal notes to everyone who had given her a party or sent her a present. She wanted her old life wrapped up and tidied away before she arrived in Monaco, and this was the tone of her final night on the liner. She swore off a group dinner in the dining room. There were dinners aplenty scheduled in Monaco. Instead, she had a snack sent to her stateroom and sat alone for an hour with Bettina Thompson, her first roommate at the Barbizon, reminiscing about the old days and shedding more tears.

When Judy Kanter dropped in, she found the two women all cried out. Grace's eyes seemed veiled and a bit distant, 'not preoccupied with specifics but focused inward'. No one talked much. The princess-to-be was consciously calming herself. This was the last night. As Grace set aside all the razzmatazz of the voyage, it seemed to Judy Kanter that she was methodically composing her resources, 'gathering some internal strength that she knew she would need'.

EIGHTEEN

The Princess from the Sea

AROUND TEN o'clock on the morning of 12 April 1956, the vibrations of the engines of the USS *Constitution* changed their tone. The 4,000-mile journey was coming to an end. There was a dullish, grey mist hanging over the sea, and the faces of Monaco's pastel villas glowed vaguely through the haze. The anchor dropped into the water, and the *Constitution* listed slightly to the landward side as all its passengers and crew crowded the rails. At precisely ten-thirty a.m., a small white craft, Monaco's antique and upright royal yacht, came veering purposefully out of the harbour. His Serene Highness Prince Rainier III was coming to claim his bride.

Grace looked magnificent. She was wearing a long, elegant, dark silk coat, with a round, white organdy hat that came out and down and shaded her eyes like a huge coolie bonnet. This hat was instantly criticized by the press. It was impossible to see her face under it, they complained. But Grace had thought hard about her new role. It was right for her to look shy and almost veiled. She was no longer Little Miss Hollywood. She was the princess from the sea, the new servant and mother of this overgrown fishing harbour. Good Catholic that she was, Grace had an instinct for ritual and symbolism. Although she was smiling, she arrived in Monaco with her eyes modestly downcast.

Clutching Oliver the poodle with one hand firmly to her chest, Grace stepped out across the gangplank that connected the liner to her fiancé's yacht. A flotilla of small boats bustled around. Speedboats, houseboats, fishing boats, dinghies – it seemed as if all Monaco had come out on the water to welcome Grace to her new home. Showers of red and white carnations fluttered down from a seaplane overhead, courtesy of Aristotle Onassis. It was Grace's grandest entrance ever.

Rainier only shook her hand politely when he met her on the deck. He was a prince on his own territory now. The couple were nervous together – it was like starting at the beginning again. They had not seen each other for nearly a month, and it did not help having Jack and Margaret Kelly with them on the yacht. Jack Kelly puffed on a cigarette, showing the strain. He had been in his element on the liner, the grand playmaster of the lodge, but now he had to take his cue from another master of ceremonies.

Waiting at the dock were a clutch of Monégasque dignitaries, adorned with the sashes, medals, tailcoats and top hats beloved of French municipal officials. There were bowings, addresses of welcome and much shaking of hands. Schoolchildren lined the streets with flags. Smiling faces waved down from balconies. It seemed as if every brass band on the Riviera had come to make its contribution to the gaiety.

'You look happy, my dear,' said the English-speaking wife of one of the Monégasque officials.

'The only thing that seems to happen,' replied Grace, 'is that I get happier and happier.'

The couple got into a car to drive through the cheering streets around the harbour and up the twisting road that led to the palace, where there were more hands waiting to be shaken – the palace servants lined up in all *their* medals. 'Do they get one for every meal they serve?' asked a disrespectful member of the visitors.

It was exactly a week before the wedding was due to take place, and the seven days until then were dedicated to an elaborate roundelay of receptions and parties, one of whose purposes was the time-honoured marriage ritual of trying to make friends of two unfamiliar and generally unwilling families. This process kicked off with a lunch in the palace on the day of arrival – twenty-four assorted Kellys and Grimaldis in formal clothes, shaking hands and making small talk – and Grace's progression from happiness to happiness ended abruptly at the reception line. Her future mother-in-law, the Princess Charlotte, known in the family as 'Mamou', made no attempt to welcome her. She was chilly and disdainful, in a black mood, which Grace's own mother did little to improve by slapping Mamou heartily on the shoulder with the greeting, 'Hi! I'm Ma Kelly!' Almost all the Grimaldis behaved with a strange reserve. It was as if they were hiding the existence of some mad cousin whom no one wished to talk about, and it took several days for the Kellys to work out the truth – that their new European in-laws disliked each other so much that there were scarcely two of them who were on speaking terms.

For a family who had managed to hold on to power for over six hundred and fifty years, the house of Grimaldi was a quarrelsome clan – and remarkably uninhibited in letting the world know about it. Rainier's parents had separated around the time of his birth, and were divorced soon afterwards. His mother, Princess Charlotte – the 'Mamou' who snubbed Grace so obviously at their first meeting – was a troubled woman who ran off with an Italian doctor in the late 1920s, loudly bewailing the formality and pomposity of her husband, Prince Pierre de Polignac. 'To make love,' she complained, 'he needs to put a crown on his head.'

Rainier was the younger child of this unhappy union, and adversity had not drawn him closer to his only sibling and elder sister, Antoinette. A conspiratorial and undersized character known in the family as 'Tiny' – she was 'Princess Tiny Pants' to the press – Antoinette had spent much of her childhood and adult years at loggerheads with her brother. In April 1956, Tiny was separated from the first of her three husbands, Monaco's former tennis champion, and she was conducting an ill-concealed romance with Jean-Charles Rey, an ambitious local notable who was one of the members of the principality's National Council. Tiny and Jean-Charles Rey had been plotting together to depose Rainier, hoping to capitalize on quite a general feeling in Monaco – prior, at least, to his wooing of Grace – that Rainier had been languid in his princely duties. Rainier 'is now disposed', reported the US consul in Nice, 'to cut off the Princess's funds,' and, on top of all this, Rainier had also quarrelled recently with his step-grandmother, the Princess Ghislaine, an actress whom his grandfather had married in later life. The prince had had her expelled from the palace.

The Grimaldi weakness for undignified feuds and vendettas was one of the reasons why every royal house in Europe had refused to come to Grace and Rainier's wedding. They sent the standard silver tray or cigarette box, but they declined, to a man, to elevate the occasion with their presence. The closest approximations to royal dignity were the Aga Khan, obese and jewel-laden in a wheelchair, and the equally overweight ex-King Farouk of Egypt, who skulked around the Hôtel de Paris in dark glasses and a fez, perpetually on the lookout for assassins.

The Grimaldis had a flashy, seaside-pier reputation, and, as is often the case with those who feel themselves scorned, this only increased their personal arrogance. Rainier had a healthy dose of it, but his womenfolk, Mamou and Tiny, were mortally afflicted. The true purpose of the Los Angeles visit of Prince Pierre, Rainier's father, while Grace was filming *High Society*, had been less to meet his prospective daughter-in-law than to discuss with his son the ways in which some of the more embarrassing family fractures might be repaired. These good intentions had backfired, however, when the prince, a slightly stuffy old gentleman with a white moustache and a taste for literature, returned to Monaco singing Grace's praises. Prince Pierre proclaimed that this American girl was exactly the woman that his son and Monaco needed – which guaranteed that his ex-wife, Mamou, came to exactly the opposite conclusion. Mamou arrived at the family lunch on Thursday 12 April with her mind already made up. Her son was marrying beneath himself, and she made her feelings obvious both to Grace and to the Kellys.

It was an incident next day, however, that really stirred the family furies. On Saturday, 14 April 1956, Matthew McCloskey, an old friend and political ally of Jack Kelly and publisher of the Philadelphia *Daily Inquirer*, announced that $50,000 worth of his wife's jewels had vanished from their room in the Hôtel de Paris the previous night – and a few hours later the bridesmaid Maree Frisby announced that $8,000 of her jewels were also missing. The two thousand or so members of the international press who had gathered in Monaco, and who had, to this point, been significantly starved of stories, rejoiced at the excitement, revelling in its echoes of *To Catch a Thief*. 'Prince Rainier III is so furious over the jewel robberies,' wrote Art Buchwald, 'that . . . he has decided to ban all jewel thieves from the wedding. This drastic measure has raised a howl of protests from jewel robbers of every nationality.'

Buchwald was closer to the truth than he imagined. The jewel thefts in the Hôtel de Paris had enraged Rainier for a very personal reason, since his headstrong mother had moved on from her Italian doctor – Mamou had tried to shoot her lover during one of their romantic disputes – to strike up a series of bizarre relationships with criminals who had been paroled from prison. The princess had come to see it as her mission in life to give of herself to redeem these fallen men, and the companion whom she had brought to Grace's wedding, dressed in a tight-fitting white uniform and accompanying her, officially, as her chauffeur, was René Girier, a jewel thief who flaunted a walking stick and went by the name of 'René la Canne' (René the Cane).

As news of the missing jewels circulated, 'the Cane' was the obvious suspect. He was on parole from a sentence for robbery, and Rainier insisted that he should leave the principality immediately. But Mamou refused to be parted from her chauffeur, and the row broke into the open when Prince Pierre joined battle on behalf of his son. At one of the prewedding receptions, the Kellys were amazed by the sight of the groom's two elderly and long-separated parents quarrelling bitterly in front of the entire party, exchanging none-too-subtle insults which, in the case of Prince Pierre, traded on the fact that his ex-wife had been born illegitimate.

Grace never liked a scene. When voices were raised, she tried to pretend that she was somewhere else, and she took Mamou's hostility particularly to heart. Her mother-in-law had been so openly disdainful that Grace doubted whether she could ever make her a friend – and so it proved. Mamou never returned to Monaco after her son's marriage to the film actress whom she had decided to despise, and though Rainier and Grace regularly travelled after their marriage to visit her in her château at Marchais in northern France, taking their children with them as they were born, Mamou never relented. Mamou's home, wrote Grace to Don Richardson in 1972, was 'cold as a witch's teat [the handwritten letter shows that Grace first wrote "tit", then crossed it out for the more decorous word]. Of course, my mother-in-law's attitude towards me does nothing to warm up the atmosphere.'

Mamou was an unpleasant reminder that life for real princesses seldom imitates the fairy tales, and the other reminder lay in the jostling multitude of press reporters and photographers who had crowded into Monaco for the wedding week. Prying, rumbustious, and more disrespectful with every passing day that did not yield them a decent story, the world's press settled on the principality like the foraging party of some invading army. Driving with Grace and the Kellys one afternoon, Rainier slowed and stopped when he saw a prostrate body lying across the road. When he got out to help, he found himself ambushed by a crowd of photographers, while the body jumped up to take some photos of his own. It was all-out war. Whenever Howell Conant saw paparazzi sneaking photographs from unauthorized vantage points, he would try to restage the picture from the same angle, then release his own version in an attempt to spoil the scoop.

Conant did this with Rainier's blessing, for the prince had become obsessed with controlling the privacy of his wedding. In America, Rainier had had to put up with treatment that he considered disrespectful, and he saw no reason to stand for it where he was master in his realm. A local school had been set aside and converted into a makeshift press centre, but its inexperienced Monégasque director took his tone from the prince, disdaining personal contact with his visitors and communicating through booming loudspeaker announcements – in French. As the pressure intensified, the harassed young man retreated into his office completely, refusing to speak to anyone.

It made for impossible confusions and resentment.

Journalists spent a lot of their time just trying to find out the scheduled times of quite uncontroversial public events – and matters came to a head on the night of Sunday, 15 April, four days before the wedding. Rainier and Grace had been attending a white-tie reception at the Winter Sporting Club beside the Hôtel de Paris, and hundreds of photographers waited patiently outside for nearly five hours in the rain. When the couple emerged, however, they dashed straight for their car, shielded by umbrellas, telling their chauffeur to drive off without delay. The outcry was immediate. The press surged around the car, angry and booing, fighting with the police and shaking their fists. 'Go home, Gracie!' someone was heard to say. Two reporters were arrested. A Monégasque policeman broke one French reporter's camera, and the Frenchman bit him angrily in return.

At one-thirty the following afternoon, Jay Kanter was enjoying a quiet lunch with his wife at the Hôtel de Paris when the summons came. Rainier had relented. He invited Grace's agent over to the palace to discuss a new press strategy. Morgan Hudgins, the MGM man, would supervise a daily press briefing – in English and French. There would be more written communiqués in both languages, and it was agreed that the prince and his bride-to-be would linger at at least one prearranged point in their programme every day to allow fresh photographs to be taken without loss of dignity.

That night Grace's whole experience of the wedding week shifted to an easier gear. The evening was scheduled as a sit-down palace dinner for the bride and groom and their bridesmaids, but the couple decided to change the occasion into a more informal gathering. A dozen of Grace's old friends were added to the guest list, and dinner was a help-yourself buffet supper off a long refectory table. There was a huge fire of crackling logs in an open stone fireplace. People ate off their laps, and Grace led off giggling parties of her friends to show them her wedding gifts and some of the sights of the palace.

Rainier was in a particularly relaxed mood, sharing in the rounds of reminiscence and joke-telling – sometimes at his own expense. 'Isn't it amazing how fluently Grace speaks French?' he described himself saying to Father Tucker. 'My Lord Prince,' the priest had replied, 'I knew love was blind, but I didn't know that it was deaf as well.'

The dinner was due to end before midnight. Both Grace and Rainier had a busy schedule the following day. But twelve o'clock came and went without either of them showing the slightest impulse to break up the party. They were enjoying themselves too much, and it was nearly dawn before the fun and games were over.

The host and hostess led their guests out into the palace courtyard and put them in their cars, but they still had no wish for the evening to end. The sky was just starting to lighten. The harbour was silent. The streets were bare and deserted. On several occasions in the chaos and stress of the previous days, Grace had remarked to Rainier how nice it would be to escape from everything, to run away and get married, just the two of them, in some remote mountain chapel. Now her prince did the best for her that he could. Without the benefit of escorts or bodyguards, Prince Rainier drove his fiancée out and down from the palace, then headed the nose of his Mercedes sports car out of Monaco and up into the hills.

They drove up into the picturesque French villages of Èze and La Turbie, getting out of the car to wander between the sleeping houses, hand in hand, climbing the steep cobbled alleyways to find a spot where they could rest, then racing each other back down the hill again. They watched the sun come up over the green-blue waters of the Mediterranean. By eight-thirty they were driving back down the winding

La Turbie road into Monaco again, ready for another hard day of social duties on the basis of absolutely zero sleep. Grace would shudder in later years at the memory of her wedding week. 'It was a nightmare, really, the whole thing,' she recalled, confessing to her friends that it was nearly a year before she and Rainier could look at their wedding photographs with any pleasure. But, up in the hills around La Turbie, the pair of them had successfully demonstrated, if ever there had been any doubt, that they were very much in love, and that there were two real people at the heart of the often undignified circus going on down below.

On the morning of Wednesday, 18 April 1956, in the throne room of the palace of Monaco, Grace Patricia Kelly went through the first of her three wedding ceremonies, the civil ceremony required by Monégasque law. A repetition of the ritual was scheduled immediately afterwards as required by the film cameras of Metro-Goldwyn-Mayer. The final and conclusive religious marriage in the cathedral would not take place until the following day.

Grace looked tired. Her night without sleep and the unremitting pace of her public engagements showed in the black rings beneath her eyes. But she exuded a strange sense of calm and strength. She was a woman on the cusp. She was moving into her destiny, the thing she had wanted and worked for all her life without knowing what it was, and nothing was going to stand in her way. The Count d'Allières, Rainier's chamberlain and chief organizer of the wedding formalities, had collapsed that morning and was in hospital, lying in an oxygen tent. The young director of the press centre was still barricading himself from the press, and the bridesmaids were atwitter over the myriad of last-minute emergencies. But Grace was entering her own stratosphere.

Photo opportunity. Grace with Prince Rainier of Monaco in the gardens of the princely palace, photographed on May 6, 1955 by <u>Paris Match</u>, who arranged the meeting.

To catch a prince. Grace and Rainier announce their engagement, flanked (above) by her parents in Philadelphia, January 5, 1956, and (right) the following evening in New York.

Rehearsing the role. Grace considers the marriage proposal of the Crown Prince (Alec Guinness) in *The Swan*, December 1955.

Farewell to life in Hollywood. Grace and her longtime friend and publicist, Rupert Allan,

carry her dresses from the MGM backlot, March 1956.

Engagement fever. Grace indulges the photographers outside her Fifth Avenue apartment.

Trousseau time. Grace selects footwear for her princessly wardrobe in the spring of 1956.

The crossing. Grace at the rail of the USS Constitution, en route to Monaco, April 1956.

Her Serene Highness. Grace about to enter Monaco's Cathedral on the rock, April 19, 1956, with her father and bridesmaids. Left: With Rainier after the ceremony.

Right: Princess from the Sea. Grace's arrival in Monaco, April 12, 1956, aboard Rainier's yacht, the <u>Deo Juvante II</u>.

Succession secured. Rainier and Grace in the palace with their first child,
Princess Caroline, born January 23, 1957.

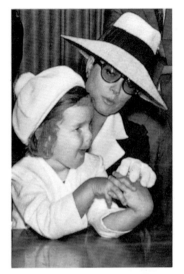

Balcony duty, November 1960. Rainier holds Caroline, while Grace holds Prince Albert, born March 14, 1958. Left: "My Baby." Grace at Kennedy Airport, New York, in 1968, with her younger daughter, Stephanie, born February 1, 1965.

A family like any other. From left: Caroline, Grace, Stephanie, Albert and Rainier, in the palace gardens, 1968.

A life of her own. Grace in the Paris house into which she moved in 1975.

Friends of her own. Swedish actor Per Mattsson, and New York model-turned-restaurateur Jim McMullen (far right).

At her side. Grace with film director Robert Dornhelm in Vienna in 1976.

1

2

3

4

5

The road from La Turbie, September 13, 1982. Police photographs taken within an hour of the accident illustrate: 1, the gap through which Grace drove; 2, the path taken by her Rover down the hillside; 3, the tree struck by the car in the course of its descent; 4, the damage to the upturned Rover. Above: 5, a close-up shows the front of the car and the relative intactness of the driver-side door through which Stephanie crawled to safety.

Family mourning. Following Grace's coffin, September 18, 1982.

A prince alone. Rainier in 1989, seven years after the death of his wife.

Grace's mass card, September 18, 1982: "Lord, I ask not why you took her away. I thank you for having given her to us."

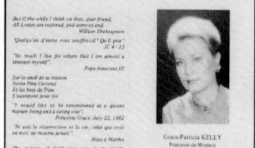

If she doubted her love for her prince or the decision she had made, she did not show it. She was on track, and there was absolutely nothing that could deflect her now.

The civil wedding and its filming was followed by an immense garden party in the grounds of the palace for the adult citizens of Monaco. They crowded in excitedly, all three thousand of them in their best suits and hats, raising their glasses to toast the health of their prince and princess, and consuming three thousand slices of specially baked wedding cake. Their tribute to the happy couple had been the most successful of the public evenings of the prewedding week, a series of folkloric singing and dancing displays on stages set up in the square outside the palace, culminating in an hour of an art form which Monaco considered particularly its own – a spectacular fireworks display. Ex-King Farouk happened to be coming out of the Hôtel de Paris at the moment that the explosions started, and he turned around and headed straight back into the safety of the lobby.

The wedding day dawned clear and bright. It was Thursday, 19 April 1956, and Grace was up early to work on her hair with Virginia Darcy. Outside, the cannon were booming in the harbour. The bridesmaids arrived at eight-thirty on the dot, and Grace had a special little joke or comment for each. It was typical of her to be thinking of her friends, trying to put them at ease. But it also struck Judy Kanter that the bride was drawing on her techniques as an actress to keep herself relaxed before she had to go on stage.

All the guests had been requested to be in their seats in the cathedral by nine-thirty a.m. and, to avoid congestion, no private cars were allowed up onto the rock. Even the grandest of guests found themselves required to step out of their limousines down by the harbour and travel up the hill to the cathedral in shuttle buses – which brought Mrs Barney Balaban, wife of the founder of Paramount Pictures (and mother of Judy Kanter), to a dead halt. She absolutely refused to countenance such an undignified method of transportation, until the waiting bus was pointed out to her. In the front seat sat the Duchess of Westminster, with the seats behind her occupied by rows of equally smart ladies and penguin-suited gentlemen.

The guests made up a striking phalanx as they took their seats in the cathedral – Aristotle Onassis, Randolph Churchill, Ava Gardner, the oriental potentates. Perusing one another intently with their assorted tans and face-lifts, they perfectly illustrated Somerset Maugham's dictum about sunny places and shady people – and the old lizard himself was to be found seated near the front of the congregation, complaining of cold in his feet and gazing balefully at the television cameras. The wedding was being broadcast live to over thirty million viewers in nine European countries, the biggest and most complicated television hook-up in history, at that date.

As the bridesmaids came down the aisle, Father Tucker directed them to their seats. It was his job to supervise this little posse of non-Catholic girls, and throughout the service he directed them to 'Rise', 'Kneel' or 'Sit' in a loud stage whisper. The service was conducted by Monseigneur Gilles Barthe, the Bishop of Monaco, with the assistance of Father John Cartin, the Kellys' parish priest from St Bridget's.

Rainier had designed his own uniform for the occasion, a chocolate soldier mishmash of gold leaf, epaulets, ostrich feathers and sky-blue trousers, which claimed to take its inspiration from the costume of Napoleon's marshals. Spattered with medals and orders, it would have looked overblown in a comic opera, but it verged on the tasteless in the ruler of a less-than-independent country that had not fought a battle in centuries and had sheltered itself behind others in the bloodshed of two world wars.

Hollywood, fortunately, had shown more discrimination in the design of the bride's elaborate but simple-looking costume – twenty-five yards of silk, twenty-five yards of silk taffeta, ninety-eight yards of silk tulle, and over three hundred yards of Valenciennes lace. Grace looked superb in this dress created for her by Helen Rose – sweeping, elegant and swanlike. With her hair pulled straight back beneath a little heart-shaped Juliet cap, there was something Elizabethan about her. Grace had lost ten pounds in the seven days since her arrival in Monaco, and it made her waist even more slender. Within the misting of bustles and puffs could be traced the silhouette of a very beautiful woman.

'Rainier Louis Henri Maxence Bertrand,' asked the bishop, 'will you take Grace Patricia here present for your lawful wife, according to the rite of our Holy Mother the Church?'

'Yes, Monseigneur,' replied the prince.

'Grace Patricia, will you take Rainier Louis Henri Maxence Bertrand here present for your lawful husband, according to the rite of our Holy Mother the Church?'

Grace did not hesitate. 'Yes, Monseigneur,' she replied.

It was a moment whose solemnity was not lessened by the whirring of the cameras and the glare of the television lights. It was personal. It was universal. A frisson ran through the entire congregation. The bishop delivered a short address in which, among several items of advice, he reminded the prince to temper his authority with tenderness, while reminding Grace that earthly beauty is but fleeting. 'He doesn't know Gracie very well,' remarked one of the bridesmaids afterwards, 'if he thinks he has to say that.'

The doors of the cathedral were pushed open, and the Mediterranean sunshine streamed inside. As Maree Frisby and her friends walked down the aisle behind Grace towards the light, they felt an extraordinary sense of closeness to their old friend – a feeling of pride and shared achievement. But they knew at the same time that she was no longer theirs. She was moving into the dimension represented by the cheering crowds outside.

The joy and applause enveloped them as they drove slowly down the road that wound from the rock to the harbour below. There had been something mystical and trancelike about Grace all day. The feeling was almost tangible, and it reached its culmination as the procession drew to a halt outside a little chapel in the corner of the port. It was the church of St Devota, the patron saint of Monaco, a martyr who had preached the gospel in Corsica back in Roman days, and whose body had been borne back to Monaco in a storm – miraculously guided, it was said, by a dove. Monaco's fishermen did homage to Devota on her feast day every January, burning a boat outside her chapel in a dark, almost pagan ritual, and Grace had come to pay homage of her own. All through the wedding ceremony she had carried a small white bible in her hand, with a spray of lilies of the valley. Now she knelt in front of this ancient shrine and laid her bridal bouquet upon its altar, her lips moving almost imperceptibly in prayer. Grace was consecrating herself – offering herself. She was Sister Inez on the floor of the chapel at Ravenhill.

Up in the palace there were photos to pose for and the wedding cake to cut. There were more than six hundred guests at the reception in the courtyard, and it was impossible for Grace and Rainier to meet every one. The bride and groom were polite, but it was clear to those close to them that they could not wait to get away. They had done their social duty for the best part of a week. Now their own time was approaching.

Soon after two-thirty they vanished discreetly, to reappear an hour later in their going-away clothes. Grace had said her farewells in private to her family and friends. Then the couple were driven, for one last, cheering, open-car ride, out through the palace gates, back past the cathedral, and down from the rock to Rainier's yacht, moored and waiting below.

The rest of the wedding party went up onto the battlements, so they could look down into the harbour, and eastward, out towards the sea. One of the bridesmaids had brought a few handfuls of rice with her from the States, and she tossed it up and into the air. Grace's light form could be seen on the bridge of the distant yacht beside Rainier, waving farewell as the boat moved away. Their wake was attended by a navy of small craft that was as busy and boisterous as the flotilla that had greeted Grace the previous week, and it was nearly five o'clock, with the sun already beginning to set behind the hills, before the thin white vessel bearing the new princess seaward had left the last of its escorts behind.

PART FOUR
PRINCESS

NINETEEN

Family Business

O N A WINTER'S night in January 1297, a group of
hooded friars came knocking on the doors of the castle
of Monaco asking for shelter. Taking pity on the holy men,
the Genoese occupiers of the fortress on the rock swung
open the gates – to be slaughtered where they stood. The
'friars' were members and soldiers of the Grimaldi family, an
ambitious clan of adventurers from northern Italy, led by
Francesco Grimaldi, known to history as 'il Malizia' – 'François the Cunning'. The attackers wore armour and carried
swords beneath their religious camouflage. They seized control of Monaco from the Genoese, and they were to remain
the rulers of the place, with just a few interruptions, from
that day forward.

The Grimaldis have always been proud of this story. When
they acquired a coat of arms, they chose as their crest the
figures of two saintly-looking friars producing swords from
their robes. Their modern guidebooks start by celebrating
the original and productive cunning of 'il Malizia' – Prince
Rainier's current yacht bears the name – and to judge from
the number of times that Grace herself told the tale, it was the
starting point for her own understanding of her new family's
history. But the American princess was not so aware, or,

305

perhaps, she chose not to be aware, of how sleight-of-hand and ruthlessness were ongoing traditions in the family business of which she was now a partner.

The rock was the foundation of the Grimaldis' power. It looms sheer and tough out of the Mediterranean, a northerly Gibraltar. When you look down on it from the mountains above, you can see how, in the age of swords and sailing ships, the man who controlled the rock controlled this corner of the coast. For centuries the Grimaldis made their living by extortion, levying their tolls on passing ships for the right of safe passage, and sallying out, effectively as pirates, to discipline any vessel that declined to pay up. They played off their more powerful neighbours against each other, winning their status as princes after they sided with Spain in the sixteenth century, then switching smartly to France when that kingdom's star moved into the ascendant a hundred and twenty years later. They never quite made it as full-scale royal princes, but they did secure the lesser rank of 'Serene Highness'.

The native Monégasques regarded their Grimaldi rulers with a reverence that approached awe. A small, quick and swarthy people who resembled the Corsicans in their mixture of French and Italian characteristics, these few thousand fisher folk and olive farmers were both enriched and protected by the strong men up on the rock. There was not a coastal community from Marseilles to Genoa that enjoyed a better deal. So the locals shut their ears to what an envious world had to say about their rulers. Princess Charlotte-Catherine Grimaldi was a byword for her promiscuity at the court of Louis XIV in the late seventeenth century. A coquette who shocked even the libertines of Versailles, 'Madame de Monaco' was said to have enjoyed affairs with both men and women, not to mention, more conventionally, the favours of the Sun King himself. But back in Monaco she was known as the protectress of the Convent of the Visitation, and it is as a pious and exemplary figure that she is recalled in official Monégasque history to this day.

The mid-nineteenth century heralded the end of ministates like Monaco. In 1861 France annexed the surrounding towns and villages – over ninety per cent of the principality's surface area – leaving it with the rock, the harbour – and not much more. But just when all seemed lost, Prince Charles III, the ruling Grimaldi, came up with the casino that was to guarantee the principality's survival into the twentieth century. Reorganizing Monaco's infant tourist business and leasing it out to the *Société des Bains de Mer*, Charles more than justified his subjects' confidence in their princely rulers, and the hill across the harbour on which the new casino stood has borne his name ever since – Monte Carlo.

The casino transformed Monaco and inspired its racy modern identity. The visitors who set the tone were the archdukes from Russia and Eastern Europe with their entourages of servants and private rail cars. They gambled in the casino at night and worked off their hangovers next morning by promenading beneath the palm trees or taking potshots at the hapless pigeons released by the dozen from baskets on the casino cliffs – the famous *Tir aux Pigeons*. Lillie Langtry, Alice Keppel, La Belle Otero, Mata Hari – Europe's most glamorous courtesans reigned in Monte Carlo. Sarah Bernhardt and Raoul Gunsbourg brought theatre and opera. Diaghilev brought his *Ballets Russes*. The glamour and naughtiness bubbled endlessly, both embellished and symbolized by the lush stucco curves of the casino building, the Hôtel de Paris, the Hermitage, and the other creamy masterpieces of Charles Garnier, supreme architect of the belle époque.

The Grimaldis themselves steered clear of the social whirl

on the hill across the harbour. Less flamboyant than some of their ancestors, they framed laws that forbade members of the princely family, or any Monégasque, from entering the casino as a player. Charles III spent the last decade of his life a total recluse, while the passion of his son, Albert, was for long voyages of maritime exploration. Albert's architectural contribution to the principality was a huge Oceanographic Museum that he raised on the rock near the cathedral, and he filled it with narwhal horns, stuffed grampuses, and the countless pale and pickled specimens that he brought back from his maritime expeditions.

The enthusiasm of Albert's son, Louis, was for soldiering. Louis enlisted in the French army, being assigned to service in North Africa, and this led to the bizarre arrangements surrounding the birth and succession of Rainier III and his sister, Tiny. In the course of his months quartered in Constantine, Algeria, Louis had a love affair with the daughter of his washerwoman. They had a child together, born in 1898, a little girl originally given the name of Louise-Juliette, but later to be known as Princess Charlotte – and eventually, in the family, as 'Mamou', the mother-in-law who disliked Grace so intensely. Having spent the first twenty years of her life under the slur of illegitimacy, Mamou found her status transformed at the end of the First World War, when the victorious allies woke up to the fact that, in the event of Albert and Louis dying, the Monégasque succession would pass to a German family – the house of von Urach, who were relatives by marriage.

Overnight the washerwoman's granddaughter became a princess, legitimized and rapidly married to a young French aristocrat, Count Pierre de Polignac. The business nature of this alliance, concluded in March 1920, was made clear by Pierre agreeing to change his surname to Grimaldi and by the count being moved up several noble stations to become an instant prince. By the normal European rules of noble succession, Pierre's children were Polignacs, but by changing his surname, the new prince had made it possible for the Grimaldis to maintain their claim, by their own rules at least, to be the one-and-only, centuries-old ruling house of Monaco.

The marriage of Mamou and Pierre might have survived without love. Without much affection or respect, the couple were doomed, and the price was paid by their children. Tiny and Rainier became pawns in the all-too-open battles that were fought between their parents. 'When we were with mother,' Rainier told Jeffrey Robinson in 1988, 'we were always being told, "When you see your father don't say anything to him about me . . ." When we were with father, we were always being told, "Don't say anything to your mother . . ." That wasn't easy.'

In 1935, the twelve-year-old Rainier, who was just starting his studies at Stowe, the English public school, found himself the object of an embarrassingly public custody battle in the British High Court that dragged on for eighteen months. The marriage that had been arranged to create the appearance of family unity and continuity had produced the very opposite.

The Second World War generated further disrepute. Monaco's substantial Italian colony, who had moved there to staff the developing tourist industry, were largely pro-Mussolini, while Prince Louis, who had succeeded his father Albert in 1922, thought along the same lines as the many French army officers who supported Pétain and his Vichy government of collaboration. Hitler was the dominant power in Europe, and Louis was willing to live with that. He received the Consul General and Military Commandant that Berlin sent to Monaco, and from 1943 onwards the principality became an R & R centre for German officers of all the services, including the SS and the Gestapo. The Germans played in the casino, which remained open for business throughout the war, and patronized the prostitutes in the ever-understanding Hôtel de Paris. Monégasque lawyers did a brisk trade in the paperwork of companies created to launder the war profits of several hundred leading Nazis and collaborationist businessmen.

On the outbreak of hostilities, Monaco's trade consuls in the United States tried to claim that the principality was technically neutral and should, accordingly, be granted the concessions that went with neutral status. But the State Department dismissed the claim with scorn. 'There is no reason for hair-splitting construction here,' wrote one official on a document in 1940. 'Monaco is, to all intents and purposes, belligerent.'

Once the Allies had invaded Europe, the Grimaldis shifted their stance in their time-honoured fashion. Rainier had spent the war comfortably and far from danger. He was a wealthy young university student in Vichy France, studying in Paris and Montpellier. But late in September 1944, three weeks after Monaco was liberated by the Allies, the young prince volunteered to join the French army, where he was assigned to the intelligence department. In this capacity he saw seventeen months of service and was awarded the medals that he wore so proudly on his wedding day.

As the new alignment of Europe took shape, State Department memos flew on the subject of Monaco's dubious war record. 'It was well known,' minuted the US Embassy in Paris on 10 February 1945, 'that the Prince and his advisers, as well as a large proportion of the people of Monaco, had been highly uncooperative with the Allies, and pro-Axis.' Using their special banking and taxation arrangements, 'these people had connived to defraud the French and other Allied treasuries.' The US Consulate in Nice sent a query to Washington. The prince of Monaco had invited the American general in charge of the area to make an official call, but the general was reluctant to do this in view of the prince's 'alleged pro-Axis attitude and sympathies during [the] occupation period'.

Washington considered the matter, then instructed the officer to make his visit. 'If the French do not contemplate any action . . . there would appear no reason why our general should not call.' It was State Department policy to leave questions about Monaco to France. 'Monaco appears to be, in theory, a Constitutional Principality,' ran Washington's briefing paper on the subject, 'but, in reality, it is a protectorate of the French government.' If France was prepared to let bygones be bygones, why should America make a fuss?

The Nazi Consul General and the SS officers whooping it up in Monte Carlo were consigned to history, and the accession of Rainier in 1949, following the death of Prince Louis, seemed another reason to forgive and forget. Rainier himself had 'not so far shown himself to be possessed of force of character or qualities of leadership,' reported Albert Clattenburg, Jr, the US consul in Nice, bringing Washington up to date on Monaco's problems at the end of 1955; the principality remained 'a hot-bed of gossip, scandal and neighbourly bad feeling.' But there was always the hope that 'an energetic young wife with a talent for running things . . . could right the present situation.'

TWENTY

Biological Equation

RAINIER AND GRACE spent much of their honeymoon cruising round the island of Corsica, taking full advantage of their yacht to explore deserted coves and beaches, where they could be on their own. It was the tonic they needed after the pressures of their wedding week. Grace was not a good sailor, and the ancient, polished-wood motor yacht was an ungainly conveyance when the sea got rough. Grace was sick for much of the time – but perhaps it was not entirely the boat's fault. When she got back to Monaco at the end of May, the doctors confirmed her suspicions. 'We're preggos!' she wrote in delight to Judy Kanter, Maree Frisby, and to every other girlfriend whose address she could muster.

Grace had fulfilled the first, and, in some ways, the most important, of her new duties with exemplary speed. It was a crude and basic business, but getting pregnant was the bottom line.

'It gives great joy to the princess and myself,' Rainier announced on 2 August, 'to share this new happiness with you . . . In light of this news, so important for me and for yourselves . . . I ask you to trust in the choice I have made for Monaco's future, and, also, to remember that the Principality has endured, and will only endure, as long as its Sovereign Prince has full and complete exercise of his power.'

Being the other half of the biological equation carried its own responsibilities. Rainier's political twist to his family announcement was prompted by the ongoing difficulties he was encountering with his elected National Council and with its leading troublemaker, Tiny's lover, Jean-Charles Rey, with whom Rainier had recently quarrelled. The two men were not to speak to each other for nearly six years. 'I see him on the golf course,' Rey told Colin Cross, a reporter for London's *Daily Express*. 'We look at each other, but we never speak. You may think it's foolish for two men to behave in such a way, but there it is.'

Grace had a great deal of shopping that she had to do for the new baby, and she wanted to do it in the stores where she felt at home. So September 1956 found her back in America again, half proud, half shy at the rapid outcome of the wedding that the world had celebrated with her only five months earlier. As she arrived in New York with Rainier, she was carrying a curiously large, almost square handbag that she had purchased on the journey from Hermès in Paris, and she was photographed holding it strategically in front of her, both shielding and concealing the little protuberance in her tummy. The bag was derived from a piece of luggage once used to carry bridles and riding tack, and it became known henceforward as the 'Kelly bag' (current price of an Hermès original in lizard – $7,131.57).

The average American reporter found it difficult to get excessively obsequious towards the girl from Henry Avenue. 'Mrs Rainier' was how several questioners addressed her when Grace and her husband went to the White House to pay a courtesy call. But the country was transfixed with her new condition. The visit to America by the prince and princess of the mile-square state of Monaco attracted far more attention than the presidents of Italy and Mexico who had visited Washington in recent months. The life and adventures of Grace had become, in some sense, part of America's own family life.

'They told me about morning sickness,' Grace told Olga Curtis in a nationally syndicated interview on the subject, 'but they didn't tell me you could be sick all day every day.' It was reported that the princess had already gained twenty-six pounds – 'My doctor,' the mother-to-be confessed cheerfully, 'says I eat too much.' As for the baby's name: 'we're looking for names that are just as good in English as French.'

America was as eager to share in the pregnancy of its own princess as it had been in her engagement and marriage, but Grace was mindful of where her new loyalties lay. 'Last season the Oceanographic Museum drew over 100,000 more visitors than did the Casino,' she told Hedda Hopper, earnestly rattling off statistics as if she were the principality's Director of Tourism. 'Over 15,000 tourists checked in at hotels in Monaco the first two months after the wedding – 3,000 more than last season.'

Rainier and Grace shopped the length of Fifth and Madison Avenues for baby clothes and equipment, then did it all over again to pick up trunkfuls of the latest electrical gadgets and labour saving appliances which had not yet reached Europe. They wanted to modernize the palace, and they also had plans to build themselves a retreat away from Monaco up in the hills above La Turbie. They packed up Grace's Fifth Avenue apartment, getting her antique French furniture crated for a return journey across the Atlantic – and they also spent as much time as they could in imitation of the most successful evening of their wedding week: relaxing in private with Grace's old friends, eating off plates in their laps, and reminiscing. Rainier was even persuaded to try his hand at charades.

'Please do not use the W.C. while the train is standing in the station,' was the first mime that the prince drew.

'I thought, "Oh, no!" ' remembers Tom Guinzberg, Rita Gam's husband. 'But Rainier just squatted down and did his stuff like a trooper.'

One late autumn weekend just before Grace and Rainier were due to leave, the group went out to the Long Island home of Marcel Palmaro, Monaco's Consul in New York. There was a chill in the air. The leaves were on the ground, and as Grace strolled through them, kicking up their dampness, she grew nostalgic.

'Oh, how I love it . . .' she said. 'It's this time of year, the smell of the leaves and the wet dirt, the colours . . .'

'It reminds me of the start of school,' said Carolyn Scott.

'And of football games and dates with new boys and first kisses,' continued Grace, almost melancholic. The East Coast girl was suddenly homesick for falling leaves and misty evenings. Then she stopped abruptly, changing the subject as she realized she might be betraying the fact that she was not totally enchanted to be returning to Monaco. In April, Grace's departure on the *Constitution* had been a euphoric leap across the ocean with scarcely a backward glance. Now, little more than six months later, the princess was less starry-eyed about the realities of life in the palace on the rock.

'The poor girl really had a tough year or so of it out there to start with,' remembers Maree Frisby Rambo. 'It was astonishing, the number of people who gave her a hard time.'

There was the butler who supervised the wine, the silver and the table settings. He resisted every attempt that Grace made to change even the slightest detail of the existing routines. 'We don't do things that way here,' he would sniff. After weeks of manoeuvring and cajoling, Grace would finally manage to get some of the lights switched off in rooms that were not in use, only to find them blazing brightly again a few days later. Grace had been looking forward to working out new flower arrangements that made use of the striking and beautiful blooms in the palace gardens, and she carefully explained her ideas to the servant who was in charge of cut flowers. He listened politely – and went on doing exactly what he had always done.

There were bonuses to living in a fairy-tale castle. The embroidery room was staffed by peasant girls whose full-time job was the stitching of beautiful designs for Grace's pillows and bed linen, as well as the hand-embroidering of her lingerie. But there were also mysterious corridors and wings that palace custom declared out of bounds, and where, Grace complained to Maree, she could not get anyone to take her.

'Grace told me once how miserable she was in those early months,' remembers Gwen Robyns, the author who became a friend of Grace in the mid 1970s. 'She used to sit there with her terrible morning sickness, and the Mistral irritating her sinuses to distraction in this gloomy old palace, longing to get cracking and to bring some sunlight into the dust, but being quite sure that everyone was snickering behind her back at her American ideas and her terrible French.'

The servants would not have been a problem if Grace had felt on surer ground with her husband. 'With Rainier,' says Gwen Robyns, 'she always felt as if she were walking on eggs.' Grace had had a taste of Rainier's moodiness during the weeks of their engagement in America, but she had not bargained for quite how imperious the prince's temper could be. Six months of romantic letter-writing and a few days of Christmas cheer had been an imperfect way to test the true mettle of her mate for life. Grace had accepted Rainier without attempting to explore the darker corners of his spirit, and, once on his home territory, she discovered that her new husband had a fearsome temper. From being sweet as pie at one moment, he could snap unpredictably in a second.

'For God's sake,' the prince yelled at her on one occasion in front of his secretary when he saw the choice of flowers that Grace had made for the guest suite of a visiting dignitary. 'White chrysanthemums are the flowers of the tomb!'

The secretary who witnessed this outburst was Madge Tivey-Faucon, an Australian lady who later provided *France Dimanche* and *Cosmopolitan* magazines with ample details of Rainier's temper and the effect it had on Grace: 'How many times have I seen the princess coming out of her room sniffling, red-eyed,' wrote 'Tiv' in 1964. "I have a cold," she would tell me, to hide her embarrassment . . . Once she had her hair cut very short against the wishes of the prince . . . He took one look at his wife, and it must have taken him three seconds to discover what was different. When he found out what it was, he became red in the face, his mouth tightened and he clenched his fist. The princess stopped in the middle of the room embarrassed. And the prince, with all his force, threw his glass on the floor.'

Rainier's troubled family background had scarcely equipped him to be a sensitive and caring marriage partner. He found it difficult to give of himself emotionally. He had never been taught how to trust or to share. His explosions were hot and human, at least. It was the silences that were harder for his wife to take, the long hours that her partner spent radiating displeasure. When Rainier was withdrawn and stewing, he was the very opposite of the sensitive and amusing soul who had tripped the light fantastic in his love letters.

If there is anything more perverse and bloody-minded than a longtime bachelor, it is a royal bachelor. Strangers encountered the phenomenon in Rainier's habit of going to sleep when he was bored. He was famous for it. In the middle of a dinner party, in the royal box at the opera, on a sofa making small talk – the eyes would roll, the head would droop, and His Serene Highness would sign off for half an hour or more, snoring, sometimes, like an old man twice his age. It was not a matter of some mysterious medical affliction, as Monaco gossip maintained. It simply reflected Rainier's regal disdain and his lack of interest in anyone who could not, jesterlike, keep him perpetually amused.

That was the princely and old-fashioned side to Grace's partner for life. But inside there was a spirit who was striving to improve – the sardonic and funny man who had wooed and won the famous film star, who was not afraid to squat and strain when his turn came round at charades. At his best, the despot could be open and unpretentious – modern not only in his love of gadgets and jazz records, but in his attempts to be a sensitive human being. If the reasons of state which impelled Rainier to marry Grace had included a vision of how his miniature country might be opened up to the wealth and influence of the new world, the prince's more personal attraction had been to the warmth with which a democratic and natural American girl might open him up as well.

Nowhere did the sensitive and human Rainier show to better effect than in his preparations to be a father in the final months of 1956. Child-rearing was an area in which the prince had made a conscious decision to do better than his predecessors. The animals in his zoo had been the only previous outlet for his parental instincts. The prince cared for them personally when they were sick, bringing baby chimps and tiger cubs up to the palace so that he could nurse them himself.

Now Rainier worked with Grace on the preparations for their own first arrival. The shipping waybill showed that the couple's loot from their New York shopping spree weighed no less than two tons, and they set out the nursery items – toys, a wicker crib and white lacquered furniture – in a room adjoining their private apartment in the palace. George Stacey, the decorator of Grace's Fifth Avenue apartment, happened to be working in France that autumn, and he came down to help them. 'He's designed a really ingenious cabinet and shelving arrangement for the baby's linen!' Grace wrote home excitedly, revealing that the colour scheme for the baby's room would be in her favourite yellow.

The original plan had been for the baby to be delivered in a small clinic in town. But Grace had been jostled on one of her excursions from the palace. A strange woman had pushed through the crowd, placing her open hand on Grace's belly and rubbing the spot to wish the princess good luck. At the time Grace had laughed, but mulling it over later, the incident made her uneasy. What if the woman had not been well-intentioned?

Grace discussed her anxieties with her husband, and Rainier agreed. The library in their private apartments was converted into a delivery room, and it was announced that the baby would be delivered in the palace. This came as a considerable disappointment to the reporters who had already started to gather. One group of photographers had bribed the ambulance driver to slow down as he passed a prearranged spot, so they could get a picture of the princess in labour.

In the middle of January 1957, Grace's gynaecologist, Dr Emile Hervet, a specialist from Paris, told her he thought that the baby would be arriving earlier than the scheduled February delivery date. Grace telephoned Philadelphia, so Ma Kelly was waiting outside the library soon after dawn on the morning of 23 January, with Prince Pierre, Tiny, and a chain-smoking Prince Rainier.

The mother-to-be was worried. 'I still can't get used to

being a wife,' she had written to Prudy a few days earlier, 'let alone a mother.' But Grace had done her homework as usual. After reading the latest childbirth and child-rearing manuals, she had decided that the infant would be breast-fed, and would also come into the world as naturally as possible, without the benefit of anaesthetic. She went into labour at three o'clock in the morning, and at 9:27 a.m. she gave birth to a healthy, eight-pound, eleven-ounce baby girl – just nine months and four days after the day she had married. The doctors handed Grace her child, and she wept.

Down in the harbour a cannon fired twenty-one blasts, and the bells of the principality's fourteen churches and chapels jangled out in merry disorder. Onassis's huge yacht, the *Christina*, led a chorus of ship's horns and sirens. A national holiday was declared. Monaco's solitary prisoner was released from jail. The new baby was given the names Caroline Louise Marguerite – and 4,000 miles away in Philadelphia Jack Kelly was asked how he felt.

'Oh, shucks,' he replied. 'I'd been hoping for a boy.'

One year and two months later, on 14 March 1958, he was granted his wish – and the cannon in the harbour sounded 101 times, suggesting that Monaco had probably felt much the same, but had been rather more considerate towards the feelings of a first-time mother. Less than two years after her wedding day, Grace had most efficiently safeguarded the succession of her adopted family and country. His voice quavering with emotion, Rainier announced that his son and heir would be christened Albert Alexandre Louis Pierre.

The family setting that Grace and Rainier created to relax with their new baby son and daughter was Roc Agel, an isolated, sixty-acre estate in the hills above Monaco, which they purchased soon after their wedding. Rainier's romantic, dawn escape with his bride-to-be up into the mists around La Turbie had been the private highlight of a hectic and overloaded time, and now Roc Agel played the same role in their family life. 'Roc Agel is the place', said Grace, 'where we close the door on the world.'

Perched at 2,300 feet above sea level, Roc Agel was an old Provençal *mas* – part farmhouse, part fortress. It had thick stone walls, huge beams and a heavy tiled roof. Even when restored by Grace and Rainier, it had a tumbledown quality about it. Literally up in the clouds at many times of the year, the place could not be overlooked from any point, and its new princely owners left most of its scrubby, fragrant terrain of herbs and bushes to run wild. A mixture of pets and farm animals – goats, rabbits, pigs, chickens and cows – were free to roam or be played with as they wished, and they might find themselves joined at the weekend by an animal or two from Rainier's zoo.

Cool, green and disorganized, Roc Agel was the very opposite of the manicured, dusty grind of Monaco in high summer, and it became home to Grace in a way that the palace on the rock never did. This was where she could barbecue her beloved hamburgers and put on the faded shirts and jeans she had told Rupert Allan that she *knew* she would be wearing in the south of France. Rainier was also at his best here, shaking off his moods and Ruritanian grandeur in the cast iron and metal workshop where he donned welder's mask and gloves. He had a big-band drum kit which he would beat to death, creating his own accompaniments to his favourite records from the swing era.

Sleepover guests were not encouraged. Rainier did not like strange faces at breakfast. Visitors were lodged down in the palace or at one of the hotels in town, and were ferried up the mountain for a rare and privileged peek. George Stacey had decorated the main living area of the farmhouse with a sombre black chintz that was a curious echo of the dark, cabbage-rose dress that Grace had been wearing when she first met Rainier, and specially favoured friends were allowed into Grace's personal bathroom. Here, at the very private heart of her very private place, the princess had decorated the walls with the mementoes of a life that had come, in only a short space of time, to seem remarkably remote – the hard-won career of a film star in Hollywood.

Early in 1960, Grace got word from Henry Avenue that her father was feeling sick. At the age of seventy, Jack Kelly's robust good health had suddenly deserted him, and in April he went into hospital for exploratory surgery. The doctors carried out a second operation at the end of May, but found there was nothing they could do for him except to sew him back up. Jack Kelly had cancer of the stomach.

Grace flew immediately to Philadelphia. Her father was lying in a private room that Ma Kelly had arranged for him at the hospital of Women's Med, and the nurse who showed Grace to the room was struck by the anxiety that made the princess's features almost unrecognizable – until the door was opened. Then the actress paused, drew a deep breath, straightened up her body, and spread a smile across her face. Daddy was in need of cheering up.

Jack Kelly died on 20 June 1960. 'My wife and children have . . . given me much happiness and a pardonable pride,' he declared in his will, a rambling twelve-page document that he had composed in his own, inimitable, grandstanding style – short on financial details and definitely long on advice:* 'In this document I can only give you things, but

---

*Having already distributed most of his shares in Kelly for Brickwork among his children, Jack Kelly showed an estate of $1,193,062.99 (just over $5 million in 1990s values). An enterprising small publisher in Philadelphia reprinted the will and sold it at $7.00 a copy.

if I had the choice to give you worldly goods or character, I would give you character ... With character you will get worldly goods, because character is loyalty, honesty, ability, sportsmanship — and, I hope, a sense of humour.'

It was classic Jack Kelly, the proclamation of tough and heroic principles that he had dared to try to live up to, and if, in life, his imperfections had sometimes inflicted pain and had caused confusion in his family, it was only right, in death, that his achievements should be granted the honour they deserved. John Brendan Kelly had pulled pretty close to his dream. His energies and paradoxes were the mixture that had made Grace what she was, and it was not surprising that she took her father's loss very hard.

Soon after she got back to Monaco from the funeral, Grace was sitting one evening beside Rainier on the little balcony that overlooked the palace courtyard. She was listening to a Chopin concert, and as the music rolled over her, she was suddenly overcome with such emotion that she had to get up in tears and leave her seat. It was a most un-Grace-like display of public distress, and people could only conclude that she was seeing herself suddenly in that same courtyard four years earlier, on her wedding day, coming down the great marble staircase, steadying herself on her father's solid and brawny arm.

Now Coach was gone. Grace Kelly, Princess Grace of Monaco, had graduated by any measure. In November 1959, she had reached the age of thirty. She had a husband, two children, her own kingdom. She would have to row the rest of the course out on her own.

TWENTY-ONE

Public Relations

THE ARRIVAL of Grace Kelly had a dramatic impact upon the financial fortunes of Monaco. As Grace had been able to boast to Hedda Hopper on her trip back to America in the autumn of 1956, hotel bookings and tourist revenues in the principality increased spectacularly in the months that followed her wedding. In the early fifties Monaco's economy had been so depressed that the employees of the *Société des Bains de Mer* had one month's pay deducted from their annual salary. By the end of the decade that situation was quite reversed.

This reflected, in part, the growing prosperity and mobility of Europe and the postwar world. The age of mass tourism was just beginning. But the attraction that gave Monaco its special aura after April 1956 was not the casino and the SBM, the Oceanographic Museum, or the historic traditions of the House of Grimaldi. It was the fairy-tale presence of Princess Grace.

This posed a dilemma which haunts the Grimaldi family to this day. Publicity was their lifeblood, but it was the death of them as well. The yellow colour scheme of the nursery, the childbirths without anaesthetic, the breast-feeding of the babies – these were the humanizing details that helped make

Monaco a destination with an identity of its own. But they were also surrenders of privacy that threatened to deny the human beings who were living the fairy tale the basic rights and decencies of an ordinary human life.

Prince Rainier had never been especially fond of the press, and the coverage of his engagement and wedding pushed his feelings to the point of loathing. 'I don't HATE, I despise!!' he wrote to Rupert Allan in April 1957, the first anniversary of his wedding. 'The mighty press can stretch like an enormous octopus and inject its poison through its stinging suction.'

Rainier was writing from Switzerland, where he and Grace had taken the three-month-old Caroline for their first family holiday. The *Daily Sketch*, a London tabloid, had reported a kidnapping attempt against the baby, and other papers had embellished the story. 'The kidnapping was a pure invention,' wrote Rainier in fury. 'It is criminal, as it could give someone the idea.'

Grace and Rainier had thought long and hard about the problems of bringing up their children in the spotlight. 'I do not want that my daughter has her childhood encumbered and poisoned by an excess of journalistic publicity . . .' the prince wrote to Allan in January 1958. 'It MUST be dosed and carefully timed so not to become saturated . . . I think we must choose a number-one magazine and give it to them and not have more than two stories a year on her.'

This was Rainier's and Grace's fatal fallacy. Both felt quite confident – Rainier, as a prince, Grace as someone who had played the Hollywood game and had emerged triumphant – that they could control their publicity and exploit it to their own advantage. The rulers of Europe's comparable royal mini-states, the principality of Liechtenstein and the Grand Duchy of Luxembourg, had a horror of personal publicity. Their pictures were never in the papers, and they were proud to be considered out of date. But even as the most precious experiences of his life were being sullied, cheapened and distorted by the mass media, the Prince of Monaco cherished the illusion that he could turn it all to his own advantage.

'Object,' ran a document that Rainier sent Rupert Allan under the title *Idea for the Organization of Press Relations Service to TSH* [Their Serene Highnesses] *the Prince and Princess of Monaco*, 'the good-taste publicity that does not seem promoted or sponsored. The dignified and true stories on TSH and the principality. Protection against the bad, ill-meaning press articles, and screening of the press demands, with elimination of a quantity of them, and a proper scheduling and programme of those accepted.'

The memo was unsigned, but it could have been drawn up by the sorcerer's apprentice. Rainier and Grace had not appreciated – and, to be fair, no one else in the 1950s seems to have considered – that controlled doses of personal publicity might not, in fact, quieten public curiosity about the lives of the rich and famous, but could actually have the opposite effect. The press coverage of the engagement and marriage of Rainier and Grace, followed by the regular, glossy magazine peekings into their family life that the couple themselves organized over the next twenty years, blazed the trail that led from the nudges and winks of Walter Winchell to the tabloid exposés of *Hard Copy*. The access might be controlled, but people came to take its relative intimacy for granted. They wanted to know still more. The world's heady dream life with Princess Grace and her growing family through the 1960s and 1970s was to provide a major stimulus to the modern, mass-market addiction to celebrity.

Rupert Allan was the man to whom both Grace and Rainier looked to supervise 'the good-taste publicity', and at first Allan worked through the American publicist, Arthur Jacobs, and the Los Angeles firm of Rogers, Cowan &

Brenner, who represented some of Hollywood's major stars and producers. As their name suggested, Rogers, Cowan & Brenner were something like a Wall Street law firm, charging high fees and operating corporately, and Rainier did not like it. He objected to the expenses that seemed to double their fees, and he took exception to the representative they assigned to take care of him and Grace on a visit to London soon after the start of her second pregnancy. 'He could not have been more useless and wrong in every sense of the word,' he complained to Allan. 'I was appalled at the idea that your company was represented by such a complete, cheap "zero".'

The solution was for Allan to work for Monaco alone, and over the years he helped Rainier and Grace create the PR network that suited them. Allan had already found the couple a press secretary who could handle day-to-day queries on the spot. Nadia Lacoste, a tough and intelligent woman of Grace's age, dealt with most European press inquiries. Based in New York, Howell Conant photographed and arranged the picture features in the big American magazines. 'If a fellow wanted a story on Grace,' remembers Conant, 'he damn well wrote a *nice* story, not some sleazy thing.'

Look magazine was the outlet of choice. 'When Bill Arthur was the editor,' remembers Conant, 'he would send over all the text to Grace for her approval.' *Look* was also willing to accept Conant's packages of photos as edited by Grace. '*Life*', remembers Conant, 'would not accept that, so we did not use them very often.'

Rupert Allan's principal work was carried on behind the scenes. The correspondence files of Hedda Hopper, now in the archives of the Academy of Motion Pictures in Hollywood, are notable for the private 'briefing' letters that were sent to the gossip columnist by movie stars anxious to curry favour – home-cooked press releases in which some of

Hollywood's most famous names grovelled to plant stories or to correct unfavourable publicity. David Niven was particularly energetic with his 'Dear Hedda' letters. In the case of Grace and Rainier, it was Rupert Allan who did the writing.

'I've never seen two happier people than Grace and the prince,' Allan wrote to Hopper from Gstaad in September 1957. 'There is absolutely no truth whatsoever – nor has there ever been – to the silly rumours made up by hungry European journalists about rifts and the like .. They are the happiest young married couple I know.'

Allan had a flatteringly personal titbit to pass on to the columnist from the princess. 'I told Grace how you thought her hair photographed better lighter, and she tells me that it is exactly the shade now that it was when she made her first films in Hollywood.' Grace's blondness had always needed a little extra assistance.

Allan also had some sterner news. Uncle George's friend, Gant Gaither, who had become part of the Manhattan House circle and had been one of the Kelly party on the *Constitution*, had published a book, *Princess of Monaco*, which had caused offence to both Grace and Rainier. Gaither had not written maliciously. The adulatory tone of his book was actually embarrassing. But he had trespassed into forbidden territory when he alluded to the rows inside the Grimaldi family – and he had also hinted at Grace's unhappiness over the newspaper series written by her mother.

'She is just very disappointed,' Allan wrote to Hedda Hopper. 'She had only given him approval on the *Constitution* to write a story on the trip on the *Constitution* and the wedding. He enlarged the scope of the book on his own and without approval.'

Grace and Rainier did not speak to Gaither for years. He was cut off – abruptly banished from the group of old friends who would visit Monaco in the summer and get together with Grace and Rainier on their regular visits to the States. The ban expressed the couple's sense of betrayal, but it was also intended, some of Grace's friends suspected, as a warning to everyone else. 'It was the first visible symptom,' wrote Judy Kanter, 'of a disease Grace caught almost at the moment she got to Monaco. It was called royalism.'

This was not entirely fair. Gaither subsequently made his peace, and was, in time, invited back into the charmed circle. It was not especially 'royalist' of Rainier and Grace to expect basic discretion of their friends. Their fault lay in wanting it both ways. It was their choice to exploit the details of their personal lives for the greater glory and prosperity of Monaco, so it was hardly realistic to get on their high horses when, from time to time, the wrong details got disclosed.

Wanting it both ways, however, was the way things worked in Monaco. It was the very nature of the place – a state which called itself independent, but which could not survive a day without the tolerance of France. Rainier's public relations campaign was a modern version of the dance the Grimaldis had performed for centuries. He was laying claim to a sovereignty and substance he did not quite possess – and his bluff was called in the spring of 1962, six years after his marriage to Grace.

It was not just tourists that were enticed to Monaco in the late fifties. Businessmen and tax exiles came too. Monaco's minimal corporate levies – and non-existent income tax – had long attracted a select group of international cleversticks and the superrich, but the wedding of the century had made it everybody's secret. By 1961 Monaco's business turnover had reached $128 million, a 400 per cent increase in ten years. For 1962 a turnover of $200 million dollars was anticipated.

Rainier had actively encouraged this process. His

country's dependence on its casino income had embarrassed him ever since his school days, when boys called him 'fat Monaco' and made jokes about his growing up to be a croupier. It was a regular theme of his interviews that the casino brought in less income than people imagined, and in 1960 he appointed an energetic young American, Martin Dale, the former US Vice-Consul in Nice, to be the economic equivalent of Rupert Allan, drumming up business publicity and new investors for Monaco.

Wiry and brainy, the twenty-nine-year-old Dale carried the title of Privy Councillor to Rainier. Jealous Monégasques called him 'the pocket Richelieu'. Endlessly scheming, Dale worked with Yves Laye, a French lawyer from Algeria, to set up MEDEC, the Monaco Economic Development Corporation, a glossy Chamber of Commerce operation, and they rapidly got results. In less than two years MEDEC attracted 103 new corporate entities to Monaco and helped arrange several hundred more business permits for foreign corporations.

The trouble was that a large number of these new arrivals were French. All that a Marseilles trucking contractor needed to do was to buy office space in Monaco, secure his business permit through MEDEC, and get Monégasque licence plates for his trucks. The vehicles could remain garaged in Marseilles, and he could go on living in Marseilles, with no disruption to his life. It was not strictly legal, but he might even rent out his 'office' in Monaco as a home to a local couple – and once he was established as a Monégasque corporate entity (the full process took five years) he would no longer have to pay fifty per cent of his profits in French corporation tax. By 1962 there were no less than ten trucking companies all based inside the mile-square state of Monaco.

Valèry Giscard d'Estaing, the French Minister of Finance, called a press conference at which he tried to telephone a variety of French businesses that were registered in Monaco. None of the businesses answered. France had tolerated Monaco's tax advantages for almost exactly a hundred years in the spirit of the protectorate, but now the junior partner was clearly taking advantage. Giscard spoke of four multimillionaires known to him personally who were supposed to be domiciled in Monaco, but who spent all their time in Paris.

The ultimate insult for France's imperious new president, Charles de Gaulle, was that many of the French colonists who were repatriating their money as a result of the war in Algeria were choosing to avoid French tax and to place their funds in Monaco. These embittered émigrés were de Gaulle's most implacable opponents. They supported and funded the OAS which, *Day of the Jackal*-style, was organizing assassination attempts upon the president's life. So the little country which France had officially protected since 1861 was using its privileges to aid and abet the sworn enemies of France's head of state.

Many of these political manoeuvrings went somewhat over Grace's head. She and Rainier had met de Gaulle on a state visit to Paris in 1959. To prepare for the trip, Grace had sent to the municipal library for a copy of the general's memoirs – then saw how huge the volume was. She asked a secretary to provide her with a résumé.

Rainier did not believe that his wife needed to be involved in the details of his government work, and Grace totally agreed. It was not her function. The prince's aristocratic view of his ancient duties precisely meshed with Grace's middle-class values from the suburbs. Playing the role of a princess was not that different from vacuum-cleaning in her pearls. Grace saw her royal duty as being the model corporate wife to her husband – the chiefest of chief executives – and she did it to perfection in 1959 when she accompanied Rainier to Paris. The congenitally anti-American de Gaulle was enchanted by her insistence on speaking to him only in French, and he found her lapses of grammar and pronunciation quite 'charming'.

Thanks to Grace's style and smoothness, the visit was a triumph. 'Grace of Monaco reigned over fifteen ministers and three hundred subjects at the Elysée,' reported *Paris Presse*. For three days Grace toured French hospitals, schools and orphanages, winning friends wherever she went. 'The best ambassador I have is Grace,' Rainier commented proudly.

The prince might have been advised to let his wife handle the details of his 1962 dispute with France. Late one night in January of that year, angry voices were raised in the palace as Rainier met Émile Pelletier, the French civil servant who, according to the Franco-Monégasque protocols, was effectively the prince's prime minister. Some reports said that Rainier actually struck Pelletier. Pelletier would only admit that Rainier had insulted him with words that were 'not repeatable in polite society' – and, worse, that the prince had made comments that slighted the honour of France.

The argument had been over the profits of Radio Monte Carlo, the prosperous commercial radio station whose transmitters were in France and whose principal audience and advertisers were French as well. Though the station made its living out of France, Rainier had sought to prohibit further French investment in its controlling company in order to protect existing Monégasque investors, and his attitude pushed de Gaulle beyond the limit. Here was the young Prince of Monaco wanting it both ways again, and doing so with extraordinary hubris.

Rainier sacked Pelletier. De Gaulle gave notice that he was abrogating France's agreements with the principality. There were six months of desultory negotiations, and then the French president stopped the talking. At midnight on

12 October 1962, on a night of pouring rain, bands of French customs officers, clad in oilskins, emerged from the darkness to block the main roads leading in and out of Monaco. They set up signs which read 'Halt – Customs', and they proceeded to stop the traffic. For the first time in nearly four centuries, the principality was under siege.

'They may enclose Monaco with barbed wire tomorrow,' wrote Grace in alarm to Prudy Wise. Grace and Rainier were in Paris when news of the blockade came, and they went hurrying back to Monaco.

The blockade was not quite what it seemed. The border between France and Monaco was clearly delineated at a few main roads, but it ran, for the most part, in a higgledy-piggledy fashion, down streets and alleys, and even, on occasions, through the middle of buildings. The Church of the Sacred Heart was built squarely across the frontier, and Monaco's professional soccer team played on a field which had one goal in France and the other in Monaco.

De Gaulle's customs officers were carrying out an exercise in tokenism. They made no attempt to control travellers arriving or departing by train. Since Monaco and France had practised free trade for centuries, and used the same currency, there were no customs duties to enforce, in any case. By checking papers and cargos, the *douaniers* were simply trying to make a nuisance of themselves. Long queues of fuming motorists built up at the exits and entrances to the principality. 'Instead of travelling for twenty minutes, I was in the car for an hour and a half,' remembered John Pochna, who commuted every day between Onassis's offices in Monte Carlo and his own home in Villefranche. 'It was de Gaulle's way of giving Rainier a spanking.'

The general meant business. The French government blocked the sale of Monégasque-produced pharmaceuticals in France. There were about a dozen small laboratories manufacturing medicinal drugs in Monaco, and the French ban immediately put three hundred technicians out of work. Another French ordinance threatened to shut down Monaco's trucking companies. If de Gaulle decided to do more than just spank, the prospects scarcely bore contemplating. Monaco's fresh water, electricity, and gas all came from plants in France.

Rainier had no choice. He had to capitulate. His negotiators did what they could to soften de Gaulle's demands, but the agreement reached in May 1963 made clear the extent of the General's victory. There was no more MEDEC – and no more Martin Dale. French investors could buy into Radio Monte Carlo as freely as Monégasques. As an incidental to the conflict, Rainier had been forced to patch up his quarrel with his troublesome National Council, which he had, at one point, suspended. Now the people of Monaco had a new constitution, limiting Rainier's power to suspend their elected assemblies.

Most significant of all, French citizens could no longer enjoy Monaco's tax privileges. They could live, work, and do business in the principality but, unless they had been registered as residents there prior to 1957, they had to pay full, French rates of tax. Monaco could continue to be a tax haven, but now this was only for the benefit of the Monégasques themselves and for people of other nationalities: Italians, Britons, Germans, Swedes – anyone, so long as they were not French.

This last provision switched Monaco overnight from being a potential drain on French government revenues to representing a significant plus, since foreign investors who came to Monaco were bringing their funds into the French monetary system – spending, living and banking in francs. Most tax evaders are quite conservative investors. They have already taken their risks and have made the major profit on their money by the avoidance of tax, which makes them prime customers for low-return, high-security investments like government bonds. So Monaco minus French tax evaders became an excellent source of financial reserves, and thus a certain underpinning to the stability of the French franc.

This may have been one reason why General de Gaulle did not go the whole way in 1962 and annex the troublesome and parasitical principality on his nation's southern flank. But another reason was undoubtedly the fact that Rainier's wife was Her Serene Highness Princess Grace. Monaco was an anachronism, and, until Grace's arrival, a not very savoury anachronism at that. The gambling, the tax evasion, the squabbling princely family, the dubious war record – who would have shed a tear, or organized a United Nations protest in 1962, if Monaco had not had its glamorous princess, and if de Gaulle had decided that he wanted the same sort of control over the place that Britain exercised over the Channel Islands, or the US over Puerto Rico?

Grace Kelly was the principal reason why most of the world had heard of Monaco, and she was the only reason why anyone – with the exception of the Grimaldi family, 3,000 Monégasques and 22,000 tax exiles – should care whether France ran the place directly or through the mechanism of a protectorate. Grace gave the place credibility – and likeability as well. It probably helped that she had charmed de Gaulle personally when she met him. More significant was the international presence and personality that she had created for her adopted home. Between 1956 and 1962 she and Rainier had visited Washington, Paris, London, Spain, Ireland and the Vatican in an official or semi-official capacity. Rainier alone did not have the charisma to command high-profile invitations to all these places, and he would certainly not have been treated by press, people and the highest government officials with the fascination and affection that attended Grace.

'The Princess of Monaco.' What magic that conjured up in the captions to newspaper photographs, which were usually printed large, on the front page, wherever Grace went. It made the principality a genuine player, a member of the world's family of nations in a way that it had never been before. It was thanks to Grace Kelly that Monaco became a real place.

TWENTY-TWO

It's Only a Movie

THE FIRST visible change that Grace Kelly brought to the life of Monaco was her stopping of the principality's famous pigeon shoot. She found it a barbaric practice. It did not make sense to Grace that her husband should be trying to preserve and regenerate wildlife in his zoo on one side of the harbour while the patrons of Onassis's *SBM* were shooting it by the basketload on the other – and it did nothing for the image of a civilized Monte Carlo. Rainier took her point. The prince had a word with Onassis, and that was the end of the *Tir aux Pigeons*.

Grace's role in her new home, as she saw it, was to soften, to humanize, and to serve. Consciously or not, she was recreating for herself a replica of the existence that she had observed her mother leading on Henry Avenue: caring for a consuming and autocratic husband, devoting herself to her children, and channelling what was left of her creative impulses into the doing of good works. Ma Kelly's focus had been Women's Med. Princess Grace's bailiwick embraced just about every charity and social concern in Monaco – *noblesse oblige* meets the Junior League.

She started in her very first year, when she was pregnant with Caroline. In the winter of 1956 Grace organized a

Christmas party at the palace for every Monégasque child between the ages of three and twelve. No parents were allowed. Five hundred children, in four shifts, were welcomed by Rainier and the heavily pregnant Grace into the august *Salle de Trône* for sticky buns, soda pop, a movie, a magician and clowns. The party became an annual event, and was matched, in later years, on another afternoon in the Christmas season, with a tea party at which Grace would go to meet Monaco's old and infirm, presenting each of them with a small gift – wherever possible, something new to wear.

Grace was a regular visitor to local homes for the elderly, as she was to Monaco's orphanage, to the hospital opened in 1958 and named after her, and to the day-care centre that she helped found a few years later for the children of working mothers. She took a practical, working interest in all these institutions, picking out colour schemes, suggesting new gadgets and equipment, and bringing back decorations from her trips abroad. At the orphanage she had the open dormitory converted with little dividers so that each child should have its own separate living area.

'We were brought up to participate,' Grace explained when she was praised for her social activism. 'My father didn't care what interests we had, but we had to be interested in something. He couldn't stand anyone who didn't have enthusiasm.'

Grace found she needed to temper her enthusiasm somewhat at the committee meetings of the Red Cross. The Red Cross had always been Monaco's masthead charity, and it was considered a signal mark of honour in May 1958, when Rainier transferred the presidency to his wife. Grace arrived for her first meeting armed with lists and agendas, and wearing her stern, schoolteacher glasses, to discover that the ladies of the charity committee had an altogether more leisurely and sociable interpretation of their duties.

It took a while to work out a compromise, the local worthies bestirring themselves to take on some of Grace's American briskness; while the princess, for her part, learned to appreciate, if never quite to share, the Mediterranean pleasures of doing things backwards. 'The Red Cross will be the end of me,' she wrote to Prudy Wise in January 1960. 'You would be amazed at how hard I have to work!'

In her letter to her old friend, Grace dared to wonder whether she was, in fact, 'cut out for charitable work,' but she need not have worried. Under her presidency, Monaco's annual Red Cross Ball became established more firmly than ever as the premier event of the Riviera's summer season. Grace used her old friendships to bring in Hollywood stars both as performers and as guests – David Niven, Cary Grant, Frank Sinatra, Sammy Davis, Jr – and she also got her committees to direct an increasing proportion of their funds towards the work of the Red Cross overseas. Without reducing the cash flow to its own local projects, Monaco's Red Cross became, proportionally, one of the most generous in the world, sending relief to the victims of wars and natural disasters from Peru to Pakistan.

Softhearted Gracie could get very serious. Early in the sixties she became the honorary president, and was one of the active founder members, of AMADE, *l'Association Mondiale des Amis de l'Enfance* – the World Association of Friends of Children. In underdeveloped countries AMADE lobbied for medicine and education. In richer societies it campaigned against such problems as violence on TV. If AMADE did not transform the world any more totally than many another philanthropy, it ranked in the plus column with those that made a difference – and Grace had no doubt that her time was well spent helping its campaigns. Her own son and daughter were so fortunate, she would explain, how could she not try to help children who had been less blessed?

It was Caroline and Albert who were at the heart of their young mother's life — and of their father's as well. When Alejo Vidal-Quadras, the Spanish painter, was in the palace in the early sixties doing a portrait of Albert, he was struck by the little boy's constant references to his ancient Aunt Leonore. She was, apparently, a funny, bent, old woman, who was definitely kind, but who was also rather eccentric, living obscurely in a distant corner of the palace. The children could not wait for her weekly visit, when she would turn up, hobbling on a cane. When Vidal-Quadras asked Grace about this mysterious fairy godmother, he was told that he had already met her. Aunt Leonore was Rainier, who put on the performance once a week.

The prince and princess revelled in their children. One of the highlights of Grace's day was when she read to them at bedtime. She would tuck them in, then throw herself into the narration of their fairy stories with such drama and feeling that the children's English nanny, Maureen King, would try to linger in the nursery to catch the performance for herself.

Rainier and Grace took their child-rearing very seriously. It was a joint enterprise that they thought and talked about a lot. If they had to go out in the evening, and knew that they would miss the rituals of storytelling and putting-to-bed, Grace would make sure that her make-up and hair-dressing left time for her to sit and talk with the children over their supper instead.

Not all her departures went so smoothly, however:

Every time her mother and father get ready to leave the palace without her [reported Madge Tivey-Faucon of the young Caroline in the early sixties] she bursts into floods of tears. The princess can never resist her daughter's tears. She turns back at the first sob. This scene usually takes place in the Cour d'Honneur. All the secretaries, hearing the little girl's screams, rush to the windows. The princess bends over the child and consoles her gently until she stops crying. This may last a quarter of an hour. But the princess never becomes impatient or angry.

Both Rainier and Grace wanted to create childhoods for their children that were more tender and carefree than their own. For Rainier, child of a broken home, the achieving of a single, stable family environment in itself represented light-years of improvement. For Grace, the objective was a parenting style that was less oppressive and awe-inspiring than that of Jack and Margaret Kelly. Like many of her generation, she was a devotee of Dr Benjamin Spock and his progressive child-rearing ideas. Grace studied her Spock as if it were the Bible, seeking new, modern solutions to the age-old dilemmas that arise from the challenge of disciplining with love. When she was bathing Albert one night and discovered that Caroline had developed the habit of biting her baby brother, she promptly sank her own teeth sharply into Caroline's arm.

'You really must not bite your brother,' she said. 'It hurts.'

The story of Grace's instructive bite was frequently repeated in the authorized magazine updates from Monaco on how royal offspring were being raised in the modern palace. Rainier and Grace were always telling interviewers what strict parents they were. 'I'm afraid I'm very severe at times,' Grace confided to Mike Wallace in 1962. But out-siders seldom saw much evidence of strictness. When her children were only three or four, Grace would take Caroline and Albert with her to picture galleries or fashion shows, where they would slide raucously up and down the polished floor or fiddle with objects of priceless value. Anything but the disciplinarian, Grace would continue to study the pictures or the fashions, apparently quite oblivious to the mayhem – while no one else dared say a word.

It was partly a question of indulgence. After long hours spent playing around her mother's feet during clothes fittings, the four-year-old Caroline asked for, and was given for her fifth birthday, a cocktail dress personally made for her by Givenchy. How could the mild and biddable little Albert not get a trifle wilful as he drove around the palace grounds in an electric car that was a present from Aristotle Onassis?

It was, more profoundly, a matter of clashing cultures. Grace was bringing up her son and daughter to be young Americans in spirit, encouraging them to speak their minds and to be themselves – in direct contradiction to the European tradition in which children should be 'seen and not heard'. When her New York and Philadelphia friends came to Monaco, they would comment on the little prince and princess with genuine approval. The kids were so bright and outgoing. Europeans and Monégasques were not so favourably impressed. In their opinion (usually whispered behind raised hands), Caroline and Albert were well along the road to becoming classic products of America's TV-and-hamburger culture – *enfants gâtés* ('spoiled brats').

Micheline Swift, the wife of David Swift, Grace's New York friend, found out just how spoiled Grace's children could be when she entertained Grace and Caroline in America. The Grimaldis had come to Los Angeles for a family holiday – 'so many new houses & buildings,' wrote Grace in excitement to Prudy, 'that it is staggering' – and Micheline persuaded Grace to let her take Caroline on a shopping expedition with her own daughter, Michele, who was about the same age.

Grace was most concerned about it. 'No one's ever been allowed to take Caroline away without me,' she said. But she agreed it would be fun for her daughter, and the party headed off to Saks Fifth Avenue. There Caroline, still a very little girl, put on the most appalling display, pulling the clothes roughly on and off her body, throwing them on the floor, and treating the staff with absolute disdain.

'This cannot be your daughter,' said the sales assistant to Micheline in horror. 'I can see that your own girl is so well-behaved. Where did you pick up this child?'

For reasons of security and to avoid alerting the press, it had been agreed that the condition for the whole excursion was absolute secrecy, but that did not bother Grace's little Marie-Antoinette.

'I'm Caroline,' she said, 'Princess Caroline – and don't you dare speak to me like that.'

Jay Kanter had never stopped sending Grace scripts and ideas for movies. He put no pressure on her – pressure was not Kanter's style – but it was his job as her agent to make sure that Grace was aware of the opportunities that were being offered her. The princess turned down everything routinely – and, apparently, quite happily. She took it as a joke when Spyros Skouras offered her a million dollars to play the Virgin Mary in *The Greatest Story Ever Told*. 'The Virgin Mary? No way,' she responded. 'Now, Mary Magdalene . . .'

The movies were behind her. They were part of another life. Princess Grace had her husband, her children, her good works, her own crowded, important, *responsible* existence. And yet, and yet . . . It struck Cary Grant when he visited Monaco in 1961 that Grace was somehow 'restive'. Rita Gam came through on her way back from Berlin, proudly bearing the film festival award which she had won for her part in *No Exit*. Grace cracked open the champagne to congratulate her old friend. 'But I sensed,' Rita Gam later wrote, 'behind her loving and generous celebration, a tinge of actor's envy.'

Grace was not as happy as she seemed in the early sixties. Her father's death had hit her hard. It left her more lonely than she cared to admit. She had no real friends in Monaco. Worst of all, she had suffered two miscarriages since the birth of Albert in 1958. 'I am actually just out of bed,' she wrote to Prudy after the second of her miscarriages. She had lost the baby at three months. 'It was a terrible experience, and has left me shaken both mentally and physically.'

Popping out babies on a regular basis had been part of the identity that Grace foresaw for herself after her marriage, and the miscarriages came as nasty surprises that undermined her self-esteem. Here was something that she could not do as well as she had anticipated. It all contributed to a curious heavyheartedness which left her uncharacteristically tired and apathetic. She would go to bed at odd times of day, spending long hours asleep on occasions. 'The telephone can ring, the visitors can wait,' reported Madge Tivey-Faucon. 'The Princess sleeps, and orders are given not to wake her.'

It was in this depressed and aimless state that Grace turned an ear to Alfred Hitchcock. The director had always refused to accept that Grace's departure from the screen could be permanent. He took her retirement as a matter of personal desertion — he had felt similarly betrayed in 1949 when Ingrid Bergman went off with Roberto Rossellini. In Grace's case, however, Hitch had worked very hard to stay on good terms. Monaco had been a regular stop on his gourmandizing expeditions to the south of France, and he had found a ready audience for his scabrous humour in Rainier. Both men could derive enormous enjoyment from such simple devices as whoopee cushions and plastic dog droppings. Hitchcock had promised the prince and princess that he could find the perfect role for Grace, and in the spring of 1962 he announced that he had found it. He sent Grace the script for a movie he had developed from a novel by Winston Graham. It was provisionally entitled *Marnie*.

Marnie played on all the themes of sexual complication that Hitchcock had explored in his previous movies with Grace, and the ending of the Hollywood Production Code and the atmosphere of the early sixties made it possible for him to be considerably more explicit. Marnie – the part to be played by Grace – is a beautiful but sexually benumbed young woman who expresses her frustrations by stealing things. One of the test titles for the movie was *I Married a Frigid Female Thief*. Her boyfriend and husband – played by Sean Connery – saves her from getting arrested and leads her back to sexual flowering and self-knowledge through helping her to uncover the truth about her disturbed childhood. In the dramatic climax to the film, Marnie is induced to recall how she slept as a child in the bed of her mother – a prostitute who brought her clients back to the house.

It was a challenging and complex role for a maturing Grace Kelly – *To Catch a Thief* meets *The Country Girl*. Whether it was appropriate for the Princess of Monaco was quite another matter. Grace and Rainier put their trust in Hitchcock to handle the question of taste. In his last three movies – *North by Northwest, Psycho,* and *The Birds* – the director had been at his most triumphantly surefooted. It was other, quite separate issues that decided the fate of Grace's bid to go back to the movies.

The main impulse for Grace to make *Marnie* came surprisingly from her husband. Rainier had not changed his view about the dignity he expected of his princess. He had discouraged the showing of Grace Kelly movies in Monaco at the time of his wedding, and the principality's tourist entrepreneurs knew better than to exploit their princess's former life with T-shirts, mugs or post-cards. Her face was on the postage stamps with Rainier's, but apart from that, Monaco studiously avoided a Grace Kelly cult of personality.

In the course of six years of marriage, however, Rainier had become significantly less stuffed-shirt. He still had his tempers and pomposities. These would never leave him. But his neurosis to control everything had relaxed somewhat, at least when it came to Grace. The prince had learned to trust his wife – and to relax a little into the comfort of his own feelings. He felt for Grace in the sadness that followed her miscarriages.

'There have been times,' he told his official biographer, Peter Hawkins, in 1966, 'when the princess has been a little melancholic – which I quite understand – about having performed a form of art very successfully, only to be cut away from it completely . . . This was not at all an individual decision of the princess to make another film. It was an idea that tickled her, and that she liked, and, quite frankly, I kind of pushed her into the solution.'

Hitchcock was planning to shoot *Marnie* in the summer of 1962 in one of the north-eastern states. Rainier and Grace had already scheduled a long summer vacation in America. It would not disrupt their family arrangements, or any public duties, if Grace got up early and went off most mornings to the set. 'I thought it would be great fun for all of us,' said Rainier, recalling the incident to Jeffrey Robinson twenty-five years later, 'especially the kids. And I knew she wanted to make more films. It would also mean working again with Hitchcock, whom she adored.'

On 18 March 1962, a press release from the palace in Monaco announced that 'Princess Grace has accepted to appear during her summer vacation in a motion picture for Mr Alfred Hitchcock, to be made in the United States.' Trying to anticipate some of the likely reactions, the communiqué emphasized that Prince Rainier was planning to be present during a good part of the filming, and that 'Her Highness will return to Monaco with her family in November.' But neither Grace, Rainier nor Hitchcock was in any way prepared for the furore that followed. In March 1962, France and Monaco were just firing the first salvos in their tax and border skirmish, and this dispute was instantly read into the equation. Grace was going back to the movies, speculated newspapers from Nice to New Mexico, to snub General de Gaulle, to prove Monaco's independence – and to raise much-needed money for her beleaguered husband. 'I don't care what Prince Rainier says,' declared Sheilah Graham in the *New York Mirror*. 'The fact that [his] wife Grace Kelly is returning to her movie career – no matter what the reason – is indicative that something in some way has gone wrong with their marriage.'

MGM added to the uproar with an indignant letter to Alfred Hitchcock. 'When Miss Kelly left the country to become Princess Grace,' wrote Joseph Vogel, MGM's president, 'there were four and one-half years unfulfilled on her contract. The unexpired portion of her contract represented and represents an important but unused asset of this company . . . So long as Princess Grace remained in retirement, we felt that we had little alternative but to sit by with an unfulfilled commitment . . . We do believe that, in all sense of fairness and equity, her return should be made with the participation of Metro-Goldwyn-Mayer.'

This had not been the idea at all. Within a matter of days an almost casual decision to take on some extra holiday work had mushroomed into an international incident with arcane business complications. Rainier kept talking in terms of summer vacation arrangements. Rupert Allan busily phoned his press contacts to insist there was absolutely nothing wrong with the marriage. The palace announced that Grace's fee for *Marnie* (over $800,000) would be going to a special foundation for deprived children and young athletes in Monaco.

It was all in vain. The impending return of the screen goddess stirred curiosity everywhere, and the widespread suspicion that Grace had found life in a palace less than totally fulfilling was, of course, precisely correct. The prospect of the princess going back to Hollywood had the horrible fascination of a piece of cinema footage being run backwards.

When Grace first told Judy Kanter the news about *Marnie* over the phone, her voice had 'bubbled like that of a teen-ager'. But the public hubbub and debate produced exactly the opposite effect. Suddenly a nice idea was no fun any more. Grace withdrew to her room again.

In 1956, during the wedding week, Rainier had censored the newspapers coming into the palace, so that Grace never saw the more negative reports. Now Georges Lukomski, Rainier's personal aide and companion, was given the unpleasant task of passing on a full picture of what the outside world was saying. 'The Princess is shocked beyond all measure . . .' reported Lukomski. 'She has been in grave danger of breaking down.'

The citizens of Monaco were particularly vociferous in their opposition to their princess's going back to the movies – 'What about her kissing the leading man?' asked one – and it was these local sensitivities that Grace cited early in June 1962, when she bowed to the inevitable. 'I am not going to make the movie after all,' she told a reporter from *Nice Matin*. No contract had been signed, and the whole project had been contingent on her approving the script in any case.

'It was heartbreaking for me to have to leave the picture,' Grace wrote to Hitchcock on 18 June 1962. 'I was so excited about doing it, and particularly about working with you again. When we meet I would like to explain to you myself all of the reasons, which is difficult to do by letter or through a third party. It is unfortunate that it had to happen this way, and I am deeply sorry.'

'Dear Grace,' responded Hitchcock one week later. 'Yes, it was sad, wasn't it . . . Without a doubt, I think you made not only the best decision, but the only decision, to put the project aside at this time. After all, it was only a movie . . . P. S. I have enclosed a small tape recording which I have made especially for Rainier. Please ask him to play it privately. It is not for all ears.'

'It's only a movie,' was one of Hitchcock's favourite expressions, and he could afford to shrug his shoulders, with more than forty movies to his credit. The director shot *Marnie* in 1963, with Tippi Hedren playing the title role instead of Grace. He had not lost much time – or any money – in the imbroglio, and all the publicity did no harm at all to the profile of the latest Alfred Hitchcock production.

Grace, however, could hardly feel so cavalier, for what she lost could never be replaced. Until *Marnie*, the possibility that she might return to the screen had been a comfort that she could always fall back on, if only in her dreams. The chance of acting again had remained in the background as a promise and a consolation – so long as she did not seek to make it come true – and by trying to turn the magic key, the door of opportunity had now been permanently closed. The public reaction to *Marnie* had given shape to what even Rainier had forgotten. Princess or actress – take your choice. Grace could not be both.

She had done her job superbly as a royal person. She was very good at smiling, at being dignified and stylish. She was simply brilliant at conveying a sustained image of humanity and concern. But that, Grace now knew, was just about all that being a princess had to offer. The register of adult challenge and emotion that was involved in her public life was really very slim. It was no coincidence that the most successful royal figures are either very old or very young. Being a day-to-day princess was not enough to occupy a mature, thinking mind. It quite lacked the intensity and exhilaration of acting – the tension and creativity, the competition, the chance of failure, the danger, the gossip, the camaraderie, the adult demands of success that depended primarily on her own original efforts and talent, as judged by the real standards of the real world.

In 1956 Grace had given all this up quite blithely, with no very clear idea of what she might be missing. Now she knew.

TWENTY-THREE

The Onassis Factor

FOR THE best part of twenty years in the 1950s and 1960s, the most striking sight in Monaco on a warm summer's night was the spectacle of Aristotle Onassis's yacht, the *Christina*, sitting in the prime berth of the harbour – 322 feet of unashamed opulence, lit from stem to stern and glowing like a Christmas tree. Onassis had bought the boat for $50,000 in 1952 – it had been a frigate of the Canadian Navy – and he had spent another four million transforming it into the supreme symbol of his power and wealth. There was a nursery, an operating theatre, a swimming pool whose floor could be raised to deck level for dancing, and nine luxury suites. The *Christina* dramatically outshone Rainier's own 135-foot yacht, the *Deo Juvante II*. When the two boats were moored side by side – a comparison that the prince preferred to avoid – the *Deo Juvante II* looked rather like a tugboat.

The *Christina* was named after Onassis's only daughter, and it was the vehicle for his fantasies and his rich man's sense of fun. The footrests of the bar stools were made of whales' teeth, and the seats themselves were of a gleaming white whale skin which Onassis described as coming from the scrotum of the animal – though sometimes he changed the story. 'Madame,' he declared to one lady visitor, 'you are now sitting on the largest penis in the world.' His sense of humour was tailor-made for the unusual young prince who was his partner in the business that was Monte Carlo, Inc.

Rainier had welcomed Onassis's take-over of the *Société des Bains de Mer* in 1953, and the fresh dynamism that the Greek brought to its activities. 'I'll build, I'll embellish, I'll renovate,' Onassis had promised, and, to start with, he was as good as his word. He added three more floors to the Hôtel de Paris, and he topped off the building with a spectacular grillroom that gave a panoramic view of the harbour and had a roof that opened to the stars at night.

Onassis controlled fifty-two per cent of the SBM's shares. Rainier only owned two per cent – a family inheritance – but the SBM's licence to operate in Monaco gave the prince the power of veto over most aspects of the company's activities. This made the prince and the shipowner the effective co-directors of Monaco's tourist fortunes, and their relationship was marked by all the pride and prickliness that two pint-sized Caesars could muster. There were occasions when their regular confabulations in Rainier's palace office took on the character of rams butting heads, but each man knew how much he needed the other, and out of the conflicts emerged an unusual friendship and respect.

'One day they would be going for one another,' remembered one of Rainier's advisers. 'Next day they would be kissing each other on the cheek.'

Grace shared her husband's ambivalence. She distrusted the ostentation that had won Onassis the title of uncrowned king of Monaco. It was insulting to the position and prestige of her own husband. But the crude vibrancy of the man was compelling. Onassis could flatter a lady with all the energy and single-mindedness of an Oleg Cassini, and he worked very hard on Grace. In the autumn of 1961, Grace and Rainier accepted an invitation to cruise the Greek islands on the *Christina* with Onassis and Maria Callas. While the two men toured the monasteries of Mount Athos, to which only males were admitted, Grace and Callas got in a little boat and sneaked as close to the shore as they could for a peek. They need not have bothered. 'The boys said the monks smelled so badly,' Grace reported to Prudy, 'that we were the lucky ones.'

Grace was finally won over by the tolerance that Onassis extended to her boisterous children. 'They would tease him, tweak his ears, and pull him into the pool,' Rainier later remembered. 'He wasn't young then, and we used to get rather worried.'

Rainier later dated the souring of his relationship with Onassis from the tycoon's love affair with Maria Callas, and the unpleasant public breakdown of his marriage that followed. 'There were nasty write-ups and gossip,' the prince told Peter Hawkins in 1965. 'He sort of shrivelled up, and perhaps because it was here that all this trouble started, he may even have taken an unconscious dislike to Monte Carlo.'

But the problem went much deeper than this. Far from disliking Monte Carlo, Onassis liked it rather too much. He enjoyed its exclusivity and cachet. His control of the SBM helped give him the class that he knew his wealth lacked, and he did not welcome the plans that Rainier was constantly urging to open up the principality to a less exclusive clientele. Rainier's recruiting of Grace had generated all the glamour and prestige that Onassis had been hoping for when he launched his own, impudent embassy to Marilyn Monroe, but now the co-directors disagreed on the best way to build on this. By a strange paradox, the prince was arguing for sausages, while the self-made man was championing caviar.

Since his accession in 1949, Rainier had nursed an expansionist vision for the future of his realm. He wished to reclaim the two shallow areas of sea at either end of Monaco, making one the site of light industry and the other the sort of beach resort which the principality lacked. Much of the rock and soil for this landfill would come from the excavation of a tunnel carrying the Nice-Menton railway line under Monte Carlo, thus eliminating the eyesore of the existing open track, and releasing more land for residential redevelopment. By the early sixties most of these plans were well on the road to completion, and Rainier had no doubt about what came next. Bring in Holiday Inn!

'My own feeling,' he explained to Peter Hawkins in 1965, 'is that the economic wealth of the principality would be greatly improved if we could start off with two thousand modern, comfortable hotel rooms of the kind at which the Americans are so good. Not super-duper deluxe, but modernly equipped, functional and agreeable hotel rooms with a maximum price of fifteen dollars a single a day.'

Even if he had not married Grace Kelly, the ambitious prince of Monaco would have been a devotee of things American, from jazz and gadgets to business techniques. The Holiday Inn chain was one of the great US success stories of the 1950s and since Rainier was, essentially, a hotelkeeper himself, he had studied the chain's mass-marketing of cleanliness, value and efficiency. A Monaco Holiday Inn would bring a new sort of traveller to the principality. It might teach the snooty and complacent Hôtel de Paris a thing or two, and it would also accomplish another of the longterm goals of Rainier, to dilute the monopoly enjoyed by the SBM.

As chief shareholder and controller of the SBM, Onassis could hardly be expected to agree with much of this. He wanted to keep his semi-private playground as exclusive as he could, and he also felt that the prince was unduly alarmist about the future of his ministate. 'Monaco will always be prosperous,' Onassis used to say, 'so long as there are three thousand rich men in the world.' Onassis felt that he, rather than Rainier, was the more careful guardian of what the principality really stood for. 'He won't be satisfied,' he grumbled, 'until Monte Carlo is nothing but hotels, tourists and tax shelters from one end to the other.'

The argument was fought out on yacht excursions and in long business meetings in the prince's study – though Onassis's Levantine style was not to confront, but rather to delay and discombobulate. 'You can speak to him for an hour, two hours, three hours,' exclaimed Rainier in exasperation. 'But when he goes out of your office you know perfectly well that nothing of what you have talked about is going to be followed through.'

Grace and Rainier still accepted invitations on Onassis's yacht. Grace felt a creative bond with Maria Callas. It was fun to be woken up in the morning by the cascading arpeggios of the great soprano practising her scales. But by 1964, it was getting increasingly difficult for business and friendship to mix. In the spring of that year, Onassis finally and reluctantly agreed to build a new luxury apartment block and two hotels in Monte Carlo, but he insisted on a guarantee that would exclude the Holiday Inn, or any other rival hotel development. Infuriated, Rainier invoked his veto to annul the whole scheme, and then went on television to attack the SBM for 'lethargy and bad faith'.

Onassis shrugged off the comment in public. Rainier's criticism, he said, had been directed at the SBM, not at him personally. But privately he was seething. When Charles Graves, an author who had written a history of Monte Carlo, met Onassis in September 1964, he found the shipowner 'obsessional' in his hatred of Rainier, fishing constantly for dirt and gossip on the prince. Onassis had always made a point never to address Rainier as 'Altesse' or 'Monseigneur' in the subservient way that many did. Only on the most formal and public occasions did he call him anything but 'Rainier', and when talking with his office staff he would refer to him as plain 'Mr Grimaldi'. Delusions of divine right, he sneered, had no place in the world of modern business.

But in the end it was the comic opera prince who proved the cleverer businessman – or, perhaps, the more skilful wielder of realpolitik. 1966 was the hundredth anniversary of the foundation of Monte Carlo, and as part of the jubilee festivities Rainier and Grace went to Paris to celebrate the now restored entente with France. In conversations with de Gaulle, Rainier secured French agreement to the strategy he proposed against Onassis, and he also got his wife to voice the official Grimaldi line in the somewhat unusual context of *Playboy* magazine.

'I don't think Mr Onassis's investment in the *Société des Bains de Mer* of Monte Carlo is of very great importance to his overall empire,' Grace said in one of the long personality interviews with which *Playboy* filled the space between its pin-ups. 'He has so many more and bigger investments than Monte Carlo. I feel that his ownership of the majority of shares, and therefore a controlling interest in the casino of Monte Carlo, has been more for his own amusement than a serious business affair.'

In June 1966 Rainier got his National Council to legislate the creation of 600,000 new shares in the SBM, all of them to be purchased and held by the Monégasque government. This forcibly wiped out Onassis's majority position at a stroke, and the tycoon promptly went to court. Since he could only sue in the courts of Monaco, however, he enjoyed little success. The Monaco Supreme Court ruled against him. The Monégasque Treasury paid Onassis $10 million for his own personal shareholding – and Rainier was, at last, the master in his own house. In the context of Grimaldi history and his family's control of Monaco, it was an even bigger coup for Rainier than the winning of Grace. The SBM was now Monaco's property, and so long as the principality retained its shareholding, the company could never be held by an Onassis again.

Grace was at the heart of the 1966 centenary celebrations, which acquired extra savour from Rainier's triumph. There were concerts, balls, ballets and recitals. The most sacred moment came on 4 November 1966, when Rainier had the bodies of his ancestors brought up from the crypt to be reburied in the apse of the cathedral. Albert the Navigator, Charles III, the creator of Monte Carlo, Florestans and Hippolytes going back to the Middle Ages – each ruling prince was now laid to rest beneath his own, grand, brass-inlaid slab of beige marble, the princely graves running in an impressive semicircle in the floor around the back of the high altar. The dynastic display provided a telling flourish to Rainier's year of victory – and it was not too long before the bulldozers moved in to break ground, down by the sea, on the new Holiday Inn, Monte Carlo.

In 1966 Grace was a mother again. On 1 February 1965, she had finally given birth to the third child she had been trying so hard to produce. Princess Stephanie Marie Elisabeth was seven years younger than her brother, Albert, and eight years younger than her sister, Caroline. She was very much the baby of the family, and she was the more treasured and pampered by her parents for the miscarriages that had preceded her.

Grace rejoiced in her new baby, but something was missing. 1966 was the tenth anniversary of her wedding, but the first flush of love had long faded. Asked by Rainier what she would like for her tenth anniversary present, she snapped, 'A year off.' Only slightly more temperately, she told Ivor

Herbert of the London *Evening News* that her greatest wish was for 'someone to take these letters off my desk and answer them – and to have ten hours sleep at night'.

'Are you happy?' was the question that every interviewer wanted to put to the princess. It was a quality check on the fairy tale. People wanted to be reassured that Grace really had lived happily ever after, and she was far too honest to fob off the query with plastic cheeriness. 'I've had happy moments in my life,' she said to Barbara Walters in another of her tenth anniversary interviews, 'but I don't think that happiness – being happy – is a perpetual state that anyone can be in. Life isn't that way. But I have a certain peace of mind, yes. My children give me a great deal of happiness. And my life here has given me many satisfactions in the last ten years.'

It was significant that Grace's answer made no mention of Prince Charming, for Grace was not personally happy in her marriage. She remained committed to her husband. In terms of public achievement, her first ten years with Rainier had been a triumph. But if Grace had come to find her public duties hard work, her private life had become even more of a trial. Life with Rainier had not proved the loving and romantic experience that Grace had dreamed, and far from softening with the passage of time, her husband's moods and arrogance had actually grown worse.

David Swift, Grace's old friend from the Gene Lyons days, got a taste of this when he visited Grace in her tenth anniversary year. Swift had become a successful film-maker – in 1960 he had written and directed *Pollyanna* for Walt Disney – and in the summer of 1966 he was in Nice directing a movie for United Artists. Invited to the palace with his wife, Micheline, he was delighted to find the old Gracie very much alive. 'Eat some of these rose petals,' the princess advised him as they toured the garden. 'Very good for sexual vigour.' But neither of the Swifts was impressed by some of the strange sides of Rainier's temper.

It was decided that the most equal pairing for tennis was for Rainier to partner Micheline Swift, while David, the strongest player, played with the princess – whereupon Rainier hit every ball, as hard as he could, straight at Grace.

'Oh, it hurts!' Grace cried as one ball hit her in the face.

'Keep your eye on the ball,' growled Rainier, and kept on hitting hard at her.

'He was just desperate to win,' remembers Swift. 'He was like a child, and it was embarrassing when he was playing with Albert as his partner. If the boy played a bad shot – and he was only a kid – Rainier went mad, shouting at him.'

The Swifts could not believe it. On one occasion Rainier even threw his racket at Albert, though the boy ducked nimbly. Albert seemed to be expecting it. Rainier's Golden Labrador was equally agile when his master missed a golf stroke and went to hit the dog with his club in his frustration. Those who lived within striking range of His Serene Highness evidently learned to keep their heads down and their wits about them.

'I came to realize then,' says Swift, 'what I have thought ever since – that Grace was a princess long before she married Rainier.'

'This is the first time since my marriage that I've been out on my own like this,' Grace confided to Micheline Swift one night, as the two women walked home through the streets of Monaco from a restaurant. Rainier had reluctantly agreed to Grace accompanying Micheline, while the two men went back to the palace by car. 'He has me cornered. I can't move. I can't go anywhere. I have no freedom.'

This was far from the happy domestic life that the Swifts had read about in the magazines, and the saddest thing was the passivity with which Grace submitted to Rainier's tyranny. She was like the little girl whom her mother and father used to cow with their anger or the threat of it. Submission for Grace was part of any intimate relationship, and in her ten years of marriage this had actually encouraged her husband to become worse.

'You can't let him control you like this,' counselled Micheline Swift. 'In marriage you have to mould a man. You have to stand up for what you want.'

Grace rationalized her timidity as being part of life's learning process. One of her favourite quotations was from the Lebanese poet Kahlil Gibran (*The Prophet*): 'When love beckons to you, follow him – though his voice may shatter your dreams as the north wind lays waste the garden. He is for your growth . . .'

It was both heroic and depressing. Grace had been brought up to see herself as the servant of those whom she loved, and this made her an enabler of her husband's difficult side. Guests at the dazzling summer concerts and soirées that she arranged at the palace noted how little trouble Rainier often took to hide his boredom. 'Another of my wife's little parties,' he would sigh to his staff, rolling his eyes.

'Rainier acted like the wallflower at his own party,' remembers an American visitor to one of Grace's evenings in the palace. It was a dinner under the stars for over thirty, with the guests seated at several separate round tables on a terrace that was lit by candles and smelled lingeringly of evening jasmine. Though the setting was entrancing, those people who were not seated at the tables of either Grace or Rainier could not help being somewhat crestfallen – until halfway through the evening, when Grace suddenly appeared in their midst. She had made arrangements to sit at every table for some part of the evening – while the prince remained stolidly, and for one period definitely sleepily, in his own spot.

360

Wherever she was in the course of the evening, Grace kept looking across the gathering in her husband's direction, anxiously monitoring his mood. It seemed that the worse the prince got, the more attention his wife paid to him. Her whole identity was tied up in being the perfect wife to this wilful and difficult man. 'Nowadays, I suppose I would say she was mistaken in being so subservient,' remarks her guest. 'But at the time, I came away feeling I had met someone who was close to being a saint.'

'She was the only member of our bizarre family,' wrote Tiny's son, Buddy de Massy, 'who had both compassion and consideration . . . She was completely truthful and trustworthy.' The difficult son of a difficult mother, Buddy de Massy was an untamed young man who could not go for long without getting into trouble at school or smashing up a sports car. Rainier had no time for his nephew, and made his contempt very obvious, but Grace always greeted the prodigal with a smile. Comforting a rebel against her husband's authority was one small way of expressing a little rebellion of her own.

Family prodigals became something of a speciality for Grace as the sixties clothed America's youth in flowers and beads and rebellion. In 1963 Peggy's fifteen-year-old daughter, Mary Lee, got pregnant and eloped to Iowa with her eighteen-year-old boyfriend, John Paul 'Bindy' Jones IV. Mary Lee was Grace's goddaughter. She had been one of the flower girls at Grace's wedding, and the FBI's nationwide search for the couple made headlines.

As the public person with most to lose from the scandal, Grace might have been expected to be particularly disapproving. 'But she was the most supportive of all the family,' remembers Bindy Jones. 'When we were finally discovered, she wanted to hear our side of the story. She did not agree with what we had done, but she was prepared to listen.

When we said that we wanted to get married, she agreed to support whatever we were going to try.' Grace invited the young couple and their baby to Monaco several times for their summer holidays. 'I know she had this cold reputation,' says Bindy Jones, 'but I must say that I never saw that. To us, she was always a very, very warm person.' The prim and proper Princess of Monaco had not forgotten the rebellious young woman who had been planning her own elopement less than ten years earlier – and she had come to feel a particular empathy with people who were lonely and disconnected.

It became a regular occurrence every summer, the phone call from the station or the airport announcing the arrival of another grubby young backpacker from Philadelphia who wanted to speak to Aunt Grace. She would send a limousine for them, take them up to Roc Agel, wine them, dine them, and lay them out on the sand with her children at the Beach Club, where the family spent sunny summer days around their cabana. She would listen fondly to the latest news from Chestnut Hill and Germantown, then send the visitors on their way, fed and rested, with tall tales to tell their college mates about crashing at the palace. She was everybody's auntie. In the absence of Jack Kelly, she was the new head of the Kelly clan, welcoming all the family to stay – particularly Uncle George, who was now in his early eighties. The old playwright could not get enough of it. 'Of courts and cities I have known,' he said, 'this is my home.'

In the absence of Jack Kelly, the rest of the family were not doing that well. By the late sixties Peggy had gone through one marriage, and was getting to the end of another. She and her second husband, Gene Conlan, were both heavy drinkers – Conlan's mutilated face bearing painful testimony to the near-fatal car crash he had suffered while under the influence. Lizanne's family life had not proved the easiest, while brother Kell was the most spectacular burnout of all. Having been flagrantly unfaithful to his wife for a number of years, he deserted his young family in the late sixties to embark on a career of philandering that was almost comical in its obsessiveness. As he brought his ever younger consorts to breakfast at the country club, his older friends remonstrated with him. But Kell just shrugged his shoulders. 'The old man pushed the hell out of me,' was all he would offer by way of explanation.

The ultimate scandal was to come a few years later when Kell started appearing at parties in the company of Rachel Harlow, the former Richard Finocchio, who had gone through a much publicized sex-change operation. A tall and striking blonde, Harlow ran a discotheque in central Philadelphia, and Kell seemed to court the notoriety of being seen in her company. 'We were at dinner once,' remembers Harlow, who dated Kell, on and off, for nearly two years. 'It was a very well-known place, and he asked me about my childhood and what it was that had given me the strength to be my own person. He told me he admired that. He said that he wished that he had had the courage to be his own person throughout his life, to go against all the odds, and against everybody's opinion in his own home town. I shall never forget what he said. "I have always been either John B. Kelly's son," he said, "or Grace Kelly's brother. I have never been myself." '

Only Ma Kelly flourished in the absence of the patriarch. Moving out of Henry Avenue to start a new life in the Alden Park Towers around the corner, she positively bloomed. 'Elbows!' she would shout gleefully at Rainier, jabbing him sharply in the ribs with her fork when the prince forgot his table manners on his visits to Ocean City. She even found herself a boyfriend, Jules Lavin, a courtly inhabitant of Alden Park who escorted her around Philadelphia and whom she took with her on at least one of her summer jaunts to Monaco.

Grace's involvement in other people's lives and problems was a very effective distraction from her own. But in July 1967, she was brought up short. The prince and princess were in Montreal, visiting the World's Fair, Expo '67, with their two elder children. They had travelled through London, where Grace had spent a few days interviewing prospective nannies. At the age of thirty-seven, she was pregnant again, expecting her fourth child the following January, and according to the official announcement she was 'very happy and very well'.

Rupert Allan was in the party, masterminding a hectic programme of engagements, when, unexpectedly one evening, he was summoned to Grace's and Rainier's hotel suite. As he arrived, Grace was being loaded onto a stretcher under the supervision of two solemn-looking doctors. Her pregnancy had gone very badly wrong.

Allan accompanied her to the hospital, sticking beside her through all the swing doors until they came to the operating room. Grace was weeping. It had been her decision that Rainier should stay at the hotel with the children, but now she wanted him there. 'In all the years that I knew her,' Allan later recalled, 'I never knew her so sad.' She reached her hand off the trolley, gripping pathetically to her old friend's fingers until the moment that they wheeled her away. Allan would break down in tears himself as he told the story.

The operation that Grace underwent was known, medically, as a missed abortion, and it brought an end to her sixth pregnancy in eleven years. The baby, a boy, had been dead for more than one month inside her. The doctors told her there could be no more pregnancies.

TWENTY-FOUR

Run-of-the-Play Contract

IN THE early 1960s, the British journalist Alan Whicker brought a BBC camera crew to film the rich and happy inhabitants of Monaco, only to find himself talking to a group of disgruntled folk who painted a picture which was anything but idyllic. Noise, dust, foreigners, rising prices – Monte Carlo, they complained, was no longer the gracious, sepia picture-postcard oasis of legend. Ruritania was turning into a building site. The beautiful old villas and their gardens were vanishing, and construction cranes now outnumbered the palm trees. Everyone seemed to be losing their sea view. Looking at the skyline, Whicker decided that the place deserved a new name. He called it 'Manhattan-on-the-Med'.

Rainier III was the driving inspiration in this orgy of concrete-pouring, and it transformed the character of Monaco in the course of his reign. The prince's twin recipes for the prosperity of his realm were the expansion of tourism and the multiplication of Monaco's tax-sheltered businesses – and both meant construction on a massive scale. Dig a tunnel here, fill the sea there – when Grace's husband got working on his plans to cram record numbers of people into the limited square footage of his little principality, he was like a boy with a Lego set. It seemed at times as if His Serene

Highness saw prestressed concrete as a virtue in its own right, and he took no little pride in the title awarded him in the travel and financial supplements: *Le Prince Bâtisseur* – the 'Builder Prince'.

The 1962 row with de Gaulle had excluded French citizens from the benefits of Monaco's special tax rates, so Rainier widened his focus to recruit tax dodgers from everywhere else. Tax exile became big business as welfare states grew top-heavy in the sixties. In Liechtenstein, Panama or the Cayman Islands, you could get away with a brass plate outside a lawyer's office. In Monaco, princely decree required that you buy or rent yourself a tangible, three-dimensional home inside the principality – which is why Vaduz, the capital of Liechtenstein, remains today a reasonable facsimile of an Alpine village, while the towering high-rises of Monaco fully justify Alan Whicker's comparison with Manhattan.

Monaco was not totally tax-free. Its annual government budget, which covered the expenses and income of the princely family, was mainly financed by TVA, a form of sales tax on all transactions, along with variable taxes on net profits. But citizens and residents of Monaco had not paid personal income tax since 1869, and it was this that attracted the flood of new arrivals. One prosperous newcomer in the sixties was one of the world's largest arms dealers, Sam Gummings, an American whose warehouses were in Britain and America, but who made Monte Carlo the headquarters of his International Armament Corporation. From its office in Monaco, Interarmco organized the supply of rifles, bazookas and even Vampire jets to such despots as Trujillo, Somoza, Sukarno, Tito and Gadhafi. Cummings preferred dealing with dictators, he would explain, because 'they have a sense of order – and they pay their bills promptly.'

Cummings did, at least, reside in Monte Carlo and operate

a genuine office there. The scandal of Rainier's tax-exile business in the 1960s and 1970s was that many of the other new arrivals did not. The façades of the new high-rises featured sun terraces and conventional sea-view apartments, but the rear of the buildings were often a honeycomb of small, dark, one-room 'studios' where a self-respecting refugee might hesitate to lay their head. Technically these studios were living units. In reality they were the equivalent of Liechtenstein's brass plates – and the chances were that the apartments at the front of the building were only occupied by their owners for a few weeks every summer.

Bogus residence was – and is – the skeleton in the closet of Prince Rainier's tax paradise by the sea. Rupert Allan found that it made the place unbearable. He had toyed with the idea of shifting his home base to Monaco in the 1960s. He could supervise his PR work on the spot, while paying less tax – but he abandoned the idea after only one winter in the ghost town. 'It grew lonesome sitting in,' he told the American reporter Linda Marx in 1983. 'I did watch movies some nights with Grace, and I ate well. But that wasn't enough.'

Rainier's plan to build a Holiday Inn in Monte Carlo proved the mistake that Onassis had always predicted that it would be. By the time the hotel opened in 1972, its high construction costs had priced it out of the reach of normal Holiday Inn travellers, while people who could afford the room rates did not want to stay in a Holiday Inn. The hotel went out of business in the early eighties and was converted into another apartment block.

The prince encountered more success, however, with the construction of what turned out to be the Loew's Hotel and Conference Center, an amalgam of all the elements with which Rainier loved to play. He would show the model to visitors with delight. There was a traffic tunnel, a helicopter pad, a cluster of convention and banqueting halls, an indoor shopping mall and a new, Nevada-style gaming room, all to be notched into the cliffs below Garnier's original belle époque casino and extended out over the sea on a forest of concrete stilts.

Rainier looked to America again, and fixed on the Loew's Corporation to build and operate the project. Under the ownership of the Tisch brothers, Larry and Robert, Loew's had demonstrated their expertise in the running of hotels, casinos and convention centres in places like Miami and Atlantic City. In 1971 Loew's formed a partnership with the SBM and the government of Monaco, along with a Franco-German partnership of investors, to build and operate the sprawling, 23,000-square-metre complex.

The Loew's Hotel was constructed where Monte Carlo's old pigeon shoot used to be, and in the eyes of all but the most fervent concrete-lover, the pigeon shoot would have been preferable. Built in the raw and angular style of 1970s architectural brutalism, Loew's encased the tumbledown cliff below the old casino in a jagged amulet of cement zigzags, which jutted out at the mouth of the harbour like so many gun emplacements. The hotel/convention centre would have seemed gaudy in Miami Beach, but ringing the entire base of Garnier's graceful masterpiece, it was cumbersome and gratingly out of scale.

Even more gaudy was the clientele that Loew's attracted. Its Nevada casino was stocked with craps tables and slot machines to attract the Las Vegas crowd – and they arrived by the planeload. It was ironic that the public relations for the hotel's opening in September 1975 was entrusted to Princess Maria Obolensky, a descendant of one of the great Russian families that had helped set the style on the top of the cliff a century earlier. The Russian princess was horrified as she saw the parade of sunglasses, shiny black shirts, and porkpie hats arriving to inaugurate the tables.

'This,' she murmured faintly, 'is the end of Monte Carlo as we know it.'

Princess Grace of Monaco took the cultural traditions of her principality very seriously. She started an annual ballet festival to help recapture the spirit of Diaghilev and the *Ballets Russes*, and when it came to architecture, she felt a strong commitment to the little cluster of belle époque buildings on the hill of Monte Carlo itself. At the height of Monaco's redevelopment fever, she successfully foiled an attempt to knock down the charmingly faded Hermitage Hotel. 'I suggested that I would nail myself to the door,' she said, 'if they moved in to demolish it.'

But that was a solitary effort. 'I'm not too keen on some of the modern buildings and their height,' Grace admitted in May 1975, and she agreed that some of the principality's new construction clashed with the 'spirit' of the place. Yet that, she stressed, was only her 'personal opinion'. She had no plans for any more threats of door-nailing. 'I protest when I can,' she explained with resignation, 'and then I have to learn to go along with whatever is the decision.'

'Why did Princess Grace participate in a modernization policy she didn't always agree with?' asked the author Steven Englund, talking to Rainier after Grace's death.

'Faithfulness to me – devotion,' replied the prince. 'She was fulfilling that part of the [marriage] contract without perhaps liking it so much.'

Grace had been trained since childhood to put on a front. She had continued the process as a film star, and now she brought it to perfection in her life as a princess. The charm of Monaco was a façade. To some observers, the uncritical overbuilding of the place reflected a greed and thoughtlessness that was no different from the something-for-nothing ethos of the casino. Rainier might have moved his country forward in crudely material terms, but it could not be said that his sponsoring of tax evasion represented any great moral or spiritual advance.

This was not an area that Grace greatly cared to discuss. Business was Rainier's side of things, she liked to say. This avoided any exploration of her own opinion – or the ethics of providing a front for gambling and tax evasion – and it allowed her to step back into the easy and submissive role in which she felt more comfortable, that of the obedient wife. Being the embodiment and inspiration of even a pint-sized mini-state was a daunting job, and the girl who had fought the Hollywood slave contracts had come to accept the compromises involved in 'going along' with the status quo.

Grace's kind heart was not in doubt. When she heard that Josephine Baker, the great black singer and dancer who had settled in France, had fallen on hard times, the princess personally organized the rescue that paid Baker's debts, helping to re-establish the 'Rainbow Tribe' of adopted children whose expenses had got the performer into financial difficulties. At palace receptions it was noted how Rainier would studiously ignore Charles Soccal, Monaco's solitary and outspoken Communist who headed the principality's union organization, while Grace went out of her way to make conversation with the somewhat isolated firebrand. She never lost her soft spot for the underdog.

But there was another part of the princess that was deeply conservative. Grace did not just tolerate, she had come actually to *believe* in the way things were, and this could have a deadening effect on her critical faculties. Journalists who were not writing admiring copy to accompany the latest set of Howell Conant photographs sometimes encountered a woman whose 'frosty, cold-shoulder' side had been chilled to the freezing point by life as the Princess of Monaco.

'She has less warmth and spontaneity than anyone I've ever talked to,' declared Leslie Bennetts, who flew out to interview Grace in the mid-seventies for the Philadelphia *Bulletin*. 'I realize she's been interviewed to death ever since she was about nineteen. Nevertheless, no matter how unusual the question, she reverts to something familiar and non-controversial, something that doesn't require thought ... She's a woman of very rigid opinions, one who doesn't question a lot of things.'

Alexander Walker, the British film critic, noticed the menacing neutrality with which Grace reacted to questions that touched a nerve. 'I really don't have much interest in films now,' she said, dismissing his attempt to open the old question of a return to Hollywood. Walker persisted, wondering whether the princess might not consider a role in the project that Joseph Losey was currently trying to put together, a cinema version of Proust – 'with roles for people accustomed to acting out the protocol of a society long past its natural term'.

The princessly lips tightened. *That* description, she said, hardly applied to Monaco. 'We have all levels of society here, all in touch with each other ... Doctors, teachers, businessmen, street cleaners . . . Here we have no unemployment, none at all. You mustn't think we're unique. Why, recently, we even had a strike!'

The strike, it turned out, had been a brief affair in the casino, and 'His Serene Highness' had put a stop to it. 'But one doesn't talk about that.'

Grace had come to treat Monaco and her status there with absolute seriousness. If she was not a princess, what else could be said about her life? Black-tie, white-tie, fancy dress – the annual summer round of galas and parties was her existence, and she dedicated herself to it with a thoroughness that made even Rainier wilt.

'They both act as if they're royal,' sniffed Rainier's usually supportive father, Prince Pierre, to Gore Vidal on one occasion. 'But they're not royal. Grimaldis are only princes.'

Grace's old friends could not understand how an American girl could feel so very comfortable with people bowing and scraping and saying, 'Your Highness'. The girl who was never invited to the Philadelphia Assemblies gave her name, and helped stage in her palace, a debutante presentation for the *Bal des Petits Lys Blancs* ('the Ball of the Little White Lilies'), a function which enabled the daughters of the nouveaux riches to 'come out' at enormous expense. But Grace had made this her destiny. It had been her dream, and now it was an article of faith.

'She actually studied for it,' says Rita Gam. 'She went to the library and got out the books on Queen Victoria. She studied English royalty. She studied the hairdos of power – big hairdos, with hairpieces and so on . . . If you are the tallest, you are the biggest. It was a calculated observation on her part. She studied the pictures and she did it.'

Her old Hollywood room-mate had noted the pleasure that Grace derived from flexing her muscles with MGM in the months leading up to her Oscar victory. Now, as a princess, Grace had even more power, and she clearly adored the slightly spurious roles that she and Rainier played on the world stage, rubbing shoulders with other heads of state. Always welcome for a glamorous and non-controversial photo opportunity at the White House or the Vatican, they were guests of the Shah at Persepolis, and were even invited to Ascot by the House of Windsor, who had decided that Grace's dignity and charm made the Grimaldis a family with whom they could associate after all.

Grace loved it. She carried it off with such style, and it

was only natural that, as a paid-up member of the grand and famous, she should tend to stick with her own. Her friends who did not live in palaces came to find her conservatism difficult to stomach. Happy to hobnob with Frank Sinatra's pal, Spiro Agnew, Grace remained a fervid defender of Richard Nixon through every sordid revelation of the Watergate crisis, genuinely puzzled that people should be turning against him.

'Grace, this is great for all of us,' said Rita Gam, eager to discuss some of the new ideas that were being advanced in the early seventies by the pioneers of Women's Lib.

'I think those women are disgusting,' Grace replied.

Rita knew that Grace had given a lot of time to certain women's causes. The princess had thrown her prestige behind the La Leche League and had given speeches advocating breast-feeding. So Rita tried again, manoeuvring to broach the subject from a different direction.

'Don't you think they are smart,' she asked, 'to put a name on what we are suffering from?'

'*Suffering* from?' asked Grace, not understanding – or not willing to understand.

'She just didn't know what I was talking about,' says Rita Gam. 'She was one of the first independent women in America. She left her home, she earned her own living, she made her bed . . . But she was also trapped by her position.'

Grace had met the challenge of putting a good face on some rather unpleasant realities by anaesthetizing part of her mind, and there were times when she sounded like any other Monte Carlo dowager. 'Take things like pornography and the sex magazines you see being sold everywhere,' she complained to Roderick Mann of the *Sunday Express* in September 1974. 'How must it be for a young girl walking past, seeing them? Either she'll turn into a sex maniac or become completely frigid.'

It was a curiously basic and extreme pair of alternatives. Grace's sense of sexual security was not what it was. 'When I pass a newsstand selling those magazines,' she told Mann, 'I go and talk to the seller . . . I tell him exactly what I think.'

It was almost comical, the picture of a news vendor welcoming the famously demure princess into his shop, to find himself hit figuratively round the ear by her handbag. Judy Kanter encountered the same contradictions one night over dinner at Rupert Allan's. Allan shared a little villa in the Hollywood Hills with his companion, Frank McCarthy, and they would invite up a few dozen friends, old and new, whenever Grace came to Los Angeles. When Judy Kanter – now in her third marriage as Mrs Don Quine – happened to mention a film she was hoping to produce about Jesus coming back in modern times and trying to get his message across through such contemporary roles as that of a TV-show host, Grace brought the party to a standstill with her anger. 'Why would you make a picture like that today?' she barked. 'Don't we have enough problems without sacrilegious films being made for mass audiences?'

Since the Quines had taken the trouble to submit their script to the Vatican, and had secured permission to shoot the movie (which was never actually produced) in Italy, this outburst made Grace more conservative than the Pope. But the extraordinary thing happened only an hour or so later. Grace had come to the party with her pretty goddaughter, Mary Lee – Peggy's daughter, who had eloped with, and was now divorced from, John Paul 'Bindy' Jones IV – and towards the end of the evening the young woman strolled out into the garden in the company of Ryan O'Neal. Rupert Allan remarked that the couple were taking their time about returning.

'Oh, to be young again,' sighed Grace with real feeling. 'I wish it were me!'

As Judy Quine remarked when she got home that night, it was like having dinner with two different people. Grace seemed to be losing her centre. Her natural, human impulses, the old frank and fallible Grace, would not be suppressed, but she seemed confused and wandering, unable to bring the conflicting components of her spirit together.

The author Gwen Robyns encountered this bewildered and in some ways immature woman in 1975 as she drew towards the conclusion of the first-ever biography of the princess. Robyns had received no co-operation from Monaco. Rainier and Grace had refused to have anything to do with her book. But undaunted, the New Zealander, who had previously written biographies of Vivien Leigh and Agatha Christie, took herself across to Philadelphia and won the confidence of Peggy, Grace's elder sister.

'Frankly,' remembers Robyns today, 'I think there was some jealousy there. Peggy really was a bright and lively mind. She was the eldest, the firstborn. According to the Kelly scenario, everything that happened to Grace should have happened to her.'

Through Peggy, Robyns met and interviewed Kell and Ma Kelly, and was passed on to Grace's Hollywood friends, who gave her a very full briefing on Grace's tangled love life before her meeting with Rainier. It was not the story Robyns had expected to write about the eminently respectable Grace Kelly, but she recorded it all faithfully in her manuscript, then sent it off to Monaco.

'I like to check my facts with my subjects wherever possible,' says Robyns. 'Grace hadn't helped me till that point, but I hoped that this might make her change her mind.'

The phone rang within days. Paul Choisit, Grace's private secretary, was on the line to invite the author to Paris to meet the princess. Grace and Rainier had always kept a pied-à-terre in the French capital and they were in the process of exchanging this for a town house in the semi-private Square de l'Avenue Foch, a green and gated little enclave leading off the Paris equivalent of Eaton Square.

When the journalist Leslie Bennetts went to interview Grace, she had encountered a snooty princess who seemed to feel she was breathing different oxygen from the rest of mankind. The Grace that Judy Kanter and Maree Frisby Rambo knew was a warm and giggly, usually unpretentious woman. Now Gwen Robyns met yet another character – someone who appeared vulnerable and curiously unempowered.

The author arrived early for her appointment, and as she sat down to wait, she was passed in the hallway by what seemed to be a schoolgirl. 'Face scrubbed, hair scraped back, a pleated skirt – I thought, "That can't be Princess Grace." But when I got inside, I discovered that it was. She was behaving exactly like a schoolgirl, very shy and anxious, and extraordinarily insecure. She sat there across the room from me, pushing back on her fingernails. She seemed to be a bundle of nerves.'

The world-respected princess was confronted by the reality of her past, and she did not know quite what to do about it. 'There are some things in the book . . .' she hesitated after some opening pleasantries, then launched into a discussion about the problems of raising daughters to be moral in the modern world. Caroline was a teenager, she explained, and was already starting to have boyfriends. Stephanie was ten. It was so important for a mother to be able to set her daughters a good example . . .

'Well,' said Gwen Robyns, catching her drift, 'we can go through the book together' – and together the two women embarked on a long and fascinating journey through the history of Grace's premarital love affairs. Clark Gable, Ray Milland, William Holden, Oleg Cassini – Grace did not attempt to deny anything. 'It would just be so very embarrassing,' she pleaded. 'Ray Milland lives just up the road from us in Monaco. And William Holden – well, my husband doesn't know about *that* one.'

Grace's frankness was quite disarming. 'How can I bring up my daughters not to have an affair with a married man,' she asked, 'when I was having affairs with married men all the time?'

Gwen Robyns was right up against her publisher's deadline. Grace was being so candid and vulnerable and human. She was little Gracie again, throwing herself on Gwen Robyns's mercy. 'What can I do to help you?' she was asking. 'I really want to help you get things right – I'll put you in touch with Phyllis.' [Phyllis Earle, formerly Phyllis Blum, had been Grace's personal secretary in Monaco for many years and had become one of her closest friends.] 'If only I had been briefed properly. If only somebody had picked up the telephone and told you are one of us.'

'All right,' said Gwen Robyns, feeling both panicked and seduced – and feeling, above all, that she wanted to do something to help this new friend she appeared to have made. 'Everything comes out.'

'I was crazy,' says the author today. 'She had told me it was true, and I should have kept it all in. But that is just not my style. She'd told me about her daughters. I already had some inkling about the state of her marriage. What would have happened to her, personally, if I had published it? I just couldn't do that to her. She had worked her spell on me.'

Gwen Robyns' biography *Princess Grace* was published in the spring of 1976. It was warm and complimentary, with scarcely a hint of scandal, and a few weeks later the author received a call from Monaco. 'I didn't believe you would really do this,' Grace said. 'Come and see me.' It was the beginning of a relationship that took rapid wing. Through the writing of her book, and through her contacts with the family in Philadelphia, Gwen Robyns already shared a curious intimacy with Grace. She had uncovered the secrets, and she had kept them. She had acted as if she were a friend – and now she became one, admitted to the private circle of women who basked in the glow of Grace's giggles and baby talk. Gwen Robyns had written about it, but she was not ready for quite how playful and kittenish Grace could be.

The author and the princess decided to collaborate on a book about flowers, a passion which both women shared. Grace came to visit Gwen Robyns' rose-decked, sixteenth-century farmhouse in Oxfordshire, and Gwen became a guest at Roc Agel. Staying in Monte Carlo at the Hermitage, she would be driven up the mountain every morning to spend long hours in the glass-ceilinged family room, strewn with piles of old telephone directories under which Grace liked to press and dry wildflowers.

Gwen Robyns was struck by how plain and almost peasantlike Grace looked in the morning, off-duty, without any make-up and with just a simple scarf on her head. 'She didn't look beautiful at all,' Robyns remembers. 'She was not a vain person, always fussing about her appearance. Nor would I say she had natural dress sense or any great sense of style. There were times, in fact, when she could look really dowdy. But she got better as the day went on. She somehow became more beautiful with every passing hour, so that by eight o'clock at night, when the hairpieces went in and she had done a little bit of what I called her "no make-up make-up" she looked truly fantastic. She wore just a light smear of foundation and some eye shadow. It was all she needed. That wonderful skin, her eyes, the cheekbones which still showed, even though her face was getting fuller – she would just knock you out. It was her business to turn herself from something normal into something big, and she really knew how to do it.'

As they worked on their book together, the two women would have long talks about life. Grace was entering her mid-forties. She was starting to have problems with her looks and her weight. Gwen Robyns had noted how much time Grace was spending up in Paris, away from her husband, and wondered if this was really just for the official reason – the need to chaperone Caroline while her daughter was engaged in her university studies.

'You know,' Grace said to Gwen one morning, as they walked together in the rose garden, 'I have come to feel very sad in this marriage.'

The façade fell away. The admired and envied Princess Grace, the face that launched a thousand magazine covers, was suddenly a lonely woman in her forties who was having problems with her husband.

'He's not really interested in me,' Grace said. 'He doesn't care about me.'

Gwen Robyns did not know what to say. In her time up at 'the farm', she had seen quite a lot of Rainier, and she had enjoyed his mildly malicious sense of fun. The prince and the author would secretly fill their glasses with vodka when Grace imposed a 'water only' ordinance upon the household. In his 'up' mood, Rainier could be the life and soul of the party.

But when he was down – or downright angry, which seemed to happen more as he entered his fifties – the prince was certainly not a man to whom anyone would care to be married. People often whispered that Rainier had mistresses. He invited David Swift on one occasion to join him on a men-only expedition to Paris, boasting of being able to obtain women who, as the prince put it, 'tore the wallpaper off the walls.' Swift declined the invitation.

If Rainier did work up the energy for infidelity, however, his dalliances were very discreet. It was not something that Grace would complain of to her girlfriends. Her problem after nearly twenty years of marriage was that her husband was devoting the lion's share of his spirit to his concrete wonderland by the sea – while he treated the interests and activities of his wife with indifference.

As her children grew older, Grace had spent more and more of her free time gathering wildflowers in the French hills above Monaco, drying and pressing them, then gluing them into collages which she framed. Several friends suggested that she should exhibit and sell some of her work, and the Galerie Drouant in Paris agreed to try a show.

Rainier made a rare visit north for the opening, which turned out to be a glittering success. Almost every one of Grace's dried flower arrangements was sold, and afterward the princely party adjourned to a restaurant for dinner. Sitting on the table was an arrangement of flowers, and Rainier plucked some petals from it and held them up against a plate.

'Sold!' he exclaimed, holding up the random arrangement of petals with clear derision. 'For three thousand francs!'

Everyone laughed, but it seemed to one of her friends that Grace had some difficulty sharing the joke. She herself had been well aware that, without her princessly imprint, her collages would not have commanded a hundred francs, let alone a show in a Parisian art gallery. But it was a cruel moment to remind Grace of the fact. Nervous and uncertain before the opening, she had swelled visibly with pride as the red 'sold' stickers began to multiply on her creations around the walls. Her friends had singled out particular pictures for special praise, pressed-flower experts had congratulated her on her technique, her ego had been delightfully caressed – and now her husband had turned it all to ashes.

This had become Rainier's way as the couple grew older.

Once proud of his wife's independent achievements, the prince seemed in later years to grow jealous of a fame and charm he could not match. *He* was Monaco. She was the import. It was a syndrome repeated a decade and a half later in the marriage of Britain's Prince and Princess of Wales. Rainier was openly slighting to Grace in company. Though she was invariably supportive of him, he would make jokes about her weakness for people-pleasing and her 'creamy smile'. His continuing fits of snoozing at the social events that she arranged showed his essential contempt for the things that were important to her. Through laziness and a self-absorption that came largely from the prince's side, the partnership had soured into a bizarre form of rivalry, with Monaco and Paris becoming the sites of the respective camps.

The deterioration hurt Grace badly at an already difficult time of her life. 'She operated on adulation,' says Gwen Robyns today. 'It was her fuel. She had got used to it in Hollywood, and she was still getting it from the outside world. In terms of the public, she was more beloved and admired than she had ever been. But that was her sadness. She was not getting it where she really wanted – at home.'

It was not just Rainier who failed to cherish Grace. Albert was a devoted son – kind and shy, and totally obedient to his mother. But his sisters were considerably less amenable, as Gwen Robyns discovered when she went to Paris to stay for a few days in the Square de l'Avenue Foch.

'Why have you come here, and when are you going home?' enquired the thirteen-year-old Stephanie, deputed to greet the visitor in the absence of her mother. 'I *hate* my mother's friends.'

Grace had prepared a lunch for her visitor, featuring Grace's favourite blood sausage. Stephanie made a face. 'I want a hamburger,' she pouted. 'I want a hamburger now.' The teenager had been at the table for some time, sitting in front of several perfectly palatable alternatives to the dreaded blood sausage, but Grace appeared to treat her daughter's tantrum as an absolute command. She called downstairs to the chauffeur, who was in the middle of his own lunch, and instructed him to take Stephanie to McDonald's.

'Why are you doing this?' asked Gwen Robyns in horror. 'You are ruining this girl!'

'Oh, darling,' said Grace, puckering up with a little girl face of her own. 'She's my baby doll. She's my baby.'

Grace had become everybody's doormat. Her welcoming of the pain of love had been exploited by those who were closest to her. Her submissiveness in public matters – not questioning, and not thinking, lest she be tempted to question – was a dreadful metaphor for the deadness of her personal life. The haughty façade of the frosty, cold-shoulder princess concealed a case of low to almost invisible self-esteem. Talking to Grace one day in these years, the Countess Donina Cicogna told her the story of a man whom she had loved passionately, but who, she had discovered, was flagrantly unfaithful to her.

'But you *did* have love,' said Grace eagerly, almost desperately. 'It's the love you had that matters, isn't it, not the pain?'

Grace was the ultimate romantic. Let the north wind come. Let it shrivel the garden. She had dreamed the fantasy, and she was determined to live it through.

'You've got to make some compromises, you know,' she said, talking to Judy Kanter one day. 'No marriage works without them . . . I love Rainier, so I do my best to make things work.'

The two old friends were discussing the pattern of Judy's divorces, and those of their other friends. Of the six light-hearted girls who had travelled to Monaco to be Grace's bridesmaids in April 1956 not a single one was now in the same marriage. All six had been through separation or divorce. 'Some of us sign on for a run-of-the-play contract – no options,' said Grace smiling wryly. 'I do not have the luxury you have.' She had rushed into a love match and found herself confined within a marriage of convenience.

Donald Spoto met Grace twice in these years when he was preparing his book, *The Art of Alfred Hitchcock*. Grace gave him a long interview in Paris during the autumn of 1975, then met him the following summer in Monaco to discuss her writing a short foreword to the book. Caroline was with her on both occasions – 'rather more princessly than her mother,' remembers Spoto. 'She [Caroline] told me she had been taking several film courses at the Sorbonne, and rattled off the names of her professors. "Would *they* have heard of you?" she asked.'

Spoto was entranced with Grace. She was warm and lively and enthusiastic, talking for three hours when their meeting had only been scheduled to last twenty minutes, then inviting the author to stay for dinner so that she could bring back still more memories of this period that had clearly been a highspot in her life.

'All these actors and actresses today,' she said, talking about *To Catch a Thief* with pride, 'they look so ugly and bedraggled – and then you look at Cary and me . . . Excuse me, but you know what I mean.'

She missed the creativity of the film business, she told Spoto, talking about Hitchcock with a special fondness. She laughed about the director's raunchy sense of humour, and remembered how he would push her to the limit to extract the performance that he really wanted.

'She was clearly very pleased to be asked about all this and to be taken seriously in her avocation,' remembers Spoto. 'But it seemed to me that there was something sad about it, this woman of forty-something who was talking so much about the past.' Spoto had the impression that Grace was a person in whose current life something was very much missing – that she was having to put a good face on many unhappy things.

'Thank you,' said Grace, when Micheline Swift complimented her on her new home in Paris. 'I can't live with him any more. It's our way of getting separated.'

TWENTY-FIVE

Angry Jaws

IN THE early 1990s, almost a decade after the death of his old friend the film star and princess, Rupert Allan was talking to Donald Spoto about Grace's final years, and the disillusionment that she came to feel with her marriage. Spoto recalled his own meetings with the princess in Paris and Monaco in 1975 and 1976, and the sad direction that her middle age seemed to take. It was clear that life with Prince Charming had turned out to be no different from life with many another mortal man. When did the marriage lose its magic? wondered Spoto. It must have been tragic for a woman who believed so fervently in romance to experience the withering and dying of romance in her own life.

Allan looked hard at Spoto. Afflicted by heart problems, the seventy-nine-year-old publicist knew that he did not have long to live.

'I have to tell you,' he said, 'that she was not entirely lonely. There was someone rather important to her – someone in Paris.'

The someone was Robert Dornhelm, a young film director whom Grace first met in 1976. Grace was then forty-six, Dornhelm just thirty, intense and hungry-looking, with a handsome shock of strong, wavy hair. Romanian by birth

and Austrian by nationality, Dornhelm spoke with an attract-
ively fractured English accent and had a knack of saying
provocative things. Dashing and slightly mysterious, he had
a touch of Lord Byron about him.

The couple met when Dornhelm came to film the introduction Grace had agreed to deliver to *The Children of Theatre
Street*, a documentary on Leningrad's Vaganova Institute, formerly the Russian Imperial Ballet school, which produced
such stars as Nureyev, Baryshnikov and Makarova. Grace had
agreed to narrate the film as part of her campaign to heighten
Monaco's cultural profile – the opening sequence of the
documentary found her on the stage of the Monte Carlo
Opera talking about Diaghilev – but the princess rapidly
became involved in the project for its own sake, and even
more for the sake of its handsome young director.

Robert Dornhelm was no Hitchcock, but he brought
passion and commitment to his film-making. *The Children
of Theatre Street* was a well-made and elegant film that earned
a nomination for Best Documentary Feature in 1977.
According to Academy insiders, it came within a whisker of
winning the Oscar. Something in Grace was rekindled by
her involvement, for the first time in twenty years, in the
excitement of film-making. 'She was a genuinely creative
person,' says Rita Gam, 'and her creativity had been stopped
right at the gate – just when she was really beginning to
fulfil herself as an actress. I think she felt an emptiness all
those years from her creative side not being realized.'

Grace and Dornhelm talked together about other projects
they might pursue. In the same tradition as *Theatre Street*, they
explored the idea of a film about child prodigies. The Year
of the Child was coming up, and Grace thought she might
be able to get sponsorship from UNESCO. They optioned
Gore Vidal's novel *A Search for the King*, in hopes of turning
it into a rock musical. On a personal level, Grace wanted to

make a film about the garden club that she had started in Monaco, while Dornhelm had long nursed the dream of making a movie about Raoul Wallenberg, the Swede who risked his life saving Jews from the Nazis and who vanished mysteriously in Russia at the end of the Second World War.

From their very different platforms, Grace and Dornhelm had ambitions to realize and ways in which each could help the other. Grace proposed herself as the casting director for the Wallenberg project, and she had her lawyer draw up a contract. From her point of view, the job provided a route by which she might ease herself back into performance – casting directors read with the actors that they are auditioning – while Dornhelm, for his part, knew that he would have no trouble getting serious actors to come and read with the former Grace Kelly.

Dornhelm's dress code favoured open shirts and flared blue jeans. On occasions he even sported a belt with a hammer and sickle motif, and this got him into trouble one day in Monte Carlo when he was sunning himself on the lawns outside the casino. Assuming that the long-haired young foreigner was the sort of drifter whom it was principality policy to kick back sharply into France, a policeman asked for his papers, and took him down to headquarters when he refused to hand them over or give his name. A phone call to Grace's private office eventually got the filmmaker released, and he angrily demanded that the agent in question should be disciplined.

'Certainly not,' the princess replied, delighted. 'We're going to give him a medal.'

Dornhelm never minced his words with Grace. 'All that time and energy that you devote to arranging dead, withered flowers,' he said. 'Isn't that the metaphor of your life?'

Far from freezing to such a comment – which trod the same dangerous ground as Rainier's auctioning of petals in the restaurant – Grace actually listened to Dornhelm and took note of what he said. The young man's rebelliousness seemed to awaken her own long-dormant spirit of independence. When the French minister of culture organized a banquet to celebrate the French premier of *Theatre Street* at the Paris Opera, he invited the Russian ambassador and numerous other dignitaries, but not Dornhelm, the director of the film, or Oleg Briansky, the artistic director. Grace politely asked the ministry if the pair could be included, and was told there was simply no room.

'Fine,' said Grace, and she boycotted the banquet. She attended the gala reception that followed the screening, but once she had shaken the requisite number of hands, she went on with Dornhelm and Briansky – along with Rainier and the three children – to a brasserie, where the party waited half an hour for a table.

'She was always a brave person,' says Dornhelm. 'Very loyal to her friends – that was one of her great qualities.'

One day the following summer, Gwen Robyns got a call in Oxfordshire from Monaco. 'Do you think Robert could come and stay with you for the weekend?' Grace asked. 'He's got to be in England for a few days on a film project.'

Dornhelm had scarcely arrived when the telephone rang. It was Grace wanting to speak to him. Gwen Robyns and her Danish husband, Paul von Stemann, held up lunch while the phone conversation went on – and on, and on. When they did finally sit down with their guest, they were interrupted after little more than twenty minutes by another phone call from Monaco, which resulted in a conversation of equal length.

'I can twist her round my finger,' boasted Dornhelm as he came back to the table again.

By the end of a weekend in which their houseguest seemed to spend considerably more time talking long distance to Monaco than he did to his hosts, Gwen Robyns and Paul von Stemann could not help suspecting that Grace and the young director had more than just film projects to discuss. A few months later Gwen's suspicions were confirmed. Driving in the hills above Monaco with Grace and Dornhelm, the author was surprised by Grace's sudden concern about her walking ability.

'Gwen, darling, haven't you got a bad knee?' she asked. 'Why don't you sit here with Paul [Grace's chauffeur], while Robert and I go off for a walk?'

Somewhat unwillingly, Gwen Robyns agreed to sit out the excursion, consoling herself by getting happily drunk with the chauffeur on a succession of brandies and water.

'Where on earth have you been, Grace?' Gwen demanded truculently when the couple finally came back down from the hills, flushed and tousled.

'Oh, darling,' said Grace, making one of her baby faces. 'It was so lovely – so lovely just being with him.'

Gwen Robyns is not sure how far Grace's friendship with Dornhelm went. 'The physical side wasn't the main thing,' she says. 'Grace just loved the flirtation. It was something to give her all the cherishing and romance which Rainier didn't.'

Dornhelm himself declines to discuss the personal aspects of his relationship with Grace. 'It is a memory that doesn't want to be disturbed,' he says. 'It's better left as it was. It is not reality any more.'

'Robert was always the gentleman,' comments Maree Frisby Rambo, who saw quite a lot of the couple together.

'Dornhelm was quite often around when I was going out with Caroline,' remembers Philippe Junot, who started dating Grace's elder daughter in 1976. 'There was never any sign of Rainier. He was leading his own life down in Monaco, while Grace was leading hers up in Paris. Sometimes we would all go out together as two couples – Caroline with me and Grace with Dornhelm. I do not know if they were lovers, but let me put it this way, I would be very surprised if they were not.'

The question of Grace's relationship with Robert Dornhelm is complicated by the fact that he was by no means the only younger man with whom she consorted in her later years. There was quite a list. Per Mattsson, a thirty-three-year-old Swedish actor who was being considered for a part in the Wallenberg project, tells an extraordinary story of stealing away with Grace from a grand dinner in New York in 1982, and her taking him up to her hotel room. According to Mattsson, he and Grace were alone in the room together until five in the morning – and spent their time doing nothing more compromising than sitting at the piano and singing duets.

It must have been confusing for a virile young man to find himself alone in a hotel room with a living icon. Was this middle-aged and now decidedly matronly lady expecting him to make the move on her?

Jim McMullen, the dashing New York restaurateur, says he could not even consider the princess in physical terms when she invited him to Monaco for a week in the mid-seventies. 'She was somebody so special. She *was* Her Serene Highness.' According to McMullen, nothing improper was even hinted at during the week he spent as Grace's guest, nor at any other time in the six years that he knew her.

McMullen, a former male model, was in his late twenties when Grace started visiting his Third Avenue restaurant with its Irish saloon atmosphere and famed chicken potpie. He remembers an excursion with Grace to the discotheque Studio 54, where the crowds outside parted in front of the princess like the Red Sea, and a surreal dinner during the week he spent in Monaco, where he found himself seated with Grace on one side of him, and Ingrid Bergman on the other.

Not without a touch of jealousy, Grace's girlfriends referred to her young men as her 'Toy Boys'. 'What she wanted was eternal glamour,' says Gwen Robyns, 'and those young men supplied it. They flattered her. They were fun.'

They were also more intelligent and accomplished than the average young stud. Jeffory Martin FitzGerald, a business executive of twenty-nine, was boarding a Concorde in London one February morning in 1980, when he found a pile of shopping bags occupying his assigned seat.

'Excuse me,' he said, trying to be polite to the middle-aged traveller seated beside them. 'Are these your things?'

Grace, who was wearing a head scarf and whom he did not recognize, apologized profusely and hastened to clear away her bags. Once they were seated elbow-to-elbow in the Concorde's narrow seats, FitzGerald tried to catch up on the paperwork of his business trip. But Grace interrupted his train of thought so persistently, tapping him on the arm to request his help with the crossword on which she was working, that the young man felt he must draw the line.

'Madame,' he said brusquely. 'I don't think I can help you with your puzzle. I'm illiterate.'

When lunch was served, FitzGerald relented. Noticing how ravenously his neighbour attacked her portion of caviar, he offered her his. 'I don't really care for caviar,' he explained, which led to a conversation about how people either love it or loathe it – which led, in turn, to a mutual exploration of backgrounds.

'Where do you live now?' FitzGerald asked, after Grace had told him about Philadelphia.

'In Monaco,' she replied, and still he did not get it. Not until she actually gave him her full name did he realize who his famous travelling companion was.

Jeffory FitzGerald was a tall and well-built Irish-American, not unlike Kell in his youth. The couple saw each other regularly whenever Grace came to New York. They would go out to restaurants in groups – McMullen's was a popular rendezvous – but they would take their leave of the party together towards the end of the night, for this was a relationship, according to some of Grace's closest friends, that definitely was physically intimate. 'I thought he'd hate my lumps and bumps,' she confided to one girlfriend delightedly, 'but he doesn't seem to mind one bit!'

She had not lost the magic! Twenty years earlier, Grace would have had no difficulty securing the attention of a busy young businessman on a plane. But in true Grace fashion, she had persevered, and she had won. Grace had not realized, until it had stopped, how much of her identity had depended on the compliment paid by crude, old-fashioned, hormone-driven, male flirtation.

FitzGerald did not have Dornhelm's artistic sensibilities. Some of Grace's friends found him rough around the edges. They would raise their eyebrows when the couple went off into the night together. But the young man certainly had it over Rainier as an attractive and vital hunk of manhood.

FitzGerald was a world traveller, as Grace was becoming in these years. The Concorde had been a very appropriate place for them to meet. They swapped tips on beating jet lag and relaxation techniques – FitzGerald was a corporate 'headhunter' who scouted out promising executives – and they fortified each other's wobbly resolves to diet.

'Watch the lunch routine,' Grace would caution in her postcards. 'Iced tea instead of beer . . .'

In the spring of 1982 the Annenberg Institute of Communications organized a tribute in Philadelphia to Grace's film career. Jimmy Stewart, Bob Hope and the fabled survivors of her era agreed to come and pay their respects to

Grace's artistry and her contribution to the cinema. It was a major honour and promised to be a heart-stopping evening of celebration, but Rainier decided that he would not have the time to be with his wife on her night. So Grace flew to New York without her husband, met up with Jeffory FitzGerald, and motored down to Philadelphia in the company of the young man who was twenty-one years her junior.

'I'm getting to the point,' Grace said angrily to Judy Quine in these years, discussing the world's expectation that she should always be perfect, 'where I don't care what you or anyone else, for that matter, thinks.'

Whenever Grace suspected that press photographers might be around, she took care to hide her young escorts in a group of miscellaneous companions, but she made no secret of them when she was with her closest friends. She saw her young men as her protégés. She was proud of their accomplishments. She introduced Judy Quine to both Dornhelm and FitzGerald, and she was particularly anxious that her old flame Don Richardson, should get to know Dornhelm.

'I'd love you to meet Robert,' she told Richardson, when Rupert Allan arranged a reunion in California. 'He's rather like you. He could be our son.'

In 1976 Grace had accepted the invitation of Jay Kanter to become the first woman on the board of Twentieth Century-Fox – a consequence of Women's Lib to which she did not object. Four times a year the appointment took her travelling in luxury, and at Fox's expense, to board meetings in exciting locations, most frequently in New York and Hollywood. Grace used these trips to meet up with Dornhelm, McMullen and FitzGerald. The young men knew about each other – McMullen and FitzGerald met quite frequently – and on one of her visits to Los Angeles,

Grace asked Rupert Allan to invite Don Richardson and his wife to his house in the hills.

Grace and her former drama coach had been exchanging letters throughout their respective careers. When Richardson went to Israel as a visiting drama professor in the early seventies, Grace had sent a donation to help the finances of his poorer students. They had not seen each other for more than a quarter of a century, but when they finally met on a cool Los Angeles night, it was as if they had never been apart.

'When I walked in,' remembers Richardson, 'she jumped up over the coffee table into my arms, and wrapped her legs around me. There was my wife, Laura, and all the other guests who were watching all this. But for Grace, in that moment, no one else mattered. We were suddenly back in days of old.'

Grace had requested a menu of southern fried chicken, and she tucked into it avidly, holding the pieces of chicken in her one hand, while she held hands with Don Richardson below the table with her other. Halfway through the evening, in her best Monaco tradition, she had the places switched around so she could sit and talk with Don's wife, Laura. What did *she* think of Women's Lib? Was she taking good care of Don?

'It was very touching,' remembers Don Richardson. 'She still had that quality you could write your dreams on – the sweet face, the wonderful eyes. But there was also something very tragic about her. It was heartbreaking to see her over-weight and gone to seed – a little drunk, the seams of her dress opened, the make-up smudged. It seemed to me that she had been hitting the bottle pretty good.'

Don Richardson subscribes to the popular theory that Princess Grace had a drinking problem towards the end of her life. This is largely based on the press photographs that show her putting on weight in her later forties and getting puffy around the face. Trying to laugh about it with her friends, Grace took to describing herself as 'Blimposaurus Rex'. In 1976, the year of Grace's forty-seventh birthday – and the year in which she started her relationship with Robert Dornhelm – Howell Conant had to make a special journey back to Monaco in order to reshoot the family's annual Christmas card. The princess had looked at the proofs of the first photo session and had decided that she was too fat.

The Grimaldi family Christmas card, a formal shot by Howell Conant of Grace, Rainier and their children, taken almost every year from 1956 onward in very much the same pose and setting, provides an extraordinary visual record of one family's expansion and development. Babies appear, change into children, then bulge and grow until, one year, they are standing over their parents as young adults. Rainier goes grizzled, then grey, then finally white. Turtlenecks, floppy collars, bell-bottom trousers, running shoes – the fashions of the decades come and go. Only Grace is the constant: tight, slender, blonde and smiling, looking even better in her early forties than she did at eighteen – until 1976, when startlingly, in just a matter of a year or so, the rose is blown.

Grace loved her food and she enjoyed her drink. From blood sausage to fried chicken, her dietary preferences were invariably fattening, while her fondness for champagne and a good stiff cocktail before dinner did nothing to help her waistline. But the reason for the dramatic change in her appearance around the age of forty-seven was not any special increase in her patterns of consumption. It was her time of life. Grace suffered from a particularly difficult and upsetting menopause.

'She rang me about it endlessly,' remembers Gwen Robyns. ' "What do I do?" she would say. "I'm getting so fat. I can't fit into my clothes, and I've got to be seen." She went to this doctor and that doctor, and they all said the same. It was water retention. It was the change of life.'

The 'angry jaws' was what Grace called it, as if turning the harsh medical word into a rhyme would make it seem better. 'The menopause with its angry jaws is catching up with me,' she wrote to Maree Rambo.

'It's not so much the physical symptoms,' she said in a conversation with Judy Quine, 'it's more an attitude, a feeling . . . I feel a bit mean, and I don't like it.'

The doctors put her on hormone replacement therapy, at quite a high dose, but it did not stop her mood swings, and it increased her bloating. Her breasts swelled, creating exactly the opposite to the problem she had as a teenager. 'I've got this dreadful thing about my bosoms,' she confessed miserably to Gwen Robyns. 'They're so big. I have to confine them.'

Menopause's undermining of the female texture is hard for any woman to take, but it was particularly difficult for one whose allure had depended so heavily on her beauty. Suddenly the geography of Grace's face was changing. Her features were shifting, in an insidious continental drift. She had sailed through more than twenty years of life – through marriage and childbirth and even the death of her father – with very little sense of getting older, and now her best friend, her body, was betraying her. She went to expensive Parisian doctors who offered blood transfusions and special injections, with no result. Desperate to hang onto her looks, Grace was engaged in a battle that she could not win, and in her disbelief she even wondered at times for her sanity.

The sad news came through in these years that Carolyn Scott Reybold, the most soignée of all the bridesmaids, had 'signed off' mentally after a number of personal setbacks and had now become a bag lady living in a shelter for the homeless in New York. Carolyn had declined the help of all her friends, including Grace. She wanted to be left alone.

'Isn't it odd that there's something about Carolyn's life I actually think of enviously?' said Grace to Judy Quine, confessing to several of her friends that she had caught her mind lingering seriously over the attractions of life as a bag lady travelling endlessly around the Paris Métro. 'I must be going "gaga" with the change,' she said to Judy Quine. 'It scares me.'

The 'Toy Boys' were Grace's defiance to the angry jaws, but they offered no real escape from the ultimate issues. How could she go on hiding behind her famous front when some of the most important components of that front were crumbling? Grace had spent her entire life pleasing others – her father, her mother, her husband, her children, the world as a whole that wanted her to *be* Princess Grace, and her church, which had taught her from her earliest days that the way to happiness lay through sacrifice to the higher cause. Prayer, confession and the mass remained Grace's consolations through the most difficult passages of her life, but, as she entered her forties, the dutiful princess did come to realize that there was a sense in which there could be no higher cause than herself.

TWENTY-SIX

Poetry and Flowers

'THE CURSE of the Grimaldis' originated in the thir-teenth century. According to the legend, the first Prince Rainier kidnapped and ravished a beautiful maiden from the Low Countries, then cast her aside – at which his victim engineered her revenge by transforming herself into a witch. 'Never will a Grimaldi find true happiness in mar-riage,' she prophesied.

History has appeared to fulfil the curse. The marital record of the Grimaldis across the centuries has been a scarcely relieved catalogue of divorces, separations and early deaths, culminating in the sad misalliance of Rainier's parents. Grace and Rainier were the first princely couple to achieve any degree of public stability in their marriage. But when it came to the marriage of their daughter Caroline in 1978, the pattern of the generations was resumed.

The Prince and Princess of Monaco had dedicated their parenting to the belief that they could give their children a lavishly funfilled and contemporary childhood, while also raising offspring who were serious and sober models of the princely virtues. This might have been possible in the sort of fairyland where witches are the only serious threat to happiness, but it proved unattainable in the Monaco of the sixties and seventies. Topless bathing, discotheques, fancy restaurants, private yachts – life in Monte Carlo provided a crash course in affluent self-indulgence, and no pupil studied with more enthusiasm than Grace's firstborn child, Caroline.

Grace came to appreciate the danger. Every year she liked to get the children out of Monaco for a spell, packing them off to healthy and hearty summer camps in Pennsylvania, and when Caroline reached the difficult years, Grace decided that her daughter would be better off in a convent. From the age of fourteen to sixteen, Caroline was a student at St Mary's, Ascot, where the principles of a convent education were reinforced by the traditions of an English boarding school. But if old-fashioned Catholic schooling had fostered conformity and polish in Grace, it had the opposite effect on Caroline.

'When Grace was growing up in Philadelphia, she went to ordinary schools where she was just one of the girls,' says Rita Gam. 'But when you are born a princess, it is difficult to be "one of the girls". The mark of God is on you, and that is a curse, in a way.'

The teenage Caroline grew up spoiled and wilful, very conscious of her privileges but not so attentive to the duties that went with them. The little girl who had asked for a Givenchy dress at the age of five graduated without difficulty to become the world's first topless princess.

'The two girls *are* Mediterranean,' Grace was wont to offer by way of an apology.

The 1990s has grown accustomed to the idea that being a princess is likely to make a pretty young woman even more vain and self-indulgent than she might otherwise be, but this was quite a novel concept in the 1970s. Princesses were presumed to be innately demure and self-effacing – rather like Princess Grace, in fact – and people found it shocking that Grace's own daughter should be pioneering the destruction of the illusion.

Grace did not like it either, but she found it difficult to be confrontational with Caroline. Jack and Margaret Kelly had never hesitated to be severe with their daughter when she fell short of what they expected, but Grace wanted something better for her own children than the series of painful showdowns she had lived through with her mother and father. When conflicts loomed she tried to be understanding. Her overriding wish was to remain Caroline's best friend. 'Whatever happens,' she would say, 'you must always leave a door open.'

In many respects, Grace secured the friendship she desired. Living together in Paris from 1974 onward, mother and daughter were like a couple of flatmates as they shared in the adventures of life in the big city. But while Grace's hope was that this life together might prove the means by which she could shape and shepherd her daughter, Caroline was working to her own agenda. She had become a teenager in the same year that her mother hit forty, and from that point onward the two women were on opposite trajectories.

Grace found it difficult to cope with her elder daughter's blossoming sexuality. One day in 1976, Earle Mack, the producer of Dornhelm's *Children of Theatre Street*, was lunching at the Grimaldis' home in Paris. Caroline and Rainier were there, along with the pianist Artur Rubinstein and his wife, who were neighbours, and the gathering proceeded through the afternoon in the leisurely tradition of the serious French lunch, until Grace noticed that Caroline had left the room and had not returned. The princess rushed to the window, her composure suddenly disintegrating.

'Where is she? Where's she gone?' she demanded frantically, no longer the suave hostess, but a panicked mother.

'Did *you* give her the car, Rainier? I know she's gone to see Junot.'

Philippe Junot has been described as the sort of man that every mother hopes their daughter will not marry – which is probably the best explanation of why Caroline did. Charming and amusing rather than conventionally good-looking, Junot was a successful businessman specializing at that time in real-estate deals in North America. He had stakes in shopping malls from Montreal to Dallas. With a father who was the deputy mayor of Paris, Junot came of solid French bourgeois stock. He was seventeen years older than Caroline – thirty-six to her nineteen when they started dating in 1976 – and he was a famous ladies' man. With his comparatively advanced age, his wit, his sense of mystery, and the nimble charm which earned him such success with women, Philippe Junot came out of the same mould as Oleg Cassini.

Caroline had inherited Grace's knack of choosing boyfriends calculated to infuriate her parents, and she took some pleasure in pushing her mother to see how far she could go. Gwen Robyns was staying in the Square de l'Avenue Foch one day when Junot came to call. 'It was in the days of tight trousers,' she remembers, 'and Junot was wearing the tightest pants you have ever seen. When he came into the room, Caroline went up to him and rubbed herself up and down against him. It was the most blatant exhibition that I have ever seen.'

' "Grace," I said, "how can you allow that in front of people?"

' "Darling," she replied, throwing up her hands as if she had long given up trying. "What am I going to do?" '

It was Caroline's equivalent of accepting jewels from the Shah.

'There are times,' Grace admitted in June 1978, 'when I see myself in her.'

Caroline was confronting her mother with the reality of her youth, her beauty and her hold over an attractive and dynamic man. She was daring Grace to do something about it. Head over heels in love with Junot, she accepted his private proposal of marriage after they had been seeing each other seriously for a year, and when her mother expressed her unhappiness, Caroline offered the alternative. She would go off and live with Philippe.

When faced with a similar impasse with her own parents over Oleg Cassini, Grace had backed down. Having toyed with the idea of elopement, she had settled for a low-key liaison removed from the public eye. But there was no chance of Caroline being so timid or discreet, and, as Grace then saw it, it was quite out of the question for the daughter of the Prince and Princess of Monaco to be seen by the world to be living in sin.

'Mommy said, "Of course he's the wrong man and you shouldn't marry him," ' Caroline remembered, ' "but now you've been compromised. You've been dating him for too long . . . What are people going to think after you've been dating this guy for two years?" '

It was Grace at her most old-fashioned and status-conscious. Her judgement as a mother, that Junot was the wrong man for Caroline, was subordinated to the need to stay looking good. Keeping up appearances had always been Grace's greatest strength and weakness – as a Kelly, as Hollywood's Ice Maiden and as Princess of Monaco. Caroline had read her mother perfectly when she proposed the possibility of just going off with Philippe. She knew the option that Grace was bound to take.

The public announcement of the engagement was set for late August 1977, and Gwen Robyns went up for dinner in Roc Agel the night before. As she entered the house, Rainier came darting from his study and motioned her aside.

'Gwen,' he said, 'you're good at getting things out of people. Take Junot for a walk in the garden and ask him what he does for a living.'

'Don't you know what he does?' the author asked in astonishment.

'No,' said Rainier, 'not really.'

Rainier was as unhappy about his prospective son-in-law as Grace was. The prince's face would blacken if Junot's name was mentioned, and he would rail biliously, when among friends, at the behaviour of the young couple. But Rainier found it as difficult to share his feelings with his daughter as he did with his wife. When he had something important to say to Caroline, he tended to write her a letter, and she found that the easiest way to communicate with her father was to write him a letter back. Rainier also shared his wife's belief that a generational rift was something to be avoided at all costs. So when Junot had come to the prince in the summer of 1977 formally to request his daughter's hand, Rainier had seemed almost encouraging. Far from being hostile, he had only mildly suggested that the marriage should wait until the following year when Caroline was twenty-one and had completed her studies at the Sorbonne.

'I never had a proper conversation with him, man to man,' says Junot today. 'Soccer, motor cars, that sort of thing, but nothing solid. I think that for him I was always a problem that he just hoped would go away.'

Rainier's hope was speedily fulfilled. Celebrated in the private chapel of the palace in June 1978, the marriage of Mr and Mrs Philippe Junot soon ran into difficulties. Junot's dinner-and-disco style of doing business while on his trips to America was reported in gossip column items and infuriated Caroline. She accused her husband of being unfaithful, though Junot today maintains that it was the other way around.

'I did not make any mistakes in the first ten months,' he says today. 'She did – she was unfaithful – and I was willing to accept it . . . She was twenty-one years old, a beautiful girl, suddenly discovering that it's a lot of fun to enjoy life, that it's great to be free, and that maybe it's a little early to be strictly married.'

Caroline later admitted that she got married less because she wished to spend the rest of her life with Philippe Junot than because she wished to escape from a home situation that she had come to find stifling.

'I was twenty or twenty-one,' she told Jeffrey Robinson ten years later, 'and didn't really want to get married . . . But I wasn't allowed to go off on vacations with him or even spend weekends with him, except at his parents' house, which was all very proper . . . Getting married was simply the correct way out.'

One day in the summer of 1980, Junot got home from playing tennis to discover a note from his wife saying that she needed to take some time out.

'Don't worry,' Rainier said when Junot phoned Monaco. 'She's not feeling well. She's a little depressed.'

The couple reconciled for a week, but then Caroline disappeared again – to England, Junot later discovered. The abandoned husband sought consolation with a former girlfriend on a trip to Turkey, which made tabloid headlines. In true Grimaldi tradition, a marriage that had been embarked on in the cause of propriety had ended up a source of scandal. Early in October 1980, Junot was served with divorce papers, to which he offered no objection, and the Grimaldis' lawyers pushed the formalities through Monaco's courts in a matter of days.

It was Grace who had put pressure on Caroline to get married, and now the notion of divorce came from Grace as well. 'Mommy, said, "You have to get divorced," ' remembered Caroline. 'I didn't dare to divorce or even mention divorce because Catholics don't divorce. You're supposed to just make the best of it ... I said, "How can you talk like that? We're a religious family." ... But Mommy said, "Religion is there to help people, not to make your life miserable." '

Grace's urging that Caroline should defy her Church's teaching reflected her practical and no-nonsense streak that could be traced back to Ma Kelly. Caroline was in pain, and Grace wanted to get her daughter started on a new track as rapidly as possible. But Grace was also displaying the less constrained character that she was starting to assume as she reached the age of fifty. Personally and spiritually she was on the move. Her relationship with Robert Dornhelm, her menopause, her growing emancipation from her husband – and even, within limits, from the conventions of being a princess – were all part of a sea change that was transforming her attitudes. Grace was finally refusing to live a life that was dictated to her by others. She was starting to live her own truths.

It was a slip-sliding, learn-as-you-go and by no means obvious process. There was no single dramatically visible break or revelation, and Grace could still revert when frightened or lazy to her old snobberies and stiffness. But shuffling sideways on occasions and picking her way around old pain, she was finally starting, as Rita Gam put it, 'to grow back into herself'.

Recapturing the joy of performance was one of the most critical elements of her rebirth, and it started, by coincidence, in the same year that Grace met up with Robert Dornhelm. In 1976 the Edinburgh Festival was being organized with themes around the American Bicentennial, and John Carroll, the organizer of the festival's main poetry recital, was looking for an American who had the right ear and speaking voice.

'How about Princess Grace of Monaco?' suggested Carroll's old friend Gwen Robyns.

'This is what you're looking for,' Gwen told Grace on the phone. 'You want an extension of your life, some way to express yourself. You can't do it in Hollywood, but this might be the answer. John is an honourable man.'

Eccentric, mildly scatterbrained, and totally devoted to poetry, John Carroll was delighted to meet Grace. 'I can't think of anything nicer,' he said, 'than going to Paris for lunch with a beautiful princess.' But the director had worked with some of England's finest actors, from Ralph Richardson to Peggy Ashcroft, and he had no intention of compromising his standards.

'I want you to do something for me,' he said once the ice had been broken. 'I want you to read this poem to me.'

The poem was called 'Nod'. It was about an old ship, and though Grace read it well, to John Carroll's ear there was definite room for improvement. The director's hearing had been damaged since childhood – he had been rejected for war service on account of his deafness – but this handicap had fine-tuned his antennae to the music of verse.

'When you read poetry aloud,' he explained, 'your projection is helped very much by the phrases, because it is not just a question of going stanza by stanza. Some stanzas need to be slightly lengthened because of the sense of the poem.'

'She took the criticism and she thought about it,' Carroll later remembered. 'She was very intelligent.'

' "Can I read that again now?" she asked.

' "It was good the first time," I told her.

'But she wanted to read it again, and the second time it was much better.

' "I am worried about my projection," she said.

'So I said, "Don't be worried, because you've got a very good speaking voice. It is a soft speaking voice, but that's

406

got nothing to do with it. It's a question of the phrasing. When you think of the poem, think about what it *means*. Bring out the meaning in the phrasing, and that will take care of the projection." '

'I see what you're getting at,' she said – and Princess Grace of Monaco became a poetry reader. It was only to be expected, perhaps, that her four recitals that September in Edinburgh's beautiful, two-hundred-year-old St Cecilia's Hall should prove to be sell-outs, but her performance also earned the praise of the festival's celebrity-wary critics. The consonants rang out clear as ever in Grace's limpid and surprisingly young-sounding voice, which was offset by the baritone of Richard Kiley, a fellow American, and by the rounded English tones of Richard Pasco of the Royal Shakespeare Company.

'At the beginning she was extremely nervous underneath,' remembers Pasco. 'But she learned from each performance. It was wonderful to watch. We somehow fed off one another, like working on the stage. You give and take. She had this gift for lifting up her spirits. It lifted up mine, and I think it lifted up the spirits of the audience as well.'

The highlight of the evening, all agreed, was Grace's rendering of 'Wild Peaches' by Elinor Wylie:

> *When the world turns completely upside down*
> *You say we'll emigrate to the Eastern Shore*
> *Aboard a river-boat from Baltimore;*
> *We'll live among wild peach trees, miles from town.*
> *You'll wear a coonskin cap, and I a gown.*

'I selected the poem,' remembers John Carroll, 'but I have to be truthful – I hadn't realized that Elinor Wylie came from the south until we were doing the rehearsal and Grace said, "It's such a lovely poem, John. I must do this with a

Southern accent." So she did it, and she was absolutely right. The accent enhanced it beautifully.' Grace's lilting, Georgia rendering of 'Wild Peaches' was chosen by the BBC's *Pick of the Year* as the finest poetry recording of 1976.

'Well,' said John Carroll. 'Now that I've launched you, would you like to do some more?'

'Yes, please,' said Grace, and for the next six years she travelled regularly to perform in poetry recitals. Dublin, Vienna, London, Aldeburgh, Stratford-upon-Avon, Chichester – Grace did the rounds of Europe's leading arts festivals, and in 1978 the American International Poetry Forum invited her on a tour of north-eastern cities that ended with tumultuous receptions in Princeton and Harvard. With the roses and the curtain calls it was just a little like being an operatic diva, and if she got a good review the next morning, she could feel that she had earned it in her own right. 'It seemed to me,' John Carroll put it delicately, 'that it came at a moment when it was very much needed.'

Grace met up on her travels with Dornhelm and Fitz-Gerald. She saw old girlfriends, went shopping, was in charge of her own life. With actors like Pasco, who was regularly teamed with her, she could recapture the collegial feeling of summer stock and work on the set – and then there was the difficult and demanding John Carroll, her deaf Hitchcock of the sonnets.

'The moment that I always waited for,' Carroll remembered in 1993, 'was the moment when Grace would walk onto the stage. It would be dark, and I would have the lights come up on her, and as she walked forward the audience always gasped, because she just looked so beautiful – her long dress, her back so straight, her blonde hair tied up above her head. Everywhere, all round the room, you heard this "Ahhh." '

Carroll had brought the legend of the princess to life.

'She had such presence,' he remembered. 'She always carried herself so well. It was a wonderful moment . . .'

The most publicized moment in Princess Grace's poetry reading career came in March 1981, when she delivered a recital in the Goldsmiths' Hall in London in the presence of Prince Charles, who had just announced his engagement and who brought along his new fiancée. It was the first formal evening appearance of the Lady Diana Spencer, and it was made the more memorable by how the young lady almost spilled out of her low-cut black gown.

'Good news,' Grace reported conspiratorially to Gwen Robyns after a session with Lady Di in the ladies' room. 'She's got them under control.' At a supper party afterwards in Buckingham Palace, Grace also passed on the benefit of her own experience when the princess-to-be confided her unhappiness at the sudden influx of reporters and photographers into her life.

'Don't worry, dear,' said the Princess of Monaco in her most comforting tones. 'It'll get worse.'

There was nothing prim or prissy about the way Grace read poetry. Many of her readings were about pretty things – honeybees, orchards and her beloved wildflowers – but her style was tough and taut, reflecting her coaching all those years ago with Sanford Meisner. Grace would drive out hard from the feeling, going with her instincts rather than trying to dress it up with thought or premeditation. It was the very opposite of the caution required of a don't-offend-anyone princess.

'She read me a Wallace Stevens poem one day,' remembers William Allyn, her old friend and colleague from her days in summer stock. 'She was using me as the audience for a recital that she had coming up. The poem was about the perfection of a flower, and, as she read it, I had to turn my head away because it was so moving. There were tears in her eyes and running down her cheeks. There was such truth in the emotion.'

Serious actors came to watch Grace perform, and went away impressed. Poetry reading is the chamber music of the actor's craft. But Grace found it more difficult to generate her husband's interest or respect.

'In 1978,' remembers Gwen Robyns, 'after Grace had done her tour in America and must have delivered a dozen recitals or more, she remarked rather sadly that Rainier had never once bothered to come and hear her perform. It so happened that she was due to give a reading later that year in London. The Queen Mother would be there. So Rainier came over. Before the end of the reading he had fallen fast asleep.'

At moments like that it could be very consoling to think of an adoring young man with a hammer and sickle belt. As a child, Grace had devised a secret life to cope with an overbearing male authority figure. Now she fell back on the same stratagem. Let Rainier slumber. Grace had developed her own new sources for her self-esteem.

She took on more television work. Father Patrick Peyton, the Catholic Billy Graham, invited Grace to work on his inspirational films, so she went to the Vatican to shoot the links for his programmes on Good Friday, the Resurrection and the power of prayer.

'She had a way of chewing the words,' remembers the director Barry Chattington. 'Everything came out so clear. She was an amazing professional. One night we were shooting late, out around eleven o'clock in the main courtyard of St Peter's, and she said, "When I was young and beautiful, I had it in my contract that I didn't shoot after five o'clock. Now I am old and fat. What am I doing here with you?"

'I said, "You *are* young and beautiful."

' "Yes," she replied, "that is the bullshit." '

What did the princess say?

'That is the bullshit,' repeats Chattington. 'That is what she said. She was just great to work with. I mean, it was funny, lots of jokes and things. She was just a natural, genuine, tell-it-like-it-is human being.'

Grace made her film about her Monaco garden club with Robert Dornhelm. *Rearranged* was a mildly farcical story of mistaken identity based on a script by Jacqueline Monsigny, the French romantic novelist who was a friend in Paris. Directed by Dornhelm, and playing opposite Monsigny's actor husband, Edward Meeks, Grace performed on screen for the first time in twenty-five years. She played herself, Princess Grace of Monaco, dealing with an absentminded professor who thought he was coming to a scientific conference, but ended up at the princess's annual flower-arranging competition.

Rearranged was no *To Catch a Thief*, but Grace dominated the action. She was warm and solid, rather like a friendly schoolteacher, her spirit calm and focused on important things. American TV executives declared that, with a little extra footage, the film could make a solid hour of prime time.

Grace's most cherished project as she entered her fifties was the creation of her own theatre, a small, summer-stock-style playhouse overlooking Monaco harbour, just below the Hermitage. For twenty years her energies in the principality had focused on good works and what other people wanted. Now her playhouse by the harbour was something for herself.

'She showed me around just before it opened,' remembers Bill Allyn. 'It had been converted from some sort of convention hall, and she had set out to make it the ideal theatre. She remembered working in the theatre, the lack of comfort in the dressing rooms, and she had got involved in making sure that every detail of *her* theatre was different.'

Dirk Bogarde was one of the distinguished actors invited to the opening in December 1981, as a 'godparent' in the French tradition. 'It cost a bomb, and sat far too few people,' he remembers, 'but it was a showcase of which she was rightly proud. I sat at her table on her left . . . She was, I remember, far more royal than our own Queen. But she was very easy to talk to . . . She watched her husband with intensity. When he grew restless, as in that crowd he was bound to be, she murmured to me, "Uhhhhu . . . The Dodo is getting bored." And when he showed unmistakable signs of very visual distress, with enormous charm and ease she brought the very long supper to a close.'

Grace's plan for her theatre by the harbour was to create a repertory of productions with actors to whom she felt close – casting, directing, and perhaps one day doing some acting herself. She could mount her own drama festival on the Riviera. 'She told us that she wanted us to come down and help her create a company of fine English actors in Monaco,' remembers Richard Pasco.

'Grace was returning to serious public performing,' remembers Rita Gam. 'She was very excited about it. It was developing into a much larger, more intensive, more time-consuming and, for her personally, a much more satisfying thing. Without creativity she had been an undeveloped woman in many ways. But now she was moving into a new, really vital and interesting phase . . . I remember that she wrote me a letter about it.'

Rita Gam received this letter early in September 1982. Less than one week later Princess Grace was dead.

TWENTY-SEVEN

'It's just easier if I drive'

IN THE spring of 1982, six months before her death, Princess Grace flew to Hong Kong with her husband at the invitation of C. Y. Tung, the Chinese shipping magnate, who had invited Grace to rededicate the USS *Constitution*. Tung had refitted the liner for luxury cruises around the Hawaiian islands, taking great pains to restore the ship to the style it had enjoyed when it dropped Grace in Monaco in the spring of 1956. Tung also invited the couple who had fallen in love on that voyage, Jack Seabrook and his wife, Elizabeth, the former UPI reporter, who first met each other on the *Constitution*.

The Seabrooks had not seen Grace for twenty-six years. Liz Seabrook had noticed from press photographs how Grace had put on weight, and when they met she found out the reason why. As they sat talking and drinking, Grace absentmindedly consumed a whole bowl of peanuts single-handed. 'Now, why do I do that?' she giggled, a little embarrassed when she realized what she had done.

Liz Seabrook knew that excessive weight and eating was often a sign of unhappiness in a woman, but she did not see any sign of that in Grace. On the contrary, the princess appeared particularly buoyant. She had great fun exploring

413

the ship, tracking down her own cabin and those of her family – and she was especially relaxed and warm with Rainier. The couple laughed and joked with each other like old and true friends. Jack and Elizabeth Seabrook found it impossible to credit the rumours they had heard about rifts in the marriage. The prince and princess were hardly young lovers, but they seemed a well-matched and contented pair.

The evolving of Grace's marriage from romantic love through discord and apathy to a new sort of tolerance and friendship was the best thing that happened to her in these years. The prince was as liable as ever to his arrogance and moods. But Grace had learned how to laugh about 'the Dodo', and Rainier in a good humour could be a delight.

Grace had stuck to her run-of-the-play contract. She had sworn she would make the relationship work, and she had persisted through the darkest moments. 'If I had the choice,' she had once confessed to Micheline Swift, 'I would divorce him. But I have no choice. He would keep my children.'

Grace was referring to Grimaldi family law and to her marriage agreement that reserved custody of the children to her husband in the event of divorce. But the issue was more complicated than that. Catholic dogma aside, Grace had not the slightest wish to give up being a princess. She might toy with the idea from time to time, but to divorce Rainier and walk away from Monaco would have been to walk out on her life. It was an admission of failure that was impossible to contemplate – and one she had no need to make. With her poetry reading, her multiplicity of interests, and her secret life with younger men, Grace had found a way to fly out of the cage and still enjoy all the benefits that went with being inside. Staying married to her husband had a great deal to offer, and when things got sticky, well, she had not been an actress for nothing.

On this detached but mutually advantageous basis, Grace

and Rainier had become each other's best friends. They had, after all, shared in the adventure that each made of their life. They had created something that the world fervently admired and believed in, and when the chips were down, they really only made sense together. They still shared the same bed – in the palace and up at Roc Agel – a capacious and voluptuous affair beneath a crucifix. For reasons both generous and selfish, the couple had come to accept each other's separate but not totally divergent paths.

'He was always very tolerant,' remembers Robert Dornhelm. 'I can remember quite a few evenings when we had dinner together, just the three of us.'

In April 1981, Grace and Rainier had reached their twenty-fifth wedding anniversary, which they celebrated with a dinner with their children and their oldest friends. Albert made a toast, as did Cary Grant and Frank Sinatra, and then Rainier got to his feet and put his better feelings into words. In his staid, slightly stern public manner, he toasted Grace and told her what she had meant to him and to the three children. There was not a dry eye in the house.

At the end of August 1982, they flew to Norway with the two elder children for a cruise. They crossed into the Arctic Circle, sailing in the same waters as Rainier's adventurous great-grandfather, Albert, the oceanographer. Grace had been complaining of headaches that summer – she had cried off some dinner parties uncharacteristically – and during the voyage the pains had got worse. But that did not stop her from organizing shipboard exercise sessions and some riotous dressing up.

Stephanie did not join them. Just seventeen, she had fallen in love with Paul Belmondo, the nineteen-year-old son of the actor Jean-Paul Belmondo, and she wanted to have her own holiday with him. Grace would not have allowed such licence to Caroline at that age, but the Junot affair had changed her thinking. After some hesitation, she let Stephanie go off with the young Belmondo to Antigua – 'She's my wild child,' she used to say with a grin. Why should her daughter not have some fun? One of Grace's private projects for the autumn was to find a place of her own where she could stay on her visits to Manhattan, not far from the apartment of Jeffory FitzGerald.

Grace's tolerance toward Stephanie had the opposite to the intended effect. When her younger daughter arrived back from Antigua on Friday, 10 September, the girl took it for granted that she could now see more of Paul Belmondo than ever. It is fashionable to talk of parents who abuse their children, but when it came to Grace's younger daughter, it is arguable that the reverse was the case.

Stephanie was due to travel up to Paris the following Monday. Having graduated, with some difficulty, from high school, she was enrolled in the Institute of Fashion Design in Paris, a prestigious and desperately hard-to-get-into establishment, where Stephanie owed her place to her name and to her mother's lobbying. But when Stephanie arrived back from Antigua, five days before she was due to start her studies in Paris, she announced that she was no longer interested in fashion. Paul Belmondo was going to attend racing-car driving school, and that was what Stephanie now wished to do – to be with Paul and learn to race cars.

Grace could not believe it. Her wild child had pushed her too far. Through Stephanie's childhood, Grace had negotiated her younger daughter through a succession of schools, meekly moving her on to a more liberal Catholic school when Stephanie complained that the nuns were too strict, and then – when Stephanie refused to attend even that – on to a private, non-religious school. Now Stephanie was planning to switch to racing-car school in the same fashion.

416

But her mother, for once, had had enough. This was something that Grace absolutely and finally would not accept.

Robert Dornhelm was in Roc Agel that weekend as the arguments raged. Grace was just mortified. All that summer she had been agonizing with her friends over what she described in her letters as the 'S & P situation'. She had tried so hard not to be restrictive, to avoid making the mistake with Stephanie that she now acknowledged she had made when Caroline fell in love with Junot. Both of Grace's daughters had clearly inherited their mother's tendency to lose all her bearings over a man, yet neither was prepared, as the young Grace had been, to bow before the ultimate authority of their parents. Sulky and obstinate, Stephanie was just as determined that she would go off with Belmondo as Grace was that her daughter would not.

Dornhelm was glad to get out of an atmosphere which was rancid and tense. He left Roc Agel on Sunday, 12 September, agreeing with Grace that they would meet up in Paris later in the week. An American TV network had shown interest in screening an hour-long version of *Rearranged*, which would require the shooting of additional scenes. Grace and the director could talk about that once Grace had dealt with her daughter. Grace's first job for the week of 13 September was to get Stephanie down to Monaco, up to Paris, and then safely into her fashion institute. When Grace spoke on the phone to Gwen Robyns late that Sunday night, she complained that her headaches had come back.

Monday, 13 September 1982, dawned clear and bright. It was a perfect, sunny, south of France late-summer day. Driving down through the broom and the pine trees with Stephanie – past the very spot where her *To Catch a Thief* picnic with Cary Grant had been set – Grace could see the yachts below in Monaco harbour and out through the haze along the Riviera coast.

Rainier had been driven down into Monaco an hour or so earlier. He had his usual weekday schedule of business to get through. Grace's chauffeur had been standing beside the Rover, ready to drive the two princesses when Grace and Stephanie came out of the farmhouse, but Grace said it would be easier if she did the driving and went down to Monaco with Stephanie on her own. She had brought out a pile of her dresses on hangers to spread across the Rover's backseat, and she explained that she did not want them to get creased.

The chauffeur later remembered that he protested a little. The dresses were not a problem, he said. He could easily come back for them, or have another car sent up from the palace. But Grace insisted that was all too much trouble.

'It's just easier if I drive,' she said.

Grace still had things she had to say to Stephanie, mother-and-daughter things that needed privacy to be expressed. It was at the forefront of her mind. She had wrangled all weekend, and the battle was still far from won. Grace had been terribly upset. As she had got into the car that Monday morning, talking properly to Stephanie had been what mattered most to her – certainly more than the fact that she hated to drive down this road. Grace knew that she was a terrible driver. After she had rammed a car broadside in Monaco a few years earlier, she had resolved that she would never drive again. But that resolution had gone the way of others, especially those about dieting. So here she was, ten minutes or so into her journey, heading down the winding CD 37 as it led out of the village of La Turbie. She had the radio shut off. She and Stephanie had serious talking to do.

Yves Phily, a professional truck driver in his late twenties, caught up with the brown Rover as it was negotiating the last of the turns before the buildings started, coming into the outskirts of the town of Cap d'Ail. Monaco itself was little more than a mile away. These final hairpins were the sharpest, and even though his semi-trailer was unloaded, Phily had put the truck into low gear so that its engine would act as a brake.

The Rover slowed as it approached a hairpin bend beside a miniature car racing track. It was the spot where local model car enthusiasts staged their remote-control competitions. The Rover made the sharp turn to the left quite smoothly, then pulled away again – until suddenly, about five hundred metres along the road, it started to wobble and waver in its tracks. The car veered from the centre of the road onto the left-hand curb, its side actually knocking into the mountain rocks. If Phily had seen a car doing this at night he would have said that the driver was falling asleep or had had too much to drink. At ten o'clock in the morning he thought it must be an illness – some sort of fainting or pain.

The truck driver sounded his horn loudly, and the Rover corrected its course. Perched up in his truck cab, Phily was looking down on the roof of the car. He could not see who the driver was. But as the Rover, now going straight and reasonably steadily, approached the next hairpin bend and reached the point where one would normally have expected the brake lights to go on, the car suddenly accelerated, shooting forward at a frightening speed – seventy or eighty kilometres an hour, the truck driver later estimated – so that instead of negotiating the bend round to the right, it careered directly on through.

'The moment that I saw it accelerate,' said Phily the next day, 'I knew that it would not make the bend. It was going too fast. The car took off straight through the corner. I literally saw the car flying.'

419

Today there are very obvious warning signs and a crash barrier where Princess Grace went off the CD 37. But in September 1982, there was nothing to prevent a car from driving straight through the corner and out into the void. To the left of the road stood a sign with a single, inconspicuous arrow indicating a corner, while straight ahead was a gap where people discarded rubbish onto the hill.

The Rover flew through the air over a drop of some forty-five metres. There were woods beyond and below the corner, and as the car sailed onward it sliced through the top of a tree – the police later found the topmost branches freshly decapitated – before starting to curve down. Thirty metres lower, the Rover struck into the trunk of another tree, then bounced upside down onto a pile of rocks, crushing the passenger-side doors and roof. The car rolled over several times noisily before tilting on its nose and roof, finally coming to rest.

Captain Roger Bencze was heading north on a drugs investigation when the call came over his radio phone. Bencze was the thirty-five-year-old commander of the gendarmerie company at Menton, which had responsibility for the French towns and countryside around Monaco. As such, Bencze was the liaison officer between the local French police authorities and the police force of Monaco itself, and that was why headquarters had called him on the phone. Gendarme Frédéric Mouniama had radioed in the news that this fairly routine mountain road crash involved two very non-routine people. The captain had better hurry and get there himself.

Bencze arrived at the scene of the accident at ten-thirty a.m. – about thirty-five minutes after the crash, and five minutes after Prince Rainier. The fact that Rainier went to the site of the crash was not revealed at the time, and has

not been known since. The Monaco police routinely moni-
tor the radio frequencies of their French colleagues, and
when they picked up the radio reports of Gendarme Mouniama, they got straight on to the palace. Rainier was rushed
along the coast road to Cap d'Ail with his private secretary,
the chief of his palace guard, and the chief of the Monaco
police in a cavalcade of sirens and flashing lights. They arrived
just in time to see the Monaco fire department loading Grace
into their ambulance and taking her back to Monaco and to
the hospital that bore her name. Confused, bruised, and
still sobbing hysterically, Stephanie was taken there at the
same time.

Newspaper reports at the time suggested there was something improper in the fact that Grace and Stephanie should
have been whisked away so rapidly to Monaco after an
accident on French soil, but the same would have happened
to any crash victim who got hurt at that spot. The protocols
between France and Monaco mandate that all medical victims should be taken to the nearest possible hospital, irrespec-
tive of territory or nationality, and the nearest medical facility
to Cap d'Ail is the Princess Grace Hospital in Monaco.

Bencze was unable to make out what condition Grace
might be in. As he got out of his car, she was being carried
away, an inert body lying on a stretcher. The police captain,
a tall, lean man who would have been well cast as the
detective in *The Fugitive*, was intent on discovering how this
crash had occurred, and he started by interviewing the people
who had found Grace and had first summoned help. Jacques
Provence and his wife Josette had been having coffee with
Jean-Claude Corneveau, a friend who was staying with
them, when they heard the Rover come crashing down the
hill outside. They ran out at once into the garden, where
they were joined by Michel Pierre, a neighbour. Pierre took
a sledgehammer to the only door of the car that was not

wrecked beyond measure – the front, driver's door on the left-hand side. Stephanie came staggering out, and while Madame Provence was comforting her and ringing the police, Jacques Provence and Corneveau were pouring water on the engine to extinguish a few sparks they had seen.

It was at this point that the Provences' landlord appeared on the scene. Sesto Lequio was a flower-seller of Italian origin, sixty-two years old, rotund, ill-shaven, and fond of a good story. When reporters reached the scene of the crash around lunch time, Monsieur and Madame Provence were nowhere to be seen. They had told the police all that they knew, but they wished to steer clear of the press. Jacques Provence was a senior manager at the Loew's Hotel in Monte Carlo. He had friends at the palace, and he did not want his name splashed all over the papers.

Sesto Lequio, however, had no such inhibitions. When the reporters found him tidying up his garden, he was only too happy to provide them with a story, and to take some money for it as well. He sold interviews to various papers at a brisk pace through the afternoon, culminating with a generous and exclusive contract to talk only to the local representative of the *National Enquirer*.

Much of what Lequio said was not borne out by other witnesses. He claimed to have extinguished a fire in the engine of the Rover with his fire extinguisher, though Provence, Corneveau and Michel Pierre all said they saw no fire in the engine beyond a few sparks. When the police forensic expert went over the car that afternoon, he found no trace of extinguisher foam or chemicals. Lequio also claimed to have been the hero who rescued Stephanie – 'I carried Stephanie in my arms' – though everyone else thought she had staggered out by herself once the door was broken down. But the flower-seller's greatest flight of fancy, which hit the newspapers next day and which continues to haunt the story of Grace's death, was that it was not Grace but her seventeen-year-old daughter who was driving – and thus breaking the law. In France you must be eighteen years old to hold a driver's licence.

When the newspaper stories started appearing next morning, Captain Bencze had already arrived at his preliminary findings. Based on the testimony of Yves Phily, the Provences, and Sesto Lequio himself – who had made no mention of his theories in his sworn statement to the police – Bencze had concluded that Grace had lost control of the car through illness or some mental lapse, and had slumped her foot on the accelerator, half in and out of consciousness, possibly in the process of trying to hit the brake.

Bencze had not been impressed with Sesto Lequio as a witness. The man had not been able to read his own statement or to sign his name to it – he had had to place his mark in the form of an X. Some of his claims to the newspapers were clear fantasy. 'I heard Princess Grace say,' he told James Whitaker of the *Daily Mirror*, ' "I want you to believe that I was driving the car," ' though all the other witnesses, including the gendarmes who first arrived at the scene, were adamant that Grace was unconscious all the time and could have said nothing. The only evidence for Lequio's allegation that Stephanie was driving, and the starting point of his entire theory, was the fact that Stephanie had emerged through the driver's door, when that was, in fact, the only possible door through which she could have escaped from the wreck.

Just the same, Bencze felt he had to investigate the allegation. He was answerable to the Procureur General in Nice who, like all district attorneys, had to take account of what was being said in the press. Passing the fingerprint brush over the steering wheel revealed nothing. 'That is usual on steering wheels,' says Bencze. 'There are hundreds of prints.'

Working out a timetable from Fred Mouniama's La Turbie sighting of Grace behind the wheel at 9:45 and the time of the crash – the clock of the Rover was stopped at 9:54 – it was clear that if Grace did indeed stop the car and change places with Stephanie, she must have been very quick about it. It was nearly a mile and a half of narrow, twisting road from the village down to the crash. From what Bencze knew about Grace, it did not seem likely that she would willingly have broken French law, but it was just possible that she had felt faint and had asked her daughter to take over for the last stretch of the road.

Bencze and his colleagues therefore embarked on a slow drive down the road from La Turbie, looking for a spot where it was possible to pull off to the side. Stopping in the road itself to change places would have blocked following traffic and would have caught the attention of someone driving by. The only possible spot was at the last corner but one, beside the site of the model car racing track. There was a gravel shoulder where cars could pull off and park. Yves Phily, the truck driver, had testified that he was already following the brown Rover at that point, but to make doubly sure, Bencze asked Phily to meet him for a second time, and drove down the CD 37 yet again with him.

The truck driver had no doubt. He had been following the Rover well before the radio-control circuit bend, he said, and the car had gone right around the corner smoothly without stopping. There was no possible way that the princesses could have switched.

Bencze dispatched a report to this effect to Nice, and said as much to reporters who took the trouble to track him down. But no one seemed very interested. The story that Stephanie was driving had already become the folkloric explanation of an event that many people found troubling. If Princess Grace could be snuffed out for no special reason one sunny morning in a car, it could happen to anyone. The reality of Grace crushed and twisted on the hillside was the opposite of the fantasy that princesses exist to foster.

The mystery might have been dispelled then, or at any time since, if Stephanie, her father, or any of their spokesmen, had issued a clear and convincing account of what actually happened inside the car. Rainier once said that Stephanie had tried to pull on the emergency brake, but the police report on the car is definite that the emergency brake had not been engaged. Some of the family's closest friends feel quite certain that Stephanie and her mother were arguing as the car went down the hill, but none will say this for the record, since, if true, it would mean that Stephanie's quarrel with her mother was, indirectly, an instrument in Grace's death.

The statements of the palace press office during these admittedly hectic and tragic days only served to deepen the mystery. The first communiqué, issued soon after midday on Monday, 13 September, stated categorically that the cause of the accident was brake failure, and the palace phoned Roger Bencze, requesting him to back up this explanation when he spoke to the press. The Frenchman refused. He had found nothing to indicate brake failure, and the forensic examination of the car at four-thirty that afternoon – which determined, among other things, that neither princess had been wearing a seat belt – could find no evidence that either the brakes or the brake lights had failed. A few days later the Rover car company sent a pair of engineers to examine the wrecked car in even more detail. They came to the same conclusion and, concerned for its reputation, the company insisted that the palace formally withdraw the accusation about the brakes failing, which was done in a statement dated 20 September.

If the crash had involved almost anyone else, French or

Monégasque, the French gendarmerie would have been able to interview the surviving passenger to find out what had happened in the car. They would have tested Grace's blood for alcohol, drugs or illness as a matter of course, and her death would have been followed by an autopsy and an analysis of the contents of her stomach.

But all these channels were closed to Roger Bencze around six o'clock on the evening of the crash. A handwritten note from Monaco's chief law officer was delivered to the police station in La Turbie, where Bencze had established his investigation headquarters. The note drew attention to the protocol between France and Monaco which exempted members of the princely family from being questioned or examined by French police officers, and accompanying the note was a photocopy of the relevant clauses from the treaty. It would be impossible for Bencze to interview either princess.

This need not have been the end of the matter. In the event of a Grimaldi being involved in a serious crime on French soil – either as witness or suspect – a writ of extradition could be sought, and Bencze looked into the process that Monday night. He contacted his Procureur Général in Nice, who, in turn, contacted the French Foreign Office in Paris. The answer came back that extradition was, of course, always a possibility, but that this process should only be launched if Bencze felt that he had good reason.

Captain Bencze decided that he did not. By the afternoon of Tuesday, 14 September, he had established to his satisfaction that Stephanie had not been driving the car, which was the only issue that had any criminal or legal implications. The girl and her mother may or may not have been quarrelling, but French law did not consider that possibility relevant to the driver error – or illness – which, the detective had come to feel, were the most probable causes of the crash.

426

The only last wrinkle was the possibility of sabotage. This was raised several years later by some of the same newspapers who had given credence to the statements of Sesto Lequio, and a scenario was created in which Grace was said to have tried, in some unspecified fashion, to cleanse the principality of gangster elements, who then retaliated by sabotaging the brakes or steering on her car. As with all theories about the Mafia, this theory had the virtue of not requiring any evidence. Indeed, the very absence of evidence was taken as proof that the Mafia must have done the dirty deed.

Roger Bencze did, in fact, specifically investigate the possibility of sabotage on the day of the crash. It was one of the issues examined in the mechanical post-mortem of the Rover, which he supervised at four-thirty that afternoon. The Procureur General had come over in person from Nice, and the investigation was conducted by Noel Anton, a professional accident investigator who conducted all such local car autopsies for insurance companies and for the Menton gendarmerie.

Printed out on its blue-and-white police inquiry form, the report is a precise document, rather sad in its cataloguing of the details of a life cut short: '1972 Rover 3500. Licence Plate 6359MC. Insurance Company: UAP [a major French company]. Coverage: all risks . . . Front windscreen: broken. Rear windscreen: broken. Ignition key: broken. Tyres: good condition on all surfaces, none burst. Hand brake: functioning, not engaged. Automatic gear: set in "Drive". Odometer: 25,540 kilometres. Radio: switched off. Steering wheel: twisted, no control. Foot brake: no control possible . . .'

'The engineer investigated these last two very carefully,' Bencze explains. 'The brakes and the steering mechanisms had been damaged badly by the crash, but there was no sign of tampering – no lines cut, no connections that had been artificially loosened. It was also clear that the prince's garage had serviced and maintained the car in very good condition.' When Rover's engineers arrived from Britain to carry out their own analysis of the car, sabotage was one of the possibilities that they examined. It would not have been a welcome discovery, but it would have helped remove the suspicion that their car had been to blame. They concluded that there was no evidence of sabotage.

Perhaps the saddest of all the entries on the Rover's crash report was the automatic-drive setting, which showed that Grace had been going down the mountain in 'Standard' drive, and had not set the shift in the special safety or 'Mountain' position that engaged the car's engine as a brake. This low gear was specifically designed for twisting gradients like the road from La Turbie, and it would have slowed her descent significantly. But, infrequent and haphazard driver that Grace was, she evidently did not see the 'Mountain' setting — or if she did, her mind was not concentrating on what it meant.

The facts about Grace's final hours became distinctly less clear the moment she was transported from France over the border into Monaco. After completing all his measurements at the site of the crash, Roger Bencze drove down at twelve-twenty to the Princess Grace Hospital, where a doctor gave him the preliminary diagnosis. Princess Stephanie, he said, had suffered only light cuts and bruises. Princess Grace was not doing so well. Her thigh bone was broken. She had also suffered a fracture of the knee, a fracture of the arm, various bruises, and unspecified head injuries that the doctor described as 'cranial traumatization'.

Bencze entered these details in his report, but when he went back to the hospital later that day for an update, the security guards directed him to the side and told him to stay in his car. A hospital official – not a doctor – came out and told him that there was no information to give. Bencze, who was wearing his French captain's uniform, repeated the nature of his assignment, but met a blank wall. 'I'm sorry, sir,' he recalls the official saying. 'You can't have any information. Blackout.' It was immediately after this brush-off that the French detective went back to La Turbie to discover Monaco's letter telling him that he would not be able to interview or examine members of the princely family.

The sinister explanation of this blanket shutdown was that Rainier wished to conceal whatever had happened in the car between Stephanie and Grace. But it was equally likely that the prince had just panicked. Rainier suddenly found himself in the middle of a tragedy. He did not want to have to make decisions. In the days that followed, his press staff were to admit with rare frankness that the prince was just lost. It was impossible to get answers out of him on the simplest things. Rainier was wrapped up in his own grief, and he did not see that half the questions being put to him and his staff were any of the outside world's business.

Grace, it turned out, was in a very serious condition. When she was rushed into the emergency room at around eleven a.m., the hospital's chief surgeon, Professor Charles Louis Chatelin, had shone a light into both her eyes. One pupil narrowed and widened as it should have, but the other made no response. This indicated more than unconsciousness. A blown eye was a sign of brain injury, and Doctor Chatelin sent immediately to Nice for Professor Jean Duplay, the chief neurosurgeon of the Pasteur Hospital there.

The routine care of a patient with suspected brain injury in most modern Western hospitals is to get a CAT scan X-ray of the brain as soon as possible. But when Duplay, an internationally respected brain surgeon, arrived in Monaco, he discovered that the Princess Grace Hospital possessed no

CAT scanner. He also found that the princess was under the influence of 'Gamma O.H.', a French narcotic drug that the Monaco doctors had administered when she was put on a mechanical respirator. This lessened the possibility of causing pain to the princess as a tube went down her windpipe, and made it possible to work on other parts of her body – notably her thorax, which needed to be cut open and cleared of air and blood. But the narcotic could only deepen Grace's unconsciousness, and it meant that no accurate reading of her brain activity could be taken until the effects of the drug had worn off.

It was nearly midnight, twelve hours after the accident, before Grace was moved to Monaco's only CAT scan machine. This was located in a clinic on the other side of town, which provided testing services for many of Monaco's doctors. Pregnancy tests, blood tests, X-rays – Monaco's inhabitants had made the trip for many reasons to the upper-floor clinic. The trouble was that the lift of the building was an ancient, open, cagelike contraption, only large enough for two or three people standing up. So in order that the CAT scan could be accomplished, the body of the unconscious Princess Grace, attended by a hand-operated oxygen tank with her IV tubes held high above her, had to be physically bumped on a stretcher up the stairs, then bumped all the way down again.

The scan showed two distinct areas of damage to the brain. One was deep in the brain and indicated, the doctors said, that Grace had suffered a stroke. The other was in the frontal area and was 'traumatic', meaning that it was the consequence of physical impact.

The stroke was only a small one, Doctor Duplay later said, and Doctor Chatelin declared that if it had happened at home, the princess might simply have lost consciousness briefly and had to sit down for a rest. But as it was, said both doctors, the stroke had caused the princess to drive off the road, thus bringing about the second, traumatic set of injuries to her head.

This was a plausible – indeed, the most plausible – theory. It fitted with the facts of the police investigation, and with the headaches of which Grace had been complaining all summer. The Kellys had a family history of strokes. In 1975 Ma Kelly had suffered a stroke that left her mentally disfunctional, and Kell was to die from a heart attack while jogging in Philadelphia in March 1985, at the age of only fifty-seven. Diet-wise, Grace had always been reckless when it came to fatty foods, gunking up her arteries with her hamburgers and blood sausage, and in the early eighties the role of cholesterol in provoking strokes and heart attacks was still only vaguely recognized.

But other doctors who studied the data that Chatelin and Duplay made public could not understand why the two French physicians went beyond what was likely, to insist that the stroke had definitely occurred before the head injuries. When questioned, the pair grew positively religious in their assertion that the stroke came first and the trauma second, even though there was nothing in the medical data to justify this degree of certitude.

A CAT scan can give a good picture of clotted blood in the brain, which shows up denser on the scan than water and other tissues. But there was – and is – no known way of determining from the scan alone whether Grace's stroke happened just before she struck her head or just afterwards. The doctors released their medical statements in the middle of the uproar over Sesto Lequio's allegations, and their vehemence seemed to be connected with that.

'It was definitely Princess Grace who was driving,' Duplay insisted to an interviewer from Radio Luxembourg.

Stroke-before-trauma fortified the proposition that Grace

was driving the car, while trauma-before-stroke allowed for the possibility that Stephanie was driving and that she took her mother over the edge.

More enduring questions, however, were raised by what happened next. Sometime on Tuesday, 14 September 1982, little more than twenty-four hours after the crash, Dr Chatelin met Prince Rainier, Caroline and Albert outside Grace's hospital room. Showing them the pictures from the CAT scan and explaining how Grace's condition had deteriorated, the doctor said that the princess was now beyond his help. There was no point, he said, in continuing with the artificial life support.

Rainier, Caroline and Albert conferred together and accepted the doctor's verdict. They went into Grace's room to say goodbye to her for the last time, then left her to the care of the doctor. Her life support machine was switched off.

TWENTY-EIGHT

'Lord, I ask not why . . .'

GRACE PATRICIA KELLY, Her Serene Highness Princess Grace of Monaco, died at ten-fifteen on the evening of Tuesday, 14 September 1982. She was fifty-two years old.

She had had no chance to say goodbye. Her last moments of consciousness were filled, almost certainly, with distressed and angry words. It was not a neat or happy ending, and the shock to her friends and to the world in general was the greater for people presuming that she had escaped from the worst of the crash. Trying to downplay anxiety, and unaware of the medical reports that were getting no further than the distraught Rainier, the palace press office communiqués had given the impression that the princess was suffering from nothing much more serious than a broken leg. Acting on these reports, a wide slew of Grace's friends – Gwen Robyns, Judy Quine and Rita Gam among them – had all fired off jokey telegrams exhorting Grace to hurry up and jump out of bed.

It was only when Gwen Robyns phoned Phyllis Earle in London that Tuesday that she got closer to the truth. Grace's friend and former assistant was helping to organize a poetry reading that Grace was due to give in Windsor the following week, and she had phoned Paul Choisit, Grace's private secretary in Monaco, to find him distraught with grief.

'Don't you realize?' he had screamed down the phone. 'It's her head! It's her head!'

The questions raised by Grace's medical treatment made things worse. The administering of the narcotic, the late-night journey across town and up the stairs to the brain scanner – might Grace have survived if things had been handled differently? Rainier seemed troubled by the same question when he spoke to Rupert Allan. 'The prince told me,' Allan said to Linda Marx in 1983, 'that the neurosurgeons told him that if all came off well, the best they could expect was that Grace would live, and be completely paralysed on her left side, which would cause a major change in her personality.'

Allan did not say when the doctors had told Rainier this, but it sounded a long way from being brain-dead. There had clearly been some stage in the hours after the accident when there was a real chance that Grace might have been saved. The rapid switching off of the machine had an imperious, Monaco-style abruptness about it. It provoked so many doubts – rather like the doctors insisting that the brain-scan image revealed things that it could not.

It was easy to be wise after the event, however. Grace had suffered terrible injuries to her head and to her chest as she was bounced around the interior of the tumbling car. The doctors had not had much to work with. Stephanie was younger, and had had the good fortune to be thrown down into the foot well on the passenger side. The most obvious and comprehensive 'if only' of the tragedy was that Grace would have stood a much better chance of survival after the crash if she had buckled herself into her safety belt before it.

The Kellys – Kell, Peggy and Lizanne – arrived for the funeral furious and suspicious. They had not discovered until just before the end how much more serious Grace's condition was than the stories in the papers, and Rainier had not considered it necessary to involve them in the decision to terminate her life support. Could he not have waited just a day or so to see what might happen, or have given them the chance to come across and say goodbye? In America such a decision involved complicated forms and notaries and second opinions.

Peggy, Kell and Lizanne did not bring Ma Kelly with them. Their mother's mind had been increasingly clouded since her stroke in 1975, and the three children decided there was no point in even telling her about Grace's being gone. Ma Kelly was to linger on until January 1990, never aware of the deaths of either Grace or Kell, or of the alcoholic decline of her eldest daughter Peggy, who was to die in November 1991. At the time of this writing, Lizanne, age sixty-one, is the sole survivor of the glittering generation of Kellys from Henry Avenue who set out to conquer the world.

Four of the bridesmaids came back – Rita, Bettina, Judy and Maree – checking into the Hôtel de Paris as they had done twenty-six years earlier, but going up to their rooms and looking out over the harbour toward the rock with emotions that were very different from what they had felt then. Crowds of onlookers and photographers pressed together outside the hotel in the style of that hectic pre-wedding week in 1956, but now they were numbed and sombre. 'We are all so sorry,' called out one old Italian photographer whom Judy Quine recognized from previous visits. 'So sorry for everyone.'

The atmosphere in Monaco, bewildered as much as sad, reflected everyone's assumption that Princess Grace could not actually die. There was much talk of her spirit living on, because people suddenly realized in her absence how kindly an inspiration she had been. Princess Grace at the garden show, Princess Grace at church, Princess Grace at the orphanage – she had worked so hard to breathe her own earnestness and care into her adopted home. The shop windows were shrouded in black. Just for a day or so the jewels and furs were taken off display, to be replaced, in unprompted tribute, by hastily framed postcards and newspaper photos of Grace that appeared everywhere like icons.

The list of dignitaries flying in for her funeral was a tribute of another kind. In April 1956 there had not been a president or crowned head of note at the marriage of Grace and Rainier, but the roll call of arrivals in the second week of September 1982 testified to the prestige that Grace had brought to the shady principality by the sea: the King and Queen of Belgium, the Queen of Spain, Prince Bertil of Sweden, Prince Philip of Liechtenstein, Madame François Mitterrand, Nancy Reagan, accompanied by more beefy security guards than anyone could imagine, and Diana the Princess of Wales, who, on the strength of one meeting, had come to consider the Princess of Monaco a friend.

Frank Sinatra was tied up by concerts in America. David Niven was already too ill with Lou Gehrig's disease to attend. But Cary Grant arrived to bring the right touch of Hollywood and the old days – and, of course, the memory of *To Catch a Thief*.

Grace looked ghastly in her coffin. The wounds on her head had been concealed by a bizarre yellow wig. Her girlfriends looked at it horrified, not knowing whether to laugh or to cry, but afterward they decided that it had to be seen as the sort of joke that Gracie at her most giggly would have enjoyed.

The funeral was held at 10:15 on the morning of the Saturday following her death. There had been a silence hanging over Monaco since the principality had woken up on

Wednesday without its princess, and the fanfare of trumpets that sounded Grace's ebony coffin out of the palace signalled an end to the holding of breath. People wept in the streets. Nowhere was mourning more tragically displayed than on the features of Rainier as he followed his wife's body through the cobbled alleys of the old town to the cathedral. Sobbing openly and frequently, the prince appeared crushed and devastated, a spirit laid waste – though people who knew the story wondered from which particular well of sorrow his unhappiness was drawn.

'They are all sorry that they were not nicer to her,' declared Virginia Gallico, widow of the writer Paul Gallico and lady-in-waiting to Grace. 'They are going to have so many regrets.'

Stephanie watched the funeral on television, lying in the hospital with her neck in a brace. But the service had scarcely begun when she broke down crying, and a few minutes later she passed out. Paul Belmondo turned off the TV.

'We are united in pain,' declared the Archbishop of Monaco in his sermon. The sudden destruction of this exceptional person, he said, 'provides no answers to the questions of life, suffering, separation and death.' The best answers seemed offered by the little, black-edged memorial mass cards that had been set out in each mourner's place: 'I would like to be remembered,' read some words from the last interview Grace had given at the end of July, 'as a decent human being and a caring one.' 'Lord,' read a quotation from Saint Augustine, 'I ask not why you took her away from me, but I thank you for having given her to us.'

After the ceremony, Rainier received the guests in the garden of the palace, shaking their hands and accepting their condolences. Suddenly overcome, he walked away to the terrace and stood on his own, standing where he could look out over the sea and all of Monaco. The prince began to cry again. Caroline and Albert walked over to comfort their father, putting their arms around him, and they began to cry as well. When fairy tales do not finish happily, their ending often tends to be cruel.

For three days the coffin lay in a side chapel of the cathedral, surrounded by flowers. Then on Tuesday, 21 September 1982, a week after her death, Grace was laid to rest in the Grimaldi family vault, taking her place in the great semicircle of princes and princesses around the high altar. 'Gratia Patricia,' read the inscription on the plain marble slab of her tomb, 'Principis Rainierii III Uxor, Obiit Ann. Dni. MCMLXXXII . . . Grace Patricia, wife of Prince Rainier III, died the year of our Lord, 1982.'

Most of her obituaries dwelt on her film career, with relatively uninspired catalogues of her innumerable good works, but one captured the spirit of her, a lyrical tribute from William Buckley, Jr, a fellow Catholic, and a very old friend.

'Grace Kelly,' he wrote in his *National Review,* was 'trained to perform professionally as an actress. But before that she had been trained by her family to perform as a human being, to control herself, and to strive for perfection . . . She had been trained to hide pain, to disguise effort – all that was a part of her character . . . If she had decided to become a nun rather than a princess, there would not have been a distinctive difference in her approach to her vocation.'

Buckley recalled how he had gone to Rome a few years earlier to appear with Grace in one of Father Peyton's religious documentaries. 'She said then,' he recalled, 'that nothing changes in respect of the opportunities, which are always there, for the individual Christian to attempt to do good, and, in doing good, to repay the great munificence of the Providence that gave us life . . . There are no princesses where she is bound, but the secular imagination must at least suppose that wherever she is, a special light will irradiate.'

Grace had shone that light on her family, on her friends and on everyone who felt that their lives had been touched by her. Most of these people had never met her. They had experienced her vitality through her movies, her photographs, and through the more general presence that goes with being a star. Even people who were not very interested in the cinema or princely personalities felt that they knew Princess Grace.

Grace's public face was her finest creation, and her greatest virtue, in an often false and artificial world, was that she genuinely strove to be as good as she appeared. She was a fallible human being, but she was always willing to learn from her mistakes, and she made real changes in her life as she came to appreciate the emptiness and cost of the dream she had been programmed to pursue. Maintaining the public illusion of happiness with a man who often made her miserable was the greatest of all her performances, and she stuck with it because that was what she had promised – and because she knew that happiness is usually complicated and is seldom self-indulgent. Grace Kelly, Princess Grace of Monaco, was authentic. Her physical beauty was the mirror of her better qualities, not a camouflage. She was lucky with her looks, but she led a life that lived up to them.

TWENTY-NINE

To Follow the Circus

O F GRACE and Rainier's three children, it was Caroline who made the most obvious recovery from her mother's death. Her marriage and separation from Philippe Junot had fired and toughened her. 'When you're young,' she said of the experience in her terse fashion, 'you make mistakes.' Suddenly Caroline grew up.

At Grace's funeral, and in the months that followed, Caroline was particularly supportive of her father. She had been in England at a health farm on the Monday of Grace's crash. She arrived back in Monaco the following morning, and she immediately started to assume something of the role that Grace herself might have played in similar circumstances.

People remarked on Caroline's physical similarities to her mother. As the puppy fat fell off her, Caroline lost the unpleasant pout that had been a trademark of her teenage years. Her features thinned and refined. She had her mother's cheekbones, and her mother's carriage. She also had Grace's elegance, and the same ability in social situations to look more intelligent and concerned than perhaps she really was. She had a lovely smile.

All these attributes made Caroline ideally suited to become the new first lady of Monaco, and she played the part seriously and well. She assumed responsibility for the ballet festival and for the ballet school. She took over the Monaco branch of the Princess Grace Foundation, the vehicle that Grace had established for her donations to charity. She opened the garden show, she visited the orphanage and the other good causes beloved of her mother, and she made a dazzling consort when she escorted her father to the Red Cross Ball.

Caroline avoided several of her mother's mistakes. After she married Stefano Casiraghi, a young Italian businessman, in December 1983, she did not serve up the three children that she had by him as fodder for magazine features, and she gave few interviews herself. She was a tough, businesslike presence, definitely less softhearted than Grace. But this toughness shielded her privacy, and probably gave her children a more natural and unaffected quality of life.

Caroline's marriage to the handsome and clean-cut Casiraghi put a smile back on the official face of Monaco's ruling family. The strange gap where Grace had always been in the Christmas cards and in official photographs was filled by Casiraghi, and the arrival of grandchildren – two sons and a daughter – helped lift Rainier out of the gloom in which he had been sunk since Grace's death. Caroline and her young family made their headquarters in a villa not far from the palace on the rock. Rainier was a frequent visitor. Monaco was back on track again – until October 1990, when Casiraghi was competing in an offshore powerboat race. He lost control of his craft, was catapulted into the air, and was killed immediately as his boat came down on top of him.

The tragedy devastated Caroline. For the second time in a decade the magazines ran pictures of her fine features riven with sorrow. She ceased appearing at public functions. She cut her hair dramatically short. She took to wearing nothing but black. Most drastic of all, she uprooted her family from Monaco and shifted them nearly two hundred miles westward into the French countryside, setting up home in a stone farmhouse near Avignon outside the remote mountain village of St Rémy-de-Provence. There the thirty-four-year-old princess rode her bicycle, did her own shopping in the local market, and took her children to the village school, seeking solace and some new direction in the texture of the simple life.

With time the wounds healed, and after a year or so Caroline was occasionally seen in some of her old haunts. She was spotted in Monaco, Paris, and even New York. There was talk of a boyfriend and perhaps of remarriage – to the French actor Vincent Lindon. But though the princess reappeared on her father's arm, doing her duty at the Red Cross Ball and particularly at fund-raising events for her mother's foundation, there was a sense in which Caroline's spiritual headquarters were no longer in Monaco, but in a farmhouse near St-Rémy-de-Provence.

Caroline's steps back towards the mainstream were helped by the announcement from the Vatican in May 1992 that her 1978 marriage to Philippe Junot had been annulled. It had taken twelve years, two papal commissions of inquiry and, finally, it was rumoured, the refusal by Prince Rainier to pay his annual multimillion franc tithe to the Church, to secure the verdict.

The granting of the annulment meant that Caroline could take communion again, and could be remarried within the church. More important from Monaco's point of view, it meant that her marriage to Stefano Casiraghi was no longer religiously invalid, and that Caroline's three children by Casiraghi – Andrea, eight, Charlotte, six, and Pierre, five – could now be recognized as both civilly and religiously legitimate. In the event of Prince Albert not producing any children, the Grimaldi succession was secured by two healthy and handsome young male heirs.

This raised the question of Albert. As the three young children of Rainier and Grace had been growing up in the sixties and were starting to display their very different characters, observers would agree how fortunate it was that it was Albert who would be doing the job. The boy was polite, obedient, dutiful and charming. Of the three children, he was clearly the one that contained the best of Grace. It was true that his stutter hinted at some unresolved conflicts – Rainier was always so much tougher with Albert than he was with the girls. But the stutter faded as Albert grew older, and the prince matured with scarcely a ripple from a bright-eyed and pleasant teenager into a bright-eyed and pleasant young man. Albert spent his college years in America, studying at Amherst, then went on for work-study experience in New York in an advertising agency and in a merchant bank. Already twenty-five at the time of his mother's death, the prince seemed firmly on course to assume the helm of the principality before many more years had passed.

Rainier came to feel that this should be sooner rather than later. He had never assumed that he would go on to the end. Princes do not have thrones and crowns and solemn coronations as kings do. It is much easier for them just to retire, and with the arrival of his sixtieth birthday in May 1983, the idea of retirement became more and more appealing to Rainier. 'I will abdicate in favour of Albert,' he told Sheridan Morley in September 1984, 'just as soon as he feels he is able and ready to take on the responsibilities of running Monaco. He is twenty-six now, and I don't want him to wait around until I die . . . I can't tell you exactly when I shall go, but it won't be long now.'

Rainier made similar remarks in other interviews at this time, and Tim Graham, the British royal photographer, was flown down to shoot a portfolio of pictures that could be released when the handover was officially announced.

That was in 1984. Ten years later Rainier remains firmly in charge of Monaco, and though he is now in his seventies, there is no more talk of the prince being in any hurry to hand his powers over to his son. 'Let us just say', Rainier once remarked on the subject, 'that as soon as Albert is in the right position, and has the moral strength to take over, I would like him to do so.'

Moral strength is the issue, for Prince Albert has failed to grow up. 'Nice', 'sweet', 'eager', 'kind' – everyone who knows the prince says the same. But words that were positive about a fresh-faced young fellow in his early twenties have a sad ring when applied to a balding man of thirty-six. Occupying his mother's former office in the palace, Albert attends meetings, delivers the speeches that his staff write for him, and turns up dutifully at official openings. But apart from competing in motor rallies and bobsled competitions, the prince has yet to do one memorable thing in his life. Grace had a tendency to blandness, and it has been Albert's misfortune to inherit that in full measure. When Caroline got her mother's tough genes, and Stephanie inherited the wild, Albert was left with Grace's eagerness to please. He is the eternal Boy Scout.

The common rumour runs that Prince Albert is gay. But there is no evidence for this, and to judge from the number of paternity suits against him, the opposite would seem the case. In March 1991, Bea Fiedler, a topless model of thirty-three, told Europe's press about a night of passion with Prince Albert in Munich – 'he tore off my panties with his teeth' – and in November 1992 the prince was served with papers by a California woman, Tamara Rotolo, who had spent a month with Albert in the summer of 1991, and claimed that he was the father of her daughter, Jasmine.

The fact that Albert slept with these women is not in serious dispute. Until the paternity suits started, the prince made little secret of his conquests, and his father would cluck indulgently over Albert's 'wild oats'. What the family lawyers are most bitterly contesting is whether these romantic adventures have truly produced any offspring, for if Jasmine Rotolo turns out to be Albert's daughter, then she will take precedence over Caroline's children in Monaco's succession. Jasmine's position will be almost exactly that of 'Mamou', Rainier's mother, the illegitimate offspring of the prince and the washerwoman's daughter in Algeria nearly a hundred years ago. Fathering a suitable heir for Monaco is the most crucial of all the responsibilities in Albert's life, and the casualness of his sexual encounters suggests the rebellion of a boy who has found no other way to rebel.

The traditional remedy for a young prince in such a state of confusion has always been to marry him off to a good, strong woman, but finding a wife for Albert has not proved an easy task. The prince can get women into bed, it seems, but he cannot get them to the altar. This may have something to do with Albert himself. Having witnessed the private toll that a very public marriage took on his own parents' lives, it would only make sense for him to be nervous of commitment.

But it also reflects the fact that becoming Princess of Monaco is not the job opportunity it once was. What intelligent young woman would welcome the prospect of two forceful sisters-in-law who have, between them, done more than anyone to diminish the prestige that was once attached to being a princess – on top of the challenge of living up to the memory of the woman who embodied the very ultimate of the type?

*

Princess Stephanie did not go to racing-car driving school, and by the time she had recovered from her bruisings and trauma in the autumn of 1982, it was too late for the fashion institute. Her mother's friend, Marc Bohan, the chief designer at Dior, arranged a fashion apprenticeship for her in Paris, but Stephanie came into the studio too late too many mornings for that to last long.

This did not halt her fashion career, however. Less than two years after Grace's death, in the spring of 1984, the Grimaldis gathered around the pool of the Hôtel de Paris to lend their support to Stephanie's first swimsuit collection, some of the costumes being revealingly modelled in the publicity photos by Stephanie herself. The venture proved a success for little more than a season, collapsing when Stephanie's talent and capacity for work had to take over from the excitement attached to her name, and the same went for her next career, in the pop music business. The princess had a hit in France with her first recording, 'Ouragan' ('Hurricane'), then scarcely sold another record. The history of her third venture, a sortie into the perfume trade with a scent labelled 'l'Insaisissable', followed a similar pattern.

'L'Insaisissable' meant 'the Unpossessable One', and it provided an ironic comment on the succession of love affairs that were Stephanie's most sustained activity through these years, since she treated her boyfriends with the same mixture of dependence and cussedness with which she had tormented her mother.

'She needs a strong man to control her,' said Rupert Allan, talking to Linda Marx in 1983. 'She's a determined young woman, selfish and egocentric, spoiled by both parents.'

Stephanie had no difficulty finding strong men, but it was not always clear where their strengths lay. Mario Oliver Jutard was a convicted sex offender. Anthony Delon, another film star's son, had been convicted of possession of a dangerous weapon. Stephanie's hurricane of a life through boyfriends and discotheques, and the hustling of her latest product, burned her out early. Friends of the family were horrified when they encountered the princess hanging out in New York and Los Angeles nightclubs. 'She was just blown away,' one remembers. 'It was extraordinary how a girl who had once seemed so sweet and nice could go downhill so fast.'

The decline and fall of Princess Stephanie prompted a question that came to be asked about all three of Grace's children in the years that followed their mother's death. How could such a lovely lady have produced such wayward offspring? Was it their royal spoiling, the lethally permissive combination of Dr Spock and Monte Carlo – or the fact that they were products of a marriage that was considerably less happy and healthy than the outside world knew?

Stephanie appeared to have plumbed the depths in May 1992, when she announced that she was pregnant by her former bodyguard, Daniel Ducruet. Posing for photographs in the arms of her lover, Stephanie proclaimed her intention to have the child out of wedlock, while Ducruet, who admitted fathering a love child by another woman less than twelve months previously, smiled fondly and placed his hand on her stomach. The couple sold the picture, along with a collection of other intimate snaps, to *Oggi, Hello!, Paris Match, People*, and just about every other magazine that had ever offended the Grimaldis.

People said that Grace must be turning in her grave, and Rainier's reaction to this ultimate scandal was a wounded 'No comment'. But two years later, at the time of this writing, Stephanie continues to live with Ducruet. Still unmarried and happily not keeping up appearances, she has borne him two children – a son, Louis, and a daughter, Pauline – and it even seems possible that Grace's much indulged wild child has finally found some kind of peace.

From her earliest days, Stephanie mistrusted the public dimension of her life. Part of her felt threatened by it. She had nightmares about being kidnapped. At her own wish, she would travel to gymnastics class in the trunk of the car to avoid being photographed, and as she grew up, she was the Grimaldi who reacted most aggressively toward the paparazzi – thus providing them, to their delight, with pictures of a princess sticking out her tongue and making obscene gestures. When the moment came for Stephanie to sound the retreat, where better to seek refuge than in the arms of a bodyguard?

Today she and Ducruet live a quiet and domestic life in their unpretentious apartment near the sea. They push the pram, and watch television. They see a lot of his mother, and rather less of Rainier, who now meets his younger daughter only rarely and privately. It is an exciting day when Stephanie and Daniel go to the town hall for the wedding of one of their young friends in the police or in the security-guard business. Their address happens to be Monaco, but it is *la vie de province*. Once upon a time Stephanie used to dream that she could grow up to lead a normal life and not become a princess, and by dint of hard work she has made her dream come true.

Prince Rainier does not pose much for photographs these days, but when he does, he usually stands in front of a painting depicting his late wife, Grace. It is a painting of Grace in the first months of her marriage, tall and slim and sheathed in silver, vibrant in that first springtime of 1956. It is poignant to see Rainier in front of it, round and droopy with the years, but you can appreciate his pride. He wooed her and won her, this vision of a woman, and that will always be Rainier of Monaco's chief claim to fame.

He makes a melancholy figure, the widower prince alone on the rock, coping as best he can with the failures of his children, whom he continues to bankroll on Grace's principle that the door should never, ever, finally be closed. He is usually overweight, frequently depressed and congenitally withdrawn. Trying to brighten the picture, Europe's press has been trying to marry him off for years – to David Niven's widow, to the widow of his friend the builder, Loulou Marsan, or to the amply endowed Princess Ira von Fursten-berg. ('Such a big girl,' commented Princess Margaret on this last prospect, 'for such a little country.')

Rainier is not interested. Grace was half his life, sometimes more, sometimes less, and he still has the other half, which is Monaco. These days it looks rather more like Hong Kong than Manhattan – a mouth into which even more buildings have been shoved, as John Vinocur once put it, like too many teeth in a denture. The eighties was a decade made for Monaco – the thump of the construction drill, the swish of the crane. Everyone made money. Real estate prices went up by 650 per cent in the period 1977–92, and in the years 1981 to 1991 the number of banks more than doubled, from twenty-five to fifty-seven. Statistics are not available for the growth rate of money-laundering, but significant transfers of Colombian narcodollars have been traced to Monaco, and a French parliamentary commission recently condemned the availability of Monégasque banks for the processing of Italian Mafia money. It was no accident that fifteen or sixteen million dollars of the illicit payments that made up the Iran–Contra scandal were channelled through Monte Carlo in the mid-eighties.

Rainier exercises a tight and rather humourless control over this modern Casablanca. Police TV cameras survey the streets, phones are routinely tapped, and notices on the pavement inform you what you may and may not wear. The locals just love it. Monaco, they will tell you, is one of the last corners of the earth where a lady can safely wear her emeralds on the street. They are correct. But since the destruction of the Iron Curtain, the principality is also the last functioning despotism in Europe.

The despot himself has no apologies to make. The 5,000 native Monégasques and 24,000 foreign tax exiles like things the way they are, and there is little more to say on the matter. At seventy-one, the builder prince puts in as many hours as ever in his office in the palace, looking at plans and models, studying traffic flows. He is half a head of state, half the mayor of Toytown, toiling away at the minutiae of his subjects' lives. It is pretty solid drudgery, and when Monseigneur does take a break, it is often at his typewriter, pecking out his long, flowing letters to his friends, full of eloquence and typing errors.

From time to time Rainier gets onto one of his favourite subjects – circus clowns. When he signs his letters, he often draws a little picture of a clown's face – the painted smile that is camouflage for melancholy. It is strange that the greatest clown ever went by the name of Grimaldi. Since 1974 one of the highlights of the prince's year has been Monaco's Circus Festival, which was his idea. The best circus acts travel from around the world to compete, and Rainier sneaks out of the office to watch the rehearsals. At the end of the festival he invites the best performers up to the palace and they sit around the dinner table telling jokes, the prince venturing out of himself in the company of the vaudevillians. In his garage, Rainier has confided to friends, he has stored a huge, caravan-style camper-bus, a princely RV that he has designed to his own specifications. In it he can be totally self-sufficient, and it is his intention, he says, when he has finally retired, to go driving off in it, and to follow the circus.

★

It is a sunny May morning in Monaco. A little band in blue uniform and white spats is playing beneath the pine trees. They are the musicians of Prince Rainier's palace guard, and they perform the hybrid selections beloved of military bandmasters – '*Marches de l'Empire*' and 'Compilation Beatles' – somehow making all the tunes sound just the same. The clash of cymbals and the oomp-pa-pa float up beside the ramparts of the pink palace. In the background is the sea.

It is the operetta scene that first drew Grace to Monaco. She believed in it. She became a part of it, and through her belief she made it more real. It has not been the same without her, and the antics of her children have made it worse. Monaco has reverted to its traditional shadiness, but Grace's presence rendered it magical – dignified, even – for a season:

> *Never by many are marvels wrought,*
> *By one or two are the dreams first caught . . .*
> *The dreamer must toil when the odds are great,*
> *Must stand to failure and work and wait . . .*
> *Must keep his faith though he stand alone,*
> *Until the truth of his dream is known.*

She stayed true to her coach's teaching. She was always someone who tried to do better, and it is this element of aspiration that keeps her memory alive today. A few hundred yards down cobbled alleys from the bandstand by the palace is Monaco's cathedral, where millions shared in Grace's marriage nearly four decades ago. Now she is buried there, and the tourists file past her gravestone reverently – thirty a minute, eighteen hundred an hour, more than nine thousand a day on a busy weekend.

The cathedral is hushed and shadowy, the stained-glass windows filtering the Mediterranean light. Around the high altar shuffle the pilgrims – modern, camera-slung folk awed to silence by the mystery. Grace lies in the great semicircle of the princes, her gravestone marked by a small vase of flowers. The visitors light their candles. The devout cross themselves and pray. GRATIA PATRICIA PRINCIPIS RAINIERII III UXOR. It could be the resting place of some medieval saint. She dreamed so hard. She earned her glory.

The Feature Films of
Grace Kelly

Grace Kelly's Hollywood career stretched from August 1950 to March 1956. She made eleven full feature films. The dates below indicate when the movie was released in North America. In many cases filming took place in the previous year.

Fourteen Hours (20th Century–Fox) 1951
Produced by Sol C. Siegel, directed by Henry Hathaway, screenplay by John Paxton from the book *The Man on the Ledge by* Joel Sayre, camera Joe Macdonald.
With: Paul Douglas, Richard Basehart, Barbara Bel Geddes, Debra Paget, Agnes Moorehead, Robert Keith, Howard da Silva, Jeffrey Hunter.

High Noon (United Artists) 1952
Produced by Stanley Kramer, directed by Fred Zinnemann, screenplay by Carl Foreman based on the story 'The Tin Star' by John W. Cunningham, camera Floyd Crosby.
With: Gary Cooper, Thomas Mitchell, Lloyd Bridges, Katy Jurado, Otto Kruger, Lon Chaney, Jr, Henry Morgan.

Mogambo (MGM) 1953
Produced by Sam Zimbalist, directed by John Ford, screenplay by

John Lee Mahin based on a play by Wilson Collison, camera Robert Surtees, costumes Helen Rose.

With: Clark Gable, Ava Gardner, Donald Sinden, Philip Stainton, Eric Pohlmann, Laurence Naismith.

Dial M for Murder (Warner Bros.) 1954

Produced and directed by Alfred Hitchcock, screenplay by Frederick Knott from his play, camera Robert Burks, costumes Moss Mabry.

With: Ray Milland, Robert Cummings, John Williams, Anthony Dawson, Leo Britt, Patrick Allen.

Rear Window (Paramount) 1954

Produced and directed by Alfred Hitchcock, screenplay by John Michael Hayes based on a story by Cornell Woolrich, camera Robert Burks, costumes Edith Head.

With: James Stewart, Wendell Corey, Thelma Ritter, Raymond Burr, Judith Evelyn, Ross Bagdasarian, Georgine Darcy, Sara Berner.

The Country Girl (Paramount) 1954

Produced by William Perlberg and George Seaton, directed by Seaton, based on the play by Clifford Odets, camera John F. Warren, costumes Edith Head.

With: Bing Crosby, William Holden, Anthony Ross, Gene Reynolds, Jacqueline Fontaine, Eddie Ryder, Robert Kent, John W. Reynolds.

Green Fire (MGM) 1954

Produced by Armand Deutsch, directed by Andrew Marton, screenplay by Ivan Goff and Ben Roberts, camera Paul Vogel.

With: Stewart Granger, Paul Douglas, John Ericson, Murvyn Vye, Joe Dominguez.

The Bridges at Toko-Ri (Paramount) 1954

Produced by William Perlberg and George Seaton, directed by Mark Robson, screenplay by Valentine Davies from the novel by James A. Michener, camera Loyal Griggs, costumes Edith Head.

With: William Holden, Fredric March, Mickey Rooney, Robert

Strauss, Charles McGraw, Keiko Awaji, Earl Holliman, Richard Shannon.

To Catch a Thief (Paramount) 1955
Produced and directed by Alfred Hitchcock, screenplay by John Michael Hayes from the book by David Dodge, camera Robert Burks, costumes Edith Head.
With: Cary Grant, Jessie Royce Landis, John Williams, Charles Vanel, Brigitte Auber, Jean Martinelli.

The Swan (MGM) 1956
Produced by Dore Schary, directed by Charles Vidor, screenplay by John Dighton based on the play by Ferenc Molnar, camera Joseph Ruttenberg, Robert Surtees, costumes Helen Rose.
With: Alec Guinness, Louis Jourdan, Agnes Moorehead, Jessie Royce Landis, Brian Aherne, Leo G. Carroll, Estelle Winwood.

High Society (MGM) 1956
Produced by Sol C. Siegel, directed by Charles Walters, screenplay by John Patrick based on the play *The Philadelphia Story* by Philip Barry, songs by Cole Porter, music director Johnny Green, orchestrators Nelson Riddle and Conrad Salinger, camera Paul C. Vogel, costumes Helen Rose.
With: Bing Crosby, Frank Sinatra, Celeste Holm, John Lund, Louis Calhern, Sidney Blackmer, Margalo Gillmore, Louis Armstrong.

The Wedding in Monaco (MGM) 1956
Produced by Metro-Goldwyn-Mayer in association with CITEL, Monaco.

Rearranged (1981 – not released commercially)
Produced by Princess Grace, directed by Robert Dornhelm, screenplay by Jacqueline Monsigny, with Edward Meeks playing opposite Princess Grace as herself.

Author's Note and Acknowledgments

I am by no means the first biographer to have written about Grace Kelly. I have been fortunate to draw on the work and discoveries of a number of other writers, and I must begin by expressing my thanks to them. Their books and articles – and the reactions to them – have been part of my story.

In the days following Grace's death and funeral, Gwen Robyns added a final chapter to her biography of the princess, which was reissued within weeks as *Princess Grace: 1929–1982*. This commemorative edition was as warm and complimentary as the original. The author did not alter the pages she had expurgated at Grace's request. But Princess Caroline considered it offensive of her mother's friend to publish the book so close to Grace's death, and she wrote to tell the author as much.

Caroline was apparently unaware of all that could have been written about her mother. She soon found out. In the summer of 1983, *People* magazine commissioned Linda Marx to research and write a major profile, 'Grace Kelly of Philadelphia', which was published on the first anniversary of Grace's death. After decades of orchestrated press coverage, it was a first serious glimpse at the vulnerable side of the icon, and it led to more. Further disclosures and some penetrating psychological analysis were delivered by the posthumous biographies *Princess Grace* by Sarah Bradford and *Grace of Monaco* by Steven Englund, which raced each other to appear virtually simultaneously in the early summer of 1984.

In 1983 Doubleday commissioned the Los Angeles writer James Spada to compile a picture-book tribute to Grace Kelly, and it was in seeking out fresh sources for his text that Spada tracked down Don Richardson and the story of his extraordinary romance with Grace. Securing confirmation of this episode from Grace's family and friends – most notably from her sister Lizanne – Spada abandoned his picture-book plans in favour of a full-scale biography, *Grace: The Secret Lives of a Princess*, which was published in 1987.

Spada's revelations provided the most profound departure to that date from the traditional image of Grace, and they prompted Prince Rainier to provide special help to two authors who were friends of the family and who would, he hoped, paint an alternative picture. The prince and his three children gave extensive and frank co-operation to the American writer, Jeffrey Robinson, and to Judy Quine, the former bridesmaid.

Published in 1989, Robinson's *Rainier and Grace* was an unabashed attempt to present the Grimaldi point of view, and it sold significantly fewer copies than Spada's book. Judith Balaban Quine's *The Bridesmaids: Grace Kelly, Princess of Monaco, and Six Intimate Friends* might have been expected to be similarly partisan – but Judy Quine proved more of a friend to Grace's memory and to her own recollections of Rainier's tempers and moodiness, which she portrayed with unflinching clarity. Her book was a bestseller.

Pondering the results of his co-operation with Judy Quine and Jeffrey Robinson, Prince Rainier came to feel, according to Nadia Lacoste, his press officer for more than twenty years, that he was damned if he helped authors, and damned if he didn't. Their books either betrayed him and sold well – or presented his own point of view and attracted little attention. In a telephone conversation on 30 July 1992, Ms Lacoste courteously and rationally explained why I should not expect any help from the princely family in the preparation of my own book, and so it has proved.

Prince Albert sent the most human and considered regrets. He signed his letter personally. Stephanie declined, briefly, through a private secretary. Caroline also replied through an assistant: 'It is not our practice to give our approbation to projects of this nature and we would ask you to verify that no mention of, or allusion to an authorization by the princely family, or members of their staff, be made in the book or in publicity associated to the promotion of this book.'

I am happy to give this verification. My book has not been authorized by the Grimaldi family, and least of all by Prince Rainier himself, who has declined a succession of interview requests. I am grateful to those of his friends who did grant me interviews.

I am also grateful for the chance to have met and talked to several of the authors on whose work I have built. My debt to Gwen Robyns is obvious from the text. Sarah Bradford and James Spada were thoroughly generous and collegial in sharing their contacts, and helping me to push the story further. As described in the source notes to Chapter one, Linda Marx lent me her research material – and though Jeffrey Robinson, an old friend, could not see the need for any more books about Grace, he conveyed his opinion with his customary wit and charm.

Philadelphia was the foundation of my research into Grace's upbringing and character, and I am grateful to the many people who helped me there: at the Order of the Assumption, Sister Dorothy and Sister Francis Joseph; Tom Baldwin and the staff of Baldwin's Book Barn; Professor E. Digby Baltzell; Hugh Best; Fran Bolno; Charleen Brooks; Lynn Brown; Jess and Selma Bulkin; Sam Bushman; Frazier Cheston; Mary-Ellen Tolan Creamer; Vincent Deeney; Jack Edelstein; Art Gallagher and Patty Gallagher; Karen Gallen; Gloria Otley Hamilton; Rachel Harlow; Betty Hess; Jane and Theodore Hughes II; Mary Agnes Hagen James; John Paul Jones IV; Harry J. Katz; John B. Kelly III; Mary Keon; Andrea Kurz; Harry Leopold; Mr and Mrs Robert Levy; Arthur H. Lewis; Bill Lynch; Jim and Carol McAllister; Don McDonough; Kathy McKenna; Joan Mateer; Philip S. May, Jr.; Glenna Costello Millar; Merrill Pannitt; Maree Rambo; Joe Regan; Jack and Elizabeth Seabrook; Dorothy Langdon Sitley; Ezra Stone; Richard Waterman; Jay and Carole Weitzman; Candie Weitzman; Alice Godfrey Waters; Emily and Harleston Wood.

Alan Wood opened many doors and was a tireless companion on my trips to Philadelphia; Charlotte Thayer was the perfect hostess and playmate; J. Permar Richards introduced me both to the fellowship of Boathouse Row and to Tully Vaughan, who took me out on the Schuylkill River with his crews and also served as a generous guide at Henley to the world of the Diamond Sculls.

In Los Angeles my thanks go to: William Allyn; Frances Brody; Lydia Bunka; Lucille Ryman Carroll; James Carville; Alex D'Arcy; Chico Day; Mel Dellar; Robert Dornhelm; Zsa Zsa Gabor; Sydney Guilaroff; Mrs Henry Hathaway; Fred Hayman; Joe Hyams; Jody Jacobs; Arthur Jacobson; Jay Kanter; Joseph Kenworthy; Stanley Kramer; Irving Lazar; Joe and Marti le Guori; Brian and Jean Mawr; Sanford Meisner; Mark Miller; David Niven, Jr.; Linda Obst; Natalie Core O'Hare; Fred Otash; Don Richardson; Herman Rush; Charles Rappleye; Tony Santoro; John Seeley, Jr.; Robert Slatzer; Mr and Mrs Tim Street-Porter; David and Micheline Swift; Bob Thomas; Gore Vidal; Jack Wiener; Tichi Wilkerson; Willie Wilkerson III.

Robert Cort and Rosalie Swedlin were most gracious and accommodating hosts; Donald Spoto was a guide, mentor and friend; and what a pleasure it was to travel up Coldwater Canyon for tea with Jean Howard!

On my trips to New York I was extended warm hospitality by Peter and Nancy Kirwan Taylor and by Barry and Sandy Cronan. My thanks to them and to: Bob Adelman; Dr Patricia Allan; Milly de Cabrol; Oleg Cassini; Dr Jonathan Charney: Richard Coons; Jean Dalrymple; James Danzinger; Dominick Dunne; Jeffory Martin FitzGerald; Paul and Gillian Friedman; Rita Gam; Lee Grant; Martin and Audrey Gruss; Tom Guinzberg; Radie Harris; Tom Hogan; Celeste Holm; Joey Hunter; Dr Gerald Imber; Zita Ingster; George Lang; Jennifer Lee; Michael and Laurence Levin; Jim McMullen; Meg McSweeney at the American Academy of Dramatic Arts; Dr Ernest Mitler; Ward Morehouse III; Ted Morgan; Helga Philippe; David Pochna; Martin Riskin; Al Rosenstein; John Springer; Rachel Taylor; Jane Ellen Wayne; Cynthia White.

Monaco was a hard nut to crack. Glossy brochures crammed

with facts about the principality abound, but, as in all authoritarian societies, real information is quite another matter. It is a strange experience to telephone a Western European country and to be cautioned, as I was on more than one occasion when phoning Monaco, 'It is not a good idea to discuss this sort of thing over the telephone.' I am the more grateful, therefore, to those residents of the principality who provided me with both information and warm hospitality in the course of my several visits. It would be poor repayment to give their names here.

In France I should like to thank Jean-Pierre Aumont; Captain, now Commandant, Roger W. Bencze; Richard Evans; Pierre Galante; Pierre and Silvita Gallienne; Adrian George and Amanda Monypenny; Xavier and Michèle Givaudon; Mr and Mrs Philippe Junot; Elisa Kitson; Nadia Lacoste; Susanne Lowry; Mike Meade; Edward Meeks; Patrick Middleton; Jacqueline Monsigny; John Pochna; Michael and Marie-France Pochna; June Sherman; Georges Charles Tomaszewski; Jane Tresidder.

I am grateful to Bryan and Greta Morrison for their enduring hospitality on my trips to England. I would also like to thank Geoffrey Bailey; Peter Bate; Lord Patrick Beresford; Kevin Billington; Sir Dirk Bogarde; Melvyn Bragg; John Carroll; Barry Chattington; John Blundell and Richard Hodgkin of Coutts & Co; Mr and Mrs Buff Crisp; Danny Danziger; Nigel Dempster; William Drummond; Peter Evans; Margaret Gardner; Tim and Eileen Graham; Ed Gudeon, visa king; Sir Alec Guinness; Gabe and Bay Gutman; Nicholas Haslam; Sanford Henry; Craig and Pamela Herron; Ruth Jackson; Howard Jacobs; David Jamison; Helene Kemble; Barbara Leigh-Hunt and Richard Pasco; Euan Lloyd; Christopher Moorsom; Sheridan Morley; Nigel Pollitzer; Catherine Portwain and R. S. Goddard at the Regatta Headquarters, Henley-on-Thames; John and Victoria Raymond; John Rendall; Gwen Robyns and Paul von Stemann; Pierre Salinger; Michael Sears; Jennifer Sharp; Donald Sinden; Alexander Walker; James Whitaker; Fred Zinnemann.

Two years of research builds up obligations for many kindnesses. My warm thanks to: Sandy Abouzeid; Betty Aldridge; Susan Allison; Chuck Anderson and Bonnie James at PBW Photo; Jayne

Barton; Carol Baugh; Cari Beauchamp; Laura Boccaletti; Nancy Brinker; Janet Brooks; Art Buchwald; Joe Carrigan; Alfred Clarke; Herbert Coleman; Howell Conant; Richard Connell; Bernie Crawford; Paul Dorman; Jacqueline Dwoskin; Josi Finsness; Sandi Fish; John Franco; Dr Stuart Goodman; Bettina Thompson Gray; Dr Iain Hassin; Dr Jack J. Hirschfeld; Evan Hunter; Maria Karlsson; Kitty Kelley; Ronald Kessler; Arthur Kudner; Wendy Leigh Karten; Earle Mack; Alvin Malnik; Emily Marschok; Linda R. Marx; Mario de Mendoza III; Dr Bill Miller; Kris Morley and Eva Ollson of British Airways Special Services, Miami; Murr Sinclair Murdoch Muirhead; Al and Tammy Nait; Jim Nicholson; Dr Paul Niloff; Chuck Owens at Advance Video; John Patrick; Eunice Ridenaur; Daniel St George; Jon Sobotka; Cathy Tankoos; Chase Thomas and Margaret Ellis; Alejo Vidal Quadras; Ralph Wolfe Cowan; Debra Wallace; Mike Wheeler.

Among librarians, I would like to thank Edda Tasiemka and the staff of the Hans Tasiemka Archives in London; Brigitte Kueppers and David Zeidberg, Special Collections, Library of the University of California, Los Angeles; Samuel Gill and the staff of the Academy of Motion Picture Arts and Sciences, Margaret Herrick Library, Los Angeles; Thomas Whitehead and the staff of Special Collections, Temple University Library, Philadelphia; Geraldine Duclow and the staff of the Philadelphia Free Library Theater Collection; the staff of the Museum of Radio and Television in New York; the staffs at the London Library and the New York Public Library; the staffs of the National Archives and the Library of Congress in Washington; Barbara Staubly and the staff of the West County Branch Palm Beach Public Library, as well as the librarians who supplied volumes through the inter-library loan system.

I met Jean-Jacques Naudet, US picture editor for *Paris Match*, when we happened to walk into the library of the Academy of Motion Picture Arts and Sciences in Los Angeles at the same minute in May 1992, each of us in search of material on Grace. From this happy coincidence has grown friendship and a professional collaboration reflected in the unique and revealing selection of photographs which have added greatly to this book. I am grateful to Michael Rand, a colleague and friend for many years, for his design of the photo pages.

At my British publisher, Sidgwick & Jackson, it has been a pleasure to link up again with William Armstrong – I first wrote a book for him more than twenty years ago – and to benefit from the calm good taste of Sidgwick's senior editor, Helen Gummer.

At Putnam's in New York, I am grateful for the support of Phyllis Grann, for the intelligence and energy of Dolores McMullan, for the sensitive copy-editing of Claire Winecoff, for the careful indexing by Cynthia Crippen, and for the beautiful jacket design produced for the American edition by Ann Spinelli. My greatest debt is to my editor, Andrea Chambers, who had the idea for this book and persuaded me to do it. Tireless, creative and forever challenging, Andrea kept me to her vision – and even to the deadline.

Morton Janklow, my literary agent, has seldom been less than an inspiration. Never in the field of literary agency have so many phone calls been returned so promptly by one man – and my gratitude is extended equally to his colleagues, Bennett Ashley and Anne Sibbald, who have matched his care and attentiveness.

This is my sixth book to benefit from the painstaking research of Jacqueline Williams. I conduct all interviews myself, but Jackie is in charge of squirrelling documentary material out of archives and libraries – Chapter 21 on Monaco's war record reflects her research into the State Department papers in the National Archives in Washington, DC. When I have completed the manuscript, she then subjects it to an intensive check against the sources cited in the reference notes – though the responsibility for errors is my own.

Lili Agee is my day-to-day assistant. Every word in this book has run through her fingers into the word processor. She has strangled more than a few ill-chosen sentences at birth, and has helped give life to many a happy phrase or concept. Making light of the practicalities of producing a 150,000-word biography, she has toiled over the photocopier, fed the fax machine, and has been at all times a loyal helper and friend.

I met my wife, Sandi, when I was writing my first book, and here we are at number twelve. It has been a passionate and exhilarating adventure together, and if I have learnt anything in the process, it has been to listen to her and to trust her judgment. Her love and faith have helped make this our best collaboration to date – with the exception of our children. The three of them got the dedication to my last book. This one is for her.

ROBERT LACEY
West Palm Beach, 9 May 1994

Source Notes

Research for this book began in February 1992 and was completed with the writing in May 1994. Full details of the books and articles cited in these source notes can be found in the bibliography starting on page 516. Interviews were conducted by the author, except where otherwise stated.

Page   THE ROAD FROM LA TURBIE

1. Shortly before ten o'clock: These paragraphs are based on Gendarme Mouniama's testimony in the French police investigation of Princess Grace's fatal car accident of 13 September 1982, and on the memories of those involved in the investigation. Mouniama's account of sighting Princess Grace driving her car was confirmed by Gendarme Rafaeli, who was with him by the crossing.

3. a reference work of the day: *Titled Americans*, 1915, compiled by A. E. Hartzell, can be consulted at the Library of Congress. It shows no publisher or place of publication. Its data is cited more accessibly in Brandon, p. 3.

1. FATHER AND DAUGHTER

A year after Princess Grace's death, *People* magazine commissioned Linda Marx to prepare a major, two-part profile on her life. Linda

Marx spent much of the summer of 1983 researching this, interviewing many of Grace's close friends and members of the family who had not spoken before, and some of whom have not spoken since. A number of these sources, including Grace's brother, Kell, and sister Peggy – who both spoke very frankly – have since died. I am most grateful to Linda Marx for making her notes and transcripts of these interviews available to me.

10.   One pose here, one pose there: The results of this July 1935 photo session can be seen in the library of the Urban Archives, Temple University, Philadelphia, which houses the archives of the now defunct *Philadelphia Bulletin*.

10.   Kelly for Brickwork had a hand in: McCallum, p. xiv and p. 5.

11.   US singles sculling championship: Ibid., pp. xv, 93.

12.   'Mr Kelly was also not qualified': Burnell, p. 25.

14.   The Federal Courthouse: *Kelly Is Brickwork.*

14.   'Never by many': McCallum, p. 221.

16.   But she revealed: Linda Marx research notes. Philadelphia interviews.

2. 3901 HENRY AVENUE

Gwen Robyns wrote the first biography of Grace in difficult and interesting circumstances which are described in Chapter 23, later collaborating with her in the writing and production of Grace's *My Book of Flowers*, published in 1980. She became a friend. I am grateful to Gwen Robyns for her generous help and support in many respects – not least for supplying me with the original notes and transcripts of her interviews with Grace's family and friends in the late 1970s. I am also grateful for the help of Arthur H. Lewis, who interviewed many members and friends of the Kelly family in the mid-1970s for his book *Those Philadelphia Kellys*. The original tapes and typed transcripts of his interviews may be consulted in the Special Collections room of Temple University Library, Philadelphia, referred to below as Temple University Archives.

17. Henry Avenue was: Lewis, p. 37.

18. never believed in the stock market: J. B. Kelly III, interview, 9 April 1992.

18. First television set: Interviews with Alice Godfrey Waters, Gloria Otley Hamilton and Dorothy Langdon Sitley, June 1992.

19. 'My older sister': Pepper, *McCall's*, p. 114.

20. Two brisk years: McCallum, p. 143.

20. Relatives and: Alice Godfrey Waters, interview, 6 June 1992.

20. 'Kell was the boy': Charles Fish, interview, Lewis papers, Temple University Archives.

20. 'The sun, the moon': Alice Godfrey Waters, interview, 6 June 1992.

20. Peggy had been: Peggy Kelly Conlan, interview with Gwen Robyns, 1975.

21. 'Why aren't you': Lizanne Kelly LeVine, interview with James Spada, January 1986.

21. The juice went: Peggy Kelly Conlan, interview with Gwen Robyns, 1975.

21. 'Grace was always': Gloria Otley Hamilton, interview, 9 June 1992.

21. 'She was always': Maree Rambo, interview, 10 April 1992.

22. 'I've always liked': Academy of Motion Picture Arts and Sciences Archives, Skolsky, 13 May 1954.

22. Grace's infant world: Peggy Kelly Conlan, interview with Gwen Robyns, 1975.

23. 'I was terribly shy': Mann, *Sunday Express*, 1 September 1974.

23. 'We were always': Bradford, p. 24.

23. 'I was always on': Pepper, *McCall's*, p. 114.

23. Grace's mother subscribed: Betty Aldridge, interview, 23 April 1992.

23. She had first met: Lewis, p. 154.

23. Margaret Majer's goals and achievements: Peggy Kelly Conlan, interview with Gwen Robyns, 1975.

24. 'I wouldn't say that Mother': Jack Kelly, Jr, interview, Lewis

papers, Temple University Archives.

24.   ' "The Boss" was what she': Charles Fish, interview, Lewis papers, Temple University Archives.

25.   'Everything was for Women's Medical': Peggy Kelly Conlan, interview with Gwen Robyns, 1975.

25.   'We were never allowed': Ibid.

25.   Peggy herself felt: Ibid.

26.   Handsome Jack took: Dan Kelly, interview, Lewis papers, Temple University Archives.

26.   On many an afternoon: Off-the-record interviews with Philadelphia friends of the Kelly family. For interviews and documentation on Jack Kelly's extramarital affairs, see Lewis, pp. 167–71.

26.   'I don't think there': Ibid.

27.   'Don't worry, son': Bradford, p. 24.

27.   'It's very difficult': Charles Kelly, interview, 17 February 1976, Temple University Archives.

27.   a grimly savoured shopping spree: Alice Godfrey Waters, interview, 6 June 1992.

29.   His satirical comedy: Bill Lynch, interview, 8 June 1992.

29.   ' . . . I've got a quarter': Lewis, p. 24.

29.   Her forte was: McCallum, p. 23.

30.   'to make a career': Englund, p. 6.

30.   loan from Walter: McCallum, p. 85.

30.   'scull practice': Gaither, p. 9.

31.   'He was one of the few': Englund, p. 6.

32.   'He was a very old-world': Dorothy Langdon Sitley, interview, 17 June 1992.

32.   Grace loved it: Ibid.

32.   'You could sit': Gwen Robyns, interview, 8 December 1992.

32.   'He is the most wonderful': Grace's application to the American Academy of Dramatic Art, quoted in Englund, p. 6.

33.   Declaiming long narrative passages: Bill Lynch, interview, 8 June 1992.

33.   . . . lecturing his young: Lewis, p. 93.

33. 'He *was* Ina Claire': Ibid., p. 97.

3. White Gloves

34. 'I am here to know Him': The Baltimore Catechism was learnt and recited by all the children at Ravenhill.

34. Ninety to a hundred: Glenna Costello Millar, interview, 8 June 1992.

35. 'I didn't have': Mary-Ellen Tolan Creamer, interview, 7 June 1992.

35. 'Any kind of rudeness': Mother Dorothy, interview, 8 June 1992.

36. 'She asked in a nice way': Ibid.

36. 'an average girl': Sister Francis Joseph, interview, 8 June 1992.

37. Once a girl could write: Glenna Costello Millar, interview, 8 June 1992.

37. She found the idea of Mary: Alice Godfrey Waters, interview, 6 June 1992.

37. ' "I hit my friend"': Mother Dorothy, interview, 8 June 1992.

38. 'Something would start': Alice Godfrey Waters, interview, 6 June 1992.

38. 'Grace Kelly was the girl': Glenna Costello Millar, interview, 8 June 1992.

39. 'The sisters were': Alice Godfrey Waters, interview, 6 October 1992.

40. 'The ceremony was': Ibid.

40. The former stable house: Jane Porter Hughes, interview, 6 March 1992.

41. 'There was one period': Kelly, as told to Gehman, *Los Angeles Examiner*, 17 January 1956.

41. 'I was terribly shy': Mann, *Sunday Express*, 1 September 1974.

41. 'She had a complex': Interview with a school friend of Grace Kelly.

41. 'Grace was not really': Jim McAllister, interview, 7 April 1992.

42. 'She was nobody's': Kelly, as told to Gehman, *Los Angeles Examiner*, 17 January 1956.

42. 'I always wanted': Ibid.

42. 'She always had': Lizanne Kelly LeVine, interview with James Spada, 8 January 1986.

42. 'When she was eight': Alice Godfrey Waters, interview, 6 June 1992.

43. 'I was not that keen': Maree Rambo, interview, 5 March 1992.

43. 'He just looked up': Bradford, p. 31.

43. Grace's stage debut: I am grateful for the help of Geraldine Duclow, curator of the Philadelphia Free Library Theatre Collection, for explaining Philadelphia's rich amateur dramatic traditions to me, and for sorting out the often confused accounts of Grace Kelly's early acting appearances. It has often been written that one of Grace's early performances was in her Uncle George's play, *The Torch-Bearers*. But though the Old Academy Players presented this in 1941 and 1946, there is no mention of Grace being involved.

43. 'I remember the first': Skolsky, *New York Post*, 13 May 1954.

44. She also displayed: Robyns, p. 40.

44. She brought the Stevens field day: Mr and Mrs Theodore Hughes II, interview, 6 March 1992.

44. In the yearbook's composite portrait: Bradford, p. 35.

44. 'She had a real': Jane Porter Hughes, interview, 6 March 1992.

44. 'She was one of': Ibid.

45. 'He's not heavy': Alice Godfrey Waters, interview, 6 June 1992.

45. 'She had the most': Theodore Hughes II, interview, 6 March 1992.

46. Grace's first serious boyfriend: Maree Rambo, interview, 5 March 1992.

46. mention in the Penn Charter Class Diary: Bradford, p. 37.

47. 'There were so many': Charles Fish, interview, Lewis papers,

Temple University Archives.

47. 'You can take': Interview with a suitor of Grace Kelly's in the 1940s.

48. 'I am sure she': Interview with a friend who dated Grace Kelly, and who was a close friend of other dates of hers.

49. 'I hope it's': Charles Fish, tape-recorded interview with Arthur Lewis, Temple University Archives.

49. 'She didn't talk': Robyns, p. 43.

49. 'If you wanted to sit': Ibid.

49. 'It's like her father': Alice Godfrey Waters, 6 June 1992.

49. Inside her own circle: Theodore Hughes II, interview, 6 March 1992.

50. It was one of the dreams: Quine, p. 46.

51. 'You want to': Alice Godfrey Waters, interview, 6 June 1992.

51. 'Jack Kelly always': Phil Klein, interview, Lewis papers, Temple University Archives.

51. 'I'm aiming for': Ibid.

52. 'I wanted to be a dancer': Spada, p. 24.

53. The Mayor gave a testimonial dinner: The dinner was held on 30 July 1947. McCallum, p. 180.

54. 'I wonder if I': Bradford, p. 40.

54. Marie Magee had been an actress: It seems clear that Marie Magee was the person who first put the idea of going to the American Academy into Grace's head. Knowing of Grace's acting ambitions, she had invited her to dinner the previous winter to meet her friend, Ezra Stone, then famous for his stage and radio character Henry Aldrich. Stone had backed up Marie's recommendation of the American Academy. Ezra Stone, interview, 23 March 1993.

55. 'American-Irish': American Academy of Dramatic Arts. Entry Report on Grace Patricia Kelly, 20 August 1947. I am grateful to the American Academy for supplying a copy of the two-page entry in their audition book.

55. 'Lovely child': Ibid.

55. 'It happened very quickly': Don Richardson, interview, 20 May 1992.

56. 'Oh, no, no!': Margaret Kelly, interview with Gwen Robyns, 1975.

56. 'Let her go now': Ibid.

56. 'None of the rest': Quoted in Englund, p. 29.

4. DRAMATIC BEGINNINGS

59. 'You could see': Rachel Taylor, interview, 16 March 1993.

60. A volunteer would go: Ezra C. Stone, interview, 23 March 1993.

60. 'The Actor is': American Academy of Dramatic Arts, p. 9.

60. 'We would be assigned': Bradford, p. 46.

60. 'We would have to pretend': Bettina Thompson Gray, interview, 23 October 1992.

61. to fall down stairs: Murr Sinclair Murdoch-Muirhead, interview, 5 April 1993.

61. 'There were guest lectures': Ibid., 22 February 1992.

62. 'I was a "swayback"': Robyns, p. 46.

62. 'Technique, technique': Rachel Taylor, interview, 16 March 1993.

62. 'It takes a trained ear': Bradford, p. 47.

63. 'You have got to': Mark Miller, interview, 21 August 1992.

63. Pitch and diction were: Bettina Thompson Gray, interview, 2 October 1992.

64. private voice lessons: Bradford, p. 47, and Ezra Stone, interview, 23 March 1993.

64. 'It was a deliberate': Dorothy Langdon Sitley, interview, 17 June 1992.

64. 'We went to': Jane Porter Hughes, interview, 6 March 1992.

64. 'They teased her': Alice Godfrey Waters, interview, 6 June 1992.

64. 'I must talk': Kelly, as told to Gehman, *Los Angeles Examiner*, 18 January 1956.

64. 'It was exactly like': Murr Sinclair Murdoch-Muirhead, interview, 14 January 1993.

65. 'The Amazon': Plath, p. 4.

65. 'They had a wonderful': Ibid., 29 March 1992.

65. 'We would go': Mark Miller, interview, 21 August 1992.

65. 'I saw this angelic': Ibid.

66. 'You'll be playing cowboy movies': Ibid.

66. 'So we did our voice exercises': Ibid.

66. 'We went to see': Bettina Thompson Gray, interview, 26 October 1992.

66. 'We might be sitting': Murr Sinclair Murdoch-Muirhead, interview, 29 March 1992.

67. 'Mother, this is': Margaret Kelly, interview with Gwen Robyns, 1975.

67. performing her exotic dances: Spada, p. 31.

67. 'Let us just say': Mark Miller, interview, 21 August 1992.

67. 'It was really strange': Ibid.

67. 'There were times': Murr Sinclair Murdoch-Muirhead, interview, 31 March 1992.

68. 'One night': Richard Coons, interview, 24 March 1993 and 29 April 1994.

68. 'I was doing': Mark Miller, interview, 21 August 1992.

68. 'I used to do': Billington, *Once Upon a Time Is Now.*

69. 'Who are you': Sister Francis Joseph, interview, 8 June 1992.

69. Back at 3901 Henry Avenue: Gwen Robyns, interview with Peggy Kelly Conlan, 1975.

69. Old Gold paid: Bradford, p. 50.

70. Somehow she usually managed: Interviews with several friends of Grace during her Barbizon years.

70. 'She wanted to be': Maree Rambo, interview, 6 January 1993.

70. 'She did it all': Local Philadelphia television news interviews with Charlie Fish, Peggy Kelly Conlan and Alice Godfrey Waters conducted shortly after Grace's death in 1982. Precise date and production details not known. I am grateful to Alice Godfrey Waters for letting me view the copy of this tape in her possession.

70. 'a candidate for': Spada, p. 34.

71. 'She was a loner': Ibid.

71. 'I can remember': Murr Sinclair Murdoch-Muirhead, interview, 31 March 1992. Anna Italiano changed her name to Anne Marno when she started work in television in the early 1950s. She did not become Anne Bancroft until she got to Hollywood. Her first movie was *Don't Bother to Knock*, released in 1952.

71. Champion scullers: Halberstam, *The Amateurs*, p. 35.

72. 'Call me': Alex D'Arcy, interview, 31 March 1992.

72. 'Girls were my hobby': Ibid.

73. 'Basically, she was': Ibid., 22 May 1992.

74. 'There were these guys': Mark Miller, interview, 23 August 1992.

75. 'I did not go': Alex D'Arcy, interviews, 31 March and 22 May 1992.

5. THE ARMS AROUND HER

This chapter is largely based on the recollections of Don Richardson, who is now, inevitably, the sole source for many of the more intimate incidents he describes. Richardson's memories are confirmed whenever they cross paths with the testimony of other people, including members of the Kelly family, and his story coincides strikingly with Grace's own recollection of the weekend when Richardson visited Henry Avenue in April 1949. She described this episode in detail in her letter of 13 April 1949 to Prudy Wise, published in full in *Paris Match*, 24 March 1994, p. 62, and in part in the Superior Auction Galleries catalogue, *Heroes, Legends, Superstars of Hollywood & Rock*, p. 117.

77. Richardson's training: Richardson's acting philosophy is set out in his book *Acting Without Agony: An Alternative to the Method*, for which Helen Hayes wrote the foreword.

77. 'She did not seem': This and all subsequent Richardson quotations from interviews with Don Richardson on 20 May and 19 August 1992.

80. 'Herbie was definitely': Murr Sinclair Murdoch-Muirhead, interview, 14 January 1993.

80. 'When I saw them': Rachel Taylor, interview, 16 March 1993.

86. 'Whenever she came': Kelly, as told to Gehman, *Los Angeles Examiner*, 18 January 1956.

86. 'Gracie, there's a man': Ibid.

86. 'I gave them the word': Robyns, p. 53.

88. 'They just didn't': Lizanne Kelly LeVine, interview with James Spada, 8 January 1986.

91. 'I hope I *am*': Maree Rambo, interview, 10 April 1992.

6. LETTING GO

Geoffrey Hellman's 1955 *New Yorker* profile, 'Philippe of the Waldorf,' is the earliest written source on Claudius Charles Philippe. Ward Morehouse, III, supplemented this considerably in Chapter 7 of his book on the Waldorf-Astoria. In addition to the interview sources cited below, I am also grateful for the assistance of Lydia Bunka, Fred Hayman, Joe and Marti le Guori, Helga Philippe and Cynthia White.

92. 'I cried so much': Grace Kelly to Prudy Wise, 13 April 1949. This letter is reproduced on p. 117 of the catalogue *Heroes, Legends, Superstars of Hollywood & Rock*, published by Superior Auction Galleries, 94780 Olympic Blvd., Beverly Hills, in March 1994.

92. 'The fact that': Ibid.

92. 'They ... made me': Ibid. This quotation comes from a page that is not reproduced in the catalogue.

93. 'It was when I': Gwen Robyns, interview, 8 December 1992.

93. 'For a month': Robyns, p. 63.

93. She told him: Don Richardson, interview, 19 August 1992.

93. 'She told me': Bettina Thompson Gray, interview, 26 October 1992.

94. Two of the best students: Ezra Stone, interview, 23 March 1993. See also Morigi, p. 74.

95. 'See one of my plays': Robinson, p. 58.

95. 'You rehearsed for': Natalie Core O'Hare, interview, 19 August 1992.

95. 'For a young lady whose': I am grateful to Geraldine Duclow, of the Philadelphia Free Library Theatre Collection, for tracking down this and other examples of Grace Kelly's early reviews.

95. Grace drove the thirty-five miles: John B. Kelly, Jr ('Kell'), interview with Gwen Robyns, 1975.

96. 'Grand Rapids furniture': Don Richardson, interview 20 May 1992.

97. no preliminaries: Don Richardson, interview, 19 August 1992.

97. 'It was like running': Ibid., 31 March 1993.

97. Soon the couple: Ibid., 19 August 1992.

97. 'The doorbell rang': Ibid., 20 May 1992.

100. 'She was definitely': Martin Riskin, interview, 26 January 1993.

100. Grace held back: Tom Hogan, interview, 24 February 1993.

101. 'You could play': Martin Riskin, interview, 26 January 1993.

101. 'We would take': Ibid.

101. 'His accent was': George Lang, interview, 24 February 1993.

102. 'He's truly in love': Martin Riskin, interview, 26 January 1993.

102. Philippe was on the rebound: Cynthia White, interview, 23 February 1993.

103. 'It's the old man': Martin Riskin, interview, 26 January 1993.

103. 'absolutely bonkers': George Lang, interview, 24 February 1993.

103. conviction for tax fraud: Philippe was indicted on four counts of income tax evasion. He pleaded guilty to one count in a plea bargain that resulted in a fine of $10,000, the maximum penalty. Ward Morehouse III, pp. 84, 85.

104. 'They went out': Maree Rambo, interview, 19 September 1992.

104. The Shah's nightclubbing capacity: Feinberg, *New York Times*, 23 November 1949.

104. 'Miss Kelly, could you please': Bradford, p. 52.

104. 'It was her first taste': Ibid.

105. 'That jewellery – ': Ibid., p. 53.

106. 'Mother, one does not refuse': Ibid.

106. 'He's asked me': Mark Miller, interview, 21 August 1992.

107. 'I can't': Quine, p. 22.

107. Ike and Leon Levy had: I am grateful to Ike Levy's son, Robert, for lending me the privately printed manuscript *Isaac D. Levy*, which tells the story of the Levy brothers and the earliest years of CBS.

107. 'It was the sort': Richard Waterman, interview, 24 March 1992.

108. 'She was a thin': Ibid.

108. 'He met me at': I am grateful to Robert Levy for lending me Hermann Rush's privately printed study, *Manie Sacks, Uncle Manie, My Uncle*.

108. 'She did not take': Richard Waterman, interview, 24 March 1992.

108. 'It was always there': Don Richardson, interview, 20 May 1992.

110. 'Her hand was in the water': Ibid., 9 March 1993.

7. Fire and Ice

111. 'Grace Kelly gives a charming': Atkinson, *New York Times*, 17 November 1949.

111. 'Only the novice': cited in Bradford, p. 56.

111. 'I read for so many': Ibid.

112. 'This is a strange': Robyns, p. 61.

112. 'She has no stove': Bradford, p. 58.

112. Grace's early television work: The records of early television drama productions have not been catalogued with the thoroughness of Hollywood movies or Broadway plays. The dates of these performances by Grace Kelly, and of those

that follow, have been taken from a research list in the file of the University of California, Los Angeles, Special Collections, no. 1032, Wolper Productions, Television Scripts and Production Materials, 1960—1964, Box 4, Grace Kelly.

113. Television had only just started: A number of these productions have been preserved and can be seen at the excellently equipped Museum of Television and Radio, 25 West 52nd Street, New York.

113. 'You only had': Rita Gam, interview, 23 July 1992.

113. 'Ten minutes before': Billington, *Once Upon a Time Is Now.*

113. Her appearances for *Lux*: The earliest reference that the Oxford English Dictionary shows for 'soap opera' or 'soaps' is in 1943.

114. 'Dozens of soaps': Nelson, p. 184.

114. 'She was one': Dominick Dunne, interview, 6 January 1992.

114. 'She was no Eleonora Duse': Englund, p. 44.

114. *The Swan* on CBS: University of California, Los Angeles, Special Collections, no. 1032, Wolper Productions, See note to p. 112, above.

115. 'I tried to find': Robinson, p. 326.

115. 'Mr Kelly loved': Jean Dalrymple, interview, 22 February 1993.

116. 'He had heard terrible things': Ibid.

116. 'You probably don't': Ezra Stone, interview, 23 March 1993.

116. 'She's twenty-something': Natalie Core O'Hare, interview, August 1992.

116. 'He treated her abominably': Ibid.

117. 'wanted her to have': Bradford, p. 54.

117. 'Oh, Grace, I hope': Ibid.

118. 'The lights were out': Ibid.

118. She was a Scorpio: Princess Grace gave her list of the Scorpio characteristics, positive and negative, on the invitation to the Scorpio party she organized to celebrate her fortieth birthday in Monaco in November 1969.

The positive read: 'sensual, brave, sensitive to beauty, creative, intuitive, ambitious, hard-working, determined, dynamic, clairvoyant, passionate, energetic, independent.' The negative: 'egotistical, egocentric, cruel, insensitive, autodestructive, pleasure-loving, lugubrious, headstrong, possessive and vindictive.'

118. 'She got terribly': June Sherman, interview, 8 July 1993.
118. 'Most of us didn't': John Foreman, interview with Gwen Robyns, 1975.
119. 'When she had something': Bettina Gray, interview, 26 October 1992.
119. 'It was her father': Natalie Core O'Hare, interview, 19 August 1992.
119. 'She had this drive': William Allyn, interview, 24 August 1992.
119. 'Grace had to make': Don Richardson, interview, 20 May 1992.
120. 'She ran her fingers': Gaither, p. 19.
120. She would sit by Harper's bedside: Charles Fish, interview, Temple University Archives. See also: Kelly, as told to Gehman, 17 January 1956.
121. 'We were childhood sweethearts': See Spada, p. 24, for an example.
121. 'shanty Irish': Lee Grant, interview, 1 March 1993.
121. 'Mother, I think': Kelly, as told to Gehman, *Los Angeles Examiner*, 19 January 1956.
121. 'He not only knew': Ibid.
121. Gene Lyons's ex-wife: Ibid.
121. 'He was not the stable sort': Ibid.

8. HIGH NOON

I am grateful to Stanley Kramer and Fred Zinnemann for talking to me about Grace Kelly and the making of *High Noon*.

123. a worthy and vaguely experimental production: Crowther, *New York Times*, 11 March 1951.
124. 'then sitting back': Schickel, p. 10.
124. 'I wasn't interested': Bradford, p. 56.

125. '*High Noon* was about': Biskind, p. 48.

125. 'I wanted somebody': Stanley Kramer, interview, 29 May 1992.

125. 'As an independent': Jay Kanter, interview, 27 May 1992.

126. 'She was wearing': Fred Zinnemann, interview, 8 December 1992.

126. 'Sort of boring': Ibid.

127. 'I told him': Ibid.

127. 'Did you kiss': Kelly, as told to Gehman, *Los Angeles Examiner*, 19 January 1956.

127. 'The presence of your sister': LeVine, *Hello!*, 10 October 1992.

127. 'Grace was odd': Stanley Kramer, interview, 29 May 1992.

128. 'She kept her own': Fred Zinnemann, interview, 8 December 1992.

128. 'She was insecure': Fred Zinnemann, interview, 17 February 1993.

128. 'Audrey had enormous': Ibid.

128. 'In some shots': Ibid.

129. 'You look into his face': *Time*, 31 January 1955, p. 48.

129. 'When we graduated': I am grateful to Donald Spoto for playing me the tape of his interview with Princess Grace in Paris on 22 September 1975, and for supplying me with a transcript.

130. 'Your imagination is': Meisner, p. 79.

131. 'Her attitude was': Sanford Meisner, interview, 2 March 1993. I am grateful for the help of his assistant and companion, James Carville.

131. 'Grace was astonishing': Nelson, p. 184.

132. 'Grace had good': Sanford Meisner, interview, 2 March 1993.

9. ROMANCING THE KING

133. 'They were very much': David Swift, interview, 28 February 1994.

133. Grace and Gene appeared: *The Rich Boy* exists in kinescope form, and can be seen at the Museum of Television and Radio in New York.

133. 'He loved his': Lee Grant, interview, 1 March 1993.

134. role in *To Be Continued: New York Times*, 24 April 1952.

134. 'Perfect!': Martin, *Saturday Evening Post*, p. 61.

135. To prepare for: O'Connor, *Sunday Mirror*, 24 August 1969.

135. remake of *Red Dust: Red Dust* was based on a play by W. Collinson, *Farewell to Women*. It was remade in 1940 as *Congo Maisie*. Conflicting MGM publicity handouts stated that *Mogambo* was a Swahili word for both 'passion' and 'big gorilla'. Neither of these meanings is correct, according to the Kenyan Embassy in Washington, whose spokesman says that *Mogambo* means the sound of something, like a shout.

135. 'I am not interested in': Lucille Ryman Carroll, interview, 18 August 1992.

136. 'None of those': Ibid.

136. 'Sit down': William Allyn, interview, 24 August 1992.

137. 'She ordered': Donald Sinden, interview, 5 December 1992.

137. Soon after her arrival: Gardner, pp. 207–10.

137. 'As far as romance': Ibid., p. 206.

138. 'They were together': Donald Sinden, interview, 5 December 1992.

138. 'both of them': Sinden, *Sunday Telegraph*, 28 February 1982.

138. 'skinny-dipping' with Clark: This extract from Grace's letter of 2 January 1953 to Prudy Wise was broadcast on *Entertainment Tonight* on 8 March 1994, and is also reproduced in the catalogue *Heroes, Legends, Superstars of Hollywood & Rock*, published by Superior Auction Galleries.

138. 'She was never much': Maree Rambo, interview, 10 March 1994.

138. 'Her little nose': Gardner, pp. 206, 207.

139. 'It's the most': Bradford p. 70.

141. 'Well, there's only ten': Ibid., p. 73.

141. 'With that, she reached': Spada, p. 68.; confirmed by Gore Vidal, interview, 19 March 1994.

141. 'No chance of': Donald Sinden, interview, 5 December 1992.

142. 'On their trek back': Skolsky, *New York Post*, 4 February 1953.

142. 'Oh, good God': Academy of Motion Picture Arts and Sciences Archives, Hedda Hopper papers, Clark Gable file.

142. 'I'm old enough': Englund, p. 132.

142. 'I remember being': John Foreman, interview with Gwen Robyns, 1975.

142. 'I was only too': Kelly, as told to Gehman, *Los Angeles Examiner*, 20 January 1956.

143. 'It was very': Ibid.

143. 'He had a guard': Mrs Henry Hathaway, interview, 19 May 1992.

143. 'I'm not speaking': See the letters on Savoy Hotel letterhead, the first headed 'Friday', with no date, the second dated 21 March 1953, in the Superior Auction Galleries catalogue.

144. 'She was just': Maree Rambo, interview, 6 January 1993.

145. The actress was denounced: Bergman, p. 273.

146. 'It has been': Academy of Motion Picture Arts and Sciences Archives, Hedda Hopper papers, Gary Cooper file.

146. 'We are sick': University of California, Los Angeles, Special Collections, Grace Kelly, Wolper Productions, research notes and materials for *Biography*, 18 January 1963.

10. SNOW PRINCESS

147. 'Anything could happen': Spoto, *The Art of Alfred Hitchcock*, p. 147.

148. 'mousy': Bradford, p. 63.

148. 'An actress like': Robyns, p. 85.

148. 'In a horrible way': Martin, *Saturday Evening Post*, p. 62.

149. ' "She's a very young" ': Jean-Pierre Aumont, interview, 10 July 1992.

150. 'She was giving': Ibid.

150. 'Neither of us': Ibid.

151. 'I loved her': Ibid.

151. 'Hitchcock filmed': Spoto, p. 352.

151. 'Hitchcock planned': Mel Dellar, interview, 28 January 1993.

152. 'snow-covered volcano': Academy of Motion Picture Arts and Sciences Archives, Hedda Hopper papers, Alfred Hitchcock file, 7 May 1958.

152. 'That Gryce!': Bryan Mawr, interview, 14 August 1992.

153. 'All the men': Bradford, p. 80.

153. 'The whole cast': Lizanne Kelly LeVine, interview with James Spada, 8 January 1986.

153. 'After the shooting': Ibid.

153. 'They made no attempt': Mel Dellar, interview, 28 January 1993.

154. 'Grace appeared': Joe Hyams, interview, 1 March 1994.

154. 'We had a long talk': Lizanne Kelly LeVine, interview with James Spada, 8 January 1986.

154. 'Grace . . . was a conniving': Mrs Henry Hathaway, interview, 19 May 1992.

155. *Confidential* was a scandal sheet: Fred Otash, interviews, February 1992.

155. After one look at Gracie: Spada, p. 83.

156. Allan told only: Rupert Allan, interview with Cari Beauchamp, 1990.

156. 'Do not fool': Friedrich, p. 406.

157. 'She and Scoop': Martin, *Saturday Evening Post*, p. 56.

158. 'Divorce was something': Lizanne Kelly LeVine, interview with James Spada, 8 January 1986.

158. Jack Kelly wanted: Gwen Robyns, interview with Peggy Kelly Conlan, 1975.

158. 'She finally got': Mrs Henry Hathaway, interview, 19 May 1992.

158. Mal Milland told her friends: Ibid.

158. 'It was a bad': Quine, p. 57.

158. 'I really thought': Gwen Robyns, interview, 8 December 1992.

158. 'At times I think': Martin, *Saturday Evening Post*, p. 62.

159. 'She's an amateur': Jean Dalrymple, interview, 22 February 1993.

159. 'She was up': Ibid.

159. José Ferrer had found: Roxanne was played by Arlene Dahl in the City Center production of *Cyrano de Bergerac*.

160. 'So I was sitting': Princess Grace of Monaco, interview with Donald Spoto, 22 September 1975.

161. 'sexual elegance': *Time*, 31 January 1955, p. 48.

162. the director insisted on supervising: Englund, p. 78.

162. 'There was a reason': Spoto, p. 372.

162. In later years: Ibid., p. 501.

162. 'I exploited the fact that': Ibid., p. 372.

163. 'I went to a girl's': Princess Grace of Monaco, interview with Donald Spoto, 22 September 1975.

163. 'I was twenty-five': Spoto, p. 88.

163. 'See what a difference': Princess Grace of Monaco, interview with Donald Spoto, 22 September 1975.

164. 'Sometimes he merely': Spoto, *The Art of Alfred Hitchcock*, p. xiii.

165. near unanimous critical acclaim: *Rear Window* opened in New York on 4 August 1954.

165. 'She was luminous': Don Richardson, interview, 20 May 1992.

11. THE COUNTRY GIRL

169. 'Grace looked absolutely': Dominick Dunne, interview, 22 February 1993.

170. 'It won't be long': Englund, p. 81.

170. 'the year of Grace': *Life*, 26 April 1954, p. 116.

171. 'I don't understand why': Quine, p. 44.

172. 'She enjoyed her': John Foreman, interview with Gwen Robyns, 1975.

172. Perlberg and Seaton: *Paramount News*, 10 July 1950.

173. William Holden was to die: See Thomas, chapter 1. Bob Thomas's *Golden Boy: The Untold Story of William Holden*, is the source for these paragraphs.

173. 'If a lovely girl': LeVine, *Hello!*, 10 October 1992, p. 72.

174. 'It was a heavy': Melvin Dellar, interview, 28 January 1993.

174. 'We fell head over': Garvan, *Weekend*, 31 August 1983, p. 13.

174. 'tears streaming': Ibid.

174. 'We kept falling': Rita Gam, interview with Gwen Robyns, 1975.

175. 'a modern apartment': cited in Bradford, p. 83.

175. In these cramped: Rita Gam, interview with Gwen Robyns, 1975.

175. 'He said that': Maree Rambo, interview, 23 March 1994.

176. 'only one week': Grace to Prudy Wise, 30 March 1956, Superior Auction Galleries catalogue, p. 125.

176. 'In more than forty': Maree Rambo, interview, 23 March 1994.

176. Slimming was a major concern: Rita Gam, interview with Gwen Robyns, 1975.

177. 'I have been': Quine, p. 110.

177. She was a warm: Interview with a producer who worked with Holden and with whom Holden discussed Grace Kelly.

177. In the days when: Don Richardson, interview, 20 May 1992.

177. 'I'd be damned': Thomas, pp. 98, 99.

179. 'that practically burns': Atkinson, *New York Times*, 11 November 1950.

179. 'George and I': Martin, *Saturday Evening Post*, p. 60.

180. 'We have big plans': Spada, p. 94.

180. 'No court on earth': Martin, *Saturday Evening Post*, p. 60.

180. 'I just *had* to': Scullin, cited in Spada, p. 94.

181. 'I never said': Levin, p. 82.

181. 'He had heard tales': Parsons, *Los Angeles Examiner*, 24 May 1954.

181. 'Bing had been': Arthur Jacobson, interview, 29 May 1992.

182. 'Fine!': Ibid.

182. 'We looked at': Ibid.

182. 'Grace, I didn't think': Englund, p. 188.

183. 'Never let me': Robyns, p. 97.

184.   'It was so like': Academy of Motion Picture Arts and Sciences Archives, Hedda Hopper papers, Grace Kelly file.

184.   'He would take us': Lizanne Kelly LeVine, interview with James Spada, 8 January 1986.

184.   'There's the man': Arthur Jacobson, interview, 29 May 1992.

185.   'If I felt the same': Thomas, pp. 97, 98.

185.   'Bing was mad for': Lizanne Kelly LeVine, interview with James Spada, 8 January 1986.

185.   'Hollywood's Newest Romance': Martin, *Saturday Evening Post*, p. 53.

185.   'Crosby was unquestionably': Kelly, as told to Gehman, *Los Angeles Examiner*, 21 January 1956.

186.   'He really wanted': Lizanne Kelly LeVine, interview with James Spada, 8 January 1986.

186.   'What else is there': Micheline Swift, interview, 20 March 1994.

186.   'Perhaps he was': Gwen Robyns, interview, 23 March 1994.

186.   'Whatever quality she had': Lizanne Kelly LeVine, interview with James Spada, 8 January 1986.

186.   'I don't think': Interview with a friend of Grace Kelly who got to know her shortly after the making of *Green Fire*.

187.   'a wretched experience': Levin, *Redbook*, p. 81.

187.   'She was very': Granger, p. 306.

188.   'No matter what': Martin, *Saturday Evening Post*, p. 58.

188.   She hired herself: Bradford, p. 94.

188.   ' . . . into the dubbing room . . .': Godbout, *New York Times*, 7 November 1954.

12. TO CATCH A THIEF

This chapter is largely based on an hour-and-a-half interview with Oleg Cassini at his home in New York on 17 June 1992, together with the transcript of a similarly lengthy interview that he gave to Gwen Robyns in 1975, and the notes of Linda Marx's interview with him in 1983. Mr Cassini has also described his relationship with Grace Kelly in his autobiography, *In My Own Fashion*. At his request, his written words have been quoted here as representing his most considered recollection of events.

189. 'Let's go and': Edith Head, interview with Gwen Robyns, 1975.

189. 'And so we went': Ibid.

190. 'There is a lot': Ibid.

190. Cassini had first met: Cassini, p. 238.

191. 'You're out of your': Ibid.

191. 'Such prosaic questions': Ibid.

191. 'I didn't tell her': Ibid., p. 239.

191. 'This was not the sort': Ibid., p. 240.

191. 'There was a pause': Ibid.

192. 'I have two': Ibid., p. 242.

192. Oleg Cassini was the son: Ibid., p. 14.

193. 'I loved women': Ibid., p. 35.

193. Cassini today recalls: Oleg Cassini, interview, 17 June 1992.

193. 'It's very simple': Cassini, p. 245.

194. 'Those who love me': Ibid., p. 248.

194. 'Our relationship was': Ibid.

194. 'There is no need': Ibid., p. 250.

194. 'We seemed to float': Ibid., pp. 250, 251.

195. 'The actual mechanics of love': Ibid., p. 42.

196. 'a form of knowledge': Ibid., p. 55.

196. They gave her the look: Ibid., p. 246.

197. 'It was as though': Nelson, p. 186.

197. dialogues of double entendre: This dialogue and the accompanying descriptions come from *The Dark Side of Genius: The Life of Alfred Hitchcock*, by Donald Spoto, who first drew attention to the suggestiveness of the script of *To Catch a Thief*, particularly in the context of the early 1950s.

198. The verbal sparring: Based on David Dodge's novel of the same title, the script of *To Catch a Thief* was written by John Michael Hayes, who told Donald Spoto that Hitchcock personally edited the script to enhance its sexual electricity. Spoto, p. 374.

199.   'I hear he's': Englund, p. 100.

199.   'to turn dead white': Spada, p. 129.

200.   When the endless takes: Skolsky, *New York Post*, 6 August, 1954.

200.   'We had a scene': Parton, *Ladies' Home Journal*, p. 215.

201.   'You've got it': Cassini, p. 254.

201.   'It was an altogether': Ibid.

201.   'the flushed enthusiasm': Ibid.

202.   'I want to write': Ibid.

202.   It was important: Ibid., p. 256.

203.   'the ethereal Miss Kelly': Ibid., p. 257.

203.   'You, Mr Cassini': Ibid., p. 259.

204.   'There is no': Ibid.

204.   'We propose a six-month': Ibid., p. 260.

205.   'I was trapped': Ibid.

205.   'They actually refused': Ibid., p. 261.

205.   a 'wop', a 'dago': Jack Seabrook, interview, 20 August 1993.

205.   He would kill the man: Lewis, p. 162.

205.   He sat through whole meals: Oleg Cassini, interview, 17 June 1992.

205.   'You can't treat': Cassini, p. 261.

207.   'If it's personal': Ibid.

207.   She lived for the most part: Lucille Ryman Carroll, interview, 18 August 1992.

207.   'I don't care what': Cassini, p. 262.

207.   letter to Cassini: Ibid., p. 263.

209.   'We both hesitated': Ibid.

13. OSCAR!

210.   'There has been': Kerr, *Toronto Star Weekly*, 11 December 1954.

211.   *Sexual Behavior of the Human Female*: Halberstam, *The Fifties*, p. 280.

212.   the virtue of her closest friends: Quine, p. 43.

212.   'She was a new thing': John Foreman, interview with Gwen Robyns, 1975.

213.   'Hollywood has overworked': Zec, *Woman's Sunday Mirror*, 13 March 1955.

214.   'There are eight people': *Time*, 31 January 1955, p. 6.

214.   expressions of modest surprise: Spoto, p. 378.

214.   'Would you all': Cassini, p. 253.

214.   There was a sense: Quine, p. 112.

215.   'as close to theatrical': cited in Englund, p. 110.

215.   'She gives it everything': Winsten, *New York Post*, 16 December 1954.

215.   'trenchant, intense': Crowther, *New York Times*, 6 December 1954.

216.   'What do you wear': Englund, p. 85.

216.   'like trying to chip': Johnson, *The American Daily*, 11 November 1954.

216.   'A Grace Kelly anecdote?': Ibid.

216.   'A person has to keep': *Time*, 31 January 1955, p. 2.

216.   Interview with Hedda Hopper: Academy of Motion Picture Arts and Sciences Archives, Hedda Hopper papers, Grace Kelly file.

217.   'We'd hoped she': *Time*, 31 January 1955, p. 3.

217.   'Last week': Ibid.

217.   His producers were constantly: Jay Kanter, interview, 8 June 1993.

218.   'Could it be': Skolsky, *New York Post*, 23 February 1955.

218.   'We are not going to loan': Parsons, *Los Angeles Examiner*, 8 March 1955.

219.   'If anybody starts': *Time*, 31 January 1955, p. 6.

219.   'right for me personally': Englund, p. 88.

219.   'The dress isn't': *Time*, 31 January 1955, p. 6.

219.   She would no longer be paid: The preceding paragraphs on Grace's relations with MGM are based on the research of Steven Englund, who was able to study MGM's files in the preparation of his book *Grace of Monaco: An Interpretive Biography*, published in 1984. In 1986 MGM was acquired by Turner Broadcasting and the studio's production files are

no longer available to researchers for legal and practical reasons that were explained to me by Andrew Velcoff, who represents Turner in this matter. It is sometimes said that MGM's files have been destroyed, but Mr Velcoff insists that this is not true. He says that they have been moved and can be made available to anyone who can show a bona fide legal cause.

219. 'bewildered and disappointed': Englund, p. 109.
220. A sudden flurry: Ibid., p. 111.
221. 'We respect Grace': Bradford, p. 107.
221. 'Many are backing': Skolsky, *New York Post*, 30 March 1955.
222. 'I just wanna say': Wiley and Bona, p. 251.
222. Holden himself made no secret: Ibid., p. 252.
222. 'The thrill of this moment': Ibid.
223. 'taking off her': Sir Dirk Bogarde, letter to the author, 1 December 1992.
223. 'Dear Judy, this is': Wiley and Bona, p. 254.
223. 'I can't believe': Ibid., p. 253.
224. 'Thank you, darling': Don Richardson, interview, 19 August 1992.
224. 'I can't believe it': Englund, p. 112.
224. 'There we were': Robert Dornhelm, interview, 2 June 1993.

14. Photo Opportunity

This chapter is largely based on interviews with Howell Conant, Jean-Pierre Aumont and Pierre Galante.

226. 'No, I don't like': Howell Conant, interview, 4 August 1992.
227. 'She'd start to smile': Ibid.
227. 'Almost everything happened': Ibid.
228. 'Grace's jawline was': Ibid.
228. eyes were oddly close-set: Ibid.
229. suspected a holiday fling: Interviews with friends who were close to Grace in 1955.

230.   'They thought she had': Beauchamp and Béhar, p. 171.

230.   'I called her': Ibid.

231.   'I found her': Jean-Pierre Aumont, interview, 10 July 1992.

231.   'I am deeply': Academy of Motion Pictures Arts and Sciences Archives, Grace Kelly biography file. Unsourced clipping datelined 13 May, 1955, by Bernard Valéry, Special Correspondent of *The News*.

232.   'Grace you can't': Jean-Pierre Aumont, interview, 10 July 1992.

232.   The photo opportunity: Pierre Galante, interview, 12 May 1992.

233.   the dress made Grace look: Quine, p. 113.

233.   'It's not like anyone': Ibid.

235.   'I think he's very': Pierre Galante, interview, 12 May 1992.

236.   the whole business had taken: Robinson, p. 72.

236.   'How was it?': Jean-Pierre Aumont, interview, 10 July 1992.

15. THE SWAN

237.   the rest of his life: Jean-Pierre Aumont, interview, 10 July 1992.

237.   'It has been wonderful': Academy of Motion Picture Arts and Sciences Archives, Grace Kelly biography file. Unsourced clipping datelined 13 May 1955, by Bernard Valéry.

237.   'no obstacles to marrying': Englund, p. 153.

238.   'I could be very happy': Academy of Motion Picture Arts and Sciences Archives, Grace Kelly biography file. Unsourced clipping datelined 13 May 1955, by Bernard Valéry.

238.   rather than Jewish: Jean-Pierre Aumont, interview, 10 July 1992.

238.   'I'd rather you married': Interview with a friend of Grace Kelly and the Kelly family.

238.   'We got engaged': Jean-Pierre Aumont, interview, 10 July 1992.

238. 'They raised hell': Ibid.

239. The couple wrote letters: Ibid., 2 September 1993.

239. 'There were a lot': Ibid., 10 July 1992.

239. 'I knew then': Kelly, as told to Gehman, *Los Angeles Examiner*, 21 January 1956.

240. 'I was pleasurably surprised': Hawkins, p. 37.

240. His correspondence had the charm: I am grateful to the friends of Prince Rainier who have showed me his typewritten letters.

241. mixture of contentment and restlessness: Quine, p. 116.

241. Grace had invited Judy: Ibid., pp. 117, 118.

241. 'But I want more': Ibid., p. 122.

242. '*The Swan* was one role': Jay Kanter, interview, 27 May 1992. According to Gaither, p. 39, it was Uncle George Kelly who suggested the idea of *The Swan* to Grace.

243. without a stand-in: Robyns, p. 46.

243. 'I love it!': Gaither, p. 46.

244. 'Think what it means': Transcribed from the final lines of *The Swan*, MGM, 1956.

244. 'There is no romance': Bradford, p. 119. See also p. 73 of Robinson, who also interviewed Rupert Allan.

245. 'Rupert, really, there is': Robinson, p. 73.

246. 'legend in decline': Evans, p. 115.

246. founder and publisher of *Look* magazine: Gardner Cowles, Jr, (1903–1985) founded *Look* magazine in 1937 and built up a large media conglomerate around it.

246. broadcasting the story in later years: This version of the story is as Gardner Cowles related it in 1975 to Gwen Robyns. See Robyns, p. 135.

247. 'Give me two days': Robyns, p. 136.

247. aura of purity she evoked: Robinson, p. 78.

247. 'I want to thank you': Ibid., p. 75.

247. Rainier had taken to Grace from the moment: Robinson, p. 78. Prince Rainier grants interviews infrequently, and seldom lets the discussions stray into personal areas. His most revealing comments about himself and his relationship with Grace were to Jeffrey Robinson in the series of inter-

views Robinson conducted for his book *Rainier and Grace: Their Story*, which the Prince regards as his final, public statement on the subject.

247. He had been a shy child: Robinson, p. 78.

248. 'someone very special': Ibid., p. 79.

248. 'My greatest difficulty': Ibid.

248. 'secret treasure garden': Ibid., p. 80.

249. 'We heard later that Rainier': Alice Godfrey Waters, interview, 6 June 1992.

249. Uncle Russ's request: Robinson, p. 76.

249. They compared him to Rasputin: de Massy, p. 27.

250. dedication for the new casino: Brandreth, *New York Times*, 14 June 1914.

250. casino opened on 13 May, 1858: Ibid.

250. construction of marble cathedral: Ibid.

251. 'He's a very nice': Alice Godfrey Waters, interview, 6 June 1992.

251. 'could knock you down': Ibid.

251. 'I'll be nice to him': Ibid.

251. Pochna was a member of the bars: Contract of 4 December 1954, between John P. Pochna and Aristotle S. Onassis.

252. 'It was this little dingy theatre': John Pochna, interview, 13 May 1992.

252. to the neglect of his princely duties: Ibid.

252. 'It simply ended': Robinson, p. 62.

252. the prince's solitary voyage: Ibid.

252. Rainier had formally notified Paris: Ibid., p. 81.

253. a Catholic Dupont, who lived in Delaware: John Pochna, interview, 13 May 1992.

253. the wife potential of Palm Beach: Ibid.

253. 'an autonomous state': Article III of the treaty reads: 'In the event of the Crown falling vacant, especially in default of an heir whether direct or adoptive, the territory of Monaco shall form, under the protection of France, an autonomous state called the State of Monaco.' *Papers Relating to the Foreign Relations of the United States, The Paris Peace Conference, 1919.* Volume IV, p. 658.

254.   'He took his pecker out': John Pochna, interview, 13 May 1992.

16. 'I HAVE MADE MY DESTINY'

In addition to newspaper reporting, the engagement of Grace Kelly was covered by the newsreels of *Movietone News*, which can be consulted in the library of the University of California, Los Angeles.

255.   on the evening of Friday, 23 December 1955: Gaither, p. 49.
255.   'I *shall* return!': Quine, p. 128.
256.   'Where's the nigger prince?': John Pochna, interview, 13 May 1992.
256.   'My father knew': Peggy Kelly Conlan, interview with Gwen Robyns, 1975.
256.   'delightfully on edge': Kelly, as told to Gehman, *Los Angeles Examiner*, 22 January 1956.
257.   'Christmas morning, I was sorry': Levin, *Redbook*, p. 82.
257.   'be over here with me': Peggy Kelly Conlan, interview with Gwen Robyns, 1975.
257.   'He all but monopolized her!': Kelly, as told to Gehman, *Los Angeles Examiner*, 22 January 1956.
257.   'then and there, that his intentions': Kelly, as told to Gehman, *Los Angeles Examiner*, 23 January 1956.
258.   'Peggy, you must take': Peggy Kelly Conlan, interview, Gwen Robyns, 1975.
258.   'We sat and played': Ibid.
258.   'I think he's very': Ibid.
258.   'She held my hand': Kelly, as told to Gehman, *Los Angeles Examiner*, 22 January 1956.
259.   The young couple could count on: Robinson, p. 77.
259.   locked in a passionate embrace: Peggy Kelly Conlan, interview with Gwen Robyns, 1975.
259.   'Gracie's home!': Quine, p. 129.
260.   'It's vital': Ibid.
260.   Bill Clothier as ideal husband material: Interview with a friend of the Kelly family who was present when Jack Kelly

first introduced Bill Clothier to Grace at the premiere of one of her films. Clothier later visited Grace in Hollywood, and also took her to a Newport, Rhode Island, tennis tournament in summer of 1955. It did so happen that Clothier had invited Grace to dinner on the evening of 26 December 1955. It was a longstanding arrangement that Grace did not feel she could break, but she left early and went home to talk about Rainier with her parents.

261. 'I am so very much': Quine, p. 130.
261. 'No shit, Grace!': Ibid.
261. 'I love his eyes': Ibid., pp. 131,132.
262. 'I acted more on instinct': Billington, *Once Upon a Time Is Now.*
263. 'as though wishing': Quine, p. 133.
263. 'Daddy was always': Peggy Kelly Conlan, interview with Gwen Robyns, 1975.
264. The pregnant Lizanne had to be escorted: Bradford, p. 127.
264. 'It looked particularly': Elliott Erwitt, interview, 31 August 1993.
264. 'a pudgy and rather unpleasant': Ibid.
264. Grace squeezed Rainier: *Time*, 16 January 1956.
264. the couple danced happily: Ibid.
265. 'I have made my destiny': Bradford, p. 126.
265. 'Daddy's making so much': Don Richardson, interview, 17 September 1992.
265. shareholding as wedding present: Jack Seabrook, interview, 20 August 1993.
266. 'I certainly told': John Pochna, interview, 13 May 1992.
266. 'any damn broken-down prince': Bradford, p. 124.
266. 'Oh! He did really': Ibid.
266. In the event of a divorce: Quine, p. 187.
267. 'If Grace worked at it': Ibid.
267. 'They'll find out': Don Richardson, interview, 17 September 1993.
267. 'Tell them you': Ibid.
268. 'She said the priest': Don Richardson, interview, 17 September 1993.

268.   'They believed me!': Ibid.
269.   'Men began proposing': Kelly, as told to Gehman, *Los Angeles Examiner*, 21 January 1956.
270.   '[It] struck Grace': Englund, p. 290.
270.   'Why couldn't she': Maree Rambo, interview, 6 January 1993.
270.   Grace phoned her mother: Quine, p. 140.
270.   'rushed out of her': Englund, p. 177.
271.   'Well, Mother, I guess now': *Movietone News*, January 1956, University of California, Los Angeles, Library.
271.   'First I had to fight': Quine, p. 148.
271.   'I knew from the start': Levin, *Redbook*, pp. 83, 84.

17. TRUE LOVE

273.   'I had spent a lot': Spada, pp. 184, 185.
273.   'She insisted on': Ibid.
274.   'At the end': Ibid.
275.   'Do you think': Celeste Holm, interview, 24 February 1993.
275.   'Well, next day': Ibid.
275.   Grace's real diamond: Quine, pp. 144, 145.
275.   'Yes, it is sweet': Celeste Holm, interview, 24 February 1993.
275.   'Did you receive': John Pochna, interview, 13 May 1992.
276.   'She was white': Celeste Holm, interview, 24 February 1993.
276.   'Someone asked': Ibid.
277.   'He's not good enough': Cited in Bradford, p. 128.
277.   engagement announcement: The fullest accounts of the Henry Avenue press conference are in the *Philadelphia Inquirer* and *New York Times* for 6 January 1956.
277.   Rainier grasped the photographer's hand: Howell Conant, interview, 4 August 1992.
277.   'I don't think so': *Movietone News*, January 1956, University of California, Los Angeles, Library.
278.   occasional work on plum roles: Schallert, *Los Angeles Times*, 22 January 1956.

278.   'So glad you've found': Summers, p. 165.
278.   'I am very happy': Englund, p. 180.
278.   'Right now, I am': Asbury, *New York Times*, 5 April 1956.
279.   MGM's salary bonus: Englund, p. 183.
280.   Grace's name kept on studio roster: Ibid.
281.   biggest shipside news conference: Englund, p. 190, 191.
281.   The dresses were a present: Gaither, p. 70.
281.   Grace paid for the socks: Quine, p. 198.
281.   'For heaven's sake': Englund, p. 189.
282.   'a floating summer camp': Quine, p. 11.
283.   'There must have been': John and Elizabeth Seabrook, interview, 20 August 1993.
283.   One of them was: Ibid.
283.   firsthand account of Grace Kelly's wedding: Ibid.
284.   NBC ran a two-week series: Gaither, p. 132.
284.   'shining example': Kelly, as told to Gehman, *Los Angeles Examiner*, 24 January 1956.
284.   'It was awful': Maree Rambo, interview, 29 September 1993.
285.   Jack Kelly called: Jack Seabrook, interview, 20 August 1993.
286.   shedding more tears: Bettina Thompson Gray, letter to the author, 5 February 1994.
286.   'not preoccupied with': Quine, p. 25.
286.   'gathering some internal': Ibid.

18. THE PRINCESS FROM THE SEA

Of the thousands of press reports filed from Monte Carlo on the marriage of Grace and Rainier, the best, by far, are those of Art Buchwald published in the *New York Herald Tribune*, 13–20 April 1956. The definitive insider's account is Judy Quine's book *The Bridesmaids*.

288.   Rainier only shook: Conant, p. 52.
288.   'The only thing': Considine, *Los Angeles Herald-Express*, 12 April 1956.
288.   'Do they get one': The details of Grace's arrival in Monaco

are minutely chronicled in Gaither and Quine.

289. 'Hi! I'm Ma Kelly!': de Massy, p. 50.

289. 'To make love': Ibid., p. 12.

290. 'is now disposed': State Department papers, Freedom of Information Act, declassified 6 April 1954: The Present Situation of Prince Rainier III; Dispatch 86, Part B(b); Albert E. Clattenburg, Jr, American Consulate, Nice, to Washington, 25 November 1955.

290. Rainier had had her expelled: White, *The Standard*, 17 September 1982.

290. obese and jewel-laden in a wheelchair: Tom Guinzberg, interview, 22 February 1993.

291. The true purpose: Gaither, p. 68.

291. On Saturday, 14 April 1956: Elizabeth Seabrook, interview, 20 August 1993.

291. 'Prince Rainier III is so furious': Buchwald, *New York Herald Tribune*, 18 April 1956.

292. Mamou had tried to shoot: de Massy, p. 13.

292. The princess had come: Ibid., p. 88.

292. René Girier: Ibid., p. 57. See also Bianchini, p. 281.

292. had been born illegitimate: Ibid., p. 51.

292. Her mother-in-law: Maree Rambo, interview, 6 January 1993.

292. Mamou never returned: de Massy, p. 255.

292. 'cold as a witch's teat': Don Richardson, interview, 15 March 1993.

293. to spoil the scoop: Howell Conant, interview, 11 August 1992.

293. A local school: US National Archives: RG59. State Department, dispatch from American Consulate, Nice, 11 July 1956.

293. harassed young man: Ibid.

294. Journalists spent a lot: Art Buchwald, interview, 15 September 1993.

294. 'Go home, Gracie!': Quine, p. 174.

295. 'Isn't it amazing': Ibid., p. 181.

295. They drove up into: Ibid., pp. 181, 182.

296. 'It was a nightmare': Kahn, cited in Spada, p. 195.

297. Ex-King Farouk happened: Bradford, p. 137.

297. the bride was drawing on: Quine, p. 200.

298. In the front seat sat: Gaither, p. 160.

299. It was a moment whose solemnity: Maree Rambo, interview, 6 January 1993.

299. 'He doesn't know Gracie': Englund, p. 201.

299. an extraordinary sense of closeness: Maree Rambo, interview, 6 January 1993.

301. One of the bridesmaids: Gaither, p. 167.

19. FAMILY BUSINESS

Objective histories of Monaco and the Grimaldi family are in short supply. It is not a subject that draws many outside historians. The most accessible papers on the principality's modern history are those of the State Department, catalogued in the National Archives in Washington under the reference RG59.

305. 'François the Cunning': Brégeon, p. 38.

306. Grimaldis sided with Spain: Monaco was under the umbrella of Spain from 1524 to 1641.

306. the favours of the Sun King: See Brégeon, Chapter 14, for a sound analysis of Saint Simon, Madame de Sevigné and the other contemporary sources on Madame de Monaco. Memoirs of her life produced in the nineteenth century by Alexandre Dumas, among others, are less reliable.

307. In 1861 France annexed: Bianchini, p. 136. Technically Napoleon III 'purchased' the towns of Menton and Roquebrune from Monaco for the sum of four million francs and various other benefits — notably a road from Nice that would bring in tourists. But Monaco had little choice in the matter. The inhabitants of Menton had voted to join France by an overwhelming majority.

307. Reorganizing Monaco's infant tourist business: Monaco's first casino opened in April 1856, shortly before the accession of Charles III, but it was an obscure gaming room

in a villa at the back of the port. It was Charles III who brought the gambling impresario, François Blanc, from Bad Homburg, and oversaw the creation of the new casino and the Hôtel de Paris on the hill in 1863.

308. Louis had a love affair: Marie-Juliette Louvet, Mamou's mother, is often described as a washerwoman or laundress. But Christian de Massy, a member of the family (son of Antoinette, nephew of Rainier and grandson of Mamou), says in his book, *Palace: My Life in the Royal Family of Monaco*, that it was Marie-Juliette's parents who ran a laundry. According to de Massy, Marie-Juliette was formerly married to a photographer in Paris, and was thought to have worked in a nightclub in Montmartre. See de Massy, p. 11.

308. the house of von Urach: The von Urach in question came from the marriage of Charles III's sister, Florestine, to Frederick-William, Count of Württemberg, Duke of Urach, in 1863.

308. by changing his surname: This was not the first time the Grimaldis had performed this manoeuvre. In 1731 the male line ran out with the death of Antoine I, and his daughter was married to Jacques de Goyon of the Goyon-Matignon family, who changed his name and was elevated to the rank of prince. While noting that the ruling house of Monaco has continued to use the Grimaldi coat of arms, genealogists list it as the house of Goyon-Matignon from 1731 to 1949 (when Rainier succeeded), and as the house of Polignac thereafter.

309. 'When we were': Robinson, p. 30.

309. He received the Consul General: Ibid., p. 35, and Hawkins, p. 25.

309. the principality became an R&R centre: Robinson, p. 35.

309. companies created to launder war profits: US National Archives, RG59: State Department file 740.00111EW (Neutrality).

309. concessions with neutral status: See US National Archives, RG59: State Department file 740.00111EW (Neutrality)

for the numerous papers on this subject.

310. 'There is no reason': US National Archives, RG59: State Department (memo) European affairs (Clark), 20 February 1940. Sovereignty of Monaco, 740.00111EW (Neutrality).

310. in September 1944: Hawkins, p. 23.

310. 'It was well known': US National Archives, RG59: State Department. American Embassy, Paris, 10 February 1945, No. 972 to Washington, subject: French attitude toward Monaco.

311. 'alleged pro-Axis attitude': US National Archives, RG59: State Department. Incoming telegram, 2 February 1945, to Washington from Vice Consul at Nice, 850B.001/2–645 CS/EG.

311. 'If the French do not': US National Archives, RG59: State Department. Washington to American Embassy, Paris, 6 February 1945, 850B.001/2–645 CS/EG.

311. 'Monaco appears to be': US National Archives, RG59: State Department (Memo), European affairs (Clark), 20 February 1940, Sovereignty of Monaco, No. 6137. 740.00111EW (Neutrality). Government–Monaco.

311. 'qualities of leadership': State Department papers, Freedom of Information Act, declassified 6 April 1994: The Present Situation of Prince Rainier III; Dispatch 86, Part B; Albert E. Clattenburg, Jr, American Consulate, Nice, to Washington, 25 November 1955.

311. 'a hot-bed of gossip,': Ibid.

311. 'an energetic young wife': Ibid.

20. BIOLOGICAL EQUATION

312. 'We're preggos!': Maree Rambo, interview, 6 January 1993.

312. 'It gives great joy': Quine, pp. 213, 214.

313. 'I see him on': Cross, *Sunday Express*, 18 March 1962. Cross reported: 'Maître Rey has known Rainier all his life, but six years ago they had a quarrel, and since have not spoken to each other.'

313. current price of an Hermès original: Price quoted by Hermès, Avenue Georges V, Paris, 25 November 1993.

314. 'They told me': Bradford, p. 159.

314. 'We're looking for names': Academy of Motion Picture Arts and Sciences Archives, Hedda Hopper papers, Grace Kelly file.

314. 'Last season the Oceanographic Museum': Ibid.

315. 'I thought, "Oh, no!"': Tom Guinzberg, interview, 22 February 1993.

315. 'Oh, how I love it . . .': Quine, p. 224.

315. 'The poor girl': Maree Rambo, interview, 6 January 1993.

316. mysterious corridors and wings: Ibid., 1 March 1994.

316. 'Grace told me how': Gwen Robyns, interview, 19 October 1993.

316. 'With Rainier she always': Ibid.

317. 'For God's sake': Tivey-Faucon, *Cosmopolitan*, p. 45.

317. 'How many times': Ibid.

317. When Rainier was withdrawn: Englund, p. 257.

318. their New York shopping spree: Robinson, p. 127.

319. 'He's designed a really ingenious': Gaither, p. 174.

319. 'I still can't get used': Grace to Prudy Wise Kudner, 10 January 1957, reproduced in the Superior Auction Galleries catalogue, *Heroes, Legends, Superstars of Hollywood & Rock*, p. 128.

320. 'Oh, shucks': Bradford, p. 162.

321. 'Roc Agel is the place': Hauptfuhrer, *Weekend*, 29 May 1975.

322. 'My wife and children': Lewis, p. 201.

322. 'In this document': Ibid.

323. she was seeing herself: Tivey-Faucon, *Cosmopolitan*, p. 45.

21. PUBLIC RELATIONS

324. Monaco's economy had been: Robinson, p. 113.

325. 'I don't HATE': Allan papers, letter of 11 August 1957.

325. 'The kidnapping was': Ibid.

325. 'I do not want': Ibid., letter of 20 January 1958.

326. 'the good taste publicity': Ibid., undated sheet.

327. 'He could not have': Allan papers, letter of 20 January 1958.

327. 'If a fellow wanted': Howell Conant, interview, 11 August 1992.

327. 'When Bill Arthur was': Ibid.

328. 'I've never seen': Academy of Motion Picture Arts and Sciences Archives, Hedda Hopper papers, Grace Kelly file, 1955 to 1959, letter to Rupert Allan, Hotel Ermitage, Gstaad, 14 September 1957.

328. 'She is just very': Ibid.

329. 'It was the first': Quine, p. 236.

329. Monaco's business turnover: Alden, New York Times Magazine, 15 July 1962, p. 11.

330. In less than two years MEDEC: Englund, p. 285.

330. All that a Marseilles trucking contractor: Alden, New York Times Magazine, 15 July 1962, p. 11.

330. By 1962 there were: Gallois, p. 171.

331. None of the businesses: Bianchini, p. 204.

331. She asked a secretary: Tivey-Faucon, Cosmopolitan, p. 44.

332. quite 'charming': Spada, p. 246.

332. 'The best ambassador': Ibid., p. 247.

332. 'not repeatable in polite society': Gallois, p. 151.

332. At midnight on 12 October 1962: Bianchini, p. 59.

333. 'They may enclose Monaco': Letter to Prudy Wise, 12 October 1962, reproduced on p. 133 of the Superior Auction Galleries catalogue.

333. Monaco's professional soccer team: Alden, New York Times, 13 October 1962.

333. 'Instead of travelling': John Pochna, interview, 15 April 1993.

333. The French government blocked: Gallois, p. 170.

334. Another French ordinance: Ibid., p. 171.

22. IT'S ONLY A MOVIE

338.   a tea party at which Grace: Robyns, p. 183.

338.   At the orphanage: Linda Marx, interview with Rupert Allan, 1983.

338.   'We were brought up': Robyns, p. 193.

339.   'The Red Cross will be': Letter from Grace to Prudy Wise, dated Monaco, 20 January 1960, reproduced on p. 131 of the Superior Auction Galleries catalogue.

339.   'cut out for charitable work': Ibid.

339.   Monaco's Red Cross became: Englund, p. 383.

339.   In underdeveloped countries: *Yearbook of International Organizations*, Volume 1, p. 1615.

340.   Aunt Leonore was Rainier: Alejo Vidal-Quadras, interview, 21 April 1992.

340.   Grace's bedtime stories: Maureen King, undated letter to Gwen Robyns.

340.   'Every time her mother': Tivey-Faucon, *Cosmopolitan*, p. 46.

341.   'You really must not': Hawkins, p. 153.

341.   'I'm afraid I'm very': University of California, Los Angeles, Special Collections, Grace Kelly, file 121–41, *Biography*, Wolper Productions, 18 March 1963.

341.   Anything but the disciplinarian: Tivey-Faucon, *Cosmopolitan*, p. 46.

342.   personally made for her by Givenchy: Roig, p. 52.

342.   'so many new': Grace to Prudy Wise Kudner, 17 August 1967, published in the Superior Auction Galleries catalogue, p. 135.

343.   'I'm Caroline': Micheline Swift, interview, 20 March 1994.

343.   'The Virgin Mary?': Bradford, p. 178.

343.   somehow 'restive': Academy of Motion Picture Arts and Sciences Archives, Hedda Hopper papers, letter from Cary Grant, 9 April 1962.

343.   'But I sensed': Gam, p. 20.

344.   'I am actually': This was one of several extracts from Grace's letters to Prudy Wise broadcast on *Entertainment Tonight* on

8 March 1994, as in the Superior Auction Galleries catalogue, p. 132.

344. 'The telephone can ring': Tivey-Faucon, *Cosmopolitan*,
      p. 38.

345. *I Married a Frigid Female Thief*: Academy of Motion Picture
      Arts and Sciences Archives, Alfred Hitchcock papers,
      Marnie file.

346. 'There have been times': Hawkins, pp, 118, 119.

346. 'I thought it would be': Robinson, p. 214.

346. 'Princess Grace has accepted': Hawkins, p. 114.

347. 'Her Highness will return': Englund, p. 296.

347. 'I don't care what': Graham, *New York Mirror*, 2 April 1962.

347. 'When Miss Kelly left': Academy of Motion Picture Arts
      and Sciences archives, Alfred Hitchcock papers, *Marnie* file,
      letter from Joseph Vogel, 28 March 1962.

347. Grace's fee for *Marnie*: *Sunday Telegraph*, 1 April 1962.

348. 'bubbled like that': Quine, p. 317.

348. 'The Princess is shocked': Hawkins, p. 117.

348. 'What about her kissing': Englund, p. 297.

348. 'It was heartbreaking': Academy of Motion Picture Arts
      and Sciences Archives, Alfred Hitchcock papers, *Marnie* file.

349. 'Dear Grace': Ibid.

23. THE ONASSIS FACTOR

351. Onassis had bought: See the books by Evans, Fraser and
      Lilly for descriptions of the boat.

351. When the two boats: Josi Finsness, interview, 19 March
      1992.

351. from the scrotum: John Pochna, interview, 13 May 1992.

351. 'Madame, you are': Hawkins, p. 61.

352. 'I'll build, I'll embellish': Evans, p. 115.

352. Rainier only owned: Hawkins, p. 140.

352. 'One day they': Fraser, p. 193.

353. 'The boys said': Grace to Prudy Wise Kudner, 30 October
      1961, reproduced in the Superior Auction Galleries cata-
      logue, p. 132.

353.   'They would tease': Fraser, p. 193.

353.   'There were nasty': Hawkins, p. 65.

353.   By a strange paradox: Robinson, p. 117.

354.   'My own feeling': Hawkins, p. 143.

354.   'Monaco will always': Evans, p. 144.

355.   'He won't be': Ibid., p. 159.

355.   'You can speak to': Hawkins, p. 65.

355.   Grace felt a creative: Robinson, p. 20.

355.   'lethargy and bad faith': Evans, p. 199.

355.   'obsessional' in his hatred: Ibid., p. 201.

355.   Onassis had always: Ibid., p. 159; and John Pochna, interview 1 May 1992.

356.   In conversations with de Gaulle: Englund, p. 330.

356.   'I don't think': *Playboy*, January 1966, p. 74.

357.   'A year off': Harrigan, *Travel Holiday*, p. 74.

358.   'someone to take': Herbert, *Evening News*, 8 December 1966.

358.   'I've had happy': Walters, *Ladies' Home Journal*, p. 65.

358.   'Very good for': David Swift, interview, 19 March 1994.

359.   'Oh, it hurts!': Ibid.

359.   'I came to realize': Ibid.

359.   'He has me cornered': Micheline Swift, interview, 20 March 1994.

360.   'You can't let him': Ibid.

360.   'When love beckons': Pepper, *McCall's*, p. 116.

360.   'Another of my wife's': Interview with a member of Rainier's staff in the early 1970s.

361.   'Nowadays, I suppose': Interview with a Philadelphia visitor to the palace.

361.   'She was the only': de Massy, p. 4.

361.   'But she was': John Paul Jones, IV, interview, 8 September 1993.

362.   'I know she': Ibid.

362.   'Of courts and cities': Lewis, p. 22.

363.   As he brought his: Patty Gallagher, interview, 4 March 1992.

363.   'The old man pushed': Lewis, p. 211.

363. 'We were at dinner': Rachel Harlow, interview, 16 April 1993.

363. 'Elbows!': Robinson, p. 52.

363. She even found: Jules Lavin, interview, Lewis papers, Temple University Archives.

364. 'very happy': *Daily Express*, 30 June 1967.

364. 'In all the years': Allan described the incident in detail to Donald Spoto in Los Angeles shortly before his death in August 1991.

24. RUN-OF-THE-PLAY CONTRACT

365. 'Manhattan-on-the-Med': Billington, *These Humble Shores*.

366. 'they have a sense': Kobler, *Saturday Evening Post*, p. 26.

367. 'It grew lonesome': Linda Marx papers, interview with Rupert Allan, 1983.

367. By the time the hotel: Jackson, p. 254.

368. Loew's formed a partnership: *Wall Street Journal*, 25 May 1971; *New York Times*, 30 May 1971.

368. opening in September 1975: Jackson, p. 254.

369. 'This is the end': Interview with an assistant of Maria Obolensky.

369. 'I suggested that': Hauptfuhrer, *Weekend* 29 May 1975.

369. 'I'm not too keen': Ibid.

369. 'Faithfulness to me': Englund, p. 366.

370. Grace's generosity toward Josephine Baker: Ibid., pp. 336, 337, and Robyns, p. 195.

370. At palace receptions: Bianchini, pp. 251–253.

371. 'She has less warmth': Lewis, pp. 279, 282. Confirmed by Leslie Bennetts, 1 June, 1994.

371. 'I really don't': Walker, p. 129.

371. 'But one doesn't': Ibid.

372. 'They both act': Gore Vidal, interview, 19 March 1994.

372. 'She actually studied': Rita Gam, interview, 23 July 1992.

373. Grace's conservatism: Don Richardson, interview, 19 August 1992.

373. 'Grace, this is': Rita Gam, interview, 23 July 1992.
373. 'Take things like': Mann, *Sunday Express*, 1 September 1974.
374. 'When I pass': Ibid.
374. 'Why would you': Quine, p. 358.
374. 'Oh, to be': Ibid., p. 360.
375. 'Frankly, I think': Gwen Robyns, interview, 17 July 1992.
376. 'Face scrubbed': Ibid.
376. 'There are some': Ibid.
378. 'She didn't look': Ibid., 8 December 1992.
379. 'You know, I have': Ibid., 17 July 1992.
379. 'tore the wallpaper': David Swift, interviews, 1 and 19 March 1994.
380. 'Sold!': Quine, pp. 423, 424.
381. 'creamy smile': Interview with a friend of Princess Caroline in the 1970s.
381. 'She operated on': Gwen Robyns, interview, 8 December 1992.
381. 'Why have you': Ibid., 17 July 1992.
382. 'But you *did*': Donina Cicogna, interview, 6 May 1992.
382. 'You've got to': Quine, pp. 317, 318.
383. 'Some of us': Ibid., p. 322.
383. 'rather more princessly': Donald Spoto, interview, 15 August 1992.
384. 'I can't live': Micheline Swift, interview, 20 March 1994.

25. ANGRY JAWS

385. Afflicted by heart: Donald Spoto, interview, 15 August 1992.
385. 'I have to tell': Ibid.
386. According to Academy: Interview with a member of the Academy.
386. 'She was a genuinely': Rita Gam, interview, 23 July 1992.
386. They optioned Gore Vidal's novel: Gore Vidal, interview, 1 March 1994.
387. as the casting director: Robert Dornhelm, interview, 2 June 1993.

387. 'Certainly not': Ibid.
387. 'All that time': Ibid.
388. she went on with Dornhelm: Spada, p. 312, confirmed by Dornhelm in a telephone conversation, 20 May 1993.
388. 'She was always': Robert Dornhelm, interview, 2 June 1993.
388. 'Do you think': Gwen Robyns, interview, 17 July 1992.
388. 'I can twist': Ibid.
389. 'Gwen, darling': Ibid.
389. 'The physical side': Ibid.
389. 'It is a memory': Robert Dornhelm, interview, 20 May 1993.
389. 'Robert was always': Maree Rambo, interview, 21 August 1993.
389. 'Dornhelm was quite': Philippe Junot, interview, 26 November 1993.
390. According to Mattsson: Spada, p. 314. Spada based his account on the article 'Per Mattsson Tells of His Meeting with Princess Grace', by Zenita Winterhall and Johan Helmertz in the Swedish magazine *Den nya Husmodern*, for 29 June 1987.
390. 'She was somebody': Jim McMullen, interview, 23 February 1993.
390. an excursion with Grace: Ibid.
391. 'What she wanted': Gwen Robyns, interview, 8 December 1992.
391. 'Excuse me': Quine, p. 428, confirmed by Jeffory FitzGerald in a telephone conversation in May 1993.
391. 'Madame, I don't': Ibid., p. 478, confirmed by Jeffory FitzGerald in a telephone conversation in May 1993.
392. 'I thought he'd': Interview with a friend of Grace who spent time with Grace and FitzGerald.
392. 'Watch the lunch': Quine, p. 442.
393. 'I'm getting to': Ibid., p. 424.
393. 'I'd love you': Don Richardson, interview, 19 August 1992.
393. The young men: Interviews with Robert Dornhelm and Jim McMullen; telephone conversation with Jeffory FitzGerald.

394. 'When I walked in': Don Richardson, interview, 20 May 1992.

394. 'It was very': Ibid.

395. 'Blimposaurus Rex': Quine, p. 441.

395. Christmas photo session: Howell Conant, interview, 4 August 1992.

395. annual Christmas card: Howell Conant took an official family portrait every year. Sixteen pictures from the twenty-six-year sequence are reproduced in Conant, pages 154–7. The Edith Head file at the Academy of Motion Pictures Arts and Sciences in Los Angeles contains another incomplete set of the portraits as sent to Edith Head in Christmas card form. I am grateful to friends of Grace who have shown me their own sets of the cards. There appear to have been a few years in which a painting of the family, or an alternative design, was used.

395. 'She rang me': Gwen Robyns, interview, 8 December 1992.

396. 'The menopause with': Maree Rambo, interview, 21 August 1993.

396. 'It's not so much': Quine, p. 444.

396. The doctors put: Gwen Robyns, interview, 17 July 1992.

396. 'I've got this': Gwen Robyns, interview, 8 December 1992.

397. confessing to several friends: Ibid., and interviews with other friends of Grace.

397. 'I must be': Quine, p. 446.

26. POETRY AND FLOWERS

398. 'Never will a Grimaldi': Robinson, p. 80.

399. summer camps in Pennsylvania: Maree Rambo, interview, 21 August 1993.

399. 'When Grace was': Rita Gam, interview, 23 July 1992.

399. 'The two girls': Billington, *Once Upon a Time Is Now.*

400. 'Whatever happens': Gwen Robyns, interview, 8 December 1992.

400. 'Where is she?': Earle Mack, interview, 30 March 1992.

401. He had stakes: Interviews with English and American business associates of Philippe Junot. Confirmed by Junot, 18 May 1994.

401. 'It was in': Gwen Robyns, interview, 17 July 1992.

401. 'There are times': Gris, *Woman's Own*, p. 27.

402. She would go off: Gwen Robyns, interview, 12 February 1994.

402. 'Mommy said': Robinson, pp. 246, 247.

403. Rainier was as unhappy: John Carroll, interview, 3 July 1993.

403. he would rail biliously: Interviews with Gwen Robyns and Murr Sinclair Murdoch-Muirhead.

403. Caroline's communication with Rainier: Philippe Junot, interview, 25 November 1993. Junot's observation that father and daughter communicated best by letter in these years is confirmed by some of Caroline's friends.

403. suggested that the marriage: Ibid.

403. 'I never had a proper': Ibid.

404. 'I did not make': Ibid.

404. 'I was twenty': Robinson, p. 247.

404. in the summer of 1980: Philippe Junot, interview, 25 November 1993.

404. 'Don't worry': Ibid.

404. 'Mommy said': Robinson, p. 247.

405. 'to grow back': Rita Gam, interview, 23 July 1992.

406. 'This is what': Gwen Robyns, interview, 8 December 1992

406. 'I can't think of': John Carroll, interview, 3 July 1993.

406. 'When you read poetry aloud': Ibid.

407. 'At the beginning': Richard Pasco, interview with Gwen Robyns, 11 August 1993.

407. 'I selected the poem': John Carroll, interview, 3 July 1993.

408. 'It seemed to me': Ibid.

409. 'The moment that': Ibid.

409. 'Good news': Gwen Robyns, interview, 8 December 1992.

409. 'Don't worry, dear': Quine, p. 466.

409. 'She read me': William Allyn, interview, 24 August 1992.

410. 'In 1978, after Grace': Gwen Robyns, interview, 17 July 1992.

410. 'She had a way': Barry Chattington, interview, 6 April 1993.

411. Grace's role in *Rearranged*: Robert Dornhelm, interview, 2 June 1993. I am grateful to Edward Meeks and to Jacqueline Monsigny for showing me their copy of *Rearranged* and for recounting the story of its making.

411. 'She showed me': William Allyn, interview, 24 August 1992.

412. 'It cost a bomb': Sir Dirk Bogarde, letter to the author, 1 December 1992.

412. 'She told us': Richard Pasco, interview with Gwen Robyns, 11 August 1993.

412. 'Grace was returning': Rita Gam, interview, 23 July 1992.

27. 'IT'S JUST EASIER IF I DRIVE'

This account is largely based on the testimony of witnesses interviewed in the course of the French police investigation of Princess Grace's fatal car accident of 13 September 1982, referred to below as 'police report'.

413. In the spring of 1982: Mr and Mrs Jack Seabrook, interview, 20 August 1993. Seabrook knew Tung – who suffered a heart attack and died just before the rededication ceremony – through the shipping business.

413. 'Now why do I': Ibid.

414. a well-matched and contented pair: Ibid.

414. 'If I had the choice': Micheline Swift, interview, 20 March 1994.

415. 'He was always': Robert Dornhelm, interview, 2 June 1993.

415. Grace and Rainier's twenty-fifth anniversary: Nelson, p. 336.

415. she had cried off: Interviews with Monaco and south of France residents who mixed socially with Grace and Rainier.

415. the pains had got worse: Gwen Robyns, interview, 17 July 1992.

416. 'She's my wild': Ibid., 8 December 1992.

416. One of Grace's private projects: Quine, p. 439. Grace also told Micheline Swift that it was her intention to find a base in Manhattan in the winter of 1982–83. Interview, 20 March 1994.

417. the arguments raged: Robert Dornhelm, interview, 2 June 1993.

417. 'S & P situation': Letters to Don Richardson, Maree Rambo, Gwen Robyns, and Rita Gam.

417. shooting of additional scenes: Robert Dornhelm, interview, 2 June 1993.

417. headaches had come back: Gwen Robyns, interview, 7 July 1992.

417. It was a perfect, sunny: Police report and Roger Bencze, interview, 22 January 1994.

418. Rainier had been driven: Roger Bencze, interview, 22 January 1994.

418. the chauffeur protested: Robinson, p. 283.

418. 'It's just easier': Robinson, p. 283.

418. After she had rammed: Robinson, pp. 280, 281.

418. She had the radio: Police report: Engineering analysis of Rover 3500.

418. Yves Phily: Englund, Bradford and Spada all identify this truck driver, incorrectly, as Yves Raimondo. Paul Raimundo was Grace's driver.

419. seventy or eighty kilometres: Police report: Statement of Yves Phily, 14 September 1982.

419. 'The moment that': Ibid.

420. Gendarme Frédéric Mouniama had radioed: Roger Bencze, interview, 25 November 1993.

422. Sesto Lequio sold interviews: James Whitaker, interview, 28 July 1992.

422. 'I carried Stephanie': Whitaker, *Daily Mirror*, 16 September 1982.

423. 'usual on steering wheels': Roger Bencze, interview, 22 January 1994.

425. The first communiqué: Ibid.

425. a statement dated 20 September: *New York Times*, 21 September 1982.

426. note from Monaco's chief law officer: This letter and its enclosure are filed in the police report.

427. '1972 Rover 3500': Police report: car engineer's report.

427. 'The engineer investigated': Roger Bencze, interview, 22 January 1994.

428. 'cranial traumatization': Police report: Report by Roger Bencze.

429. 'I'm sorry, sir': Roger Bencze, interview, 22 January 1994.

429. Grace rushed into emergency: The medical details in these paragraphs are based on the report by Lawrence K. Altman, M.D., in his column 'Doctor's World', in the *New York Times*, for 21 September 1982. Dr Altman interviewed both doctors Chatelin and Duplay by telephone, as well as several unnamed American doctors who passed their judgement on what the French doctors said.

430. thorax needed to be cleared: Bradford, p. 222. Sarah Bradford obtained her account of Princess Grace's medical treatment in an interview with Dr Chatelin.

430. was a cagelike contraption: I am grateful for the memories of the Monaco residents who used this clinic in the early 1980s.

430. The stroke was only: Vinocur, *New York Times*, 17 September 1982.

431. Kell was to die: *New York Times*, 3 March 1985.

431. 'It was definitely': *Philadelphia Inquirer*, 17 September 1982.

432. There was no point: Robinson, p. 286.

28. 'LORD, I ASK NOT WHY . . .'

434. 'Don't you realize?': Gwen Robyns, interview, 8 December 1992.

434. 'The prince told me': Linda Marx, interview with Rupert Allan, 1983.

435. Ma Kelly was to linger: *New York Times*, 8 January 1990.

435. Peggy's death: See the *Main Line Times*, November 1991, for a tribute to Peggy by her friend Selma Edelstein Bulkin.

435. 'We are all': Quine, p. 462.

436. Grace looked ghastly: interviews with several guests at the funeral.

437. 'They are all sorry': Interview with a guest at the funeral.

437. Stephanie watched: Robinson, p. 288.

437. 'We are united': Vinocur, *New York Times*, 19 September 1982.

437. After the ceremony: Linda Marx research papers. Interview with Congressman Tom Foglietta.

438. 'She said then': WFB, *National Review*, p. 1265.

29. TO FOLLOW THE CIRCUS

440. 'When you're young': Howell, *Sunday Times Magazine* (London), 13 May 1990.

442. Caroline's annulment: According to the *National Catholic Reporter* of 16 April 1993, Caroline's marriage to Philippe Junot was formally annulled in June 1992 'after ten years of study by two papally appointed commissions'. In February 1993, the Pope signed a further rescript rendering Caroline's children legitimate.

443. 'I will abdicate': Sheridan Morley, interview, July 1993. Rainier made these remarks about Albert following an interview he had given Morley on the subject of David Niven. Morley asked Rainier if he could publish what he said, and Rainier agreed. Morley wrote an article, from which these words are taken, published in the *Daily Mail* for 2 October 1984.

444. Rainier made similar remarks: James Whitaker, interview, 28 July 1993.

444. 'Let us just say': Hawkins, p. 168.

444. 'he tore off': Clare, *The Sun*, 28 March 1991.

444. the prince was served: Interview with a member of Tamara Rotolo's family, *Washington Post*, 19 January 1994.

445. Albert's 'wild oats': Interviews with friends of Albert and Rainier.

446. 'She needs a strong man': Linda Marx papers, interview with Rupert Allan, 1983.

446. possession of a dangerous weapon: Benson, *Daily Express*, 10 February 1987.

447. 'She was just': interview with one of Grace's artistic collaborators.

448. 'Such a big': Nicky Haslam, interview, 28 July 1992.

449. like too many teeth: Vinocur, *New York Times Magazine*, 18 June 1978.

449. money-laundering in Monaco: See Bianchini, Chapters 1 and 2, on the recent scandals involving Monégasque banks, including under-the-counter payments to French soccer players.

449. Iran-Contra scandal: United States Senate, Committee on Foreign Relations, etc., p. 386.

450. When he signs his letters: I am grateful to several of Prince Rainier's friends for showing me his letters and his drawings of clowns.

Bibliography

BOOKS

Academy of Motion Picture Arts and Sciences. *The Players' Directory*. Los Angeles: Academy of Motion Picture Arts and Sciences, 1938.

American Academy of Dramatic Arts. *Annual Catalogue: Sixty-Third Year, 1947–48*. New York: American Academy of Dramatic Arts, 1947.

Beauchamp, Cari, and Henry Béhar. *Hollywood on the Riviera: The Inside Story of the Cannes Film Festival*. New York: William Morrow, 1992.

Benhamou, Serge, and Stanislas Choko. *Grace Kelly: Princesse du Cinéma*. Paris: Editions du Collectionneur, 1992.

Bergman, Ingrid, and Alan Burgess. *Ingrid Bergman: My Story*. New York: Delacorte, 1980.

Bianchini, Roger-Louis. *Monaco: Une Affaire Qui Tourne*. Paris: Editions du Seuil, 1992.

Biskind, Peter. *Seeing Is Believing: How Hollywood Taught Us to Stop Worrying and Love the Fifties*. New York: Pantheon, 1983.

Blume, Mary. *Côte d'Azur: Inventing the French Riviera*. London: Thames and Hudson, 1992.

Bradford, Sarah. *Princess Grace*. London: Weidenfeld & Nicolson, 1984.

Brandon, Ruth. *The Dollar Princesses: The American Invasion of the European Aristocracy 1870–1914*. London: Weidenfeld & Nicolson, 1980.

Brégeon, Jean-Joel. *Les Grimaldis de Monaco*. Paris: Criterion, 1991.

Burnell, R. *Henley Royal Regatta: A Celebration of 150 Years*. London: Heinemann, 1989.

Cassini, Oleg. *In My Own Fashion*. New York: Simon and Schuster, 1987.

Conant, Howell. *Grace*. New York: Random House, 1992.

de Bernardy, Françoise. *Histoire des Princes de Monaco: de Rainier I à Rainier III*. Paris: Plon, 1960.

de Massy, Christian, and Charles Higham. *Palace: My Life in the Royal Family of Monaco*. New York: Atheneum, 1986.

de Vilallonga, José Luis. *Gold Gotha*. Paris: Seuil, 1972.

Englund, Steven. *Grace of Monaco: An Interpretive Biography*. London: Sphere, 1985.

Evans, Peter. *Ari: the Life and Times of Aristotle Socrates Onassis*. London: Jonathan Cape, 1986.

Fraser, Nicholas, with Philip Jacobson, Mark Ottaway and Lewis Chester. *Aristotle Onassis*. London: Weidenfeld & Nicolson, 1977.

Freu, J., with R. Norella and J. B. Robert. *Histoire de Monaco*. Monaco: Ministère d'État, 1986. (2 volumes).

Friedrich, Otto. *City of Nets*. New York: Harper & Row, 1986.

Gaither, Gant. *Princess of Monaco: The Story of Grace Kelly*. New York: Henry Holt & Company, 1957.

Gallois, Jean-Pierre. *Le Régime International de la Principauté de Monaco*. Paris: Editions A. Pedone, 1964.

Gam, Rita. *Actress to Actress*. New York: Nick Lyons Books, 1986.

Gardner, Ava. *Ava: My Story*. New York: Bantam, 1992.

Grace of Monaco, with Gwen Robyns. *My Book of Flowers*. New York: Doubleday, 1980.

Granger, Stewart. *Sparks Fly Upward*. New York: G. P. Putnam's Sons, 1981.

Guest, Edgar A. *Collected Verse of Edgar Guest*. Chicago: Reilly & Lee, 1934.

Halberstam, David. *The Amateurs*. New York: Morrow, 1985.

———. *The Fifties*. New York: Villard, 1993.

Hawkins, Peter. *Prince Rainier of Monaco: His Authorized and Exclusive Story*. London: William Kimber, 1966.

Jackson, Stanley. *Inside Monte Carlo*. New York: Stein and Day, 1975.

Kenward, Allan Richard. *Star Bound: A Comedy in Three Acts*. New York: Samuel French, 1939.

Labande, Léon-Honoré. *Histoire de la Principauté de Monaco*. Monaco: Imprimerie Nationale de Monaco, 1934.

Lewis, Arthur H. *Those Philadelphia Kellys: With a Touch of Grace*. New York: William Morrow, 1977.

Lilly, Doris. *Those Fabulous Greeks*. London: W. H. Allen, 1971.

Longstreth, W. Thacher, with Dan Rottenberg. *Main Line Wasp*. New York: W. W. Norton, 1990.

McCallum, John. *That Kelly Family*. New York: A. S. Barnes, 1957.

Meisner, Sanford, and Dennis Longwell. *Sanford Meisner on Acting*. New York: Vintage, 1987.

Michelin. *French Riviera: Côte d'Azur.* Clermont-Ferrand, France: Michelin, 1992.

Modleski, Tania. *The Women Who Knew Too Much: Hitchcock and Feminist Theory.* New York: Methuen, 1988.

Morehouse, Ward, III. *The Waldorf-Astoria.* New York: Evans, 1991.

Morigi, Gilda. *The Difference Began at the Footlights: A Story of Bucks County Playhouse.* Philadelphia: Bucks County Playhouse, 1973.

Nelson, Nancy. *Evenings with Cary Grant.* New York: William Morrow, 1991.

Plath, Sylvia. *The Bell Jar.* New York: Harper & Row, 1971.

Quine, Judith Balaban. *The Bridesmaids: Grace Kelly, Princess of Monaco, and Six Intimate Friends.* New York: Weidenfeld & Nicolson, 1989.

Richardson, Don. *Acting Without Agony: An Alternative to the Method.* Boston: Allyn and Bacon, 1988.

Robinson, Jeffrey. *Rainier and Grace: Their Story.* New York: Avon, 1990.

Robyns, Gwen. *Princess Grace.* London: W. H. Allen, 1982.

Roig, José Luis. *Carolina.* Barcelona: Ediciones B, 1993.

Schickel, Richard. *The Stars.* New York: Bonanza Books, 1962.

Sheehy, Gail. *The Silent Passage.* New York: Random House, 1992.

Shepherd, Donald, and Robert F. Slatzer. *Bing Crosby.* New York: St Martin's Press, 1981.

Spada, James. *Grace: The Secret Lives of a Princess.* New York: Dell, 1988.

Spoto, Donald. *The Art of Alfred Hitchcock* (2nd Edition). New York: Anchor, 1992.

——. *The Dark Side of Genius: The Life of Alfred Hitchcock.* New York: Ballantine, 1984.

Summers, Anthony. *Goddess: The Secret Lives of Marilyn Monroe.* New York: Onyx, 1986.

Superior Auction Galleries. *Heroes, Legends, Superstars of Hollywood & Rock.* Los Angeles: Superior Auction Galleries, 1994.

Taki, (Taki Theodoracopulos). *Princes, Playboys, & High-Class Tarts.* Princeton: Karz-Cohl, 1984.

Thomas, Bob. *Golden Boy: The Untold Story of William Holden.* New York: St Martin's Press, 1983.

Union of International Associations. *Yearbook of International Organizations.* Munich: K. G. Saur, 1993.

United States Government. *Papers Relating to the Foreign Relations of the United States. The Paris Peace Conference, 1919. Volume IV.* Washington: US Government Printing Office, 1943.

United States Senate, Committee on Foreign Relations, Subcommittee on Terrorism, Narcotics, and International Operations. *The BBCI Affair, Hearings of February 19 and March 18, 1992.* Washington: US Government Printing Office, 1992.

Walker, Alexander. *'It's Only a Movie, Ingrid': Encounters On and Off Screen.* London: Headline, 1988.

Wayne, Jane Ellen. *Grace Kelly's Men.* New York: St Martin's Press, 1992.

Wiley, Mason, and Damien Bona. *Inside Oscar: The Unofficial History of the Academy Awards.* New York: Ballantine, 1986.

ARTICLES

Alden, Robert. 'The Chips Are Down for Monaco.' *New York Times Magazine,* 15 July 1962.

——. 'France Harasses Monaco's Border.' *New York Times,* 13 October 1962.

Archives du Palais Princier. 'Annales Monégasques: Revue d'Histoire de Monaco.' Nos. 1–15, 1971–1991.

Asbury, Edith Evans. 'Grace Kelly Bids Regal Au Revoir.' *New York Times*, 5 April 1956.

Atkinson, Brooks. 'At the Theatre – "The Father." ' *New York Times*, 17 November 1949.

———. 'At the Theatre – "The Country Girl." ' *New York Times*, 11 November 1950.

Benson, Ross. 'Stephanie of Monaco: The Wayward Princess, Day 2.' *Daily Express*, 10 February 1987.

Brandreth, J. B. 'Monte Carlo's Profits Last Year Were Over $4,000,000.' *New York Times*, 14 June 1914.

Buchwald, Art. 'Buchwald in Monaco.' A series of reports to the *New York Herald Tribune*, 13–25 April 1956.

Clare, George. 'He Fathered My Boy, Says Topless Girl.' *The Sun*, 28 March 1991.

Considine, Bob. 'Monaco in Wild Ovation.' *Los Angeles Herald-Express*, 12 April 1956.

Cross, Colin. 'Is Abdication Near for Grace and Her Prince?' *Sunday Express*, 18 March 1962.

Crowther, Bosley. 'Man and the Mob: "Fourteen Hours" Focuses on a Classic Theme.' *New York Times*, 11 March 1951.

———. 'Screen: Crosby Acts in "Country Girl." ' *New York Times*, 16 December 1954.

Daily Express. 'Now Grace Expects Her Fourth Baby.' 30 June 1967.

de Vilallonga, José Luis. 'Princess Grace.' *The Star*, London, 30 October 1979.

Feinberg, Alexander. 'Shah at Princeton Sees Arab Library.' *New York Times*, 23 November 1949.

Garvan, Frank. 'How Hollywood's Golden Boy Destroyed Himself.' *Weekend*, 31 August 1983.

Godbout, Oscar. 'Star on the Ascendant.' *New York Times*, 7 November 1954.

Graham, Sheilah. 'Hollywood.' *New York Mirror*. Dates as per the citations in the source notes.

Gris, Henry. 'Does Princess Grace Really Want Caroline to be Mrs Junot?' *Woman's Own*, 24 June 1978.

Harrigan, Stephen. 'Feeling Flush.' *Travel Holiday*, February, 1993.

Hauptfuhrer, Fred. 'The Problem on Mother Kelly's Doorstep.' *Weekend*, 25 May 1975.

Hellman, Geoffrey T. 'Philippe of the Waldorf – Very, Very Cordial.' *New Yorker*, 19 February 1955.

Herbert, Ivor. 'Grace: Champagne Princess with a Bit of the Shepherdess.' *Evening News*, 12 August 1966.

Howell, Georgina. 'Serene Test.' *Sunday Times Magazine*, 13 May 1990.

Johnson, Erskine. 'Rich Girl Makes Good.' This biographical series was syndicated in *The American Daily* and other newspapers in October and November 1954. The dates and newspapers are as per the citations in the source notes.

Kahn, R. T. 'Amazing Grace.' *Ladies' Home Journal*, September 1982.

Kelly, Mrs John B., as told to Richard Gehman. 'My Daughter Grace Kelly: Her Life and Romances.' Published in both the *New York Journal American* and the *Los Angeles Examiner*, 15–24 January 1956.

Kerr, Carson. 'Grace Kelly: Record-Breaking Bombshell.' *Toronto Star Weekly*, 11 December 1954.

Kobler, John. 'The Man with the Crocodile Briefcase.' *Saturday Evening Post*, 24 March 1962.

Levin, Robert. 'Why Grace Kelly Became a Princess.' *Redbook*, February 1957.

LeVine, Lizanne Kelly. 'Princess Grace of Monaco's Sister Lizanne Kelly LeVine Recounts Exclusively for *Hello!* the Fascinating Life of the Kelly Clan.' *Hello!*, London, 9 September and 3, 10, 17, 24 and 30 October 1992.

Life. 'Hollywood's Hottest Property.' 26 April 1954.

Mann, Roderick. 'Why Princess Grace Gets Mad at Stories About Her Daughter.' *Sunday Express*, 1 September 1974.

Martin, Pete. 'The Luckiest Girl in Hollywood.' *Saturday Evening Post*, 30 October 1954.

Morley, Sheridan. 'How I Miss My Grace.' *Daily Mail*, 2 October 1984.

New York Times. 'New Monte Carlo Hotel Due.' 30 May 1971.

——. 'Monaco Palace Retracts Brake-Failure Story.' 21 September 1982.

——. 'John B. Kelly Jr, U.S. Olympic Chief.' 3 March 1985.

——. 'Margaret Kelly, 91, Grace Kelly's Mother.' 8 January 1990.

O'Connor, Ulick. 'Princess Grace Drops a Secret.' *Sunday Mirror*, 24 August 1969.

Parsons, Louella. 'Louella O. Parsons.' *Los Angeles Examiner*. Dates as per the citations in the source notes.

Parton, Margaret. 'What Makes Grace Kelly Different?' *Ladies' Home Journal*, March 1956.

Pepper, Curtis Bill. 'Princess Grace's Problems as a Mother.' *McCall's*, December 1974.

Philadelphia Inquirer. 'Doctor: Grace Had Stroke in Car.' 17 September 1982.

Playboy. 'Interview: Princess Grace.' January 1966.

Schallert, Edwin. 'Critic Sees Monaco's Gain as Filmland Loss.' *Los Angeles Times*, 22 January 1956.

Scullin, George. 'The Girl Who Dares To.' *Motion Picture*, March 1955.

Sinden, Donald. 'With Sinden on Safari.' *Sunday Telegraph*, 28 February 1982.

Skolsky, Sidney. 'Hollywood Is My Beat.' *New York Post*. Dates as per the citations in the source notes.

Sunday Telegraph. 'Princess Grace to Get £357,000.' 1 April 1962.

Time. 'The Girl in White Gloves.' 31 January 1955.

——. 'Pennsylvania: The Philadelphia Princess.' 16 January 1956.

Tivey-Faucon, Madge. 'Inside the Palace with Princess Grace.' *Cosmopolitan*, March 1964.

Vinocur, John. 'For Princess's Family, The Parting Is Forlorn.' *New York Times*, 19 September 1982.

——. 'High Society.' *New York Times Magazine*, 18 June 1978.

——. 'Princess Stricken Before Crash, Doctors Say.' *New York Times*, 17 September 1982.

Wall Street Journal. 'Loews, 2 Firms Abroad Plan $35 Million Complex For Monaco in Late 1974.' 25 May 1971.

Walters, Barbara. 'How Now, Princess Grace?' *Ladies' Home Journal*, November 1966.

Washington Post. 'Problem Child or Royal Scam?' 19 January 1994.

WFB (William F. Buckley). 'Princess Grace, RIP.' *National Review*, 15 October 1982.

Whitaker, James. 'I carried Stephanie from the car . . .' *Daily Mirror*, 16 September 1982.

White, Sam. 'Grace and the Monaco Match-maker.' *The Standard*, 17 September 1982.

Winsten, Archer. ' "The Country Girl" at Criterion.' *New York Post*, 16 December 1954.

Zec, Donald. 'Grace, the Queen of Hollywood.' *Woman's Sunday Mirror*, 13 March 1955.

Zolotow, Maurice. 'Grace of Monaco.' *Cosmopolitan*, December 1961.

PRIVATE PUBLICATIONS AND PRIVATE PAPERS

Isaac D. Levy. A memoir by Isaac D. Levy. Published privately in Philadelphia.

Kelly is Brickwork. A brief company history and publicity brochure, produced under the chairmanship of John B. Kelly, Jr, sometime after 1979.

Paramount News. A publicity newsletter produced by Paramount Studios in the 1950s. It can be consulted today in the library of the Academy of Motion Picture Arts and Sciences.

Uncle Manie. A memoir of Manie Sacks by Herman Rush. Published privately in Philadelphia.

DOCUMENTARY FILMS AND FILMED INTERVIEWS

Billington, Kevin (Director). *Once Upon a Time Is Now . . . the Story of Princess Grace.* NBC TV, 1977. Producers: William and Sandra Allyn. Presenter: Lee Grant.

—— (Director and Producer). *These Humble Shores: A BBC TV Tonight Presentation*, 1963. Presenter: Alan Whicker.

Dornhelm, Robert (Director). *The Children of Theatre Street.* Peppercorn-Wormser, 1977. Producer: Earle Mack. Associate producer: Jean Dalrymple. Artistic director: Oleg Briansky.

Photo Credits

526

PHOTO CREDITS

Index